2000/1

# CHILDREN INTO EXILE

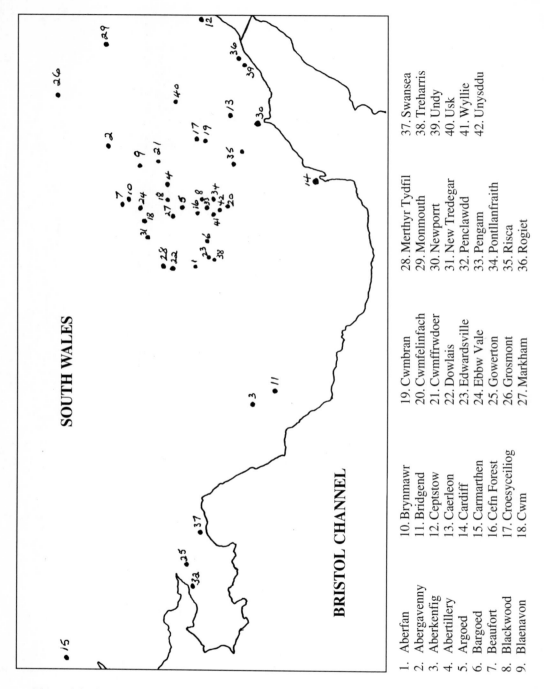

## SOUTH WALES

## BRISTOL CHANNEL

1. Aberfan
2. Abergavenny
3. Aberkenfig
4. Abertillery
5. Argoed
6. Bargoed
7. Beaufort
8. Blackwood
9. Blaenavon
10. Brynmawr
11. Bridgend
12. Ceptstow
13. Caerleon
14. Cardiff
15. Carmarthen
16. Cefn Forest
17. Croesyceiliog
18. Cwm
19. Cwmbran
20. Cwmfelinfach
21. Cwmffrwdoer
22. Dowlais
23. Edwardsville
24. Ebbw Vale
25. Gowerton
26. Grosmont
27. Markham
28. Merthyr Tydfil
29. Monmouth
30. Newporrt
31. New Tredegar
32. Penclawdd
33. Pengam
34. Pontllanfraith
35. Risca
36. Rogiet
37. Swansea
38. Treharris
39. Undy
40. Usk
41. Wyllie
42. Unysddu

*Most of the locations in South Wales to which the children of Dover, Folkestone, Deal and Sandwich were dispersed to during World War II.*

# CHILDREN INTO EXILE

The story of the evacuation of school children from Hellfire Corner in the
Second World War

## Peter Hayward

Buckland Publications Ltd
Barwick Road, Dover

DEDICATION:

to all those in the South East of England
who were exiled as children from their homes
in the Second World War 1939-1945

Published in 1997 by Buckland Publications Ltd
Barwick Road, Dover, Kent CT17 0LG

ISBN 07212 0970 X

Printed in England by Buckland Press Ltd, Barwick Road, Dover CT17 0LG

# CONTENTS

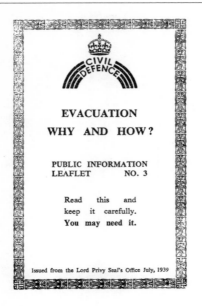

CIVIL DEFENCE

# EVACUATION
# WHY AND HOW?

PUBLIC INFORMATION
LEAFLET        NO. 3

Read     this     and
keep   it   carefully.
**You may need it.**

Issued from the Lord Privy Seal's Office July, 1939

## WHY EVACUATION?

There are still a number of people who ask " What is the need for all this business about evacuation ? Surely if war comes it would be better for families to stick together and not go breaking up their homes ? "

It is quite easy to understand this feeling, because it is difficult for us in this country to realise what war in these days might mean. If we were involved in war, our big cities might be subjected to determined attacks from the air—at any rate in the early stages—and although our defences are strong and are rapidly growing stronger, some bombers would undoubtedly get through.

We must see to it then that the enemy does not secure his chief objects—the creation of anything like panic, or the crippling dislocation of our civil life.

*One of the first measures we can take to prevent this is the removal of the children from the more dangerous areas.*

## THE GOVERNMENT EVACUATION SCHEME

The Government have accordingly made plans for the removal from what are called " evacuable " areas (see list at the back of this leaflet) to safer places called " reception " areas, of school children, children below school age if accompanied by their mothers or other responsible persons, and expectant mothers and blind persons.

The scheme is entirely a voluntary one, but clearly the children will be much safer and happier away from the big cities where the dangers will be greatest.

There is room in the safer areas for these children; householders have volunteered to provide it. They have offered homes where the children will be made welcome. The children will have their schoolteachers and other helpers with them and their schooling will be continued.

## WHAT YOU HAVE TO DO

### Schoolchildren

Schoolchildren would assemble at their schools when told to do so and would travel together with their teachers by train. The transport of some 3,000,000 in all is an enormous undertaking. *It would not be possible to let all parents know in advance the place to which each child is to be sent but they would be notified as soon as the movement is over.*

If you have children of school age, you have probably already heard from the school or the local education authority the necessary details of what you would have to do to get your child or children taken away. *Do not hesitate to register your children under this*

*scheme, particularly if you are living in a crowded area.* Of course it means heartache to be separated from your children, but you can be quite sure that they will be well looked after. That will relieve you of one anxiety at any rate. You cannot wish, if it is possible to evacuate them, to let your children experience the dangers and fears of air attack in crowded cities.

### Children under five

Children below school age must be accompanied by their mothers or some other responsible person. Mothers who wish to go away with such children should register with the Local Authority. *Do not delay in making enquiries about this.*

A number of mothers in certain areas have shown reluctance to register. Naturally, they are anxious to stay by their menfolk. Possibly they are thinking that they might as well wait and see; that it may not be so bad after all. *Think this over carefully and think of your child or children in good time.* Once air attacks have begun it might be very difficult to arrange to get away.

### Expectant Mothers

Expectant mothers can register at any maternity or child welfare centre. For any further information inquire at your Town Hall.

### The Blind

In the case of the Blind, registration to come under the scheme can be secured through the home visitors, or enquiry may be made at the Town Hall.

### PRIVATE ARRANGEMENTS

If you have made private arrangements for getting away your children to relatives or friends in the country, or intend to make them, you should remember that while the Government evacuation scheme is in progress ordinary railway and road services will necessarily be drastically reduced and subject to alteration at short notice. Do not, therefore, in an emergency leave your private plans to be carried out at the last moment. It may then be too late.

If you happen to be away on holiday in the country or at the seaside and an emergency arises, do not attempt to take your children back home if you live in an " evacuable " area.

### WORK MUST GO ON

The purpose of evacuation is to remove from the crowded and vulnerable centres, if an emergency should arise, those, more particularly the children, whose presence cannot be of any assistance.

Everyone will realise that there can be no question of wholesale clearance. We are not going to win a war by running away.

Most of us will have work to do, and work that matters, because we must maintain the nation's life and the production of munitions and other material essential to our war effort. For most of us therefore, who do not go off into the Fighting Forces our duty will be to stand by our jobs or those new jobs which we may undertake in war.

Some people have asked what they ought to do if they have no such definite work or duty.

*You should be very sure before deciding that there is really nothing you can do.* There is opportunity for a vast variety of services in civil defence. YOU must judge whether in fact you can or cannot help by remaining. If you are sure you cannot, then there is every reason why you should go away if you can arrange to do so, but you should take care to avoid interfering with the official evacuation plans. If you are proposing to use the public transport services, make your move either BEFORE the evacuation of the children begins or AFTER it has been completed. You will not be allowed to use transport required for the official evacuation scheme and other essential purposes, and you must not try to take accommodation which is required for the children and mothers under the Government scheme.

For the rest, we must remember that it would be essential that the work of the country should go on. Men and women alike will have to stand firm, to maintain our effort for victory. Such measures of protection as are possible are being pushed forward for the large numbers who have to remain at their posts. That they will be ready to do so, no one doubts.

—

The " evacuable " areas under the Government scheme are:—
(a) London, as well as the County Boroughs of West Ham and East Ham; the Boroughs of Walthamstow, Leyton, Ilford and Barking in Essex; the Boroughs of Tottenham, Hornsey, Willesden, Acton, and Edmonton in Middlesex; (b) the Medway towns of Chatham, Gillingham and Rochester; (c) Portsmouth, Gosport and Southampton; (d) Birmingham and Smethwick; (e) Liverpool, Bootle, Birkenhead and Wallasey; (f) Manchester and Salford; (g) Sheffield, Leeds, Bradford and Hull; (h) Newcastle and Gateshead; (i) Edinburgh, Rosyth, Glasgow, Clydebank and Dundee.

In some of these places only certain areas will be evacuated. Evacuation may be effected from a few other places in addition to the above, of which notice will be given.

*The Civil Defence authorities issued a range of Public Information Leaflets. This one, Leaflet No. 3, issued in 1939, dealt with the question of evacuation.*

# ILLUSTRATIONS

# FOREWORD

EVACUATION CHANGED all our lives. It certainly made an impact on the rest of my life. It broke down class barriers and helped me see the other person's point of view. Some boys and girls from pre-war working class homes were welcomed into the homes of the middle class in rural areas, but for many of those evacuated from East Kent to Wales, it was a case of middle class youngsters being welcomed by miners, steelworkers and others engaged in heavy industry.

We saw the best, and occasionally the worst, in human nature. Occasionally we saw some homes taking as many evacuees as possible in order to boost incomes. But usually it was a case of families showing great kindness to a boy or girl whose parents remained in danger in 'Hellfire Corner'.

It wasn't much fun for the foster family or for the evacuee. I remember on one occasion, lugging a battered suitcase, joining a group and going from house to house with a policeman trying to find billets. I remember the look of semi-disgust as the woman of the family, told she had to take one of us, surveyed the group to select the least objectionable boy. Grubby me was about the last to be picked out from the slowly diminishing group.

During my four and a bit years in Wales I was billeted with six or seven families, three or four in the first four months at Pontllanfraith and associated communities. In four years in Ebbw Vale I had three homes.

In one I remember coming home from school only to have to stand in the garden, in the falling snow, until my foster mother returned home. She later relented and allowed me to stand in the garage! But who can blame a house proud mother, with a daughter of her own, from preventing a noisy, potentially damaging eleven year old having the run of her middle class home.

But I also remember the great kindness of a very wealthy (for the area) childless couple who took me into their home for two years, trying to persuade me not to run wild in a town that became crowded with American troops. And of their kindness to me when they had to tell me that my brother had been killed on active service.

I remember the early years when we shared desks with the boys and girls of Ebbw Vale County School. They went to classes in the morning, Dover County School for Boys in the afternoon. The next week it was vice versa. There was certainly conflict as the Welsh boys found that their girls were taking too much interest in the 'new boys' in town.

I remember the excitement when one of our number tried to 'escape' by running away back to Dover. And how one, now a Dover licensee, was caught trying to walk through the Severn Railway Tunnel!

Most of us hated it there, despite the many kindnesses shown. We had a little ditty that went something like this:

> There is a mouldy dump
> Not far away,
> Where we get axle grease
> Four times a day.

Butter we never see,
We get slag dust in our tea,
And we are slowly
Fading away!

    Can you wonder our Ebbw Vale foster parents got a little fed up with us? But best of all I recall catching the train home when evacuation ended. Parents back home, with the shelling ended, but the war still on, demanded the return of their children. There had been a steady unofficial return after the last 'All Clear' was sounded. Now parents demanded all to return. The authorities relented. Ebbw Vale breathed a sigh of relief, but scores turned out at the railway station (now closed) to see us off to the noise of thunderflashes and fog signals on the line. What a happy journey that was, made even happier when the girls from our sister school, who had been evacuated to Caerleon, joined us at Newport.

    They were days I'll never forget. But how many of us ever showed our appreciation to those who looked after us through those desperate days? A few, but not many, and not enough.

Terry Sutton, MBE

*After the war, Terry worked for 46 years as a journalist in Dover, retiring from the* Dover Express *newspaper in 1994 as associate editor*

*Terry Sutton with Jeanne Fairweather (now Mrs Ruddick) at the reunion for evacuees
in Dover in May 1995*

# INTRODUCTION

WHEN WAR AGAINST Germany was declared on the 3rd September, 1939, I was just two and a half years old, and living with my family in St James Street, Dover. At that age I was blissfully unaware of what was happening in the world. Hitler, Chamberlain, war and evacuation, all meant nothing to me as I played in the River Dour or watched the Gordon Boys' Pipe Band, or was transported in my pram by my elder sisters down to Dover seafront to watch the roller skating.

On the day of evacuation, Sunday, the 2nd June, 1940, when the bulk of the schoolchildren of Dover, Folkestone, Deal and Sandwich left for unknown destinations in South Wales, my only memory is of getting lost amid a sea of legs on the platform at Dover Priory Station. My mother had been persuaded by the authorities to let me be evacuated together with my three older sisters despite my being under school age.

My sisters, Pearl, Jean and Mary, and I all ended up in the small mining town of Blaenavon in Monmouthshire. Jean and Mary were sent to separate billets, but Pearl, the eldest, had had strict instructions from Mum, not to let me 'out of her sight', so, for a while, Pearl and I managed to stay together.

At the time of our evacuation, troops from the besieged town of Dunkirk were landing in their thousands at Dover and other ports in the South-East, and my father was among them. One can only imagine what anguish my mother went through at that time; four of her five children being taken from her and sent to some strange place in South Wales; my father narrowly missing death on the beaches of Dunkirk and being whisked away to some unknown destination to have his injuries treated; and the threat of enemy invasion as the Germans overran the French channel ports! The experience that my mother went through was typical of what many hundreds, possibly thousands, of families were going through at that time.

It wasn't until more than fifty years later that I realised that, although books on evacuation had been produced, nobody had written about the East Kent evacuees, and I felt this to be an important missing chapter in the social and oral history of the Second World War. This book, therefore, attempts to tell their story.

I will brush briefly on Government plans for evacuation before war had even started, and will also cover those evacuees who, in 1939, were sent from London and the Medway Towns to East Kent, and their subsequent removal as the danger of invasion loomed ever nearer. But the bulk of this book is the story, told by themselves, of the children of Dover, Folkestone, Deal and Sandwich, who in 1940 were wrenched away from their parents and, for many, were also separated from brothers, sisters and friends. Most of these children suffered from culture shocks, as they found themselves in a strange and totally different environment.

This book also includes memories of those in Wales who still remember the evacuees. It also mentions a few of the tragedies which occurred during the separation of children and parents.

There is also a chapter on the schools' perspective of the evacuation, drawn mainly from school log books, but there are also several personal accounts from teachers who went with the children.

Some evacuees suffered terribly, with lice, scabies, malnutrition and general abuse, but the majority of evacuees found billets with loving foster-parents and made life-long friendships with the Welsh families.

This book is dedicated to all those war-time children who underwent the experience of evacuation, and to those present and future generations of children who, hopefully, will never know the trauma of evacuation.

Peter R. Hayward

---

KENT EDUCATION COMMITTEE

# Emergency Arrangements for

# Schools in Reception Areas

**TO PARENTS**

**Please read this carefully and keep it handy for reference.**

P. R. MORRIS,
Director of Education,
Springfield,
July, 1939.                     Maidstone.

---

*The front page of a leaflet issued before the outbreak of war by the authorities to prospective foster parents in Kent who were expected to receive evacuees*

Chapter One

## THE SCENE IS SET

AFTER THE FIRST World War, developments in both bomb and aircraft power intensified fears about the potential effects of bombing on densely-populated areas should another conflict arise. As early as 1931, the Committee of Imperial Defence formed a sub-committee to discuss plans for civilian evacuation from key areas, although these plans were never published. As the likelihood of another war with Germany grew, the subject of evacuation became ever more important and was discussed in the House of Commons.

By the end of 1938, the responsibility for overseeing evacuation in the event of war was placed with the Ministry of Health under the direction of Sir John Anderson. Britain was soon divided into three distinct areas – evacuation, reception and neutral areas. It was also decided that priority should be given to school children (who would be evacuated as school units), to mothers with pre-school children, to pregnant women, and to handicapped adults.

By early 1939 local authorities began planning. The designated evacuation areas started to arrange for would-be evacuees to register so that some idea of numbers could be gained. Meanwhile, the threat of war became more real as newspapers and radio carried stories of invasion and atrocities in Europe. On 31st August, 1939, Hitler gave orders for his forces to invade Poland. On the same day, the British Government ordered the evacuation to start. On Friday, 1st September, the evacuation machine went into action although the official declaration of war against Germany did not come until 3rd September. The Government was anticipating immediate and widespread bombing on Britain's industrial centres.

The evacuation, the first of several, proceeded swiftly and within three days nearly 1,500,000 people were conveyed under the Government Evacuation Scheme, of which over 800,000 were unaccompanied children. Most evacuees went by train and stations were packed with children, with labels attached, carrying sandwiches and the inevitable gas masks in cardboard boxes.

One of the greatest ironies of the evacuation was that the towns of East Kent, later themselves to become front-line towns, were at first designated reception areas. They received evacuees from London and the Medway towns. The following two long-range plans issued by Southern Railway show the numbers of evacuees from London and the Medway area who were scheduled to arrive in East Kent:

LONDON EVACUATION

Understood to take place on three days (document dated 13th April 1939)

| | | |
|---|---|---|
| Railhead provisionally fixed | Deal | |
| Number which may arrive | 4,710 | |
| Railhead Officer | Town Clerk, Deal | |
| Numbers which may be billeted in District | Deal Borough | 3,720 |
| | Eastry R D | 990 |

| Railhead provisionally fixed | Folkestone Shorncliffe |
| Number which may arrive | 13,000 |
| Railhead Officer | J. A. Wilkinson, Folkestone Borough |
| Reception Officer to local | J. A. Wilkinson, Old Harvey Grammar |
| authority for billeting area | School, Foord Road, Folkestone |

EVACUATION - LONG RANGE PLAN - 1939 - MEDWAY TOWNS

2nd July 1939 - Medway Evacuation (understood to take place on two days)

| Railhead provisionally fixed | Canterbury East | |
| Number to be detrained | 9,000 | |
| Nos. allocated to District | Canterbury C B | 2,500 |
| | Bridge-Blean R D | 3,500 |
| | Elham R D | 3,000 |

| Railhead provisionally fixed | Dover Priory | |
| Number to be detrained | 2,000 | |
| Nos. allocated to District | Dover R D | 2,000 |

| Railhead provisionally fixed | Deal | |
| Number to be detrained | 1,300 | |
| Nos. allocated to District | Deal Borough | 1,300 |

| Railhead provisionally fixed | Sandwich | |
| Number to be detrained | 5,300 | |
| Nos. allocated to District | Sandwich Borough | 1,300 |
| | Eastry R D | 4,000 |

Medway evacuation to take effect on and from 2nd July 1939.

Issued by: Southern Railway, Traffic Manager's Office, Operating Department, Waterloo Station. 26th June 1939.

*Evacuation poster issued by Southern Railway, just prior to the outbreak of war*

*This poster reflects just one aspect of work done by women during the war*

*Prior to the issue of the Long Range Evacuation Plan for the Medway Towns, dated 26th June, 1939, there must have been further plans to send Medway evacuees to the Borough of Dover, as the following letter shows:*

Brook House,
Dover.

W. L. Platts, Esq.,
Clerk of Kent County Council,
Sessions House,
Maidstone.

25th March 1939

Dear Sir,

Evacuation of Medway Towns

I am in receipt of your letter of the 24th instant giving particulars of a provisional time-table prepared by the Southern Railway in this matter, from which I note that provision is made for certain numbers of persons to be evacuated from the Medway towns to be detrained at Dover Priory Station.

I would refer you to my letter on the subject to the Ministry of Health, of the 16th January last, a copy of which I sent you with my letter of the 17th idem, suggesting that the Borough of Dover should not be a reception area. I have had further correspondence with the Ministry and the matter is still apparently under further consideration by them, with the result that my Council have not yet undertaken any Survey of Accommodation, and do not propose to do so unless and until definitely required by the Ministry, and I have asked the Department to receive a deputation from my Council on the subject before any decision to this effect is made.

Yours faithfully,
S. R. H. Loxton,
Town Clerk

*In the event, Mr Loxton's protests, and the rapidly changing nature of the war meant that, as far as can be ascertained, no evacuees from the Medway towns were ever billeted in the Borough of Dover. Indeed, by the middle of 1940, the children of the south-east coastal towns, including Dover, were themselves to be evacuated to safer areas.*

*Those London evacuees who did arrive in East Kent included the girls from Eltham Hill School. An article written by **Jill Bobe** and **Brenda Tarrant**, both of the Upper VI, appeared in the school's magazine in the 1950s, giving an account of the school's preparation for evacuation, and consequent removal to Deal and later to Folkestone:*

'Great Britain is now in a state of war with Germany.' This announcement on 3rd September, 1939, was to start a new era in the history of Eltham Hill School. A week before the declaration of war, the school had been preparing for evacuation and, as the weather was fine, the girls were kept occupied by various team games on the field. Girls had been prepared for departure at any moment, and rucksacks containing only the necessary requisites were brought to school and examined by staff to judge the suitability and adequacy of the contents. Other schools would be going to the station at the same time as Eltham Hill and speed was likely to be essential, so a special road drill known as 'waving' was practised, by which a hundred girls at a time crossed the road by all stepping off the pavement in one long line. Numbers of younger brothers and sisters signed on with Eltham Hill School. Meanwhile, Miss Ozanne and her staff were anxiously awaiting orders for evacuation from County Hall. Finally, on Friday, 1st September, the school left Well Hall Station for an unknown destination. The bombing of Warsaw had begun that morning and everybody wondered whether any of London would escape – this might be a final farewell.

We arrived at Deal, where, after much difficulty, billets were found for everyone, including the nursery contingent, and even then some of the staff did not know where Miss Ozanne was staying or how to contact her the next day. The summer holidays had not yet ended, and small groups – small, because the authorities were afraid of air raids – spent days on the beach in the lovely weather. School studies would have been difficult in any case, since there was no grammar school for Eltham Hill to share, and the buildings we were offered had no laboratories. At the end of a fortnight, therefore, our second evacuation began. This time we did not go so far, only some twelve miles to Folkestone.

Again there was a hunt for billets (a term hitherto known only in history lessons, but one that was now almost daily on our lips) and, although we shared the Girls' County School, the threat of air raids made the authorities forbid us to assemble in large numbers in any one place. We therefore made use of two Baptist churches, two Anglican church halls, a convent and a deep sea mission, situated by the harbour, with its lingering smell of fish. Westbourne House was also used; it was a boys' preparatory school (the son of Earl Haig had been a pupil there) whose members had been evacuated to a safer part of the country. It was delightfully situated, with views of the sea from many windows and from the spacious grounds. Eltham Hill School finally gained permission to use the whole of Westbourne House and all our furniture was sent from Eltham including desks, chairs, cupboards, laboratory equipment, library book-cases and books. Even a hostel was established there because the billeting situation remained difficult. Miss Wilson, the art mistress, had a grand time painting iron bedsteads in cheerful reds, greens and blues. There was an Aga cooker in the kitchen, and the school began cultivating some of the grounds to ensure a steady supply of our own vegetables.

*Growing vegetables at Westbourne House inspired one girl to write the following poem:*

### GARDENING AT WESTBOURNE HOUSE

With spade and fork we go to dig,
    With rake and trowel we weed;
Until the earth is clear and fresh
    And we can plant the seed.

Onions, carrots, beans and peas
    Are planted, grown and sold,
We help to tend our varied crops
    In weather hot or cold.

The 'Dig for Victory' campaign
    In which our food we grow
Is carried out by all the girls,
    Who rake and weed and hoe.

With spade and fork we go to dig,
    With rake and trowel we weed,
By growing all the food we can
    We help our country's need.

*Joyce Healey*, Form IIp

*A linocut by the girls of Eltham Hill School, depicting both Abertillery and Folkestone, which appeared on the cover of their first school magazine produced in Wales in 1940*

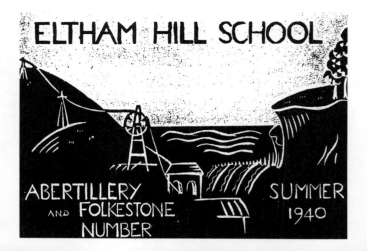

*Other poems by the girls of Eltham Hill School, while they were in Folkestone, gave small glimpses of the war and include the following:*

### A Day In My Life – by Our Host's Small Son

At seven o'clock one sunny morn
   I tumbled out of bed,
And ran into the girls' bedroom –
   'Wake up, wake up,' I said.

We had a pillow-fight, of course;
   I won, I always do;
Then quickly we put on our clothes,
   And down the stairs we flew –

We ate a hearty dinner, and
   Got ready to go out.
We climbed some hills and raced down fast;
   Oh my! How we did shout!

We fought his soldiers, killed them all,
   We brought his bombers down;
We chased a spy – her name was Viv,
   Pursued her through the town.

They answered not a single word.
   'They're still asleep,' I cried.
But no, for there beneath the sheets
   Two pairs of eyes I spied.

To have a hasty breakfast, for
   There was homework to be done.
We did our Maths and History –
   Homework can be such fun.

Then hungry we walked home at last,
   And after eating tea
We played at fighting Hitler,
   We bombed his ships at sea.

At last 'twas time to go to bed,
   So Daphne read to me;
Then up the stairs, and soon, I thought,
   In slumberland I'll be.

                                         **Vivienne Webb**, IIIG

### A Letter Home.
#### (Immediately before Christmas)

Dear Mum and Dad and Cousin Ray,
We've had a lot of snow today;
It's rather cold down here, you know;
Oh, by the way, have you had snow?
I've heard from Auntie May and Lu
Poor Uncle Ted has had the 'flu.
Has Ruby found her puppy yet?
Now what else was it? – I forget!
Oh! Yesterday when we were out
Something strange was bobbing about,
And eight men standing on the beach,
Lassoing the object, out of reach,
At last attached it to a line;

They hauled it in; it was a mine!
A harmless one enough, thanks be,
Or else we'd not have stayed to see.
Isn't Christmas getting near?
The shops are very gay round here.
I'll send a postcard soon to say
When I arrive on Saturday.
We break up Friday night, instead
Of Saturday noon, as I have said.
Kind regards from Mrs Dann,
And I must close –
Your loving
Nan, (**Nancy Dalziel**, Form II)

                    *       *       *

*When Sir Roger Manwood's School at Sandwich reassembled at the end of the summer holidays in September 1939, great excitement was caused by the sudden appearance of two hundred boys from Gillingham Boys' County School. This school was evacuated to Sandwich as a 'safe' area, so, for eight months before its own migration began, Manwood's found itself playing host to a school already caught up in the war. It was difficult enough running two schools in one set of premises, but a war-time regulation which forbade more than one hundred people to be under one roof at any one time without air-raid shelters, made things almost impossible. It became necessary to bring into service the most unlikely teaching spaces – the local Congregational and Methodist church halls, rooms in private houses like the Ramparts and Dunearn (now Manwood Lodge), and the Salvation Army and Scouts' H.Q.*

*With boys dispersed in classrooms all over the town of Sandwich, masters had to become adept in moving from one period to the next. By December 1939 the completion of the air-raid shelters enabled the usual numbers to be taught on the school premises again. These shelters, which stretched in a long line along the top of the Home Field, were fortunately never used – at least not for their official purpose.*

*Another effect of the war on the school in these early months was the blackout. With so many windows in the building, only certain rooms could be effectively screened; elsewhere blue and orange electric light bulbs shed their ghostly glow at intermittent distances. 'The journey from one haven of light to another is fraught with danger,' reported the vice-captain of the school,* **W. Middlemass.** *'The common herd has to grope its way by sense of touch alone and, since shadows have no identity, it is necessary to be polite to all whom one encounters.'*

*By the end of May 1940 war was raging dangerously close to the Belgian and French ports. The first result was an immediate increase in the number of air-raid warnings which brought the boarders at Manwood's down at night from the big dormitory to the supposedly greater security of the headmaster's staircase, and in the hectic days of Dunkirk, Sandwich found itself in the front line. Hastily improvised fortifications transformed the appearance of Sandwich Bay, the bridges on Sandown Road, and the senior boys in the OTC spent at least one early summer night in vigil on St Clement's church tower watching for signs of invasion.*

*It was now obvious that Sandwich was no longer a suitable reception area, and the departure of the Gillingham boys to a safer place was almost immediately followed by a warning to Sir Roger Manwood's School, to make preparations for the evacuation of their own pupils.*

**Jim Cullen** *was eleven years old when war was declared. He remembers with vivid detail, the months leading up to the evacuation of Sir Roger Manwood's School in Sandwich:*

Finally, war came. Listening to Chamberlain's broadcast my parents were in a sombre mood, but the children of Woodnesborough Village were excited. My elder half-brother had put on his uniform and cycled off to join his TA unit at Sandwich. A searchlight unit had been positioned on some high ground and we were thrilled by the sight of an aged Lewis gun mounted on a post, which was the only means of defence against the bombers that were sure to come.

I had won a scholarship to Sir Roger Manwood's Grammar School in Sandwich, but the start of term was delayed and then we worked half days for some time to allow for a system to be worked out to enable us to share facilities with a school evacuated from the Medway Towns.

The bitter winter of 1939/40 came and went; the 'Phoney War' was enlivened for us by the sinking of the *Graf Spee*, but after the boarding of the *Altmark* in February 1940, the war intensified. Norway and Denmark were quickly overwhelmed by the Germans in April, followed in May by the opening of the Blitzkrieg on the Western Front. War was coming nearer – and very quickly too, as the Germans broke through and the sound of the guns in France could be heard once more on the Kent Coast.

Rumours of impending evacuation spread through the school and at last it was confirmed that we were to leave. No-one seemed to know our destination and when it was finally disclosed – Penclawdd – no-one knew where it was! I can remember going home to tell my parents that the school was on the move and I said that I wanted to go. To me it was an adventure; to them it must have been heartbreaking, but the decision, probably the first of any importance that I had made, had a material bearing on my future.

As the day of departure neared, the school books were packed, lists of what we could take with us were issued – one suitcase, one rucksack and 'Don't forget your gas mask and Ration Book!' In those days Woodnesborough village had a saddler, for there were still many working horses on the farms, and he made me a stout but unsightly haversack from black canvas, which was totally 'unwearoutable' and is probably still doing yeoman service somewhere in Kent. Anyway, we were to leave on the following Sunday, 2nd June, 1940.

*As late as May, 1940 the authorities were still contemplating sending a further 400 evacuees into the Eastry Rural District. Protests against this proposed action are recorded in a meeting of the Eastry Rural District Council:*

EVACUATION

The Billeting Officer reported that the number of evacuees in the billeting area at present was 206 made up of 162 unaccompanied pupils, 14 accompanied, eight mothers, ten teachers and 12 helpers. The decrease in the number of unaccompanied children was due to the fact that scholars who had succeeded in passing the recent examination had returned home to seek employment. The health of the unaccompanied children had been maintained. Some 224 people who had taken in evacuees had qualified to receive the Queen's message.

With regard to further evacuation, it had been decided not to send any children to the northern part of the area, but it was possible more would be sent to the remaining part of the district. It had been pointed out to the Ministry that the area was an agricultural one and that owing to men having been called up, women were absent from their homes from early morning until evening engaged on farm work, and it would therefore be unwise to billet children with farm families where there would be no-one to look after them during the day. The Ministry replied that they were not contemplating moving children from the area; and, in fact, the area must be prepared to receive a further 400, even if it meant applying compulsory powers. As to unsuitability, whatever the conditions they would have to take them.

Mr Holness asked if the Council were going to sit down under that. They had been told it was very important that more food should be produced, but in spite of that being pointed out by the Executive Officer the Ministry proposed sending them more. The matter should be taken up by the County Agricultural Committee. It was unreasonable to expect more food to be produced when the men had left the land leaving the women at home to do the greater part of the work formerly done by the men. It was a difficult question and he thought they should communicate with the War Agricultural Committee. Most of the women went out to work in the fields and they could not attend to evacuated children, much as they would like to do so.

The Chairman said the matter had been under consideration and they had avoided putting the children in undesirable cottages as much as possible. The Billeting Officer said that Northbourne where they had a school canteen was the only place where children could be looked after throughout the day. The

I WISH TO MARK, BY THIS PERSONAL MESSAGE, my appreciation of the service you have rendered to your Country in 1939.

In the early days of the War you opened your door to strangers who were in need of shelter, & offered to share your home with them.

I know that to this unselfish task you have sacrificed much of your own comfort, & that it could not have been achieved without the loyal co-operation of all in your household.

By your sympathy you have earned the gratitude of those to whom you have shown hospitality. & by your readiness to serve you have helped the State in a work of great value.

*Elizabeth R*

19

*'The Queen's message' issued to foster parents after a period of qualification in looking after an evacuee*

evacuated children had been removed from Deal.

The Chairman suggested a resolution could be sent to the Ministry to the effect that they considered the district a very undesirable one to which evacuees should be sent on the grounds that it was a danger area as well as being an agricultural district in which the wives of the men were out at work all day.

On the motion of Mr Cable seconded by Mr Holness it was agreed to protest to the Ministry and also send a copy to the War Agricultural Committee.

*Frank E. Davies* *reflects on his memories of the first few months of the war:*

When war was declared in September 1939, I was aged fourteen years and ten months. I travelled by rail each day to attend Dover County School for Boys. We were aware of terrible happenings in Germany, when German Jews joined our school, sent out of their country by their parents for their safety. I was friendly with one boy, Hahn, who was a brilliant pianist.

1938-39 enabled this country to prepare for war. All the civilian population was issued with gas masks (officially called respirators) which we carried about in cardboard boxes. We were also prepared for attack from the air. We had practices, both at school and at home, to run to shelters. The ones at home, called Anderson Shelters, were archways of metal, half buried in the earth in the garden. I helped to dig ours in. They would only give modest protection, and would certainly have been useless in the event of a direct hit.

We also received pamphlets about ARP (Air Raid Precautions) and Air Raid Wardens were appointed. In the war we had to 'blackout' our homes. Yards of blackout material were sold and fitted to windows. Not a chink of light was allowed to show, and Air Raid Wardens, even when no aircraft were about, could be heard bellowing, 'Put that light out!' at the sight of any glimmer. We were aware from the newspapers, of the devastating effects of air warfare, having read accounts of German aircraft attacking targets in the Spanish Civil War.

This was the background for the beginning of the war on the Home Front. War started on Sunday, 3rd September, 1939. I was organist at a beautiful Norman church in Nonington, about three miles from my home in Aylesham. I either cycled along the roads or walked across the fields, a short cut, on clearly defined footpaths. We had been told that day by the Prime Minister that we were at war with Germany, and this was very much in my mind as I walked to church that morning. I was over half way there when the air-raid siren sounded. I was frightened, being near a railway line and a coal mine, obvious targets for air attack, and I ran the rest of the way to church, to find other people there, equally disturbed. We heard later that it was a false alarm.

There followed a quiet period nicknamed the 'Phoney War'. At home in Aylesham, we were part of the reception area for evacuees; children evacuated from London and the Medway towns, into a supposedly safe area. We had an evacuee, Grace, from Gillingham. Every Sunday her mother came by train to see her. My mother was kindness itself to her, but she was very homesick and after some months of the phoney war, she returned home as did many others.

As far as we were concerned, life proceeded as before. I was in the 5th form at school, preparing for School Certificate Exam. Sometime in the new year, we noticed that the trains were only using one track in the very long tunnel we used to go through on the way to school. The reason was that a huge gun on wheels was hidden in there. We saw it occasionally, surrounded by soldiers of the Royal Artillery. It was capable of firing shells across the Channel. The tunnel provided perfect protection in the event of an air-raid.

In the second week of May 1940, the Germans commenced a Blitzkrieg; in five days Holland was beaten, and the Germans swept into Belgium and France. By 27th May, Admiral Ramsay, in Dover, began to evacuate British troops from Dunkirk. Dover gave its little ships to this historic evacuation – peacetime pleasure launches, old paddle steamers, fishing boats etc. They came back, packed to their limits, with exhausted troops to Dover, Folkestone and Ramsgate, whence they were dispersed by rail to reception camps throughout Britain.

It was thought at the time that the invasion of Britain was now imminent. Immediately, the whole coastline was covered in concrete obstacles, barbed wire and gun emplacements. The shore was out of bounds and the civilian army, known as the Local Defence Volunteers, was formed. They later became known as the Home Guard. Soon it was to be the turn of the school children to be evacuated, and I was to be one of those to go.

*Ted Green* *was nine years old, living in Trevanion Street, Dover, when war was declared and later was to be evacuated to South Wales with his two sisters, Marie and Margaret.*

On the 3rd September, 1939, I was sitting on the rear wall of our house in Trevanion Street, when I heard from other children over the wall that war had just been declared. It didn't seem serious to me at the time. In the following weeks we all had to go to St James' School Hall in St James' Street to be fitted with gas masks. I thought they gave off a terrible smell, but alas we all received one and had to carry it wherever we went. I suppose it was a little frightening to us children, not knowing what was going to happen.

During the first few weeks after war was declared, the families in the part of Dover where we lived started using the Trevanion Street caves. One cave was in the yard of a scrap merchant and the other one was situated near to the Buffs Drill Hall close to Liverpool Street. Every evening at about sunset we would all go to the caves, which were damp and musty. There were old bunks and bedsteads in the caves, provided by the locals. The air-raid sirens would sound most evenings, and off we would go to the caves. I don't think we slept very well, but I can see it as if it were yesterday. I know now how much danger we must have been in. ARP wardens were always at the entrance of the caves.

The people were always friendly and helpful towards each other during those early war days. I remember as we sat in the caves, we could hear distant rumbles of guns, or bombs exploding. From the entrance of the caves we could see the skies lit with searchlights. Soon we had to leave Trevanion Street because it was getting too dangerous, and we moved to a safer part of Dover near Buckland Hospital. Soon, Anderson shelters were delivered to every household and we had to get busy helping to set them into the ground in the back gardens. It was not long, however, before we heard that the schools were to be evacuated.

*Dover resident,* *Elsie Hayward**, remembers the day that war was declared:*

I can remember the day war broke out. I was cook at Doctor Elliott's. They had kippers for breakfast. They had an old-fashioned radio powered by gas. The doctor's wife had just sent me upstairs for some blackout material. When I was coming down the second flight of stairs, I bumped into the doctor and he said, 'War has just been declared.' I dropped the blackout material and ran. 'Where are you going?' asked the doctor. 'Home,' I said, 'because the children are on their own.' Peter was only two years old. Then the siren went. Minutes later George arrived with my gas mask! The doctor said to him, 'You are a brave boy!' Anyway, the doctor wouldn't let me go home, and said I should go down to the shelter. Then the 'All Clear' went and we all laughed! It was frightening though!

*Although she didn't know it at the time, four of Elsie Hayward's five children were to be evacuated in due course.* *Duncan Turner** was living in St James' Street, Dover, before the war, and went to St Mary's Boys' School. He reflects on those days before evacuation:*

My memories of Dover in 1939 are still strong even though a lot of time has passed by. As young as I was, a change was taking place and I don't think I realised that we were at war.

Instead of green downs above the cliffs, defence trenches were dug everywhere and heavy gun emplacements were built. Then came the first awesome sound of the siren warnings.

I remember well many of the air-raids, the heavy thump and roar of our defending guns. I remember some of our fine ships in Dover Harbour, that we later lost in various naval engagements – the *Hood, Nelson, Rodney* and some others. On one occasion, I went to Deal for the day and there was great excitement on the sea front. Two ships had collided with each other trying to avoid a floating mine. It was in Dover Harbour, in the dock area, we saw the first captured German U-boat, which I found very exciting.

*Brian Hedgecock was nine years old when war was declared. He was living at the time, in the village of River, just outside Dover.*

My mother had three sisters and a brother, all married, as well as her mother, all living close to hand in the village including my three cousins, brothers Colin and Keith, and Jean. We were frequently to be found in each other's houses. Keith was older than Colin, Jean and me and in 1939 went to Dover County School, whereas we three went to River Elementary School. We all lived in an idyllic environment with loving families in a lovely sleepy village, roaming far and wide over unspoilt fields and woodland. We played by, and in, the river where we caught tiddlers, tadpoles and newts, and floated our boats. We picked primroses, bluebells, cowslips, knew about the birds and found their nests – it was wonderful!

I can't remember our lives as children being unduly affected by the phoney war except that we now had air raid shelters in our gardens and had to know what to do if there was an air raid warning, especially if we were out somewhere without our parents – and we had gas masks. Having assimilated these new things our lives largely went on as before. I became ten years old in January 1940 and soon things were to change rapidly!

In May came the events leading up to Dunkirk; Red Cross trains going one after the other up the railway line away from the port of Dover. Then came the radio announcement that many areas were to be designated evacuation areas and others were to be reception areas. I can well remember the announcer saying that Dover was to be an evacuation area and then my mother turning to my father and saying, 'That doesn't mean us though, does it?' – a forlorn wish, born out of dread, I am sure, based on the fact that our village of River was just outside Dover! Well, of course it did mean us and so we waited for the evacuation instructions, my mother and father with an ever-increasing sense of dread, fear and anxiety. When the instructions were published we learned that evacuation was to be by schools, and we were effectively to be placed in the care of our teachers who thus had a tremendous responsibility thrust upon them. Not enough has been made of the debt of gratitude we all owe for what they did for us in the ensuing years.

*Doris Fisher joined the staff of the Dover County School for Girls in the month that war was declared. Here she relates her own experiences prior to evacuation:*

I joined the staff as senior English mistress in September 1939. I had hoped to book in for a few nights at the Lord Warden Hotel, but it had already been taken over by the navy. I had already rented a flat at the bottom of Park Avenue, but had had no chance to furnish it, so I was homeless! A member of the staff kindly gave me a bed for a few nights until I could move in. My flat was the first floor of a large house that had been made into three flats. The top flat was occupied by a retired nurse, the ground floor flat rented by the War Office, who had taken over all unoccupied property in the town. For my first few weeks it was filled by a group of ATS, who entertained noisily most of every night until the number of local complaints prevailed and they were removed. By that time, the headmistress, Miss E. M. Gruer, had kindly insisted that I sleep at her house as I was the only member of staff living entirely alone.

Prior to my going to stay with her, we had a number of noisy nights with our ships being bombed right into the harbour. We had also a number of raids in the district during the day, and spent a lot of time in the school air-raid shelters. So we received the news of evacuation with a certain amount of relief, as teaching had become a total farce. The children were listening, not to us, but to the 'planes coming overhead. Some of our girls had already left Dover; sent by their parents to safer areas, but the bulk of the school joined the evacuation train on 2nd June.

*Dover Grammar School for Girls as it is today – very much the same as it was at the time of evacuation.*
*Photo – Peter Hayward*

*By 10th May, 1940, that period of inactivity in Western Europe which had become known as the Phoney War came to an abrupt end. By 14th May Holland fell. By 20th May, German tanks had reached the Channel coast and encircled the British Expeditionary Force and three French armies. On 26th May Operation Dynamo commenced, with a view to lifting up to 45,000 of the British Expeditionary Force from the beaches and port of Dunkirk. However, by the 4th June, over 338,000 had been rescued, Operation Dynamo was terminated and the brave and battered town of Dunkirk finally surrendered. Soon Dover was to become the centre of 'Hell-Fire Corner', and she and her sister towns of Folkestone, Deal and Sandwich were all to become 'Frontline Towns'. Rumours of a civilian evacuation of East Kent were circulating prior to the evacuation of British and Allied troops from Dunkirk, prompting the issue of the following notice which appeared in the* Dover Express *on 17th May 1940:*

THE EVACUATION RUMOUR – A DEFINITE CONTRADICTION

The rumour which has been widely spread as to the evacuation of Dover, is entirely without foundation. There is no intention to evacuate anyone, children or otherwise!

Do NOT spread rumours.

Do NOT believe the stories of threats to Dover.

The advance of the Germans into Holland, however, makes more than ever necessary all the ARP precautions which have been displayed for months.

Black Out properly.

Carry your gas mask.

Keep under cover when there is gunfire.

Put bonfires out before dark.

*Just nine days later the Ministry of Health issued evacuation plans which appeared in the* Dover Express *on 31st May, 1940:*

DOVER AN EVACUATION AREA

The Ministry of Health announced on Sunday that a number of towns on the south and east coasts were to be declared evacuation areas. They were: Great Yarmouth, Lowestoft, Felixstowe, Harwich, Clacton, Frinton and Walton, Southend, Margate, Ramsgate, Broadstairs, Sandwich, Dover, Deal, and Folkestone.

Arrangements are being made for the despatch to safer districts in the Midlands and Wales of those children whose parents want them to go. They will travel by special trains next Sunday. A similar movement of school children on the same day is being made from Chatham, Gillingham, Rochester and Sheerness which have already been made evacuation areas. An advertisement in another column gives particulars of the method being adopted at Dover. It should be studied. Information should not be given to strangers and those purporting to represent the press.

MORE EVACUEES LEAVING

On Tuesday it was announced that the Government has decided to remove evacuated children from rural and urban areas within approximately 10 miles of the coasts of Suffolk, Essex and Kent, and part of Norfolk. This follows the removal a fortnight ago of evacuated children from areas on the coast.

The decision does not apply to children normally living in these districts. The areas now affected in Kent are: Bridge Blean RD, Dover RD, East Ashford RD, Eastry RD, Elham RD, Strood RD, Swale RD.

*Also appearing in the Dover Express for 31st May, 1940, was a notice from the Town Clerk:*

GOVERNMENT EVACUATION SCHEME
SCHOOL CHILDREN

School children and their younger brothers and sisters who have been registered for evacuation will assemble at their schools before leaving for the station at a time which will be told to parents as soon as possible. In order to prevent crowding, parents and the General Public cannot be allowed to come to the station to see the children off. There will be plenty of helpers.

S. R. H. Loxton
30th May 1940                                                                        Town Clerk

*Unlike the inner cities' evacuation of September, 1939, the schools in Dover, Folkestone, Deal and Sandwich had little time to prepare for the evacuation of their own children. Just seven days notice was given for schools to issue registration forms, register the children for evacuation and generally prepare the schools for departure to reception areas in South Wales. Thus the scene was at last set for the evacuation of the school children from Hellfire Corner.*

*East Kent buses deliver children to Dover Priory Railway Station on the day of evacuation,*
*2nd June, 1940 – Peter Hayward collection*

Chapter Two

## THE EXODUS BEGINS

*WITH THE WAR IN EUROPE rapidly deteriorating and the threat of invasion looming ever nearer, the time had come to start removing the children from East Kent to safer places. The first to go from the coastal towns were those children who had been evacuated into East Kent from London and the Medway area. On Sunday 19th May, 1940, some of these evacuees took their leave of Deal and Sandwich. The following article which appeared in the East Kent Mercury on Saturday, 25th May, recorded their departure:*

### EVACUEES LEAVE – SCENES AT DEAL AND SANDWICH

Early on Sunday morning the school children who had been evacuated to Deal and Sandwich took their departure in special trains to take up new quarters in South Wales.

At Deal the party of 397 were seen off by the Mayor (Councillor E. J. Dobson, JP), Mr D. A. Daniels (Town Clerk), Mr Brigg (District Secretary of the KEC), Mr A. J. G. Marsh (Evacuation Officer), a large number of teachers, foster-parents and others who had been associated with the housing and education of the evacuees. In many instances considerable reluctance was apparent on the part of both foster-parents and the children to say goodbye, and many were the expressions of appreciation of the happy time spent during their stay in Deal. Through the kindness of Mr Colgrave, of Messrs R. G. Waters Ltd., the children who wished were given a bottle of milk to drink before they left.

The first of two comfortable corridor trains arranged for by Mr Gardner (Stationmaster at Deal) left at 7.25 and conveyed 268 children to their destinations in South Wales, at Magor, Osaweeru, Bassaleg and Rogerstone. In the second, which steamed out at 9.25, were the 129 Secondary School scholars who were to be provided for at Rogerstone. The Mayor and Town Clerk passed up and down the trains shaking hands with the teachers and wishing the children a happy and comfortable journey. Quite a number of children, it is understood, had been taken back to their homes by their parents, who did not wish them to go so far from home.

There are indications that the removal of the children has caused some anxiety as to the possibility of sinister steps being taken in other directions, but up to the present there has been no hint of the likelihood of a general evacuation order being made. There is certainly no foundation for such rumours, which should be received with caution.

### AT SANDWICH

Some 60 evacuees joined the trains at Sandwich, and here too, they were seen off by the Mayor (Cllr W. V. J. Precott-Westcar, DSO, JP) and other officials connected with the evacuation arrangements. The party was all that was left of between 400 and 500 children who came to the district in September, and again many of the foster-parents were reluctant to part with the youngsters who had been in their care during the past six months. All the children took with them hand luggage and a day's rations, and it was expected they would reach their destination early in the evening.

*The evacuees to Folkestone left on the same day, 19th May, 1940. Among those that departed were the girls of Eltham Hill School. **Margaret Downie** of Lower VI wrote in the first issue in exile of the school's magazine, the following account of the journey from Folkestone to South Wales:*

The scene is Radnor Park, Folkestone; the time, eleven o'clock on Sunday, 19th May, 1940. One of a group of about 250 excited Eltham Hill School girls, surrounded by their Folkestone foster-parents and all carrying as much of their personal luggage as possible, I waited for the train which was to take us further out of the danger zone. Excitement was the predominant feeling, although this was slightly damped by the sadness which we nearly all felt at leaving Folkestone. It was a hot summer day and the wait in the park was not a very pleasant experience. At last we made our way on to a platform of the Central Station and, after farewells had been said and promises of letters exchanged, the train, whose windows were all crowded with cheerful faces, slowly drew out of the station.

We settled down to enjoy what promised to be a most interesting journey. The attractive Kent scenery before us as we started and the beauty of the day aroused a greater interest in the windows than any paper or magazine. The usual pleasure of a walk along a gently rocking corridor was also indulged in by many of us when the scenery had become a slightly less powerful attraction. Our train took us through the counties of Kent, Surrey, Berkshire, Wiltshire and Gloucestershire, until we finally went through the famous Severn Tunnel.

The arrival at Newport, where we learnt that our destination was Abertillery, awoke in most of us the feeling that now we were really among Welsh people and we looked forward eagerly to the end of our journey. Suddenly we were surrounded by mountains and we saw, many of us for the first time, the shafts at the heads of the pits, about which we had all heard so much.

We arrived at Abertillery at half past six, and were surprised and flattered when we left the station to find the streets filled with welcoming crowds. There was never the least doubt about the warmth of our reception. Anyone who looked weary was immediately relieved of her load, and many were the remarks on our sad fate at being separated from our parents. Our age and size also called for comment; certainly we could not succeed in looking like the 'little girls' whom they had been led to expect.

We had been told at the station that the Tabernacle Congregational Church was very kindly going to give us tea but we were not prepared for such a feast as we saw on entering the hall. (Other members of our party fared just as well at the Ebenezer Baptist Church.) We eagerly ate the meal and were very grateful to the Abertillery people who provided it for us.

# Thank you, Foster-Parents . . . we want more like you!

The Secretary of State, who has been entrusted by the Government with the conduct of evacuation, asks you urgently to join the Roll of those who are willing to receive children. Please apply to your local Council.

*An example of one of the many notices issued by the Government, which encouraged families to 'take in' evacuees.*

After tea, various members of the town made speeches of welcome, to which Miss Ozanne responded with a vote of thanks. We were medically examined and then waited to be taken to our billets. By half past nine we were all settled in our new homes and feeling already that we were going to be very happy there; a feeling that time has only confirmed.

*Also in the Eltham School magazine appeared the following poem:*

The Travels of an Evacuee

**A**s soon as the war began, our school
**B**ecame a flock of evacuees,
**E**vacuated from a mother's rule
**R**ight into the 'Land of the Leas'
**T**hen after a while we were moved.
**I**n leaving Folkestone we realised we loved,
**L**ovely seatown backed by high hills,
**L**eft to the mercy of tyrants' wills.
**E**ver moving for several hours,
**R**elieved when rest at last was ours.
**Y**ou must guess where Eltham School now resides;
    For a clue the beginning of each line provides.

***Muriel French***

*Just one week after the departure of those children who had been evacuated to East Kent, plans were laid for the evacuation of local school children from Dover, Folkestone, Deal and Sandwich. Various reports were published in the local press, including the following in the* East Kent Mercury *for Saturday, 1st June 1940:*

SCHOOL CHILDREN TO GO – REGISTRATION AT DEAL AND SANDWICH.

It was announced by the Ministry of Health on Sunday night (26th May) that in view of the fact that Holland with parts of Belgium and Northern France were in enemy occupation, the Government have decided that a number of towns on the east coast between Great Yarmouth and Folkestone should be declared evacuation areas.

Amongst those towns of course are Deal and Sandwich. Registration of children for evacuation began on Monday and up to mid-day on Wednesday there had been given in at the various schools in Deal, 1,477 names of the 2,700 children on the registers.

These with some 100 teachers and helpers are expected to leave tomorrow (Sunday) though up to the present their exact destinations have not been made known.

At Sandwich there were 466 out of 845 registered, including Manwood Grammar School with 191 out of 250. The majority of other boys of the school are being privately evacuated. At Sandwich Central School only 122 of 322 registered, probably because many of the scholars live in villages not being evacuated. Arrangements for the reception of the children have been worked out. It was emphasised that children who have not registered will not be evacuated.

Mr Malcolm MacDonald, Minister of Health broadcasting on Sunday night on the new evacuation areas, said: 'We have chosen these places deliberately on the facts of the situation before us. The change is to be confined to the stretch of coast nearest to the territory, across the narrow seas, which is at present in the enemy's occupation and it is to be further confined to certain urban centres on our coast which are fairly closely populated. There is no question of compulsory evacuation of school children, but it is highly desirable from the point of view of their own safety, as well as on other grounds, that as many as possible of these children may be evacuated at an early date.

Mr MacDonald added that he knew how hard it was for parents to determine on separation in time of danger and that the Government could not guarantee safety to everyone in the reception areas, but if they did not register their children, they might speedily rue it.

*The article continued with a list of items the school children needed to take with them on evacuation: gas mask, identification card, ration book, food for a day, change of underclothes, night clothes, handkerchiefs, spare stockings or socks, house shoes or plimsolls, warm coat or mackintosh, toothbrush, comb, towel.*

Parcels should not be of greater proportions than a child can carry. Other necessities can be sent on by parents at a later date. Ration books and identity cards should be packed with the children's luggage and not given to them to hold. Each child will be supplied with a postcard, and in the course of a day or so their parents should hear where they are stationed. The evacuation arrangements apply also to private schools.

*Before the Deal children left, the chairman of the Deal Education Committee bade farewell to the children in this open letter:*

FAREWELL MESSAGE

Dear Boys and Girls,

The Editor of the *Mercury* has kindly allowed me to say goodbye to you on your removal from Deal. I do so with much regret, but I feel that the Government has done wisely in evacuating you to a safer area and that parents who have refused to take advantage of the decision are very foolish. They may be assured that under the wise and helpful guidance of their teachers, assisted by a band of loyal helpers, you will be well cared for, and your education continued as far as possible. All I ask is that in your new abode you prove worthy of the town which has been your home.

I wish you and your teachers every happiness and success in your new surroundings and trust that in happier times, not, I hope, far distant, we may all be re-united.

Needless to say you will never be absent from my thoughts, and I shall be always wondering how you are getting on, and hoping that you are all doing well.

With every good wish that God may bless and protect you.

Yours sincerely,

Draycott                           ***J Waller,***
Church Path, Deal                Chairman
May 30th, 1940           Deal Education Committee

*On Sunday, 2nd June, two special trains conveyed the Deal children to South Wales under the government evacuation scheme. The first train left at 10am carrying the following:*

Parochial School: 130 children, 10 teachers and 2 helpers;
St Mary's School: 102 children, 5 teachers and 4 helpers;
South Deal Council Junior Mixed School: 153 children, 9 teachers and 4 helpers;
South Deal Infants: 21 children, 3 teachers and nil helpers;

making a total of 406 children, 27 teachers and 10 helpers, who all detrained at Bridgend. In the same train were the following schools:

Methodist School: 67 children, 4 teachers and 3 helpers;
North Deal Council: 11 children, 5 teachers and 1 helper;
Lower Walmer School: 105 children, 6 teachers and 3 helpers;
Upper Walmer School: 43 children. 3 teachers and 1 helper.
Great Mongeham School: 36 children, 2 teachers and 2 helpers;

making a total of 262 children, 20 teachers and 10 helpers, who detrained at Pyle.

*In the second train, which left at 11.15am were:*

Central Boys: 332 children, 13 teachers and 16 helpers;
Central Girls: 379 children, 11 teachers and 16 helpers;

a total party (which included younger brothers and sisters of Central School scholars) of 767. These all detrained at Merthyr Tydfil.

*The first train was due to arrive at Bridgend at five o'clock and at Pyle at 5.25, but it was one and a half hours late. The second train, due at Merthyr Tydfil at 6.40, arrived at 7.05. The mayor and town clerk of Deal, the chairman and several members of the Deal Education Committee and the Glynn Vivian Mission Band were on the platform to see both trains depart.*

*The route taken was via Redhill, Reading, Swindon and Newport. The weather was perfect, but the sun which blazed down all day, made the heat in the trains somewhat trying. However, much needed supplies of drinking water, were given to the children on the spur of the moment at various stopping places on route by ladies, railway men, soldiers, nurses etc. The children were well-behaved and the whole journey seemed to have been made without mishap.*

*On the same day, Sunday 2nd June, the Sandwich children departed. It was shortly after nine o'clock in the morning when 482 scholars with 50 teachers and helpers were despatched from Sandwich to Gowerton, near Swansea in South Wales. Here again was a large gathering of parents and relations and the mayor and the town clerk (Mr L. N. Watts) also attended to see the children off. The following week, the* East Kent Mercury *printed a short but moving article on the evacuation of the Deal and Sandwich children:*

## IMPORTANT NOTICE

## EVACUATION

The public throughout the country generally are being told to "stay put" in the event of invasion. For military reasons, however, it will in the event of attack be necessary to remove from this town all except those persons who have been specially instructed to stay. An order for the compulsory evacuation of this town will be given when in the judgment of the Government it is necessary, and plans have been arranged to give effect to such an order when it is made.

You will wish to know how you can help NOW in these plans.

THOSE WHO ARE ENGAGED IN WORK OF ANY DESCRIPTION IN THE TOWN SHOULD STAY FOR THE PRESENT.

OTHER PERSONS SHOULD, SO FAR AS THEY ARE ABLE TO DO SO, MAKE ARRANGEMENTS TO LEAVE THE TOWN—PARTICULARLY

    MOTHERS WITH YOUNG CHILDREN
    SCHOOL CHILDREN
    AGED AND INFIRM PERSONS
    PERSONS WITHOUT OCCUPATION OR IN
      RETIREMENT.

All such persons who can arrange for their accommodation with relatives or friends in some other part of the country should do so. Assistance for railway fares and accommodation will be given to those who require it.

Advice and, where possible, assistance will be given to persons who desire to leave the town but are unable to make their own arrangements.

Information about these matters can be obtained from the local Council Offices.

    (*Signed*) AUCKLAND GEDDES,
        *Regional Commissioner for Civil Defence.*

    **2nd July, 1940.**

(393/4177A) Wt. 19544-30 70m 7/40 H & S Ltd. Gp. 393

*One of the many leaflets issued by the Ministry of Information. This one was issued a month after the bulk of schoolchildren had already left 'Hellfire Corner'.*

## CHILDREN EVACUATED – SCENES AT DEAL AND SANDWICH
### TEARFUL BUT HAPPY

Sunday was the day that will live long in the memory not only of those children belonging to the Deal and Sandwich schools old enough to realise its meaning, to the parents who were sending their young ones out on a great adventure, but also to all those who assembled to bid God-speed and a safe return in the near future to the boys and girls upon whose shoulders will rest the moulding of the new world that will arise out of the present dark troublous days.

In all, some 1,500 children left Deal for South Wales and, as they passed through the entrance hall on to the station, tiny tots of three and four years of age clung to the hands of their elder brothers and sisters, with looks of wonder in their eyes.

*In the same issue appeared a letter from the headmaster of Deal Boys' Central School, about the journey to South Wales and the reception they received from the people of Merthyr Tydfil:*

### WONDERFUL GREETINGS AT MERTHYR TYDFIL.

Dear Mr Editor,

I hope these few lines will be in time for insertion in this week's *Mercury*, as I know how anxious many of your readers will be to hear of their children's reception at Merthyr Tydfil on Sunday last. The long train journey down was trying in the heat of a summer day, but all the children kept up wonderfully, and we were proud of the way they did so.

All the way along from the Severn Tunnel we passed parents and children waving a welcome from houses and embankments. We arrived at Merthyr Tydfil shortly after 7pm. Other large parties from Folkestone and elsewhere had arrived some time ahead of us and were still being billeted on our arrival. In spite of the town officials being thus busily occupied, we were welcomed most warmly at the station by the mayor and later, at the large Miners' Hall, the children were given a civic welcome to Merthyr.

All the streets of the various parts of Merthyr Borough were packed with men and women out to show a real welcome to our children, and many plainly showed an emotion that beat in sympathy with the feelings of the parents that had been left behind.

The billeting of our children was not complete until late in the evening, but the arrangements made had been most carefully planned beforehand and no mishaps occurred. Parties of the Deal children in their family groups were billeted in the various wards of the borough which extends for some seven miles from Merthyr Town along the valley of the Taff, and includes several smaller centres of population. It has been a busy time making contact with all our parties, which we found, however, safely in the care of their own teachers and helpers.

From Merthyr along the Taff Vale, through Abercannaid, Troedyrhiw, Aberfan, Merthyr Vale to Treharris, I have found our children happily billeted and well looked after. There will doubtless be a few misfits, but we have been assured that these will be rectified as soon as possible.

The most striking feature has been the wonderful reception of our Deal children into the Merthyr homes, and real sympathy and readiness to assume responsibilities for the children's welfare are everywhere apparent. The Education Authority is working hard to place all our children into schools suitable for the continuance of their education and within easy distance of their respective billets, and full-time instruction will commence next week.

Most of our children have by now written home, and as soon as possible I hope to get our home letter scheme working, by which all news will reach parents once a week at least.

Before closing, may I make an appeal for any discarded boys' clothing and underwear that may be kindly given to us. Some of our boys have arrived very poorly clad with no proper change, and I am sure the Deal parents will agree that the local inhabitants who for years have suffered from industrial depression should not have their kindness and generosity overtaxed.

Yours sincerely,

**H. *Mainwood*,** Headmaster,

Deal Boys' Central School.

*The following extract, concerning the arrival of East Kent evacuees into South Wales, appeared in the* Free Press *newspaper during June, 1940:*

Nearly 1,000 children evacuated from Folkestone and Dover arrived in the Eastern Valley with their teachers, one of whom said he went to bed the previous night by the light of burning Calais. Another said it was possible at his home to smell oil burning in Rotterdam when the wind was in the right direction. Thousands of local people welcomed the evacuees, and at Blaenavon, they were greeted by the Blaenavon Colliery Band.

### DOVER CHILDREN TO WALES

The evacuation of 2,899 Dover schoolchildren to Wales, in conjunction with those from Folkestone, Deal and Sandwich, also took place on Sunday, 2nd June. With the Dunkirk evacuation at its height and thousands of survivors crowding into the town, the children were assembled at their schools, where farewells with parents were said before leaving for the station, on foot or in buses. The mayor and other civic heads and officers were at the station to see the children off to their new war-time homes. The first train steamed out of the Priory Station at about 7.45am with 707 children, 54 teachers and helpers aboard.

The next train, bearing among others the children of the Dover Boys' and Dover Girls' County Schools, left at 9.20am, its total complement being 687 children, 59 teachers and helpers. The third train left at 10.40am with 744 children, 64 teachers and helpers, and the fourth and last train left at 12.40 with 761 children, 58 teachers and helpers. The destinations of the various Dover schools were:

*Blackwood, Monmouthshire (Bedwelty Urban District:* Astor Avenue, St Martin's Boys and Girls, St Bartholomew's Boys, Girls and Infants, River Mixed.

*Ebbw Vale Urban District:* County School for Boys, St Paul's (RC) School

*Caerleon Urban District:* County School for Girls

*Cwmbran Urban District:* Christ Church Boys and Infants, Holy Trinity Boys and Girls, Pier Infants.

*Blaenavon Urban District:* St Mary's Boys, Girls and Infants, St James' Girls.

*Severn Tunnel Junction (Chepstow Rural District):* Buckland Girls.

*Risca Urban District:* Buckland Infants.

*Ynysddu and Pontllanfraith (Mynyddislwyn Urban District):-* Barton Road Boys, Girls and Infants, Charlton Boys and Girls.

The South Wales Argus *reported the arrival on 2nd June of the thousands of Kent evacuees:*

Tired but happy after many hours of travel, thousands more evacuee children passed through Newport on Sunday singing their way to the Home of Song. They were on the last stages of their journey to reception areas in South Wales and Monmouthshire, and train after train from Chatham, Gillingham, Dover, Rochester and Folkestone passed through Newport with clockwork precision. First to arrive were the children from Rochester and Medway, bound for Risca, Blaina and Nantyglo.

All, under the supervision and care of their school teachers, wore labels giving their destination, and were provided with postcards to send back to their parents on arrival. They had been travelling since seven o'clock in the morning, but their spirits were still high as they raised the roof with song as their train steamed into Newport Station. Carriages and corridors were packed with boys and girls of all ages, and their temporary halt was the occasion for a barrage of questions. 'Where's Risca?' 'Any coal mines?' 'Are we the first?' 'Any hills?' 'How much further?' and 'Can you get us some water?'

Anticipating thousands of thirsts, Newport Railway Station staff improvised travelling buffets, filling milk churns with water, and ladling it out in cups, bottles and an amazing variety of receptacles. They laughed and chattered away until the whistle blew; the train bearing its precious cargo slowly gathered momentum and away they went, one tiny figure in the very last carriage of all, leaning out, two grubby little thumbs uplifted.

Speaking to a *South Wales Argus* reporter, a teacher said, 'It is a great responsibility, but all the children have been wonderfully good-tempered. Only two have lost their labels, but we know who they are.'

*Alderman J. J. Panes, chairman of the Monmouthshire County Council, wrote the following message to the people of Dover:*

The people of Monmouthshire came out in large numbers to give a royal welcome to their visitors. The day was made pleasant by glorious sunshine, and the hearts of our people went out in compassion as they opened their doors to give hospitality to the children. Monmouthshire people are warm hearted, generous and kindly disposed, and these qualities were much in evidence as they met their new little guests. Traditionally religious, fond of music, and lovers of learning, our people have always taken a keen interest in education, and the University Colleges of Wales are monuments to their enthusiasm, zeal and sacrifice for this good cause. Educationally we shall do our best to meet the needs of our visitors; we shall share our schools and give every facility for their instruction. Our schools are not all we would like, yet it can be said that we have made good progress over the last few years in the building of new elementary and secondary schools and technical institutes. The homes of our people are not elaborate or luxurious, but they are clean and comfortable, and all the children I have had the pleasure of meeting are happy and contented. They came to Monmouthshire in glorious sunshine, and despite the long journey they had travelled, they were happy. Having said a few things about Monmouthshire and its people, may I assure the parents who have allowed their children to come to us that all that can be done will be done to keep them happy. The local government officials, the councillors and aldermen, the school teachers and, last but not least, the foster-parents, all contributed to make the children's entry into Monmouthshire a happy one, and I ask the parents who remain behind in Dover not to worry unduly, we shall do our best so that your children shall be happy as long as they must stay in their new homes in Monmouthshire.

*Mrs Blapham, who travelled with the Dover County Schools on the day of evacuation, sent back the following report which appeared in the* Dover Express *on Friday, 14th June, 1940:*

Last Sunday morning (2nd June, 1940) the two Dover County Schools started out on their great adventure. By some happy mischance, or perhaps through the wisdom of some understanding railway official, the two schools shared the same train. This experience in co-education made a success of a long, hot and crowded journey. No disciplinary voice was heard, nor necessary throughout the long day. Each school tried to outdo the other in gallantry.

It was a triumphal progress through the English countryside. Throughout the whole route kindly people came to cheer the children on their way. On and on went the train towards the west and made its first stop at Salisbury, where the WVS and the VADs were indefatigable in handing cups of very cool water to the children and cups of very hot tea to the staff. There were happy meetings here, some of the Salisbury helpers being old friends of some of the staff.

Cheered and refreshed, the travellers were able to enjoy the lovely country they now entered, through wooded valleys where boating and bathing parties lazed away the sunlit day, past ancient stone houses, stately and gracious, and so on to Westbury, where the train again stopped and for the first time was heard the homely west country burr when a stalwart member of the St John Ambulance Brigade pulled down the windows and inquired if anyone wanted a drink.

On again and presently through the Severn Tunnel, and after that a different feeling was evident throughout the train. It was coming near to the new country, to the new homes and every mind was curious and wondering what was in store. At Newport, the girls disembarked for Caerleon and the boys went on up the valley. And now they chattered now longer, but stood staring rather thoughtfully out of the windows.

Just after six the train steamed into Ebbw Vale station and immediately hands were outstretched in welcome. Smiles and warm hearted greetings were there on every side. When one of the staff inquired, 'Do you mind us coming?' the answer was, 'We have been longing for you. Come and look outside at the crowds who have been waiting for hours to welcome you.'

Quickly the boys were driven in buses to a school. Again the lovely welcome. No set speeches to tired children, but a good tea and that feeling everywhere that the boys were wanted. One official said, 'The people are clamouring for them. They want to help.'

In the months to come the indebtedness of Dover to these generous, warmhearted people will grow and grow, but if for nothing else it should be eternally grateful for the wonderful welcome given to its boys, the amazing kindness and generosity shown on every side and the anxiety that the boys should be happy. By 10 o'clock (pm) all were safely bedded down and awoke on Monday morning to hot brightness and a new world of a long green valley where mountain ponies roam on the hillsides, where long-tailed sheep with their lambs trotting beside them trot unconcernedly along the rocky roads quite oblivious of the motor buses which are driven, with the verve, skill and audacity of Pyrenean drivers, along roads which the East Kent bus drivers would certainly class as quite unsuitable.

*Charlton C. E. Primary School, Dover, (Picture taken in 1996 by Peter Hayward)*

In this remote valley all the inhabitants still rush out from their homes to view, as a novelty, a solitary aeroplane flying overhead. Such is the quietness and the feeling of remoteness that one feels that the older ones who have come here should daily utter this prayer: Dear Lord, let me not be complacent. Let me not forget that at the other side of England a brave and untiring navy keeps the seas, and men are fighting and giving up their lives that we may live here in peace in this lovely land.

*Another letter received by the* Dover Express *highlighting the reception given to the boys of Dover County School on their arrival in Wales was from* **Mr Llewellyn Langley**, *a distinguished teacher at the school, writing from 14 Raglan Terrace, Beaufort, Mon.:*

Our boys have met with amazing kindness from every section of the population. No effort is being spared to make them happy and comfortable in their new surroundings. I have questioned hundreds of boys, with the same result, 'A lovely bed!', 'Fine breakfast!' and so on. Dover County School has been taken to the hearts of the people of Ebbw Vale and Beaufort. Today we have been exploring the countryside in groups under supervision. Tomorrow, we are occupying the County School building all day, to find our way about. Work and play will alternate, and no boy will find time to be bored. Let no parent be anxious for, if there were even a small complaint, investigation and adjustment would follow immediately. I have yet to see a down-cast face under a County School cap. We are all full of gratitude for what has been done for us.

*Two more letters appeared in the* Dover Express *on 7th June, 1940, concerning the Girls' County School. The first was to the Mayor by* **Mrs Mary Young** *of 19 Cardiff Road, Newport:*

Dear Sir,
.   Yesterday my husband and I went out to Caerleon to see the girls of Dover County School arrive. This was a great delight for us, as we were sent here from Dover last September, and have only met one Dover man since we arrived. We saw many girls we knew, and went to the houses of several in which these girls are to live – and I should like, through you, to let the Dover mothers know what a wonderful welcome was given to their children.

Fleets of cars, an ambulance, doctor and girl guides all turned out to help in any way they could. The Dover girls arrived well up to time, all looking very happy if somewhat tired, and I can assure you that the people of Caerleon are quite ready to make the children as happy as possible. It is a perfectly delightful place, with the river running through the centre of the village and wooded hills surrounding it.

We shall go out very often and see the girls of the Dover County School; it looked a little bit like home to see the red band on their hats, as we had seen them for so many years in Dover.

*The following is a letter from* **Mr G. H. Jones** *of Caerleon, dated 3rd June, the day after the children arrived:*

I have had a request to get the *Dover Express*, the weekly edition. As you know, there are 250 of your children here. Could you arrange to send me some? May I say what a fine lot of girls they are, and you may tell their parents they are all in really good homes and will be well looked after, this being a residential town. So you may feel quite at ease, they will be all right.

*Reports on other Dover schools in Wales were also received by the* Dover Express *during the first few weeks of evacuation. At St Mary's Church one Sunday, Canon A. B. Richie said that he had received a letter from* **Mr A. J. Wheldon** *(headmaster, St Mary's School), reporting that the children of St Mary's Schools had settled down very happily in Wales. They were attending school together and were receiving the same religious instruction as when in Dover.*

**Mr V. Gutsell**, *headmaster of Holy Trinity School, writing from 84 Llantarnum Road, Cwmbran, said:*

Just a line from Cwmbran, where children from Trinity and Pier Council Schools, Christ Church Boys and Belgrave Infants arrived on Sunday evening at 6.40. On the station platform were members of the local UD Council, St John Ambulance Brigade, representatives of the clergy, school medical service, Birmingham evacuees and local teachers. Passing through crowds of sympathetic residents the children made their way to the reception station. Here, in a speech of welcome, Mr A. Jenkins, MP, Pontypool Division, said he hoped the children would be happy and enjoy their visit. After a meal, Red Cross vehicles, ambulances and private cars took the children and their teachers to their new homes.

*At St Paul's Catholic Church on Sunday, a letter written by the children of their school, who have been evacuated to Ebbw Vale, was read. It stated that they were having a very happy time riding on ponies and they had pet lambs, and they asked their parents not to worry about them.*

*At a meeting of the Dover Education Committee, held shortly after the departure of the Dover school children:*

*Belgrave Infants School, Dover. The buildings are now used as a Community Centre – Photo, Peter Hayward*

The secretary said that he could now give some idea of the work entailed in the evacuation. The elementary school children and those under five years old amounted to 2,338, with 126 teachers and 58 helpers; and the county schools to 561 scholars, 45 teachers and 6 helpers; a total of 2,899 scholars, 171 teachers and 64 helpers.

The position as far as he could estimate, was that on 24th May the numbers on the rolls of the elementary schools, were 4,210. The number of scholars on the registers who had been evacuated was 2,232, leaving a balance of 1,978. There was really no information on the number who were evacuated voluntarily either at that time or before, but as far as he could gather from conversations with head teachers, it would appear that about 500 children were dealt with in that way, so that it would appear that there was something like 1,478 of school age left in the borough.

On the chairman's instructions, he had written to the station master, expressing sincere appreciation and thanks for the excellent work carried out by himself and his staff in the evacuation. To entrain nearly 3,000 children, a large proportion under seven years of age, was no mean task, and the calm and sympathetic manner in which it was carried out without mishap invoked the admiration of all concerned.

*A few days after the departure of the Folkestone school children for South Wales, the* Folkestone, Hythe & District Herald *received the following account from Merthyr Tydfil:*

YOU WILL GET A SQUARE DEAL
by a Master of the Harvey Grammar School

Before anything else let me say this, that the warmheartedness of the Welsh folk in Merthyr Tydfil is not only overflowing but at times embarrassing. Mothers who are naturally concerned about the welfare of their children need not have a moment's anxiety. All the boys are settled in billets and the number of readjustments that will have to be made is surprisingly small.

*Cyfartha Castle, Merthyr Tydfil*
*– Peter Hayward collection*

## First View of Wales

Our journey down was comfortable and fairly well to time. We were greeted along the line by people who had come to cheer the troops from Flanders, but they were equally enthusiastic to the younger generation passing by. The weather was sunny and it was something of a thrill when we came out of the Severn Tunnel for a first view of Wales. How pleasant it was. Broad valleys, dotted with villages, fine ranges of green hills, and an exhilarating sense of space.

The train was met at the station by the mayor and a number of prominent townspeople. Over the platform hung a banner with 'WELCOME' on it, and further on, beyond a line of flags, another with, 'YOU WILL GET A SQUARE DEAL HERE, FOLKS'. That was a good start anyway, but we weren't prepared for what was to follow.

The whole town had turned out in the streets to welcome us as we walked to a large hall. Policemen kept a way for the long line of boys and girls. There was no doubt about the warmth of the welcome. We could feel it. As we halted now and then the townspeople, particularly the women, who were in the front of the lines often five or six deep, chatted with the boys and girls and assured them that they would be happy in Merthyr Tydfil. We have been here a few days only and these people are making good their word.

## Courage and Cheerfulness

After the assembly for checking, medical examination (the second that day), and tea, the school were sent in groups to separate halls, one in each ward of the town, and from there they were taken by billeting officers to their new homes. Perhaps in some future note I shall be able to give you an idea of Merthyr Tydfil and its people, of the prosperous and distressing times and of the unfailing courage and cheerfulness of its people. After the last week we had spent in Folkestone when children slept, if they could, through the sound of gunfire and were taken from their beds at the sound of the siren, Merthyr Tydfil seems like a new world. There is no place like home, but this will be a home from home. It is quiet down here.

Arrangements for the re-opening of the schools are almost complete. We again appear to be fortunate and, if things go well, the boys will have their lessons in Cyfarthfa Castle. This noble building standing in a large and lovely park, with flower gardens and lakes, and overlooking the distant hills, was the home of Mr William Crawshay, an iron and steel magnate, who for a nominal sum offered it to the education authority.

The boys are in splendid spirit. There will be plenty to do. The country abounds in attractive walks and already I have seen groups of boys looking at fishing rods in the shops. The parents of boys of the Harvey Grammar School may rest assured that Mr Downing, the headmaster, and his staff will undertake their new responsibilities with a single purpose – the happiness and welfare of the boys.

*Another message shortly after the children had arrived was sent by the president of Merthyr Tydfil Chamber of Trade and Commerce, **Mr D. W. Wood**, to his counterpart in Folkestone.*

The Merthyr Tydfil Chamber of Trade desires to express its sincere sympathy with you in the circumstances that have made the evacuation of your little citizens a matter of such urgency, and because of the consequent effect of the evacuation upon you as a trading organisation.

It is a pleasure to be able to reassure you and through you, your fellow citizens, that your little ones have come to a town with a long reputation for the warmth of its heart towards those in adversity. Our people will do everything possible to compensate the children of your town for the loss of the loving care which has obviously been lavished upon them; they are already looked upon as our 'Honoured Guests'. By service, courtesy and kindness, we, as traders, will do our utmost to fill the places in the lives previously filled by our confreres at Folkestone.

In conclusion, we pray that the parting will only be of short duration, and when the happy day of reunion comes we trust that a link of affection and esteem will have been forged between our two towns that will never be severed.

*The following poem appeared in the* Dover Express *shortly after the children had left. The poem probably mirrored the thoughts of many hundreds of mothers who suddenly found their homes silent and empty:*

Home from morning school they come,
Shouting, 'What's for dinner, Mum?
And what's for afters? Rice again!
That blinking stuff gives me a pain.'

What's this in his trouser pocket?
Some marbles, a damp squib and a rocket
That's been let off – a piece of string
Oh, and that's not everything.

'Mum, we're going to be evaporated,' teacher
'Could I stay up, not go to bed          [said,
So early, I've such a lot to pack,
And could you make me a haversack?'

The tears fall on a money box,
'Dad, buy me one that really locks,
So's I can save up for a bike,
I've seen one that I think I like.'

Dad, his shoes are through again,
I've mended his trousers – but in vain,
Just look at those mud marks on my floor,
Don't think I'll polish any more.

A piece of plasticine I find,
And – looks like toffee to my mind,
That fondly to the lining clings,
And what? Some of my curtain rings.

Now they have gone, dear girls and boys,
I sit and sort out all the toys,
That once I grew so cross about,
Threatened so often to throw them out.

No comics now upon the floor,
No finger marks upon the door,
The whole house has a hollow ring.
Its neatness is an empty thing!

\*     \*     \*

*The following, from the* Folkestone, Hythe and District Herald *for Saturday, 8th June, 1940, covers the journey to South Wales of the children from Folkestone:*

WALES WELCOMES OUR CHILDREN
Greetings Banners at Railway Stations
Crowded Streets on Arrival
Honoured Guests

The Mayor of Folkestone (Alderman G. A. Gurr, JP) and the Deputy Mayor (Alderman R. L. T. Saunders) were among those at the Central Station on Sunday, when 3,063 school children were evacuated to various parts of South Wales. The majority of parents said goodbye to their children before they left for the station. As the children passed through the streets in buses many people lined the route cheering and waving.

At the station, writes a *Folkestone & Hythe Herald* reporter, all was in readiness for the arrival of the children. Mr J. A. Wilkinson (Clerk to the Education Committee) and Mr T. L.

Higham (Deputy Clerk) were in charge, assisted by members of the Folkestone Education Department led by Mr Amos, and Southern Railway officials. Besides the Mayor and Deputy Mayor, there were present on the platform during the morning, Alderman J. W. Stainer, JP, (Chairman of the Education Committee), Councillors A. E. Bayliss, E. P. Bridgland, W. H. Wright, H. Johnson and H. Hughes, Mr A. M. Morley (HM Inspector), Mr J. G. Gibbard (District Secretary, KEC) and Mr G. E. Wythe (Folkestone Education Committee).

Mr L. B. Easton (Corps Secretary) was in charge of about 30 members of the St John Ambulance Brigade who did efficient work during the day. Alderman G. Spurgen, JP, paid a surprise visit to the station in the afternoon. Parents were not allowed on the up platform, although many of them had bought platform tickets and watched their children depart from the other side. I noticed only one very small boy in tears. The rest seemed to me to be very excited and happy and appeared to look upon it as a holiday more than anything else.

As the trains drew out of the station the children waved and cheered, and a long row of heads could be seen taking their last look at Folkestone. 'This has been a harder job than all the others,' Mr Higham told me just before the first train left. 'That is due to the fact that we have had such a little time to get ready. There has been a remarkable response from Folkestone parents. I think it is probably due to the fact that we have had a few air-raid warnings recently. Naturally we could not expect a 100 per cent answer, but in the circumstances I am very pleased. All the children had to be certified fit before they were allowed to travel, and I don't think the officials in Wales will have any cause to complain about their health.'

The first train left for Merthyr Tydfil at 9am, fifteen minutes late, carrying nearly 800 children. The individual figures were as follows: Harvey Grammar School, 352; County School

---

. E V A C U A T I O N                    1st June, 1940.

ADDITIONAL   PARTICULARS   FOR   PARENTS

1.   Country boys will be picked up by bus.   The bus will
        call at *Eythorne Post Office*
        at    *7.40*

2.   Other boys must be at School on the Astor Avenue playing
        field by 8.20 a.m.

3.   Be sure that your son has his food for the day, his
        ration books, his gas mask and his identity card.

4.   It will be a great help if he has a stamped post card
        with him to send home immediately.   His new address
        is likely to be in Monmouthshire.

5.   Parents will remember that, where possible, they are
        expected to contribute towards the cost of billeting,
        but any such contribution is based on family income
        and is not likely to exceed 6/- per week per child.

                                    J. C. BOOTH.

*Instructions issued to the parents of Dick Langford by Mr Booth,*
*headmaster of Dover Boys' County School.*

38

for Girls, 216; The Grange (Technical School), 135; Stella Maris RC School, 98. There were about 60 teachers and helpers. The second train, which carried the biggest number, left just over an hour later. Those travelling to Chepstow were: St Peter's, 105; Garrison, 72; Christ Church, 105; Sandgate, 35; Athelstan, 29. Those travelling to Monmouth were: Dover Road, 257; St Eanswythe's, 94; Cheriton Horn Street, 77. They were accompanied by 64 teachers and helpers.

The third train, which left at 11.15 for Caerphilly, was composed of George Spurgen, 302; Cheriton All Souls, 167; Mundella, 335; and 63 teachers and helpers. The last train, which was nearly half an hour late, left at 1.45pm, carrying St Mary's, 298 who were to detrain at Pontypool Road; Harcourt School, 277, and Morehall, 152 who were travelling to Abergavenny. They were accompanied by 57 teachers and helpers.

Mr Wilkinson and Mr Higham also travelled to South Wales on Sunday, in order to superintend the billeting and arrival of the Folkestone children. They stayed a few days.

*The following account of the journey of the children to Wales, and of their arrival and the welcome they received was written specially for the* Folkestone and Hythe Herald *by an official of the Education Department who travelled with the children:*

### They welcomed us with Open Arms

'Good luck and I hope you all come back soon,' said Alderman J. W. Stainer, as the fourth and last train steamed out of the Central Station at 1.45pm on Sunday last. The children were all in good spirits and were evidently looking upon the journey down to South Wales as a wonderful adventure. As the train passed through Shorncliffe, Morehall and Cheriton, the roads and gardens were lined with waving folk, and in this particular case many were fathers and mothers of the scholars, as some of the children were from the Morehall and Harcourt schools.

Once through Cheriton the children settled down to lunch and out came all manner of good things to eat, ranging from ham sandwiches to oranges, apples and packets of crisps. These all soon disappeared and then came the exciting part of the journey, picking out familiar objects and, as the journey advanced, the unfamiliar objects and scenes.

To more than one little child this was their first journey in a train and even the train running through the tunnels was a thrill. At Tonbridge, Redhill and Reading, where the train stopped for a few minutes, kind-hearted folk handed up drinks of lemonade to the now thirsty children. Actually, we were sharing the good things which had been prepared for the BEF soldiers who were passing through after their arrival in England.

This train eventually arrived at Pontypool Road Station at 7pm, where we were received by Alderman A. Jenkins, MP, and Mr D. Brymar Morgan, Director of Education for Monmouthshire. The children were then loaded on to buses and taken to a nearby school where doctors and nurses were in attendance. After passing before the doctor the children were provided with refreshments, formed into suitable groups, put on the buses and distributed to the various villages. There a great reception awaited the children for it seemed the whole population of the villages had turned out to welcome us. Billeting was soon put in hand. Brothers and sisters and friends were billeted together. Cars were ready to take us and our belongings to our new homes and soon the children were experiencing the wonderful hospitality of the Welsh people. I am sure it was not long afterwards that many a tired boy or girl was tucked up in bed to enjoy an unbroken night's sleep in rural peace and safety.

The bright morning sun, the call of the cuckoo and the bleating of the lambs awakened the children on the first morning and then they had their first real view of Welsh scenery – rolling fields sweeping to the foot of mountains topped by clumps and plantations of trees.

The village of Goytre, where there are 80 scholars from St Mary's School, is situated in a valley. The village is grouped round the school with a number of cottages and houses somewhat more scattered. This village is typical of many of the villages where the children from other schools are billeted. St Mary's School is distributed over the Pontypool Rural District and there are 80 children at Goytre, 85 at Cresyceiliog, 25 at Gwehelog, 22 at Llantrisant, 33 at Llanhennock, 25 at Llangibby and 33 at Llanfrechfa.

The Harcourt and Morehall schools are in the Rural District of Abergavenny. There is no doubt that, in the districts and villages which I have visited, the children have been received with open arms, and very keen disappointment has been expressed by householders where there were not sufficient children to go round. On all sides one has heard the expression that they are 'such nice children'. Householders have without fail spoken of their good behaviour and nice manners. Indeed, one feels proud to have been associated in the movement with the children of Folkestone who, throughout this upheaval, have shown such fine courage.

They have already made friends with their foster parents and in passing round the countryside one could see a boy with the Folkestone school cap sitting with his farmer host on a farm van taking round the milk, or perhaps a girl going round with the lady of the house collecting eggs. The children of the villages have taken our youngsters in charge and are showing them the whys and wherefores of country life.

And now just a last word to the mothers and fathers left behind. Please don't fret about the boys and girls; they have gone into homes showing wonderful hospitality and, although the children may feel a little homesick at times, left to themselves they will soon settle down and be perfectly happy. Schooling is being arranged and parents may rest perfectly assured that the Folkestone teachers and helpers are doing everything in their power to see that the young folk left in their charge are happy and well cared for.

*After the main evacuation, more children left from Dover, Deal, Sandwich and Folkestone for South Wales. The following appeared in the* Folkestone Herald *for Saturday, 29th June:*

### MORE CHILDREN LEAVE FOR SAFETY AREAS

The second evacuation of Folkestone school children, numbering 159, was carried out without a hitch on Tuesday morning. The children left Folkestone Central for various parts of South Wales and Monmouthshire where their schools are already situated.

Children carried gas masks, identity cards, ration books and hand luggage with them, and were accompanied by 14 teachers. As the train drew into the station at 8.50am, eager faces of children evacuated from Sandwich, Deal and Dover could be seen, looking from the carriage windows. Folkestone children boarded the rear part of the train, and the whole operation was carried out in under ten minutes. Mr T. L. Higham, who was superintending the arrival of school equipment from Folkestone to Wales, travelled with the children.

*The following report from a master of the Harvey Grammar School, was in the* Folkestone Herald *on 6th July, 1940. It highlights the confusion that must have occurred in many of the areas where the expected groups of evacuees did not arrive, but were replaced by others:*

### HARVEY GRAMMAR SCHOOL

If these notes are brief it is because there is little to report and parents may read into this simple statement a good deal of comfort. When they hear the news I hope that they will remember that where we now live is just a small part of a very large area called South Wales.

I was amused to hear the following story, which, unlike most evacuee stories, is true! On the day we arrived, a large number of children from a poor quarter in a northern town was anticipated, and a lady, expecting two little girls, decided that the first thing to do was to put them in a bath. She made the necessary arrangements. The evacuees arrived. One was a six-footer of 15 stone, the other a shade smaller, and both from our own Vb. There the story ends!

News comes through of our old boys, some killed, some missing, or prisoners, some with stories to tell of strange adventures, and all of them young. To the sorrowing parents of those who have fallen, we who were boys at the school with them or who had the privilege of teaching them, extend our deepest sympathy.

*Folkestone County School for Girls, accommodated in Cyfartha Castle, Merthyr Tydfil, produced a school magazine during their stay there, in which the following poem appeared:*

AN EVACUEE

A small lone figure
  Patiently waits,
In the midst of her luggage
  By the station gates.
When the bustling crowd
  Has gone on its way,
She thinks of her journey
  And breathless day.

We've come to a station,
  The loudspeakers blare,
While the porters are rushing
  About everywhere.
Then passing through London,
  Two hours yet remain,
A luncheon at Lyons
  And then off again.

The dash to the station!
  The guard's whistle blows,
Then parting and waving;
  The trees and hedgerows
All rushing along
  At a wonderful rate,
While she dismally thinks
  Of her coming fate.

A snug corner seat
  With a book on her lap,
Sandwiches lying
  Above in the rack.
Feeling impatient
  For what lies ahead,
Yet knowing well also
  Strange feeling of dread.

'Is your name Eliza?'
  Says a voice close at hand,
As she wakes from her dreaming
  With a start brought to land
'You're my new daughter;
  I hope you'll like me,
Now come quickly along dear,
  Or we'll be late for tea.'

*Peggy Freezer*
Lower 5, Age 14

*Miss J. B. Scott, head of Barton Road Infants' School at the time of the evacuation, wrote back to Dover, giving a word of advice to parents about following their children to Wales:*

It might be of interest to some of the Dover people to know that the children of Barton Road Infants' School are very happily settled in Pontllanfraith. We have come to a very lovely district, and the children are looking well and happy. The people are kindness itself to them, and on all sides we hear good reports from the foster-parents as to the good behaviour and charm of our children. The homes are visited regularly by the staff and we are made most welcome by the people. The only difficulty that presents itself is that of finding suitable accommodation for parents. As there is a large number of evacuees arriving this week-end, parents would be well advised not to come to Pontllanfraith at present, as every available billet will be occupied.

*Initially at least, adequate clothing for the younger evacuees appeared to be a problem, as shown in **Miss Scott's** appeal to the editor of the* Dover Express:

Would you be so good as to allow me to appeal through your paper for any articles of clothes suitable for children (boys and girls) from the ages of four to eight years. We shall be able to make very good use of any garments that people are kind enough to send us.

**Mr R. Roberts**, *headmaster of Barton Road Boys' School, wrote of the journey and the welcome given on arrival in Wales:*

It is difficult to write without emotion of the wonderful welcome which the warm-hearted people of this 'Proud Valley' have given to the children of Dover. We have been overwhelmed with kindness – a fact which must bring great comfort to the parents who have sacrificed their natural desires for the sake of the safety of their children.

We left Dover quietly and unhurriedly on a Sunday afternoon, which must assuredly remain as a milestone in the memories of all of us, teachers and children alike. A long journey was anticipated, and it proved very long indeed, in fact we did not arrive at our destination till nearly midnight. Children are thirsty creatures

*Barton Road Boys' School, Dover, (taken in 1996) is as it might have looked in 1940, except that the air-raid shelters have now been bricked up and the blast walls removed – Photo, Peter Hayward*

and, although water had been provided on the train, it had all disappeared before we reached London. This might have been a serious matter on such a hot afternoon, but good fortune brought us to a long halt at Wandsworth Road, where a large number of the local inhabitants who were on the station platform came to our rescue with buckets, baths and cups to replenish the supply. These good working folk had been at it for days doing the same Samaritan service for the Dunkirk heroes and they did not hesitate to give equal generosity to the Dover refugees.

The same scenes occurred at Salisbury and Westbury. At Bristol, a working man handed up two boxes of ice-cream bricks for distribution. One could only regret the lack of miraculous powers of multiplication. So at last, after a sulphurous passage of the Severn Tunnel, we entered Monmouthshire. At Risca, a very tired company of Buckland Infants were detrained. There were so many eager local workers awaiting them that each child seemed to have his own attendant. Some of the youngest were so sound asleep that they were gently carried off without disturbance of their dreams.

The rest of us came on to Newport, and then in the gathering darkness our train puffed up the steep valley to Ynysddu. After some uncertainty as to the destination of the various schools, detraining commenced, and the young travellers trod solid ground again after nearly ten hours of train journey. As we moved down a rocky path to the waiting buses, we began to realise that we were the central figures of a great occasion. The streets were crowded, in spite of the lateness of the hour. And what a royal welcome we received! The people had been waiting for hours, but they cheered and clapped as though we were conquering heroes instead of refugees.

We were taken to a large hall where crowds of eager helpers waited to give the children a meal and to arrange for their billets. This was inevitably a lengthy process, and it was not until the small hours of the morning that the last child was safely tucked up in bed.

So ended the great adventure, accomplished safely and successfully in spite of inevitable difficulties arising from the great strain on the railway workers in these days. It only remains to be said that the children are very happy and thoroughly well cared for. These good people have taken them to their hearts and have bestowed kindness and sympathy in such generous measure as to allay any anxieties which might have been felt. They are a religious people and they have not forgotten the words. 'Inasmuch as ye have done it unto one of the least of these my little ones, ye have done it unto Me.'

*Another extract from the* Dover Express *for Friday, 14th June, 1940, was written by a Welshman who witnessed the arrival in Markham of the children of St Martin's School, Dover:*

This week I have been thrilled. I have gone through an experience the like of which I shall never know again. It was not heralded by pomp and trumpet; it belonged not to the palace or mansion; it was just the spontaneous expression of the fellow-feeling of the everyday citizen. It was simply that I saw the reception of the children of St Martin's School, Dover, when they came to Monmouthshire.

I am a Welshman, but never have I been more proud of my race. For over two hours we waited the arrival of the youngsters, and we knew they had come when a tremendous burst of cheering was heard outside the school. All the village was out, and grandfather made himself as hoarse as little Tommy. I heard expressions such as 'Aw, poor darling!', 'God love them,' 'The poor dears are tired,' from the waiting women helpers. We ushered the children and their teachers into the assembly hall, where they just flopped into desks. They had had tea previously. There was not a tear. I spoke to some of the kiddies, and they were already thrilled with the mountains. They wanted to know where the coal was! Growing like gooseberries, maybe!

What a day their teachers must have had, and with never a grumble. But the weather was glorious, and has been ever since. Thank you, Dover, for bringing it. Then, after medical examination came the billeting. No-one was allowed to choose a child, but in every instance the evacuee was personally considered. There were five from one family. No house was big enough here to accommodate them; we put three together, and two next door. Sisters were fixed up in the same house, friends put together and singles were snapped up quickly. The biggest trouble was that we hadn't enough to go round. Mrs Davies said, 'Quick! Give me one. Mrs Jones has got two!' 'Look here, why can't I have a little one? Mrs Jones is after her.' We really quarrelled with some because we had no children to offer! All the children were fixed up in an hour – a feat made easy by the motherliness and sympathy of the new foster-mothers.

On Monday, taking two evacuated teachers with me, I visited the new homes of a number of the children. They were delighted with the characteristic Welsh cleanliness and love that was demonstrated. Every single child was happy. Some had already been taken to see their new 'grandmother' a few miles away! I only wish the real mothers could have been there to see. All day the children have played on the splendid field and hill on which their new school is built. The building is recent, and is nearly 1000 feet above sea level, so that it can be imagined what beautiful air the kiddies are breathing. But above all, there is peace. One child on Monday said she hadn't heard the guns the night before! My purpose in writing this is to give the mothers of Dover a few facts which will make them as full of joy as the people in Wales were to receive their children. They may rest assured they are in good hands, that they will be well fed and tended, and that they will be given as good a substitute as possible for the greatest power on earth – the love of the mother.

*During the first week of evacuation, the chairman of the Dover Education Committee, Alderman Powell, received the following letter from* **Councillor F. C. Walker**, *JP, chairman of the Chepstow Rural District Council:*

I must write you personally to let you and your residents know your Buckland Senior Girls arrived at Rogiet, Mon., in good spirits. The children were given a cheering reception from our inhabitants. Within one half-hour of the examination the children were in their billets. Every child has been placed in purely voluntary billets, and I have made a tour today and find all the children have settled down in their new homes. You can assure the parents of the Buckland Senior Girls that the interests of the children will be closely watched.

*The following letter from 8-years-old* **Stephen Coombs**, *a pupil of Charlton Boys' School, to his parents at 27 Charlton Green, appeared in the* Dover Express *on Friday, 14th June, 1940:*

1, St David's Avenue<br>
Woodfield Side<br>
Blackwood.

Dear Mam and Dad and all,

I am quite happy here, and my new Mam and Dad are quite good to me. We have not been to school this week, and I have been having a nice look round.

I have been over the town of Blackwood, and we have a swimming pool here, that I have been in. We have another little girl here that came from the same street as I came from, but she is living with the other people in the other rooms in our house.

I have a nice pal here with John Bennett, and we are getting on quite well together. I think we are starting school on Monday this week, and I have been having a nice look round. Our school will now be Pontllanfraith.

My new Dad works down the mine, getting coal for the Navy, and he is very good to me. I have had pennies off him this week, and I get some off my new Mammy. They have got a lot of chickens here too, and I go out and feed them and bring in the eggs, and I have had a few to eat.

We had five lovely baby chicks born last Tuesday, and I am going to bring one home with me when I come back home. That is all.

I remain,<br>
your loving son,<br>
Stephen

*(Author's note – One can only wonder how Stephen's parents in Dover felt at reading his letter, and of his new 'Mam and Dad'.)*

*More news from Wales reached the* Dover Express *for its 2nd of August 1940 edition. This particular item highlights the problem the authorities encountered in many areas where evacuees were drifting back to their homes and, of course, back to the danger of enemy action:*

**Mr A. B. Taylor**, *Headmaster of Christ Church School (Dover), in a letter from Pontnewydd speaks of the excellent health of the boys:*

They are high up, the air is bracing and appetites are good. Dover parents who have paid a visit all comment on the lads' appearance and their good fortune at finding a home from home. The kindness is really exceptional and the warmth of welcome on arrival has in no way diminished. Though there have been some sirens, there had been no incidents. It is regrettable that children from London suddenly and in increasing numbers are whisked away overnight without warning, to their homes in vulnerable areas, largely as a result of unfounded and misleading reports. This does not however apply so much to Dover parents, particularly those who have been down and seen for themselves. A sudden whisking away by parents of children without a thank you and without even consulting any authority is greatly to be deprecated. It is not only an insult to the great kindness shown by the people of Wales, but it is not in the interest of the children themselves.

*Almost two weeks after the Folkestone children left, it was decided by the authorities that the children from Hythe should also be evacuated. On Sunday, 24th June, 1940, the Hythe children left for South Wales. The following article appeared in the* Folkestone, Hythe and District Herald *for Saturday, 29th June, 1940:*

### HYTHE CHILDREN LEAVE

Early on Sunday morning some 450 Hythe children including between 20 and 30 from Saltwood, with teachers and helpers making the number up to about 500, were evacuated to the rural district of Cemaes, Pembrokeshire, Wales. The children assembled at the schools before 7 o'clock, and at an early hour preparations were being made in the many households affected. A large crowd gathered at the point of departure.

Everything was carried out with the minimum of fuss, and there was not a hitch in the arrangements. Motor coaches drew up in front of the school in succession, and as each was pulled up the exact number of children filed along to fill it. A few more minutes and each coach started on its short journey to Hythe Station. The children waved as they left. The teachers travelled with the children, whose departure was witnessed by Mr H. Stainer (Town Clerk), who is the local evacuation officer. Mr Stainer travelled to the station in one of the coaches. At the station the children entered the train immediately, and here there were smiles and cheering galore. Many parents were present to see their children off.

The Mayor (Councillor G. Few), with his daughter, Mrs Sylvia Whittle (the Mayoress), travelled from Seabrook with the children of the school there. The Mayor acted the part of unofficial conductor on the bus on its way to the station, and kept everyone happy and bright. Before the party left, the Mayor had a few words with each of the teachers. He walked the full length of the train exchanging remarks with the children, and was tremendously pleased with the high spirits of the young people.

The final farewell, a last cheer and waving of hands, and the train left to schedule, commencing a journey that it was anticipated would take practically 12 hours.

\* \* \*

*It is surprising to find that rivalry, friendly or otherwise, should erupt between two Welsh villages when, after being in South Wales for just a few days, it was decided to move Sir Roger Manwood's School from Penclawdd to Gowerton. The following article appeared in the* South Wales Evening Post *newspaper which highlighted the situation:*

### PENCLAWDD VILLAGERS ANGRY
### Plan to remove boy evacuees opposed

If the 250 boys of the Sandwich Grammar School who have been evacuated to Penclawdd are removed to Gowerton, as suggested, there is likely to spring up a feud between the two villages. When the boys from Sandwich arrived in Gowerton on Sunday last, complete with school ties, blazers and straw boaters, there were misgivings when it was learned that they were to be billeted at Penclawdd, the little Welsh cockle village. Many were of the opinion that the boys would never fit in there, and that local residents would resent having the school billeted there.

Indeed, so greatly did the fear grow that almost immediately efforts were on foot for the transference of the boys from Penclawdd to Gowerton, where the County School is situated.

This news reached Penclawdd and the residents are up in arms about it. 'Do they think that Penclawdd is not good enough for these boys,' asked one housewife interviewed by an *Evening Post* reporter yesterday. 'I have two boys staying with me. They are fine fellows and they like being with us. I am not going to allow them to be taken away.'

Many other householders were of the same opinion, and it is likely that a protest meeting will be called if efforts to move the boys to Gowerton are continued.

One angry husband said, 'Why is Gowerton considered so much better than Penclawdd? If they take the boys away from here we will have a banner placed across the road at Berthlwyd Colliery, warning every Gowertonian that Penclawdd is out of bounds for him.'

## BOYS ARE HAPPY

There were many humorous stories told about the boys' first few days at Penclawdd, but all the people to whom I have spoken are indignant over the suggested removal, and were firm that the boys should not be taken away from the village. The boys themselves seemed to be perfectly happy among the cockle folk, many expressing the wish to remain in their new homes.

## COUNCIL DISCUSSION

The affection that has sprung up between the people of Penclawdd and the evacuees was the subject of a resolution proposed by Alderman W. H. Davies at yesterday's meeting of Gower Rural Council. Mr L. M. Pugh, Clerk to the Council and billeting officer for the Gower area, reported on the work done on Sunday in receiving the 614 evacuees, in which were included 200 boys of Sir Roger Manwood's School, Sandwich. These boys, students at a famous public school 400 years old, had arrived complete with matrons, cooks and maids, and had been billeted in Penclawdd. Their settlement in the village had given rise to a problem, he said. There were no educational facilities available in Penclawdd, and the boys had to go into Gowerton. It had been ascertained that the cost of conveying the pupils from Penclawdd to Gowerton would be about £400 per annum.

## 'GREAT AFFECTION'

'The boys are extraordinarily nice,' said Mr Pugh, 'and a great affection has sprung up between them and the people. I could give you several instances of the good manners of the boys, and they themselves don't want to be moved.' Alderman Davies said the boys were perfectly happy and contented, and that their headmaster had told him the night before that they were settling down comfortably. 'It would be a pity to move these boys now,' said Alderman Davies. 'They have found good homes, and are liked very much by the people. If they are moved, the attitude of the villagers will have to be considered when the time comes for new evacuees to be billeted. I have no hesitation in saying that in Penclawdd I shall require the full assistance of the Council to start the reception work again.'

Dr W. E. Moreton, who strongly condemned the discussions taking place between representatives of the Board of Education and the Welsh Board of Health about moving the young men to Gowerton, told the Council, 'You have lit a spark in Gower of very definite interest, but you are going to kill that spark if you go chopping and changing these boys.'

Several members were of the opinion that bad feeling would result in Penclawdd, and in other parts of the Gower, if the boys and other evacuees were taken away. The public school boys had proved lovable and considerate, many of them getting up early in the morning to light the fire and lay the breakfast table for their 'landladies'. During the discussion it was reported that between 500 and 2,000 children might be coming to Gower from Liverpool.

*(Author's note: In the end, neither Penclawdd or Gowerton played host to the boys of Sir Roger Manwood's School because school accommodation forced the headmaster to move his school to Carmarthen.)*

\* \* \*

*A mother's love for her child can be a powerful driving force.* **Mrs L. Brenchley** *of 4 Dawson Road, Folkestone cycled to see her son in Wales and described her experiences in the* Folkestone, Hythe and District Herald *of 24th August 1940:*

People told me I would have a dreadful time trying to find my way, but everybody I met was most helpful. I found my boy very happy indeed when I got there and I hope to make another journey to see him later. It was a very cool morning when I left Folkestone at 8am, but got very hot towards the middle of the day. I first stopped at Wrotham for a cup of tea and then later on I ate some sandwiches in a children's playground. Then on through Riverhead, Westerham, Limpsfield and across the common. It was extremely hot so when going through Brasted and seeing 'Swimming' in big letters, I took a dip in the swimming pool and felt very refreshed.

After this I went on to Godstone where I finished my tea. I felt I ought to do a bit more before stopping that day so I went through Redhill and Reigate and reached Dorking. Here I found a bed in the village which was very welcome. Next morning I reached Guildford. I found it a nice place with lovely shops and a cobbly street. Someone put me on the Farnham road and I was well away with a slight wind behind me.

After a good long stretch I arrived at Swindon and stayed the night at the Hardwick Hotel. I arrived in Gloucester the next day and from there on the country was really lovely through Ross, Whitchurch, Monmouth, Raglan and Usk. It can be seen better on a bike than any other way. That evening I reached Llangibby and met Mr and Mrs England, Peter's foster parents and their family and Peter. I stayed with them two days and was shown all over the farm. I haven't the least doubt that Peter is with one of the best-hearted families in Wales.

*Mrs Brenchley made the return journey by cycle covering a total of some 600 miles.*

Chapter Three

INTO EXILE

*IN SPITE OF the wonderful reports of enthusiastic welcomes for the evacuees that appeared in the East Kent newspapers to reassure parents, actual experiences of the journey, reception and billeting procedures were often far from perfect. The first shock to the system of many young evacuees was when, on arrival in South Wales, they suddenly found themselves separated from their brothers or sisters, usually because of the different schools they attended, or because of accommodation problems in the areas to which they were assigned.*

*The evacuees not only had to contend with the terrible realisation of being parted from their parents, but now had to accept being parted from brothers and sisters as well, sometimes by many, many miles. Last minute instructions of 'Look after your little brother,' 'Stick together' or 'Don't let them part you', issued by anxious mothers and fathers, suddenly had no meaning for many of the evacuees. The personal accounts of this chapter go some way to illustrate the mixed experiences of reaching 'a place of safety'.*

**Jean White** *(now Mrs Craig) lived in the Tower Hamlets area of Dover and attended St Bartholomew's Junior School. She recalls the day of her evacuation:*

I can remember my mother crying bitterly when we left early on the morning of 2nd June 1940. My father was taking my younger sister, aged 7 years, and me, aged 10 years, to the school. I was really puzzled over the crying of my mum because I thought we would only be gone for two weeks. I remember saying to her, 'Don't cry, mum, we will be home soon.'

At the school we were all put into our respective classes and walked to the station with teachers and parents; my dad holding on to both me and my sister. Dad really impressed on me that as I was the eldest, I must always look after my little sister, but on the train, Nanette was put with her teacher and class mates and I was put with my teacher and friends.

I remember waving out of the train window to dad, and arriving in Blackwood in the dark, but everything else is completely gone. I know that my sister and I had our small suitcases, our gas masks and my sister had a teddy bear. When we arrived in Wales, we got off the train and stood in lines. I was very worried because I couldn't find my sister, and can remember an adult twice putting me back in line after I had tried to look for her. It turned out that the train had been split into two and the younger children taken to another town, but nobody told us that.

I was taken with two or three other girls to the Bloomfield Road area of Blackwood where we were dropped off one by one, all reasonably close to each other. I thought I had a very rich foster home because they had a light bowl hanging from the ceiling – we only had shades back home. My memories are very blurred of that first night. I suppose I was very tired, but the following morning one of my Dover friends telling me we were to report at the school that afternoon. I thought we were going to have a holiday, but we soon settled into a routine.

As to what happened to my sister Nanette, it was three weeks before I knew where she was. My mother kept writing to me, but I had no news of her whereabouts. Eventually, dad wrote to the education people and they told him where Nanette was. My parents then wrote to me with her address and I was able to take a bus to New Tredegar to see her.

*Brian Hedgecock* recalls his first day of evacuation:

Evacuation day for me was a day I shall never forget. We had to be outside our school (River Elementary School) at about 7am, with our cases, sandwiches and gas masks, and with a label tied somewhere on us saying who we were. Buses arrived to take us to Dover Priory Railway Station and, having said our last goodbyes to our parents, we were herded aboard the buses for the couple of miles or so to the station. I think we had a sense of bewilderment mixed with one of adventure. We travelled up the same railway line on which we had seen the Red Cross trains and our teachers got us to take a last look at our home village through the train windows before we settled down for our journey to we knew not where!

I remember very little about the journey itself, but quite late in the afternoon we got off the train in a place called Blackwood, but where was it? We all marched across a level crossing through a crowd of people, many of whom were women who were crying, presumably because they were sorry for us. Then came the first clue as to where we were. We were put aboard brown and maroon single-decker buses on the side of which were the words 'Western Mon' – we were in Monmouthshire. The buses drove to Aberbargoed, where we got off at the school, which was being used as a reception centre. Here we were given something to eat and drink and then we sat and waited, tired and missing our parents.

We became aware of an increasing number of people present at the school; they were our prospective foster parents and our numbers gradually dwindled as our friends were taken away by them. I can vaguely remember such statements as 'I'll have that one' and 'no, that one over there,' until there were not very many of us left. All a very unsettling experience for very young children. Finally, a lady arrived who said she would have me and I was led off to her house. I have a dim memory of being shown my bedroom and the bathroom, but nothing more.

*Remains of Blaenavon Ironworks, drawn by Don Lewis*

49

**Mercy Webber** *was living in Walmer near Deal at the outbreak of the war. Her father was stationed at that time in the Royal Marine Barracks in Deal. She used to travel daily from Walmer Station to attend the Dover County School for Girls:*

I was aged twelve and a half and in the Lower Fourth form. Details of the journey are rather hazy now, but I do remember that although we had been told to bring sandwiches, no drinks were allowed on the train. It was a very hot day and we stopped at several stations where drinks were given out. We passed through the Severn Tunnel and arrived at Caerleon station during the afternoon, where we were taken to the local elementary school and – horror of horrors – had our hair examined for 'nits'! What indignity! We were also asked if we wet the bed. After that we were taken in groups to find our billets. I went with one group to Lodge Road where we stood on the pavement while the householders came out and chose which girl they wished to take. I was left until last. We were told to call our foster parents, our host and hostess.

**Dot Larkins** *(now Mrs Parrett) was ten years old at the time of evacuation, and was attending Barton Road School in Dover:*

I was ten, my sister Kitty was eight and my younger sister Linda was just about six years old. We stood together in a queue outside Dover Priory Station with our parents, and my mother was constantly telling me (as the eldest) that I must look after Kitty and Linda! As we moved to board the train, our parents rushed from the station to get a last glimpse of us as the train went over the bridge at the bottom of Union Road [now Coombe Valley Road]. Our home was at 46 Union Road which was to be demolished by a land mine later in the war.

The journey to Wales seemed unending. I knew my sister Kitty was in the same carriage as me and that my younger sister was in the next carriage along the train, so I felt content they were both near. We eventually arrived at a village in South Wales called Ynysddu quite late at night. We all got out of the train and we must have looked a sorry lot, with our gas masks and labels, plus our small cases or bags. You can imagine how shocked I felt when I discovered that the front half of the train had gone off to another destination taking Linda with it!

The rest of us were taken into a hall, given something to eat, seen by a doctor and given a one week's emergency ration card. We were then taken by bus to the next little village called Wyllie, where we all ended up in the village hall. There was still no sign of Linda and nobody seemed to know anything. We were given a piece of paper with somebody's name on it and when the name was called out, you had to go with them. Kitty and I were in tears because we were not together. Lots of other sisters who had been split up were also in tears. I suppose nobody minded taking one evacuee, but not many wanted, or indeed had the room for two.

The name I had was Mr and Mrs James and when the name was called out I had to go to their home at 13 Pen-ny-Cwarel Road, where I was to spend the next two and a half years.

**Ted Green** *remembers the day his school, St Bartholomew's in Dover, assembled outside Dover Priory Station before leaving for South Wales:*

We had to get be at the station promptly at 2 o'clock. So there we all were with our carrier bags, little cases and gas masks, all lined up outside the Priory Hotel. We had labels attached to each of us – like a parcel! The day was hot and sunny, and some parents were crying while telling their children to be good, and to listen carefully to the teachers' instructions.

We seemed to be standing outside the Priory Hotel for ages, when there came a strict command, 'Stay together and in line as you move forward to the station entrance,' and there we were, being seen off by our parents. We children were ushered along slowly, looking round to see if brothers and sisters were close by. My older sister Marie had been told by mum and dad to keep us together and to watch out for us little ones. Now we boarded the steam train and crammed into the compartments. There was not a lot of room to move around. About half an hour after leaving Dover, somebody said they were hungry. At the mention of food we all grabbed for our carrier bags and boxes and tucked in. We were not aware of course, that the food we were carrying was all we would get for hours to come.

Very late in the evening the train came to a stop and we heard lots of noise as some of the children left the train. We all made for the doors and stood on the platform; we didn't know where we were. Somebody said, 'We've arrived.' I was looking out for my sisters, Marie and Margaret, and eventually they saw me. Marie said, 'Stay together now.' The next thing that happened was that all the boys were ordered back on the train by Mr Gubbins. We all climbed back on to the train and so I was separated from my sisters who stayed on the platform.

We continued our journey and much later, when it was quite dark, the train stopped again and we all got off. I didn't know it at the time, but we had arrived in Pontllanfraith. The next thing I remember was being marched to green buses (Griffin Service), single-deckers.

We boarded a bus and it trundled off over a railway crossing. Ten minutes later we arrived at Pontllanfraith School and, once inside, we had something to eat and drink. After a while we were piled back into the bus and moved off. The bus stopped frequently, dropping off my friends, one or two at a time. Then suddenly there were only two of us left, myself and my friend, Henry Plant. When Henry was taken off, I heard somebody shout, 'There's only one left,' and then I saw a jolly-looking stout lady, who said, 'I'll have him; come on, son.' Then she turned to a big man standing near her and said, 'John, take the poor lads indoors,' and, with that, he picked up both of us, one under each arm and carried us indoors and up the stairs.

*Ted's elder sister,* **Marie Green** *(now Mrs Pucknell) tells her story:*

We were all very upset to think that we were going away from our mum and dad, and our little sister Rosemary – she was only four at the time. The next we knew was that mum had packed three carrier bags; one for my little brother Ted, one for my sister Margaret and one for myself. Each contained our nightwear and a change of clothes, together with a tin of food for our foster parents when we arrived at our destination. My tin of food was corned beef.

The next day, the 2nd June, mum made sure that we had our carrier bags, gas masks and a clean handkerchief. We were all ready for our long walk to the railway station. At Dover Priory, there were lots of children from all different schools in the town. We were each given a tag with our name written on it, to put around our necks, which we had to keep on all the time

It seemed ages before the train arrived. mum and dad were upset because we were going, but they knew it was for the best. Finally it was time to go and we said our goodbyes. I felt a feeling of excitement inside me because I had never been on a train before. We boarded the train with our teachers and, although we didn't know where we were going, it didn't really seem to matter.

After a very long time on the train we arrived at our destination, which turned out to be the Severn Valley Junction. All the girls were taken off the train and ushered into a church hall. When I asked my teacher where my little brother Teddy was, she told me that he had to stay on the train because the boys were going to another place. I told her that they couldn't do that. I had promised mum and dad that I would take care of both Margaret and Ted. I was terribly upset, I felt so responsible for them, even though I was only twelve years old at the time.

In the hall we were given a hot drink and something to eat, and the local people started choosing the children they wanted, like a cattle market! Eventually, my teacher came in and said that I would have to go with her to my foster parents who were two miles away. This was even more traumatic; brother Teddy had gone to some unknown destination, and now I was being parted from Margaret. We were all separated, and I had promised to take care of them.

***Margaret Green*** (*now Mrs Brian*), *Marie's sister, also recalls her first day of evacuation:*

I was evacuated to South Wales with the staff and girls of St Andrew's Girls' School at Buckland. It was a hot Sunday morning, and I remember clutching my mother's hand tightly as we walked from our home in Barwick Road, down Union Road, together with my older brother Ted and sister Marie. Our younger sister Rosemary was also with us, however she was staying behind with mum and dad. On the way to Dover Priory Station we met hundreds of other children and parents also making their way there. I remember how painfully sad it was to leave mum, dad and Rosemary, but the excitement as I had never been on a train in my life.

I was wearing my new blue blazer and we were carrying our gas masks and a few belongings. We also had name-tags attached to our clothes, which seemed rather strange to me. Our train left the station, with frantic waving from parents and children to each other, and we were on our long journey to Wales. It was a comfort to have our teachers with us. Our headmistress was Miss Radford, a very pretty lady with black curly hair.

I didn't see my sister Marie or brother Ted once I had got on the train. We must have kept in our own classes with our respective teachers. Miss Thomas is a teacher I remember well. A welfare officer, Miss Welles, was also looking after us. We must have looked very dirty when we arrived at the Severn Tunnel Junction, which was the end of the journey for St Andrew's girls. We had kept the train windows open all day long, even through the Severn Tunnel! It was a tearful goodbye to Ted, because his school was going on to Pontllanfraith and Blackwood.

After getting off the train, we were put on to coaches that took us to Rogiet School. Miss Welles saw that we all had drinks of Horlicks, and a school nurse looked through our hair. Then they took my sister away and put her on a coach for the next village of Undy, near Magor.

The rest of us were taken to Rogiet Village Hall. It was all very strange. I was nine years old, one of the youngest children there. I had never been alone in my life before nor without my brothers and sisters; I hardly knew any of the other children. I hid myself in the farthest corner while the billeting officer was taking details of the children they had chosen for the villagers. Eventually, only the officials and I were left. Then a Red Cross worker, Mrs Pritchard, spotted me but all the villagers had gone! She persuaded the billeting officer and his wife, Mr and Mrs Walker, to take me. I later found out that Mrs Walker had recently had an operation and was advised not to take an evacuee; however,Mrs Walker, holding my hand, took me to her home.

***Brenda Rainsley*** (*now Mrs Brown*) *was evacuated with her brother and sister:*

I was only six years old when evacuated from 15 Oswald Place in Dover with Buckland School. I remember my mother at the gate, holding my little sister and crying, but I was really looking forward to the adventure. Looking back now I suppose I must have seemed very uncaring to my mother, but I was quite independent even as a child and felt very grown-up. I was with my older sister, Joan, who was also from Buckland School, and my brother William from Barton Road School. I can't remember the journey, except that we had teachers travelling with us – Miss Holloway, Miss Marsh and Miss Hine. Arriving in a big hall, I was practically the last one to be taken by foster parents. I was very tired and was put straight to bed.

The next morning when I opened my eyes, a girl and boy were sitting on my bed impatiently waiting for me to wake up. They were Betty, who was a few months older than me, and Martin who was a little younger. The first surprise I got was the bathroom – we didn't have one at home – just a big bath that was filled every Friday in front of the fire.

The town I was evacuated to was Risca. My sister and brother just seemed to have vanished, but I later found out that Joan had been sent to Rogiet and William to Ynysddu.

**Duncan Turner** *went with St Mary's School Dover to the mining town of Blaenavon:*

I don't think any of us realised what was happening. Most were led to believe that we were going on holiday. On the day we departed, we all stood on the station with our gas masks and our labels – and a packed lunch. I had a carrier bag with towel, soap and toothbrush – no personal possessions of my own. During the journey we saw lots of trains full of soldiers, and they were being given refreshments by members of the WVS. Eventually we arrived in Blaenavon Low Level station. There were waiting crowds of strange faces and a babble of strange accents. We were escorted by our teachers to Park Street School, where hot drinks and a meal was provided. When that was done we were placed into groups to be distributed to foster parents willing to take us. It seems amusing now, but then it was like trading in human cattle.

**Evelyn King** *(now Mrs Jenkin) was living in Stanhope Road, Dover, before the war. She first attended Charlton School before obtaining a place at the Dover County School for Girls.*

After watching the troops landing from Dunkirk, I think we accepted anything that might be offered and almost overnight the whole family went in different directions, wondering if we would ever see each other again. My father walked to the station with us. My school shared the train with the boys' school which seemed very exciting at the time. I can't remember much about the journey, but we finally arrived at Caerleon, South Wales, where we assembled in the village school. By nine o'clock that night everyone had been housed except Marie, who came from Deal, and me. No-one seemed to want us. We were quite big girls – perhaps we looked as if we would eat too much! People would look at us and walk away. Eventually, someone took us, but we had to share a single bed, and we shared that bed for as long as we were there.

*North Street, Blaenavon, drawn by Don Lewis.*

*Dick Langford joined Dover County School for Boys as war was declared:*

I was born and brought up in Eythorne and started at the Dover County School in 1939 but we only did part-time for the first two terms. We were evacuated during our third term – just after starting full-time! We assembled at school on the day of evacuation and could see much activity in the Channel and the smoke from fires in Calais. We made our way to our train. It seemed an interminable journey; to where we did not know. We finally arrived at Ebbw Vale. While we were awaiting dispersal, I looked up at the rows and rows of terraced white-painted cottages on the mountainside. We later found out that it was Newtown. We wondered about the nameplate 'CWM' on the buses, guessing wrongly that it was an abbreviation, perhaps Central Welsh Motors. We didn't know it was a town just down the valley!

Our group set off to Beaufort Hill School where we were kindly received, then we were taken to our billets. I went with a classmate to Mrs Williams in Beaufort. On opening the door she said, 'But I ordered girls!' On being told that all the evacuees were boys she said, 'Right, bring them in.' I stayed with Mrs Williams and her husband, who soon became auntie and uncle to me, until the school returned to Dover in 1944.

*James Mack, another Dover boy, was evacuated from Barton Road School:*

I don't think the normal twelve year olds gave much thought to Mr Chamberlain's statement on 3rd September 1939, or how it might affect their lives. The war was on but nothing much was happening as 1939 rolled on into 1940. Soon, we had two new words added to our vocabulary – invasion and evacuation. Before long, parents were being called on to decide whether or not their children would become evacuees. So on a lovely summer morning, I was one of the Barton Road group waiting to board the train at Dover Priory station. It was late morning when we slowly pulled out and began our journey towards another chapter in life. As we had no idea of where we were going, we certainly weren't prepared for such a long journey.

It must have been close to midnight when the train started to slow down and finally stop. We still didn't know where we were. The local people sounded strange and we were unable to pronounce the place where we had stopped – it turned out to be Cwmfelinfach. Our main concern now was tiredness, hunger and the need of a good wash after all those hours in a steam train. It took time to empty the train but at last some local people lead us to the village hall where we saw tables all set out with food and drinks. But we were getting very weary, as by now it was one o'clock in the morning. I doubt if any of us had ever been up so late.

Most of us had difficulty in understanding the local dialect, but we realised that someone was starting to call names from a list. All the local people who had volunteered to take evacuees were in the hall now and as a name was called, that person came forward and they were presented with the number of boys that they had promised to take. The name of Mrs Pritchard was called and I found myself, Gordon Saunders and Tony Lay put forward. Poor Mrs Pritchard! She had promised to take three girls – not boys. She put on a brave face, I must say, but you could see her disappointment. We later found out she had three grown up sons of her own, and was looking forward to having some girls in the house.

*Eileen Neville (now Mrs Lacey) lived in Deal but attended Dover County School for Girls:*

One morning in May 1940, the headmistress announced that the school was to be evacuated. She did not know where we were going, but our parents would all be receiving a letter to this effect. They then had to sign the letter if they wished us to go. My heart sank. I didn't want to leave my family and I was convinced that my parents wouldn't let me go.

I took the letter home. My two sisters also had letters from their school. My parents must have discussed the possibility of evacuation and decided that it was a sensible thing to do – I was devastated. I was the eldest of the children and had always looked after my sisters. To be told that you were to leave your family and go to an unknown destination was too much to bear. No-one knew how long the war would last and we couldn't guess how long we would be away. I cried every night and would creep into my parents' bed and cuddle up to my mum. She was also upset; to be losing three of her four daughters must have been awful. Kit the youngest was not at school so it was decided she would stay at home. This didn't seem fair to me. Betty and Pam were not quite so upset, because they were to be evacuated together, and they were probably too young to realise the implications of war.

We went two days before my twelfth birthday! We were all packed up with our little bundles of clothes, gas masks and packs of food. The gas masks had been issued at the outbreak of the war, and we had regularly practised using them. They were horrible smelly things and quite hideous to look at. We were also issued with an identity card, with our own personal number. Mine was DHIJ343. I was told to be ready at nine o'clock on the morning of the evacuation. We were to board a bus on Deal seafront, which would take us to Dover Priory Station. There we would catch a train to some unknown destination. My mum and sisters came to see me off; my sisters weren't going till later, and many tears were shed that day.

We had been given a postcard so that when we finally arrived at our new homes we could let our parents know. On arrival at Dover Priory we were met by the rest of the school and some of the teachers who were going with us. We all boarded the train and as it pulled out of the station there was much waving and more tears. So our journey into the unknown began. We ate our food and watched the passing countryside as we chattered and wondered when we would get there, and where it would be. Finally, after many hours we arrived in Newport, and from there we went on to Caerleon, a small village with a Roman amphitheatre as its claim to fame.

This was to be our home for the foreseeable future. We stood outside a school, with our pathetic little bundles, waiting like cattle to be picked by our prospective foster parents. I was eventually taken with my friend Ellen, by a young couple, Mr and Mrs Cook. They took us home and gave us a meal. They had no children of their own and were possibly a little daunted by being allocated two twelve-year olds, but they were very kind. We were put to bed in a little room with two small camp beds. We were thoroughly exhausted. The situation suddenly hit us and we both started to cry, sobbing uncontrollably that we wanted our parents. Mrs Cook came to calm us down and eventually, we fell asleep utterly worn out.

*Alan Avery* recalls his day of departure:

Our home was at 91 Manor Road, Maxton, Dover, immediately below the cross-channel guns positioned on the hill above our houses. I had just completed my first year at Belgrave Infants' School at the outbreak of the war. The headteacher was Miss Wiseman and two other teachers that I can remember were Miss Turtle and Miss Bowles.

I woke up very early on the day we were being evacuated, feeling very happy and excited at the thought of a long train journey. I was keen to get to the station and wave goodbye to my parents! As I have grown older, I have often thought about how my parents must have felt as their six year old son and thirteen year old daughter were taken away from them amid the likelihood of an imminent invasion. Would this be the last time we would ever see each other?

As a family man with children of my own, what would I have done in my parents' position? I dread to dwell on it! On that day my mother took me to school and had to leave me there while we were checked that we had our belongings – a small pressed cardboard case with my wash things, pyjamas, clean pants, socks and shirt – no toys or comforter! With my gas mask over my shoulder, we marched in crocodile fashion down Belgrave Road and along Folkestone Road to Dover Priory Station. Here we joined other schools and my school joined up with Christchurch School, whose headteacher was Mr A. B. Taylor. After the war he became head of St

Radigund's Primary School and chairman of the English Schools' Football Association.

As we approached the steps down to Dover Priory, there were crowds of parents waiting to see us off. My parents waved goodbye and my mother's best friend, Mrs Cheney, thrust into my hand my two favourite comics, *Rainbow* and *Chick's Own.* Meanwhile, my sister Pat was doing the same things except her school, Astor Girls' School, approached the station down the steps from the Tower Hamlets side of Dover Priory. My mother's last words to her were, 'Look after Alan – don't let him out of your sight!' My poor sister never saw me at the station as one of the trains being used for our evacuation was commandeered to transport troops arriving from Dunkirk. What a responsibility to face a thirteen year old in such frightening times. Unlike me, she appreciated the seriousness of the situation. Seven days were to pass before she, in Pengam, found out that I was billeted at Upper Cwmbran, many miles and valleys away!

I remember very little of the train journey, which seemed to go on for ever; at times we were stationary for very long periods. It was late in the day when our long journey stopped at Upper Cwmbran, and we had finally arrived at our destination.

*Dawn Terry (now Mrs Vodka) was living at 1 Townwall Passage, Dover, attending St James' Girls' School with her friend Pearl Hayward, who lived close by at 64, St James Street:*

When all the children were being evacuated, I wanted to go. To me at that time, it seemed like they were all going on holiday. My friend Pearl was going and I wanted to go with her. In my mind it seemed like we would be together all the time. When they gave out the evacuation papers at school, I took them home to my parents, but they would not sign them. They gave me all sorts of reasons – I wouldn't like being away from home – they didn't want me to go – I should stay with my sisters! My sisters incidentally, were too old to be evacuated.

Nothing would change my mind! Pearl was going and I wanted to go, so when I called for Pearl the next morning to go to school, I asked if her mother would fill out my papers to be evacuated. Pearl didn't bother asking her mother. Pearl filled out the forms and signed them on behalf of my parents, and I took them to school. When my parents found out what I had done, they were very angry and said I couldn't go. I had to go back and tell my teacher, but the teacher in turn said that as the papers were signed, I had to go! So I went!

I remember the day we were leaving. I was all excited. I was so sure it wouldn't last very long. We would soon be back home and things would return to normal. I never ever thought things would turn out the way they did, but I guess none of us did. Pearl and I were separated from the start when we got on the train. I expected to be with her when we got to our destination, but I never saw her again! I never knew what part of Wales she went to, and completely lost track of her. I went to Blaenavon where I lived in a beautiful farm house. It belonged to one of the wealthier families in the area. I remember when I first saw the place I was feeling very fortunate at having such a lovely billet, but there was a lot I was to find out.

*St. Martin's County Primary School, Dover.*
*(Picture taken in 1996 by Peter Hayward)*

*A group of boys from St Martin's School, Dover, pictured at Fairview School,
Pengham, South Wales – Peter Hayward collection*

**Audrey Turner** *(now Mrs Rickman) went with her twin, Vivienne, and younger sister, Josie:*

Vivienne and I started together at St Martin's School in 1935. Our home was at 13 Church
Road, Dover, where we lived with our mother and father and younger sister Josie. On the day of
evacuation I remember my mother saying, 'Don't, whatever you do, get split up! When you get
to your destination they have got to take all three of you.' Mum kept saying over and over
again, 'You are not to get split up!' Josie was only four years old.

We thought the evacuation was a big adventure. We took a little suitcase and my mother had
made some nice little dresses to take. The journey to Wales at first was very exciting, but after a
while we started to realise that it was something more serious. Two of the teachers that went
with us were Miss Harmer and Miss Beverton. Finally we reached our destination, the village of
Markham. I don't remember disembarking, but I remember we went into a hall; we were kept
standing and we were awfully tired. Women started choosing the children. I remember one
woman saying, 'I'll have the twins.' We clung together then, and said, 'No, Josie must come
too!' but she didn't want three.

Gradually the children got fewer and fewer and I remember one tall skinny boy left standing
there. They were obviously picking out the nice looking children first; the pretty girls, etc.
Mother had told us that we were pretty, but nobody wanted to take the three of us. Josie was
really pretty, and lots of people wanted to take her. I think that had we not stuck together, Josie
would have been very unhappy, but we would have probably been able to see her, and perhaps
we would have gone to better billets. In the end, the woman who only wanted us twins said she
would take all three of us, but she didn't really have the accommodation. Still, we were
together, and that was the main thing.

**Violet Lamoon** *(now Mrs Gregory) was attending Astor Avenue School in Dover at the time
of the evacuation. Her sister and brother were at St Bartholomew's School:*

I was eleven years old when I was evacuated. My sister was nine and my brother was seven
years old. When we reached Wales I had no idea where my brother and sister were. I was
billeted in Pengam with a nice family, Mr and Mrs Jones. After a while I found out that my
sister and brother were at Blackwood, so one day I walked from Pengam to the Blackwood
schools and eventually found them.

**Rosina Wells** (now Mrs Elson) was at Buckland Girls' School, Dover, at the age of nine:

I can remember my mum and my auntie talking about the children of Dover having to be evacuated. I asked if I could go, and mum refused so I cried and said that I wanted to go. My younger sister also wanted to go; we both thought that we would be going on a holiday! We didn't realise at the time, that we were going to have to stay. However, Mum must have eventually agreed for us to be evacuated.

When the day came for us to go, we all had to meet at school, where we had name-tags put on our coats and gas masks, and on the bags with our clothes in. We then went to Dover Priory Station to catch the train. All the parents were there, saying their goodbyes, and some were crying. Anyway, the train pulled out and the journey seemed to go on for hours and hours. On one occasion the train stopped, and none of us knew where we were. As I looked out of the carriage window, there was a man standing on the track. He said, 'Hello!', then he gave me some coins and the train moved on. I can still see him now with his big cap on.

My most traumatic memory of the journey was when I lost my sister on the train. I had gone to the toilet but when I returned to the compartment we were in, there was no-one there, just the carrier bag with my clothes in it. She was gone! The next thing I remember was standing in a big hall, waiting to be picked out. I remember going with an old lady, then waking up in a young couple's house. Their names were Mr and Mrs Jones. I found out later that I was at a place called Undy, and that my sister was billeted in Risca.

*Dee Croucher* (now Mrs Samuel) recalls the first day of evacuation:

The long, long train journey to Wales seemed never-ending. I felt the movement of the train for ages afterwards. I was just nine years old and was from St Martin's School, Dover. After many hours we finally arrived at a small town called Blackwood. There, we were taken to a school hall and given tea. Afterwards we went taken bus to a school hall in Argoed where we were handed over to a lady who took a group of us to our billets. I was lucky. I had a very good home with a miner's family. They had a daughter of twenty-seven years, and I shared her bedroom. Some of the evacuees weren't so lucky and didn't stay long. My sister had two billets before being settled, and she lived about three miles from me. As she was soon to leave school, she wasn't there long. She had a job to find out where I was at first.

*Sylvia Hedgecock* (now Mrs Dunford) remembers her experiences of those first few days:

I was seven years old and in the infants at Barton Road School, Dover, when I remember bringing home these bits of paper about the evacuation. Mum wasn't keen at all about letting us go. I kept pestering her, saying that I wanted to go because all my friends were going, and she said, 'Well if you are going, I want your sister to go with you.' Well, she hadn't yet started school, because she wasn't five until the September, but I suppose we had time for her to be attached to the school. Mum agreed then, but she really didn't want us to go.

I can remember that we gathered at school and got on a double-decker East Kent bus and went to Dover Priory Station. We ended up at Newport, and then went to a hall where we all went on view, waiting for foster-parents to pick us out. It got to midnight and we were the last two there. I can still see us sitting there, not really understanding it all.

Anyway, there was a couple waiting to take an evacuee; they didn't want two children, but they were persuaded in the end to take both of us. The couple, Mr and Mrs Jones, took us to Pontllanfraith. Meanwhile, my dad, who was in the Royal Engineers, was evacuated from Dunkirk. He didn't stop in Dover; I don't know where he went to, but as he was passing through Dover, he managed to contact Hayhoe's the bakers and Quested's the butchers, two local shops down at the harbour, supplying provisions to the ships. Dad managed to get them to relay a message to my mum, to let her know that he was safe. You can imagine what my mother must have been going through – my dad over there in France, and we two girls in Wales. Anyway, we arrived in Pontllanfraith and, eventually, Mrs Jones put us to bed. We curled up together and we cried for most of that first night!

***Jean Simpson*** *(now Mrs Gladish) was evacuated with her thirteen year old sister*

I was evacuated from Dover with Barton Road School at nine years old. I recall, quite clearly, being led round the streets of Cwmfelinfach in the dark looking for a billet, until a woman came forward and said she would take the little girl with curls. I had my thirteen year old sister with me, and she said that we weren't to be separated, so the woman took my sister as well. We were to find out what a good billet we had compared to some of the other children.

***Dora Hedges*** *(now Mrs Riley) and her sister Brenda were evacuated to Blaenavon:*

We were all living at 5 Church Place, in Dover at the outbreak of the war, and I was attending St James' Girls' School. Poor dad was left waiting for his call-up papers. His mother sent for my mother, as dad wouldn't go to work and was 'letting himself go'. Normally he was so hard working, but it was dreadful for him seeing his family being split up because of the war.

I thought that we would only be away a few weeks, and we would be altogether in a big hall, with rows and rows of beds. I wondered what it was going to be like living in a strange place. Anyway, we arrived in Blaenavon and the children were being billeted out. Most people only wanted one evacuee, but I would not let go of my sister, Brenda. Finally, Mr and Mrs James took us in, and we sat together in an armchair, just crying quietly for our mother.

***Bob Hadley*** *was ten years old when he was evacuated:*

I lived at the Ropewalk, in Dover, and was attending Holy Trinity School in the Pier District. On the day of evacuation, it was like going on a day's outing, but things soon changed once we reached our destination. I was evacuated with my brother Ray, aged six years, and my sister Mary who was five years old, and we all went to Cwmbran. When we arrived, we were all lined up along a fence outside the station. I was with Ray, but sister Mary must have been somewhere along the line. People started picking children out of the line. Someone wanted me, but they were told that we were brothers and couldn't be split up. I suppose being so young and not really realising what was happening, we just forgot about our sister Mary! Anyway, we were taken to a house alongside a canal bank, shown our bedroom and given a banana. We found out later that Mary was living with a childless couple, and apparently kept crying that she wanted her Bob. Not knowing what she meant, the couple gave her a shilling! We were soon reunited.

***Alan Bell*** *was living in Deal and going to the Dover County School for Boys:*

I normally travelled to school by train, but on the day of evacuation I believe the train services were somewhat disrupted, and a coach was provided for the Deal boys to be taken to Dover to join the rest of the school on the train to set off for an unknown destination. About ten of us had to travel in the guard's van as the train was so crowded. As there was only one small window in the door on each side, our view was rather limited, so the journey was somewhat tedious, taking about ten hours. We reached Newport and started going up one of the western valleys, seeing coal mines. Just before arriving at Ebbw Vale station, we passed the Richard Thomas steelworks, which seemed to be belching out flames and smoke of various colours. We had been expecting to be taken to a quiet rural area, and here we were apparently arriving in a highly industrialised part of the country; perhaps a prime target for enemy bombers.

Incidentally, my sister, who was four years younger than me, had gone with her Deal school to an entirely different part of Wales, near Bridgend and it was some time before I knew where she was. At Ebbw Vale station were crowds of local people who had come to see the arrival of what they referred to as 'vacuees'. They had been expecting to see a crowd of ragged, bewildered little children, so were surprised when a crowd of boys in school uniform, some over six feet tall, get off the train and form up into their classes. The dispersal to foster homes was efficiently organised, so by about nine o'clock in the evening we were all in our billets.

**Bessie Laurie** (now Mrs Newton) of Clarendon Place, Dover, was at the County School:

At the start of the phoney war in September, 1939, we immediately went over to part-time schooling. But things started to happen at the time of Dunkirk. My father was working down at the harbour at the time, and I think the whole docks area became an exclusion zone. Soon a letter came for our parents to sign if they wanted us to be evacuated. My father didn't want us to go, but my mother, who was the disciplinarian, said, 'Well, they will have to go!' My older sister had already left school, so that left me and my twelve year old brother, Harry at Christ Church School, up Military Hill. Dad came home very worried. He had already seen our troops landing at Dover and he changed his mind about us going. I think it was only on the Friday that we were told we were going on the Sunday morning, 2nd June, 1940.

We reported to school with our suitcases. I looked on it as a bit of an adventure, having never been on a long train journey before. I had been to Folkestone, but that was about it!

Our cases were taken to the station by lorry, then we all marched in crocodile fashion with the teachers, to Dover Priory. Parents were not allowed on to the platforms. My mother told me later that my father had tears streaming down his face as he watched us all leave. Apparently mum didn't shed a tear! She had had such a hard life as a child, it had taken the emotional side out of her. Brother Harry left with his school on a different train, and it was some time later that I found out he had gone to Cwmbran. Anyway, our train left and nobody knew where we were going. The first thing I noticed was that all the station signs had been removed, presumably because of the expected German invasion. It wasn't until we got into Wiltshire and we saw the 'White Horse' that we found out we were heading west.

We finally arrived at Caerleon at about eight o'clock in the evening, where we were taken into a hall and 'sorted out'. The local people had been primed to have these evacuees, so we were picked out and allocated! I didn't think much of the way we were billeted out, but at least my friend Betty and I managed to stay together with Mr and Mrs Jones, who were very kind people. We went to a cottage by the river, and put into a bedroom where we shared a bed – but the lavatory was down the end of the garden! We had both been used to flush toilets back home.

As we looked out of the bedroom window we could see these things moving about. They were water voles, but we thought at the time that they were rats. I said to Betty, 'Don't unpack your suitcase.' We didn't even undress; we just sat in our clothes all night. In the morning I said to Betty, 'Get your suitcase, we are going up to the school.' We had been told to assemble there at nine o'clock – I think. Mrs Jones gave us some breakfast and afterwards I said to her, 'Sorry, we were only staying for the night,' and off we went! Poor Mrs Jones just looked blank as she watched us walk away.

***Robert Dunford*** *remembers the day he and his brother Sam were evacuated:*

At the time of the evacuation we were living in the High Street in Dover, at the corner of Peter Street, and I went to St Mary's School. In May 1940 I had my tenth birthday, and soon everyone was talking about evacuation. My brother Sam and I were on the list that came home from school. I remember my father saying, 'I don't care what you do. If you want to go, you can go. If you want to stay, you can stay.' Well, I was only ten and my brother was eleven, but it was up to us. So I said, 'Well, all our mates are going – so we will go.' We packed our kit bags; we literally had small white canvas kit bags – just like the soldiers and sailors used to have in those days, but smaller. On the day of evacuation we assembled at school then marched up to Dover Priory Station, but our parents never came to see us off! Well, they still had five children at home, and missing two was a bit of a relief I always imagined.

Like most kids in those days, we had never known any great travelling. So when we went on this epic journey down to Wales, it was a great adventure! I think we left Dover at about ten o'clock in the morning, and to the best of my knowledge we didn't get to Blaenavon until about half past six in the evening. I remember we stopped at one or two places on the way, and there were these great ladies handing out cups of tea and buns. It was quite a journey really. I remember the highlight was the Severn Tunnel. We had all been looking forward to that.

After getting off the train at Blaenavon, we marched up to one of the schools where a meal was laid on for us. After we had eaten, we were taken in groups of about ten, to various distribution points around the town. Our distribution point was the greengrocer's shop in Broad Street. Because my brother and I wouldn't be separated from each other, we were the last two there. It was getting late in the evening by now but we continued to tell the billeting people that we were going to stick together. Eventually, a woman agreed to take us both. She lived opposite the greengrocer, in a little company shop called Edwards and Fowler, a sort of baker and general grocer. Anyway, the family we were to live with were Mr and Mrs Challenger, and we stayed with them for about three months.

*Astor Avenue School, Dover,*
*now Astor Primary School*
*– Photo, Peter Hayward*

***Joyce Hawkins*** *(now Mrs Purssord) was ten years old and her sister Jean, eight years old, when they were evacuated with Barton Road Girls' School:*

My mother's last words to me were, 'Take care of Jean!' We had all been given a small notebook in which to write a composition of our evacuation from Dover. The journey seemed to go on for ever, but I got an 'A' for whatever I wrote in my notebook.

We finally arrived at a small village called Wyllie, between Cwmfelinfach and Pontllanfraith. The village stood on top of a small hill and included a coal mine, the railway station, a community centre, Baptist chapel and a general store with post office.

It was dark when we arrived and we were shepherded into the community centre to await billeting. All the while I kept very close to Jean. When Jean's name was called I remember shouting out that we must stay together, and that my mother had said I must look after Jean, but Jean was taken nevertheless. I started to cry and someone told me I could see Jean in the morning. I sat there crying until I was almost the last one left. I remember thinking that no-one wanted me but I had been allocated to the lady in charge of billeting, so I had to wait until she had finished sorting out everyone else. Mrs Jones turned out to be one of the kindest people I knew, but I think I cried myself to sleep that first night, wondering what had happened to Jean.

*This group of children are girls from Astor Avenue School, and boys from St. Martin's School, Dover, pictured at Pengam, South Wales.*
*TOP ROW: Richard Turner, Cyril . . . . . , Lenny Turner.*
*MIDDLE ROW: Joyce Pullman, Phyllis Baker, Joan Turner.*
*BOTTOM ROW: Hazel Shelf, Betty Whiting, Violet Lamoon, Gwen Taylor.*

**Bob Cain** *was nine years old when he and his four sisters were evacuated from Dover:*

I am one of five children, the others being girls. At the time of the evacuation, my eldest sister June was twelve and attended Astor Avenue School for Girls; my sisters Josephine (eleven) and Rose (eight) attended St Martin's School for Girls, and I was at St Martin's School for Boys, while my youngest sister Barbara (six) was at Belgrave Infants' School.

In the pre-war days, going away for holidays was very rare and, although working-class people from the cities and industrial areas would take their charabanc trips to the seaside, since we already had the sea at Dover, there was little point in going elsewhere. Since we didn't go anywhere, we had no suitcases. Mother therefore had to find anything that would hold clothes for the five of us and, as a result, we arrived at Priory Station festooned like Christmas trees with an assortment of Scouts haversacks, brown paper parcels and those awful brown paper carrier bags with string handles – and of course, our gas masks, and our name tags.

Most of the evacuees left Dover on 2nd June, so you can imagine the scene at the station – weeping children, wailing mothers, teachers trying to assemble their own particular flock, and the fact that troops were still coming through from Dunkirk, did nothing to lessen the confusion.

Well, eventually, we started the worst train journey I have ever experienced. It was not so much the journey, which I believe took about twelve hours, that got me down – after all, we were going to Wales which had lovely mountains, I was with my friends and there was a certain euphoria about this great adventure we were embarking on. No, it was the awful, nagging thirst. I don't recall whether we had taken any bottles of water with us but, if we had, mine must have gone quickly, for even today I can recall that terrible thirst. I know that trains in those days had 'Not Fit For Drinking' signs above the taps in the toilets, but in our case, it was academic for there was no water at all on the train. As far as I can recall, I didn't quench my thirst until we arrived in Pengam, South Wales, where somebody there gave me a drink of water.

Apart from the thirst, the only other thing I clearly remember from that journey was that on many garden fences that backed on to the railway line from Dover, were large notices, mostly painted on white sheets saying, 'WELL DONE, LADS' and 'WE ARE PROUD OF YOU' etc. – these, of course, were for the soldiers returning from Dunkirk who were travelling on the same line.

And so we arrived in Pengam, Monmouthshire, where there were dozens of people (who looked very important to a nine year old) to receive us. A lady with a megaphone stood on a dais and bellowed, 'Have any of you got sisters or relatives in Astor Avenue Girls' School?' I put up my hand and was whisked away to join my eldest sister June, and it was only then that I realised that she was on the same train. My sister and I were then handed over to a Mr and Mrs Jones, and the evacuation of four years, six months and eight days had begun.

Rose and Josephine ended up in Argoed, about fifteen miles from Pengam (although I only found this out by chance, three months later), and my youngest sister Barbara had gone to Cwmbran, about forty miles away. Being on her own at the age of six was obviously not satisfactory, so my mother arranged for her to join my other sisters at Argoed.

*Joyce Heath* (now Mrs Larner) was evacuated with Barton Road Girls' School, aged 12.

We all lived at 1 Alexandra Cottages, Dover, before my brother and I were evacuated to Wales. I can't recall much of the train journey, but I know it was very long and we were all very tired when we finally arrived at at place called Ynysddu. We were all eventually billeted out. I didn't know where my younger brother was. However, the next morning I found him billeted a few streets away. When I saw him, I promptly burst into tears. I was so upset at being parted from him that his foster parents, Mr and Mrs Williams, took pity on me. They told me that I shouldn't be separated from my brother, and promptly made arrangements to foster me as well.

*Peter Prescott* was a pupil at the Dover County School at the time of evacuation:

The great withdrawal from Dunkirk was still going on. Train loads of troops were leaving the Marine Station in Dover. It was a hot, dry day when we turned up at the Priory Station to be loaded on to a train, which had, as I recall, the County School girls at the front; the two staffs in the middle and us in the rear. It may have been the other way about, but I distinctly remember that the staff were in the middle to prevent any unseemly or licentious behaviour on the train.

The journey took all day and was very boring. We passed through London and I distinctly remember women standing on platforms, handing bottles, sweets and sandwiches to troops on a train passing slowly through a station. When we arrived at Newport the train was split. The girls went off to Caerleon and we chugged up the valley to Ebbw Vale. It was many years later that I learned that we should have gone to Caerleon, which was geared up to receive us, and the girls to Ebbw Vale. This explains the reluctance of mothers to receive strapping great youths into their homes when they were expecting girls! It also explains the smiles of the girls who, with their mothers, formed the welcoming party. We were quickly found billets and I found myself, with George Cropton, at number 37 Hillside Terrace, Waunllwyd with the Atkins family. We were received, fed and watered, and shown to our room which we were to share for over a year.

***Rowland Powell*** *was another Dover County School pupil at the time of the evacuation:*

That Sunday morning in early June dawned bright and clear, which was more than could be said of my waking mood; for one thing I had to be at school by eight o'clock and for another, the eight miles trip had to be undertaken by bus instead of the normal train journey, and buses always tended to make me sick. Worst of all though, I would be leaving home on a one way ticket for an unknown destination. Selfishly, I had not given any thought to what the upheaval might be doing to my father; since my mother had died in 1938 there had been just the two of us – and I was leaving. If I was downcast that fine morning, how must he have been feeling?

We arrived at the pick-up point for a brief farewell before I had to climb on board the bus with my one allowable item of luggage plus raincoat, gas mask and food for the journey. Unlike our normal behaviour when travelling daily to school by train, we were all thoroughly subdued during the short trip to the school where buses and cars were disgorging their loads, to be mustered into our groups of classes before being marshalled into what must have been the longest crocodile in the history of Dover County School for Boys, for the trek to the station.

Led by our headmaster, Mr Booth, we stepped out somewhat glumly, the younger boys at the front with the seniors bringing up the rear to avoid stragglers. As we neared the station our flagging spirits were given a much needed boost as we spotted a similar procession approaching from the opposite direction; it was the Girls' County School, but our joy was to be short-lived as we were directed to the rear of the train and the girls to the front, while the centre had been occupied by the staff of both schools, presumably to prevent any possible fraternisation.

We had a last longing look at the sea as we travelled between Dover and Folkestone but the rest of the early stages of the journey have been lost in the mists of memory as gradually, youthful resilience overcame our earlier low feelings at leaving homes and parents. By mid-day we had travelled quite slowly by deviated route to Clapham Junction where we paused just long enough for a fresh locomotive to be attached to our end of the train before we were off once more. This time we went south-westerly through Surrey and Middlesex, across rural Hampshire and into Wiltshire for another engine change at Salisbury before heading north-west to Bath.

It was late afternoon when the train ground slowly to a halt once more, this time on a high, curving embankment overlooking a long row of terraced houses on the outskirts of Bristol. By then the long journey and the oven-like heat in the carriages from the sun blazing down on us all day had left even the most ebullient in a state of near exhaustion. We must have looked a sorry sight, with the open windows crammed with boys and girls seeking a breath of cool air. Suddenly, the embankment seemed to come alive with people from the houses below, carrying bottles of pop, jugs of tea and water; we had stumbled upon a veritable oasis which had given us a most welcome, if brief, respite. All too soon the signal changed and we were on our way again, refreshed by a spontaneously warm, generous and unforgettable gesture of kindness.

Onward we rolled, plunging under the River Severn to re-surface in Wales, and within an hour of our last stop we had pulled into Newport Station where, for the first time, we were allowed on to the platform to stretch our legs. We were soon herded back into the train and, with a jerk we were on our way yet again only to be cast into deep gloom as lookouts at the windows reported that the girls had been left behind. Later we learned that they had gone in the opposite direction to Caerleon.

The air of depression that had settled upon us at leaving the girls behind became even deeper as the two tubby tank engines that had been hitched on at Newport, started to huff, puff and chuff as they piloted us into a valley, hauling their load up an ever increasing incline. Gone now were the earlier sylvan summer scenes; we were entering an industrial region which did nothing to lift our depression as the slopes on either side of the track became steeper and higher until they almost disappeared from view; deeper into the valley and climbing all the time; under a sky-high viaduct, through colliery pit-head workings until, at a junction in the line we had entered an even narrower valley. Its sides were thickly covered in trees that seemed to hang so far over the line that the train appeared in imminent danger of being swallowed. The sun no longer beat down on the carriages and there was a definite chill in the air.

Onwards and upwards through another colliery and then alongside a vast industrial complex that seemed to go on for ever. Finally we passed beneath a very high bridge and came to a halt at a long empty station with seemingly deserted station buildings. It was time to disembark, bag and baggage. Apart from the station there was a high bank of trees opposite and, beyond the station, a few whitewashed cottages in the distance. We appeared to be miles from anywhere, with little sign of life except for a couple of official looking gentlemen standing waiting.

A sudden fanfare of car horns heralded the arrival of a convoy of just about every make of pre-war car available and we were swiftly counted off and loaded into them for the next leg of the journey. Our first impressions, as the overloaded cars groaned away from the station, had been that we were heading for some moorland hideaway as, for the first time, we encountered sheep and ponies wandering at large across wide open spaces, but we need not have worried. We suddenly took a left-hand turn and came face to face with a largish town, and in no time at all we were being ushered into Willowtown School which lay in the shadow of a brickworks.

We were then quickly absorbed into a warm and welcoming gathering where food and drink waited for us. As we relaxed, our prospective foster parents wandered among us and, while we sized each other up, we learned where we were. Our one-way tickets had expired in Ebbw Vale.

*Keith (Mac) McInnes was eight years old when the evacuation took place:*

Before the war our family home was in Elms Vale Road, Dover, and my father was a chief engineer on the cross channel boats. When my brother and I were evacuated, I was at St Martin's Primary School, and Ian was at the Boys' County School. Because we were at different schools, we were evacuated to different places in South Wales. I went to Cefn Forest and Ian went to Ebbw Vale, both in Monmouthshire. I was billeted with Mr and Mrs Sankey, a childless couple. He was a miner. The postcard I took with me, to post when I got to my billet, was filled with the words, 'I want to come home!'

*Peter Elgar was, at first, evacuated privately. He recalls the period of his first evacuation:*

I was evacuated to four different places during the war years. Life became a mixture of peaceful existence when the hostilities seemed very remote, interspersed with periods of living in frontline situations. My first experiences were very much a case of 'from the frying-pan into the fire'. In spring, 1940, the phoney war was coming to an end. My home town of Dover was about to become 'Hellfire Corner'. In May, at the age of ten, I was taken by my mother to stay with relatives in Portland, Dorset. At first it was all wonderfully idyllic in that lovely warm summer. In nearby Weymouth, where we frequently went for shopping, people were holidaying very much as usual. There were long and happy days of country walks and exploring the rocks and beaches of the Chesil Bank with my cousins and their friends. There was a farm at the bottom of the High Street where we were living. Cows were regularly driven along the picturesque narrow streets near the beach – rather alarming for a town boy! At the corner shop we could buy Milky Ways and other sweet delights for a penny. I attended the local school with a number of other evacuees. Being mixed, it was another new experience.

Everyone must have realised that it wouldn't be long before Jerry turned his attentions to the important naval dockyard and installations close to where we lived. Air raids became frequent about mid-June. We often had to shelter under the desks. The noise of the Junkers 87 dive-bombers was deafening and frightening. Sometimes there were up to fifty aircraft over the island. When we were indoors we had to shelter under the stairs. After one particularly heavy attack, we saw large clouds of smoke rising from the harbour area. The naval defence vessel *Foyle Bank* was sunk. Seaman Jack Mantle continued firing his guns at the raiders though mortally wounded. Later we heard that he had been awarded a posthumous Victoria Cross.

One day we walked up the hill towards the next village to see a German aircraft which had nose-dived into the ground and had remained in a vertical position. On another occasion we were all walking over the bridge towards the mainland and Wyke Regis. A large black ball of smoke appeared in the air above. Seconds later a tremendous explosion almost blew us into the front of a house where we had run for shelter. We later heard that it had been a landmine.

After about three months we left Portland to stay with other relatives in Kensal Rise, London – another unwise move! The Blitz began almost immediately and we spent many anxious nights huddled under the stairs. The days were relatively free of raids and we could visit Harlesden, Kilburn and other shopping centres, or the local parks where I first began to enjoy cycling.

Soon we returned to Dover and our coach passed many scenes of destruction in London's south-east suburbs. We could see the huge pall of black smoke from the Surrey Docks fires until we were well into the Kent countryside. After the Dunkirk evacuation and the fall of the French channel ports, Dover had become a front-line town and would remain so for the next four years. The Battle of Britain was already well under way and there were dogfights almost daily. The harbour and convoys in the channel were frequently attacked. In one such incident the destroyer *Codrington* was bombed and sunk at her moorings.

I remember walking with my father on High Meadow which overlooked the town. An aircraft flew low over Dover castle. Like all boys I believed myself to be an expert at aircraft recognition and calmly stated that it was one of ours. The next moment, a couple of flaming barrage balloons were on their way to the ground, including the one moored a few yards away from us. We lay flat as the raider zoomed overhead, the pilot clearly visible. He shot up a number of other balloons and, within seconds, was well out to sea before anti-aircraft guns had barked into action. He must have given the secret radar installations at Swingate quite a scare.

The town was now well within range of enemy guns on the French coast, and regular shelling was another serious hazard to be endured. The population of Dover had been reduced to about 15,000. My school, St Bartholomew's, had been evacuated to Blackwood, Monmouthshire, about the time we had left for Portland. For the sake of my education, it was decided that I should go and join them. As I boarded the coach in the Market Square I little thought that it would be three years before I saw my home town again.

I've always been a good traveller and was about the only one who wasn't ill on the journey to London. We travelled by train from Paddington to Newport, where I was met by my new foster-parents, David and Bessie Williams. I travelled the last leg of my journey to Blackwood in their car. Both were teachers and he was on the staff of the school opposite their house, a portion of which had been set aside for our school. I enjoyed being reunited with many school friends.

*Frank Davies recalls his memories of the day of evacuation:*

Soon it was the turn of the schoolchildren of Dover to be evacuated, and this affected me. My brother Ron remained at home to attend, as usual, Aylesham Secondary School. My friend, who was a pupil at Simon Langton's School in Canterbury continued to travel each day from Aylesham to Canterbury by train. But on that beautiful Sunday morning on 2nd June, 1940, I had to say goodbye to my family on the platform and get into the train with my fellow pupils, our gas masks and a suitcase, having been told what to take, but not where we were going.

The train moved across southern England, avoiding most of London. Thirst became a real problem as the day went on – there was no water on the train! It was early evening by the time we reached Newport where we stopped for a while. It was at Newport that the Dover County

School for Girls left us and went in a different direction to Caerleon.

Some time later our train moved off again, along the valley towards Ebbw Vale. A few miles south of Ebbw Vale the train was halted again and I was among those told to alight. We had been a whole day on the train, hot and exhausted, and very bewildered. Now we heard Welsh voices, kindly directing us to walk from the platform to a local hall, where people had been waiting for a long time for the evacuees to arrive. They were expecting young children!

There I stood, over two hundred miles away from home, and anxious, when a well dressed man came up to me and said, 'I am Gurnos Worthing, could you find another boy to come with you?' I looked around for friends, but could only see one member of my form. He was over a year older than me, having been kept down in the fifth form because he had failed his school certificate exams. We were taken from the hall and found ourselves walking back in the direction of the station, to a small road alongside the railway. Halfway down we turned into a house where Mrs Worthing was waiting. She was quite young and attractive, and couldn't hide her surprise, saying, 'Well Gus, what has happened?' She was expecting two little girls – I was nearly fifteen years old and six feet one inch tall, and Harold was older and roughly the same size! Their black spaniel, Jet, fussed over us, and then we were given a meal. We were starving. After the meal we talked for a while and then went off to bed. It wasn't a very large bed, and we had to sleep together. I didn't like this much, and neither did Harold! I was exhausted but found it difficult to sleep; so much had happened. On the following day, we assembled at the tiny station, and it was then that we found out the name of the village – it was Cwm.

*Alma Collis* (now Mrs Cork) was a pupil in Folkestone:

The war broke out the day after my tenth birthday – I remember my father rushing into church to tell everyone, and sent me rushing home as the sirens were going. At this age I knew nothing about war except for the stories my father told of his experiences in the first world war.

Shortly after this, three boys moved into the house next door. They were evacuees from London. I well remember thinking how dreadful they must feel, having to leave their mother and father behind, little realising that it was going to happen to me in June 1940.

I attended All Souls School in Stanley Road, Cheriton, but my elder and younger sisters were at Harcourt School in Surrenden Road. This meant that I had to join them to be evacuated together. The first I knew of that day was being told that I was going to the country for two weeks with Helen and Anne – Mother would see us later. I loathed being labelled, carrying my gas mask and suitcase, getting in line with masses of other children and I cried all the way to Wales! By the time we reached Abergavenny it was dark and we were cold and tired.

*Alma, Patricia, Edie and Gillian Collis. Picture taken at Grosmont Castle, 1941 (Alma Cork)*

Like all other evacuees, we were shepherded into the 'cattle market' to await selection by whoever fancied us. A lovely cuddly lady with white hair said she would take my sister and me, but she was outbid by another lady who, I was to learn later, was held in high esteem. This upset me even more, as I was to learn that the first lady had a large white house at the top of a village called Grosmont. However, we were all bundled into a car and driven to a manor house three miles outside the village and all down hill! The house is called 'Part-Y-Seal', pronounced 'Porty Seal', and our host and hostess were Captain and Mrs

Pope. Anne and I had twin beds in a very large bedroom, but Helen, being older, had her own room. There was a lovely housemaid called Eileen and a cook. Eileen was young and very kind to us, but cook treated us very badly.

*Folkestone evacuee, **Raymond Harris**, remembers the day he and his sister left for Wales:*

I was born in Cheriton, Folkestone, the youngest of six children, and I attended Morehall School first, then went to Harcourt School. I was evacuated at the beginning of June 1940 at the age of nine, together with my fourteen years old sister, who, although she had already left school, was allowed to accompany me after some 'string pulling' by our headmistress.

I remember the day we left. We had our gas masks and identification labels tied to our coats, and mum walked with us to the station. I didn't realise what was happening until the train pulled out, leaving all the parents on the station, many of them weeping. I don't know how my mum coped after having six children round the table. She was left with one seventeen year old son after my sister and I left; three of my elder brothers had already gone into the forces; one at the time was reported missing believed killed. We found out later that he was a prisoner of war.

Anyway, we were on our way to some unknown destination, with our escorting teachers making the journey into a geography lesson, and explaining different things such as the Severn Tunnel. Finally, after many hours on the train, we arrived at Grosmont, not far from Abergavenny. We were ushered into the village hall where there were two rows of chairs back to back. We were told to sit n these almost as though we were going to play musical chairs.

Then the villagers entered and walked around us on a tour of inspection, almost like a cattle market really. They asked us questions and one motherly lady came back to find us being questioned by another who said, 'Too late! They're mine, I've already booked them.' She turned out to be a Mrs Jehu who, with her husband, had a farm about half a mile out of the village. They were a lovely couple, kind, gentle and, with their son Derek, a few months younger than me, made us more than welcome. When we arrived at the farm that first night, we were miserable and homesick, and ate very little. Later, we were shown to our bedroom which was very large, but very comfortable, where Mrs Jehu later found us sobbing our hearts out. She sat with us, hugging us, until we fell asleep.

*__Ivy Campbell__ (now Mrs Pieri) from Stella Maris School in Folkestone, was evacuated to Merthyr Tydfil with her sister and three brothers:*

I remember being very upset on the day of evacuation, and I cried a lot at the station before we left. When we arrived in Wales, we must have looked like a lot of orphans, sad and dirty after many hours on a steam train; standing there with our parcel of clothes, gas mask and a label with our name on it. I was with my sister and three brothers, and we were taken to a large hall. I can't remember how we were allocated to our foster parents, but we were all sent to different homes. I went to Dowlais and my sister and brothers went to Pennydaron. I was very upset at our being parted and it was several days before I saw them again.

*__Joyce Pellett__ (now Mrs Pascoe) remembers her first day of evacuation:*

It was on the 2nd June 1940 that my sister Vera and I were evacuated to South Wales. I was nine years old and my sister was eleven. We both went to St Mary's School, Folkestone. I can't remember whether we gathered in the school or at the railway station, all I know is that we had a label with our name on it, and our gas masks hanging round our necks.

My first sight of Wales was the mountains and the word 'CROESYCEILIOG'. When we arrived at Croesyceiliog we were taken to the school, the Highway. We were given a bun and a drink and, if my memory serves me right, we had to undress to our vest and knickers to be examined; looking through our hair and in between our toes, etc. My sister and I clung to each other all the time. After this, we were taken by some ladies to our foster home. They wanted to part my sister and me, but we said that our mother had made us promise to stay together. Luckily for us, Mrs Kidner who was going to have just one agreed to take both of us. She was very kind.

*Another pupil from St Mary's School, Folkestone, was* **Margaret Hodges** *(now Mrs Brooker).*

On the 2nd June 1940, just prior to my eighth birthday, I was evacuated from Folkestone to Croesyceiliog, South Wales, where I lived until November 1943. My foster-sister Edith was twelve years old at the time and was put in charge of looking after her 'little sister'.

All the children lined up in the playground wearing school uniform together with gas mask in its cardboard box, and a label giving our name, address and group number, which I recall was '15'. There was a terrible feeling of anxiety for both parents and children, not knowing where we were actually going, or for how long we would be separated.

After a very long train journey on a hot summer day, we arrived at our destination, and were transported by coach to the local school at Croesyceiliog to be billeted out in the community. This was the first traumatic experience of my life, still vivid in my memory after fifty-five years. Edith and I were the last children to be found a home, because we refused to be parted. I held on to Edith, feeling very frightened. Eventually, late that night, it was agreed that we would be given a home together, with Mr and Mrs Charles. They had one daughter of Edith's age. They were a lovely couple and I stayed with them throughout.

**Ena Colquhoun** *(now Mrs Colquhoun-Flannery) was ten years old :*

I can remember all the children, including myself and my sister Jean, gathering in the playground of All Souls School, Cheriton, and then being taken by bus to Shorncliffe Station. I remember my mother telling me that I was the 'big girl' and must keep Jean with me at all times. I cannot imagine how the mothers must have felt at that time, not having a clue as to where their children would be living. Now having four children of my own, I have often tried to imagine myself in that situation.

I recall lots of food stands on the stations as we passed by. Somehow I think that they was for the soldiers who were returning from Dunkirk. We eventually arrived in Caerphilly, in South Wales. We were then taken to a hall where the local people were waiting to pick out the children they would be giving a home to. Jean and I were very well dressed so we were soon picked out; even so they tried to split us up, but I kicked up such a fuss that we managed to stay together. We were taken in by a lovely couple, Mr and Mrs Davies, who had no children of their own, and they showed us much love and kindness.

**Jeanne Fairweather** *(now Mrs Ruddick) recalls the build up to evacuation:*

My world changed at the end of May 1940. The German army was just twenty-five miles away from my home. The British forces were trying to escape back across the English Channel. Every available ship, large and small, from around the south-east coast was used to bring back the troops. Many thousands if lives were saved by the 'miracle of Dunkirk'.

I was almost twelve years old at the time and attending St Mary's school, Dover. My parents debated for several days whether to send me and my nine-year old sister. Finally they agreed that we should go. So on that Sunday, we assembled at our school with our gas masks, a label on our coats and one small suitcase each. We left at about ten o'clock in the morning, our mother waving goodbye with tears streaming down her cheeks. To us children it was a great adventure but none of us at the time realised that perhaps we might never see our parents again. We travelled all day and passed many trains carrying troops, many of whom were bandaged.

After a long time we arrived at Blaenavon. The town band was waiting to escort us through the main street to a dispersal area. We were feeling very tired and bewildered. Many of the local people were there and they started picking us out like cattle, to take us to their homes. My sister and I were chosen by Mrs Edmunds; she and her husband were childless, so we were very fortunate and had a lovely home. During the next few days we found out where all our friends were living and we started to settle down. Everyone was homesick for a while; my sister and I had left loving parents and had never before been separated from them.

**Helen Crick** *(now Mrs Gerard) was living in Deal when evacuated:*

I was living with my family at my grandmother's house in Water Street and went to Deal Central School for Girls. On evacuation we travelled with our own school with our head-mistress, Miss Rutherford, teachers and helpers with us. All pupils were in school uniform.

On arrival at Merthyr Tydfil station there were buses laid on for us which took us to what I think must have been the town hall. There we had refreshments and soft drinks and were put into groups before leaving by bus for Merthyr Vale. When we arrived, it seemed the whole village was out in the streets; I had never seen so many people. It was getting very late as we walked through Crescent Street and children were being taken off to their billets. I was still with my brothers, Edward, Walter and Bob. Edward was the first to be billeted, to a house in Taff Street. Walter and Bob were billeted together at the end of Taff Street with Mr and Mrs O'Brien. Then came a hitch! They hadn't got a place for me.

The man who had been walking round with us took my hand and bag, saying, 'Beattie will take you in.' With that, we all went back to a woman who was standing on her doorstep with her daughter talking to neighbours. She was tall with grey hair. The man asked the woman to take me in but she said, 'No! I told them – I don't want an evacuee!' Then the girl standing beside her mother tried to persuade her to change her mind. The lady suddenly had a change of heart, took me by the hand and we all went inside the house. She did make the condition that it would only be temporary. Finally, I went up to bed with Nodene, the daughter, who was the same age as me. As we were getting ready for bed, she said to me, 'Don't worry, I won't let you go.' I loved it with Nana Sullivan and Nodene and spent over four and a half years with them!

**Jean Randall** *(now Mrs Lilly) recalls her memories:*

During May 1940, I was living in Deal and attending the Central School in Mill Road. Towards the end of the month we spent a lot of our time up at the seafront, watching the wonderful ships that saved thousands of soldiers from Dunkirk. We could see a lot of smoke and hear the guns and bombs. Then we were told that we were going to be evacuated to safety.

We were to take with us a change of clothing and a packed lunch and we had to be at Deal station at 9 a.m. on 2nd June. I was the youngest of a family of eight. One of my brothers couldn't go because he had measles, so it was just my brother Eric, aged 13, and myself, aged 11, to go. On the day of evacuation everyone was crying. Yet I thought we were only going for a little while, and to go on a train was a big adventure! My mum couldn't come to the station, so my aunt and two sisters took us; we were labelled with our names!

The last thing my mum said to Eric was that he was to take good care of me and we were not to be parted. As soon as we got on the train, he told me to 'clear off' as he was going with his pals, but I didn't mind because I soon found my two friends, Joyce and Betty, who were twins.

On the long journey we waved to other trains packed with soldiers. We arrived finally at Merthyr Vale station in a valley with mountains on either side. After getting off the train, we were marched to a miners' welfare hall where we had something to eat and drink. I was extremely tired by then. Soon, women were coming in to choose those children they would like to have in their homes. A lady came to me and I told her I was not to be parted from my brother. She looked at Eric and said that she didn't want any boys. So, instead of being one of the first to be billeted, I was one of the last. The same lady came back later and said that she would take us both – but just for the night. It turned out in the end that she kept both of us – and had our youngest brother who arrived in Wales a month later.

**Olive Hopper** (now Mrs Divito) was another pupil from Deal:

I was thirteen years old when I left with Deal Central School for Girls. We all thought it was going to be a month's holiday. Many of us in those days never went away; there was no need as we were already at the seaside! My feelings were different from a lot of other kids, as my mum and sister were coming with me – at least they were on the same train. My sister attended the Methodist School, going to a different part of Wales.

Before we left we were given an orange and a bun and had a luggage label tied to us. The journey was very long and the orange was very sticky. When we arrived at Merthyr, they took us all into a large hall and we were fed and watered – and were very tired. Then the billeting started. Peggy Hopper (not related to me) and I were taken to a house in Bethesden Street. The cottage was a bit basic with the loo miles down the end of the garden. There was a lovely dog, but it was full of fleas. Peggy and I slept in a big double bed and we were quite happy at this first billet, though we did not stay there long. We were taken away, perhaps because we were covered in flea bites from the bed. Peggy, being very pale and white, got the worst of them – I must have been tougher. My mother and sister had ended up in Bridgend, many miles away.

**Vanda Brown** (now Mrs Martin), 11, and her brother Teddy left their parents behind in Deal:

Papers given out at school about evacuation caused much excitement. One was a list of 'goodies' we were to take for the train journey – like nuts, raisins and barley sugar. I did not take in the real implications until we got on the train. We didn't know where we were going. While we were queueing outside the station, two children disappeared because they didn't want to go. Our parents were not allowed on to the platform to see us off. There were lots of tears especially from me! Mum and dad appeared with my brother's blazer and they looked so sad. What had we done? When would we see them again?

My brother Teddy and I had labels tied to our coats which said 'not to be separated'. I can't remember if we had suitcases or not, but I do remember my brother had a brown paper carrier bag with a jar of Brylcreem in it which got broken during the journey. It made such a mess. The journey itself seemed endless and we were all very tired. We finally arrived at Aberkenfig, near Bridgend. We made our way to a queue outside the village hall. People gathered, looking at us and talking to us; they were very kind. The couple who were to billet us were, for some reason, unable to take us, so we stayed in the hall until everyone else had gone. We didn't know what was going to happen to us. An elderly couple, who had been helping with the evacuees, decided to take us home with them. They were so kind. They actually gave us their own bed for that first night, because they thought we had had such a gruelling day and we looked so tired.

**Marjorie Taylor** (now Mrs Cockerill) used to live in Canterbury, was sent to Deal to live and ended up as an evacuee in Aberkenfig, South Wales:

Our mother died in January 1938 so my father sent my younger sister and me to board at St Mary's Roman Catholic School in Park Street, Deal. The school was joined to St Ethelburga's

Convent in Queen Street. When war broke out in September 1939, some of us older girls helped the local St John Ambulance and Women's Voluntary Service by being 'patients' for their instructional evenings. This went on for several months. As conditions deteriorated and German invasion seemed imminent, some of the boarders returned to their home towns but in June 1940 we joined all the other local schools and boarded a train for a journey to South Wales.

I distinctly remember all the children milling about carrying battered suitcases and bundles – and the necessary gas masks. All the children seemed very excited at the thought of a train journey, so rare to most of us then. I think the general idea was that we were all going on a holiday. After what seemed for ever, we finally arrived in Bridgend where we were all medically examined. Then our school went by bus to Aberkenfig, to a hall where we were united with the families who were to take us in.

*Jim Cullen* left Sandwich with Sir Roger Manwood's School for Penclawdd.

On Sunday, 2nd June 1940, we got up early, had a full breakfast and then old Burton, who drove the local taxi, arrived at the door with Dennis, my half-nephew (a year older than me); we drove to Sandwich station, picking up another Manwoodian on the way. None of us wanted our parents to see us off; they must have been feeling dreadful. Our military position seemed desperate – would they ever see us again? Stiff upper lips prevailed. The train was already there, in an unfamiliar livery of chocolate and dark cream. The masters were mustering their forms. Strangely, there was little confusion and then some 200 of us from Manwood's plus other local children were all on our way to unknown hosts in Wales, almost a foreign country. I remember the lengthy halts, particularly at Paddock Wood where a troop train had stopped. It was filled with soldiers evacuated from Dunkirk who were being given tea and biscuits by the WVS; the soldiers drank the tea and passed the biscuits to the ever hungry schoolchildren.

My longest rail journey had been to Folkestone, but this seemed never-ending, as did the Severn Tunnel when we finally reached it. We were in Wales, but still a long journey ahead. Another lengthy stop on a wooden bridge high above a town. Finally, we reached Penclawdd, a small seaside village, where we were fed sandwiches and buns while we awaited our fate. Our numbers diminished as we were allocated to our hosts – the singles first and then the twos and threes who wanted to stay together, such as Dennis and I.

Our hosts were a miner and his wife who lived with their two sons in a small whitewashed cottage. These good people took us in for less than 50p a week. The Davies family was not well off, but they were very kind-hearted. They looked after us as their own and we soon learned to take a bath, the water second or even third hand, in front of the coal-fired range.

Lessons were impossible. There was insufficient accommodation and classes were held whenever possible in the open air, where our teachers fought a losing battle to retain our interest in such arcane subjects as algebra and geometry. Cricket and rounders were popular, but it couldn't last, for we were not homesick and we were still excited by the novelty of our existence. But we were to be educated, like it or not, and we subsequently moved to Carmarthen, where we shared accommodation with Queen Elizabeth's Grammar School and its adjoining girls' school.

*Leonard Fry* recalls the evacuation, feeling 'left behind':

I was born in Folkestone in 1931 at 12 New Street. I was attending Dover Road School at the time of the mass evacuation of children, but I didn't go during the initial stages for reasons I can't remember. My elder sister went even though she was fourteen and had already left school.

I had a cousin, Ron Curry, who was nearly my own age and I must have been influenced by him. We soon discovered that it was no fun at all with all our friends gone and all the schools

DOVER COUNTY SCHOOL FOR BOYS

GOVERNMENT EVACUATION SCHEME

## TO PARENTS

As you know, the evacuation of school children will begin on Sunday next, the 2nd June. Whether it will be possible for all the children to go on the one day will depend upon how many there are to go. If there are too many for them all to go on Sunday, the rest will go on Monday, and, if necessary, on Tuesday, and following days. In order that trains may be ready to take the children whose parents wish them to go, we must know <u>at once</u> how many parents intend to send their children away. If you wish your child to go, please register them at their schools as soon as you possibly can, <u>and in any case not later than 12 (noon) on Wednesday, the 29th. May</u>.

Please remember:-

(1) that only those children whose parents register them at the school, as explained above, before 12 o'clock (noon) on Wednesday, will be taken:

(2) that when the children have been taken to safer areas, parents will be expected to leave them there until the Government decide that it is safe for them to return.

------------------------

Arrangements to be made when evacuation is ordered.

(1) Children will assemble at places and times of which they will be told before the end of this week. The children will travel by train and will go in school parties. They will be accompanied by their teachers, who will stay with them in the safer areas to which they are sent.

(2) <u>Cleanliness</u> After evacuation had taken place last September, complaints were made by householders in the receiving areas that some of the children were not clean. You will wish to be sure that this cannot be said about your own child and to do everything possible to make sure that he goes away with clean clothes, clean hair and clean body, for every mother will wish her child to arrive at his new home in a state in which he will be gladly welcomed. There will be a Medical Inspection of all boys at the School on Friday next, the 31st May.

(3) <u>Clothes and equipment</u> Your child should bring with him the following articles:-

| | | |
|---|---|---|
| Gas mask | Change of underclothing | Warm coat or mackintosh |
| Identity card | Night clothes | Tooth brush |
| Ration book | Handkerchiefs | Comb    House shoes or |
| Food for the day | Spare stockings or socks | Towel    plimsolls. |

He should wear his warmest and thickest boots or shoes. The child's clothes should if possible be packed in a rucksack or haversack which he can carry on his back so as to leave his hands free, rather than in a suitcase. <u>The luggage must not be more than a child can carry</u>. The other clothes that he will need can be sent later on.

(4) <u>Ration books</u> Be sure your child has his ration book with him. If pages of coupons out of his book have been deposited with retailers, ask for their return and pin the pages in the ration book. If the child leaves before the pages have been recovered, forward them to your local Food Office.

Both the ration book and identity card should be securely packed in the child's luggage and not given to him to hold.

PLEASE keep this notice for reference, and register your child(ren) at school immediately if you want him to take part in the evacuation scheme.

*J.C. Booth*    Headmaster. 28th May, 1940.

Country boys are included because their School is evacuated.

*Instructions issued to all parents of pupils of Dover County School for Boys, by the Headmaster, Mr Booth, 28th May, 1940* closed. Eventually there was another round-up of children and this time we went!

The only part of the journey I can remember was travelling on a rail-car from Chepstow to Monmouth. We were put with other Folkestone children at Lord Raglan's house, Cefn-Tilla Court, near Usk. We were living in the former stable staff quarters and sleeping in camp beds. Ron and I were immediately depressed. After a few heart-breaking letters home, Ron's mum came and took him away. I also left and was put with my sister at Llynos Farm, near Abergavenny, where I was to stay for three years.

*Bill Collard wasn't evacuated with the bulk of the Dover children. He passed for the Dover County School and joined them the following year in Ebbw Vale:*

I was attending Waldershare Park School when I passed the scholarship to go to Dover County School. We were living at Great Napchester Farm and I used to walk part of the way to school across the fields. Three of us took the scholarship for the county schools that year and, although I didn't know it at the time, being only eleven years old – one of the three was to be my future wife. She later joined the girls' school in Caerleon. I joined my new school a year after it had been evacuated to Ebbw Vale, so I was faced with the journey to Wales on my own, a week after my eleventh birthday, but Peter Bean, the son of our postman at Whitfield, was already at the school and agreed to take me. I remember being very miserable carrying my case down to Kearsney station, meeting Peter there.

I remember very clearly arriving in Ebbw Vale. It was early evening and we were met by Mr J. C. Booth, the headmaster, whom I later came to respect as a great chap. He directed me and other arrivals to the Ebbw Vale Council Chambers. We stood there around the walls and waited. In came the ladies who had volunteered to take us in. They looked around the room and I heard comments like, 'I'll have him, he looks a nice one!' The evacuees gradually left for their new homes – all except me! Nobody seemed to want me. In the end Mr Booth took me to a temporary billet where I was made very welcome but I cried myself to sleep for the next week.

After a few days, I moved on to 42 Harcourt Street with Mr and Mrs Rees. They were quite elderly but he was still working. They lived in a small terraced house and they made me very welcome, but had no experience of looking after little ones. My main memory of that billet was having a bath every Friday night, in a tin bath in front of the fire. After six months I was moved to Mrs Domin at 3 Aynho Place. This was to be my home for the next eighteen months.

*Edna Maynard (now Mrs Gibbs) was living in Whitfield Avenue, Dover and attended Barton Road Girls' School. She was ten years old when evacuated:*

Our school had to report outside Dover Priory station at 10.30 on that sunny June morning. We were told to take a gaberdene raincoat or winter coat with us as we would need it later. We each had to take a haversack (no cases), a packed lunch and our gas masks. We also had

*Barton Road Girls' School, Dover, now part of Barton Road Junior School*
*Picture taken in 1996 by Peter Hayward*

*Barton Road Girls at Wyllie, South Wales – Peter Hayward collection*

labels pinned to our coats. Our train left Dover at about eleven o'clock and we made many stops along the way. It was dark when we arrived and, due to the blackout, we could not see the name of the station. I think it was Newport. By this time we were all tired and bored. I can't remember anyone crying, but we were all asking the same question, 'How long before we get there?' – wherever 'there' was! Anyway, we got off the train and were transferred to buses. The school was divided and we were sent to various villages. So now, after being separated from parents and sisters, even my school was being sent in different directions. I was one of about twenty children taken to Wyllie, a small mining village near Pontllanfraith. I was finally billeted with Mr and Mrs Morgan and my life in exile began.

*Joyce Spratling* (now Mrs Bignell) remembers the day she, her sister Pearl and brother Ernie left Dover to face life with strangers in South Wales:

Mother took us to school that morning and I remember her saying to me, 'Now you make sure you keep an eye on the other two. I'm only letting you go because you have got to look after them.' I was thirteen years old! Anyway, we all tripped down to Astor Avenue School, with kit bags and gas masks, and once we had all assembled, we were marched over to Priory Station. As we waited for our train we saw many of the troops who had been rescued from Dunkirk. It was at that point that I suddenly realised that I had no idea where my brother was – he was only six! And I couldn't see my sister either. Anyway, we finally got on our train and eventually left Dover for some unknown destination.

After a very long journey, we arrived at Blackwood where food and drinks were waiting for us. I managed to see one of our teachers, Miss Twyman, and I asked her if she knew where my brother was. She didn't know but said that someone would find out when we got to our destination. We left Blackwood and then went by bus to Cefn Forest where the local people were waiting for us. The children were starting to be billeted out and, when my turn came, I refused to go. I kept telling the people that I wanted my sister and brother with me. I had no idea where my sister and brother were. I was eventually taken to a billet and, when I was shown the bedroom, I couldn't believe my eyes. There was no mattress on the bed – just old coats, and the floor was just bare boards! I couldn't sleep. I just had one of a grey blanket to cover myself up. So there I was, hundreds of miles from home and separated from my brother and sister.

*Winnie Delahaye (now Mrs Barrow) and her twin sister Peggy were evacuated with Deal Central School to the Merthyr Tydfil area, and was eventually billeted in the village of Aberfan:*

There was just one week to get lists sorted out, details arranged and all school stock packed, then early on Sunday, 2nd June, 1940, about 800 girls and boys of the Deal Secondary Schools left Deal Railway Station for some unknown destination in South Wales. The day was an emotional one for both parents and children. My sister and I wondered if we would ever see our parents again. All we were allowed to take with us were our gas masks and a few belongings.

For a while on its slow journey to Wales, the train followed the same route as trains carrying the troops back from Dunkirk. We didn't realise it at the time, but we were caught up in the drama of Operation Dynamo. After a very long journey, it was evening when we finally arrived in Merthyr Tydfil, but our journey wasn't over even then. Some of us were transported to Aberfan where we were marched to a big hall and given something to eat and drink while we waited to be allocated billets. Because we didn't want to be separated, my sister and I had to wait longer for a home. We were finally allocated a billet and eventually got to bed. However, we couldn't sleep; we cried a lot but we had managed to stay together!

*Michael Cox was almost eight and a half years old when he and his brother Ken left Deal:*

I have many memories of those early days of the war in Deal and of the planned evacuation. My father, who was in the merchant navy, had arranged for my brother and me to go to the USA; I had just started a stamp collection and was looking forward to collecting many American stamps. Later, my brother and I were called into the sitting room to find my mother's will had prevailed and, instead of going to the USA, we were going to Wales with the rest of Canada Road School in Walmer. My one concern was that Wales was a different country and they would have different stamps! So I was eager to go.

The journey was quite remarkable, not only because of the length of time it took, but also because it was during the time when all the troops were being evacuated from Dunkirk. As we pulled into a station, ladies would rush forward with sandwiches and drinks, only to find them being snatched out of their hands by grubby schoolkids. The journey seemed endless, but I remember our excitement as we reached the Severn Tunnel, and the warning to keep all the windows shut. Next was the parish hall in Pyle, Glamorgan, where we were to meet our hosts. .

There my brother and I were immediately separated! He was claimed by a Mrs Davies, and I was by Mrs Hamer. Unfortunately for Mrs Hamer, I was going down with tonsilitis, and since there was a diphtheria scare at the time, I was packed off to an isolation hospital at Cefn Cribwr for a few weeks. Thus I entered Wales and my troubles were just beginning!

*Bernard Burgess was head boy at Sir Roger Manwood's School, Sandwich:*

I must have been one of the oldest child evacuees of the Second World War, for I boarded the special evacuee train on the morning of my 19th birthday. I was revising for the Higher School Certificate examinations, which had been postponed for a few weeks because of the war. Up to a month before, it had been assumed that Sandwich was in a safe area, so Sir Roger Manwood's School was sharing its premises with a Medway school which had been evacuated. When the Germans blitzed through Holland and Belgium, the Medway school was sent elsewhere and we settled down to life as before. But the speed of the German advance suddenly made the invasion of East Kent seem quite likely, so hurried arrangements were made to move us away.

A crowd of anxious parents saw us off at the station in brilliant warm sunshine. All the senior boys had a number of juniors to look after, each with a label on his lapel, and carrying a small suitcase. As we waved goodbye I believe the special train travelled northwards via the Minster loop and then to Canterbury, Ashford and Tonbridge. No one knew where we were going.

A sharp reminder of the serious turn in the war came when we reached Tonbridge. Our train was held up for half an hour opposite a troop train carrying soldiers who had been evacuated from Dunkirk. Some were bandaged, but all were unshaven, unsmiling and exhausted. Women volunteers on the platform were giving them cups of tea and biscuits. I felt terribly embarrassed because some of these soldiers were younger than I, and here was I wearing a school blazer!

We left the weary soldiers behind and our train slowly made its way across the south of England via Redhill, frequently stopping to allow scheduled services to pass. The journey across Hampshire, Wiltshire and Gloucestershire seemed interminable, but eventually we passed through the Severn Tunnel and realised we were bound for Wales. I can't remember whether the train finished at Swansea or Gowerton, but our final destination was Penclawdd, where we arrived in buses. Penclawdd was a small Welsh-speaking fishing village, which must have found our arrival very inconvenient. It was now evening and we were taken to a church hall where, beginning with the youngest pupils, we were matched with our hosts.

***Joyce Brown*** *(now Mrs Markwick) was attending Folkestone County Technical School:*

I was living in Bethersden where my parents farmed, but travelled daily to attend Folkestone County Technical School and when the evacuation of the schools was announced, I had to go to complete the last one and a half years of my education. The train left Folkestone Central Station soon after 7.30am on Sunday, 2nd June, 1940, and we didn't arrive at Merthyr Tydfil until late afternoon. It was a tedious journey, although it was all new ground for me. For a start there was little or no drinking water on the train. It was an extremely hot day and we were very crowded in the carriages. Once our small supply of water ran out, we just suffered from extreme thirst.

The train was constantly stopped and put into a siding to allow the troop trains through; we noticed that, when these troop trains were halted at the stations, the troops were given plenty to drink. We soon realised the awful conditions these troops had endured being evacuated from Dunkirk so our 'envy' soon waned. When we arrived at Merthyr Tydfil Station it was such a relief to find our feet on solid ground again and being in the fresh air after the stuffy train journey was unbelievable. After getting off the train we formed a very long crocodile and marched through the streets carrying our own luggage, one large suitcase, shoulder bag, tennis racquet, winter coat and the inevitable gas mask!

We marched to the town hall where we were at last given a drink of water; the relief after hours without a drink was enormous. We were welcomed in a speech by the mayor of Merthyr Tydfil, although we didn't understand much because of the strong Welsh accent, but everybody was so kind. The people had lined the streets and clapped us all the way from the railway station to the town hall. Even after all this time, it still brings a lump to my throat when I remember that welcome. By this time it was about 6pm and, after leaving the two Folkestone Grammar Schools at Merthyr Tydfil, my school and one or two of the primary schools were put into coaches and we travelled to Treharris, a mining village. Here we were taken into one of the local schools to be medically examined, after which we were all lined up for billeting!

Chapter Four

## UNHAPPY BILLETS – PROPAGANDA VERSUS REALITY

*IF THE REALITIES of the journey and the welcome received at the destination differed from the idealistic propaganda reports which appeared in the local newspapers, the experience of living in strange billets was sometimes even more traumatic. Children, already uprooted from the familiar warmth of their parents' care, now found themselves in totally different surroundings. Some culture shocks must certainly have been evident. The following accounts reflect the trauma experienced by some of the less fortunate evacuees.*

**Dawn Terry** *(now Mrs Vodka), from Dover, remembers her unhappy time in Blaenavon:*

The people I stayed with seemed very rich with a huge farm. All the family worked on the farm and they didn't have any outside help. At the time of going to live there, another girl was billeted with me. She hated it so much that she got her parents to come and take her back home.

The farm house was huge but we all lived in the back part where the servants quarters were. The rest of the house was never used and I was never allowed to go into any of the other rooms. I always wondered what the rest of the house was like, but in all the years I lived there I never did see the rest of the house. People used to think that I was so lucky to be in such a grand place with wonderful people, but I remember how much I hated living there..I wanted to go home so badly, but my sisters would write and tell me how bad the bombing was in Dover and that I should stay in Wales where I was safe. My parents used to write a weekly letter and send me a shilling for pocket money. The family I was living with used to open the letters and read parts to me, saying I wouldn't understand the writing. The shilling, they said, was for them to get me something I needed, but I never got anything! They told me I had to write back to my parents each week, but they always had to read what I had written before the letters were posted.

I was told that I had to work on the farm and that I was very lucky to be living with them. I didn't think so; I hated every part of being there. They would make me go all over Blaenavon after school, with a big sack and collect pig food, scraps of food that people saved. People would have all these scraps piled up in their back yards, and I would have to go round picking it all up with my hands and put it in the sack. Oh, the flies and the smell were terrible! I would put the sack on my back and hope that I didn't meet any of my school friends. If I did see any, I would hide until they had gone; I was just too embarrassed.

Sometimes the people I collected the pig food from would give me money and would ask why I was going around collecting the stuff, but I didn't dare tell them. I didn't have any choice. I was afraid if I said anything, it would get back to the farm, and they were constantly telling me how lucky I was to be living there. Whenever I did get enough money, I would buy a loaf of bread and eat it in a back alley because I was so hungry. I knew I couldn't go back to the farm to get something to eat, at least not until late in the evening when everybody came in from working. The old lady cooked dinner late in the evening and it was

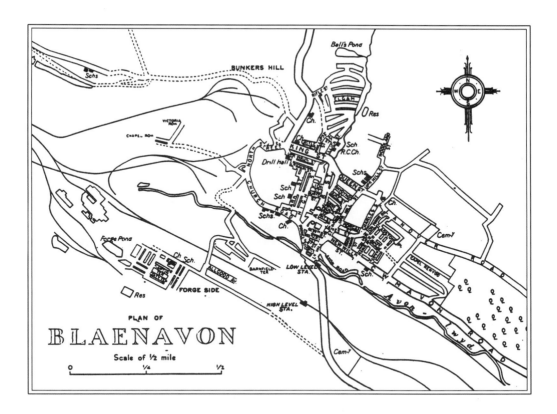

*Plan of Blaenavon in the 1940s showing High Level and Low Level railway stations, both of which are now gone with the passage of time – Peter Hayward collection*

always very sparse. I was never allowed to eat anything unless they gave it to me. I remember one time coming home from school, I was so hungry that I got myself a slice of bread and butter. The old lady who ran the farm like a drill sergeant, caught me. I was in big trouble. She told me how food was rationed, and that I was to be punished. I never again took any food – I was too frightened!

They used to kill chicken and make me go out into the yard and pluck them. I used to hate to see the chicken's necks wrung. Occasionally a sheep would be slaughtered. They would cut it up and hang it in an outbuilding, then later on cook it for meals. They even made a stew out of the head. All the time I wanted to go home. I can never remember having any holiday time like Christmas. Every day was the same.

It is true I had a bedroom to sleep in, but the floor always seemed to be covered in potatoes laid out to sprout. When I went to bed I had to be careful where I stepped, and at night I would hear the mice scratching and running about. During hay-making time I would come home from school – I didn't dare be late – and go out into the fields to gather hay.

Once there was a singer coming to perform in Blaenavon, someone called Frank Littleton. He stayed in the grand part of the house and wouldn't have known about the back part where we all lived. Anyway, they needed a maid to wait on him and serve his meals. They had a little black dress made for me to wait on this Frank Littleton and serve him his meals. They told me that I was always to tell people I had such a good life on the farm, and that they were always so very good to me, when all the time I was being treated like a servant!

*Audrey Turner (now Mrs Rickman), from Dover, recalls the time she, her twin sister Vivienne and baby sister Josie shared the same billet in Markham, South Wales:*

We hadn't been in Wales long before we were bitten all over by lice and our foster mother claimed we had brought them with us. My mother was furious when she found out.

All three of us were put into a double bed. Although Josie had been potty trained, she was very upset and started wetting the bed. So we were sleeping in a wet bed and it always seemed that I would get the thrashing for the bed being wet. It wasn't me who was wetting the bed, but I always got the blame for it. Can you imagine two little nine year olds looking after a four year old! We never had to look after Josie when we were back home in Dover. It was mum's job to bath the children, but in Wales it was very different. We were filthy! I remember we used to wash our knees, and the dirt used to run down the backs of our legs. Our foster mother just didn't take care of us. She was really wicked. The woman had three sons but I don't remember much about their father except he was a miner and seemed to drink a lot.

On 1st April, our foster mother told us there was a chocolate for us in the pantry. We were so excited and we looked and looked, and she kept saying, 'You're not looking in the right place.' After a while we said, 'We can't find it.' She then laughed and said, 'April fools!' Can you imagine anyone doing that to children! Once our teacher said we were dirty, so our foster mother put neat paraffin on our hair to get rid of the lice, and sat us in front of a coal fire!

I remember carol singing at Christmas. A woman offered us half a crown each, but we said, 'Could we have a piece of bread instead?' People didn't seem to realise how hungry we were.

Parcels were sent from home quite regularly but of course we never even got to see them. Our foster parents had friends who had twins, a boy and a girl, and I remember once seeing these twins, who were about our age, in new jumpers. I said to them, 'Cor, my mummy knits us jumpers like that.' We found out later that they were our jumpers, sent by our mum. Our foster mother was opening our parcels and selling the clothes to the mother of the twins. In the meantime we were going round scruffy and wearing badly fitting shoes. The foster mother told our teacher that nothing was ever sent for us, which was untrue. Mother told us later that she sent lots of parcels for us containing sweets and goodness knows what, and we never received any of them. I am also fairly sure that our foster parents got parcels for us from the Red Cross, which we never received.

We were really poorly off. I don't think we ever saw meat. She had our ration books of course! I can remember an awful lot of potatoes with gravy on them, and greens out of the garden – and cocoa with no milk or sugar. You can't live like that for any length of time!

Any letters we wrote home were always read by our foster mother before they were sent, but we managed to see our brother Derek. He wrote and told my mother that he wasn't happy about the way we were, and he also wrote and told her about the poor conditions he was living in. Father came and took Derek back with him. Later on mother came to visit us and said that she would come back and get Josie. It was about this time that the authorities were trying to stop parents taking their children home because of the danger of being killed by enemy action.

I remember pulling a piece of paper out of my school exercise book, and writing on it 'I want to come home,' and I repeated this over and over again on this piece of paper, but not saying why. I was allowed to put my letter in an envelope and I posted it home to my mother. I think it was then that my mother realised how badly we were being treated.

The next time dad came, we were shovelling coal from the pavement to the coal house. We were filthy dirty, but we both jumped all over him. He said, 'Come on kids, let's get your bags packed, I'm taking you to East Grinstead.' We didn't know where East Grinstead was, we just thought anywhere is better than here. When we started on our journey, dad said to us, 'I'm not taking you to East Grinstead, kids, I'm taking you home!'

***Bob Cain*** *from Dover had several billets during his stay in South Wales:*

Arriving in Pengam, my sister June and I were finally billeted with Mr and Mrs Jones, and the evacuation of four and a half years had begun. We were treated very well but Mrs Jones had a heart attack and we had to move after only a few months. My sister went to another family but whenever I went to the house to try and visit her I was told to go away, so I saw very little of her until she went to Treharris in 1941 to join Folkestone Girls' Technical School.

I was moved to a family which already had two evacuees, and thus began two years of absolute misery! There were two grown-up daughters who were always very kind to us, but were very much under the thumb of their mother, who was an absolute tyrant. We had very little to eat and were always hungry. Breakfast, which we had to prepare, was porridge with salt on it – we never saw any sugar! Lunch usually was a piece of bread, again with salt on it, and dinner was tripe and onions, which we found almost inedible.

We would regularly sneak out in the middle of the night to raid the local allotments for cabbages, swedes or anything remotely edible, for she kept a strict watch on all food in the house. I recall one day she went to Newport to do some shopping and, on her return, measured the loaf announcing that someone had taken a slice. It was mid-winter, with thick snow, but we were forced to stand in the garden in our pyjamas for hours until one of the other chaps confessed that he had eaten it. The only respite from this continual hunger was when we started to collect money for Mrs Churchill's 'Aid to Russia' fund, for which we received a 'thank you' letter from Mrs Churchill, which our landlady kept! We sang carols at people's doors at Christmas, collected empty jam jars (shops paid a halfpenny for the pound size and three farthings for the two pound size), we collected rosehips from the hedgerows (and sold them for a penny a pound to make rosehip syrup), and finally caught white butterflies. I can't recall how much we received per hundred, but there was a government campaign to catch as many as possible, the theory being that they ate cabbages and therefore, hampered the war effort.

Anyway, with these 'unrecorded' funds (she watched our pocket money like a hawk), we were able to take the occasional halfpenny, and buy a bag of 'cracknel' – the crispy bits left in the fryer at the fish and chip shop – what a feast for the starving!

Some of the St Martin's boys went to Pengam School, but the majority were at Fair View School under our own teachers, Mr Weeds and Miss Baker, who were absolutely wonderful people. On reflection, we should perhaps have complained to them about our treatment at our billet, but I suppose we were too terrified to say anything. As well as being starved, we also had to do most of the work. In addition to preparing the porridge, we had to cook the food for the chickens (potato peelings mixed with some kind of meal), collect eggs, and clean out the chicken sheds – which were inspected afterwards.

I am not sure whether it was compulsory or not to take in evacuees, but in any case our landlady must have made a good living out of it. Three evacuee incomes and virtually no expenditure, plus free manual labour – a bit like winning the Pools! I was fortunate enough to pass the scholarship to Dover Boys' County School in 1942, which meant that, not only was I leaving a living hell, but I was also able to return to Dover for a month in July/August 1942 to make all the necessary arrangements – uniform etc., and this was probably the most wonderful month of my life. The sun shone, I had plenty to eat, lots of cuddles and, although we had shelling and bombing constantly, I had a bunk in Winchelsea caves, where we had a canteen, toilets, baths and lots of friendly people.

I returned to Pengam to collect my remaining bits and pieces and ration book and, on 1st September, set off for Ebbw Vale. By this time I had somehow acquired a suitcase, so, after a terse goodbye from the 'Dragon' and envious looks from the other two evacuees, I picked up my suitcase and gas mask and off I went. I should mention that some lads were utterly sick of being evacuated and we occasionally had an 'escapee'. I don't know how many managed to get back to Dover, but quite a few were picked up by the police en route. These boys were treated with some reverence when they were returned, but the real heroes (apart from those who actually made a 'home run') were those who had 'made the river'. This was the River Severn, which was much more difficult to cross then than it is today, and anyone who managed to cross it before being picked up was almost beatified on his return!

*Jean White (now Mrs Craig), another Dover evacuee, looks back on her stay in Blackwood:*

My foster parents were Auntie Rene and Uncle Ivor who had one son, Brian, aged about five. Uncle Ivor was a really nice man, but I feel his wife must have been pushed into taking evacuees in, because she didn't like me. All she wanted was a young person to work for her.

As well as her son, the woman had her niece aged about four, from London and, later, another evacuee called Peggy, but I was the one that had to do most of the donkey work. I was up at six o'clock preparing breakfast, then I had to wash, dress and feed the other children, prepare myself for school, and then take auntie's breakfast upstairs whilst she lay in bed. I think I did this almost every morning I was there.When school was finished for the day, there were bedrooms to be done, windows to be cleaned another day, polishing, ironing then washing up after dinner before getting the others ready for bed! My parents never, to my knowledge, had a cross word, but auntie and uncle had fights and would even throw things at each other; it would be my job to go round picking everything up. I complained to my teachers about my billet but, because I was always clean, well-fed and healthy, they thought I was just being ungrateful.

One Christmas spent in Wales, when I was ten years old, I was beginning to doubt the truth of Father Christmas, but desperately trying to hang on to the magic. That Christmas Eve after getting the other children to bed, I was given four pillowcases and four piles of presents, and told which presents belonged to which child. I had to pack them including my own, and put them at the bottom of the beds. I recall not wanting to wake up on that Christmas morning.

When auntie was allocated another evacuee named Peggy, I was very pleased because she was only months younger than me. However, after spending the first night, it was discovered she had wet the bed. When we got home from school on that particular day, I was told to go and make the beds. When I went to our room I was surprised to see no mattress on the bed – just brown paper, which we had to sleep on until Peggy stopped wetting, which was quite a while!

Peggy had caught scabies; nasty pus-filled blisters all over her body. Each morning I had to bath her and wet all the blisters until they popped. Then I had to plaster her in ointment. Needless to say I also caught scabies, but only on my hands which cleared up fairly quickly.

The post became very erratic due to the shelling in Dover, so I often went two or three weeks without a letter. I would go home each day and ask if there was a letter for me, and very often the reply would be that I wouldn't be hearing from my parents any more as they were probably dead! Another time it was announced on the news that the Germans had reached Calais. I burst into tears because I told them that we could see the town of Calais from Dover. I was called a liar – and every other name she could lay her tongue to.

Mum, dad and my younger sister and brother came to see me in September, 1941. I went to Newport station to meet them. I walked past my father before I realised who he was. We both laughed and cried and we cuddled. We were all going to New Tredegar for a few days, to stay at my sister's foster home, but first I had to go and get my case. Although mum and dad had been travelling nearly all day, they were asked by my foster parents to sit outside on the lawn, while I had to go in, eat my dinner and wash up for all the family before I was allowed to go.

We had a lovely two weeks altogether, but it soon came to an end. Nanette and I went with mum, dad, little sister and brother to the station at Blackwood to say our goodbyes. After the rest of the family had gone, I was going to take Nanette back to New Tredegar, but when I got to my foster home I was really crying badly, and this was the one and only time that my foster mother hit me. She told me to do a pile of ironing, but I grabbed Nanette's hand and fled up the

*Astor Avenue Girls' School at Pengam, South Wales, 1940.*
*TOP ROW (from left): Betty Scrivens, Joyce Spratling, Pat . . . . ., Miss Esling (Teacher),*
*Grace Croucher, Joan Schroeder, Grace Ward*
*2nd ROW (from left): Joan Newman, Shelley Powell, Nora Curran, Edith Hoare.*
*3rd ROW (from left): Violet Cook, June Cain, Jean Gamble, Mavis Blaskett,*
*Vichy Magrino, Connie Cornfoot.*
*FRONT ROW (from left): Muriel Miles, Mollie Driscoll, Doreen Ahearne, Pat Avery, Ivy Chivers,*
*Jean Durban, Barbara Brinkworth, Hazel Sedgewick, Joan Constable – Bob Hollinsbee collection*

fields at the back of the house. We climbed a tree and both sat there crying our eyes out.

We stayed there until we saw her go out shopping. I went back indoors and got my ration book, gas mask and identity card and we caught the bus back to New Tredegar. I was crying with fear all the time. At Nanette's foster home I must have asked if I could stay. I can't remember what was decided, but I was going to stay that night. Later that evening there was a knock on the door and I remember my name being mentioned. I tried to hide under the table, but I can remember a policeman's arm pulling me out. I was taken back in a police car and was told what a naughty and ungrateful girl I was.

The next morning I was sitting on the back lawn crying, when Mrs Dyer from next door asked me what was wrong. I told her how unhappy I was. She went indoors and got a sheet of writing paper and a pencil and told me to write and tell my parents, and she (Mrs Dyer) would post the letter for me. I managed to do this without auntie finding out, and for the next few weeks I was a very frightened little girl. However, one day as I was getting in from school, Uncle Ivor asked what mum had to say in her letter to me. I replied that I hadn't heard from her, so he reached up and brought down an opened letter from a very high mantle shelf.

I was thrilled to find out that the very next day, 11th October, 1941, one of dad's friends who was visiting his parents in Wales, would be taking me back to Dover with him. I was thrilled to bits, but for some reason auntie didn't want me to leave and tried all sorts of bribery to get me to stay. She even took my wristwatch, dresses, shoes and toys, saying I could have them back if

I stayed, but I just wanted to get home. Uncle Ivor did all he could to help, and even made sure he was there when dad's friend came to fetch me. That was a day I shall never forget.

My worst fear on my journey home was that, when I turned the corner of my street in Dover, the home I loved would be bombed or shelled, but everything was fine and Mum was waiting on the doorstep with open arms. I remember my younger sister and brother laughing at my accent, but I don't think I kept it for long. Mum eventually went back to Wales to get Nanette as her foster aunt had died. Mum also went to see my 'auntie' and I think there must have been words because when mum got back to Dover, not only was Nanette with her, but she also had my watch, dresses and presents as well.

It seems very strange that only sad memories remain with me. There must have been happy times because we, the evacuees, were taken to Weston-Super-Mare for a week's holiday, but I can't remember anything about it at all. I just thank the Lord that I had such sensible and well-adjusted parents, who helped me to get over those unhappy times. I have never been back to Wales since that day in October 1941, and I have never wanted to go back. Having said that, many of my school friends had very happy times whilst in Wales, and went back for holidays. Some even married Welsh boys so it wasn't all bad. I was just one of the unlucky ones.

*Grace Croucher (now Mrs Frogé) was evacuated with Astor Avenue Girls' School, Dover:*

My sister and I were evacuated because our father had died. Our mother had to work to support us, and she was worried about us being on our own during the bombing and shelling, especially as the schools would be closed. The journey to Wales was spent mostly playing games. The worst thing was being locked in and also not being allowed to walk through the train to see my sister. Our teacher who went with us to Wales was Miss Esling. The Severn Tunnel seemed unending and many girls were very frightened. I did not see my sister when we arrived in Blackwood and it was some time before I found out where she was.

My time as an evacuee in Cefn Forest was not a happy one. The most memorable thing about it was the hunger. My friend and I carried penknives in our blazer pockets and I used to go through the allotments on our way to and from school. We went to Fairview School in Pengam. The gardeners were happy to give us vegetables which we ate raw. If no-one was about we would help ourselves, but only took what we could eat. Whatever was in season we tried, potatoes, carrots, peas, beans, cabbage, sprouts, swedes and rhubarb.

To this day I still love raw vegetables and always sample them when preparing a meal. When they were about we enjoyed wild blackberries, blueberries and even hawthorn berries – it's a wonder we survived. Although we often walked the three miles or more to Argoed to see my young sister, sometimes we went because we were sure of a good meal when we got there.

The man of the house where we lived was a miner who always worked the afternoon shift. We had to be in bed and out of the way by the time he came home, so that he could have his bath in front of the fire. He used a tin bath and the water was heated on the fire, which was also used for any cooking, and was the only heating in the house. We put our coats on in bed during cold weather. He never washed his back! He said that it would weaken it, and also when we did the ironing, we were not allowed to iron the back of the vests or shirts for the same reason. We thought the Welsh were very strange. Only once a fortnight did we girls have a bath, other times we had to wash in cold water at the sink in the scullery, from the one tap in the house. Occasionally we went to the swimming pool and it was heaven to have a warm shower.

On coal delivery day, which was one day each month, a ton of coal would be tipped in the road outside the house, and after school we had to round up friends to help us carry it through to the coal shed at the back of the house. Lots of time was spent walking, and we loved to go to the pit heads to see the ponies that had been brought up top for a rest. When our parents visited us they were so shocked by how much weight we had lost, that they decided to take us back home. I had been in Wales for about a year.

84

***Mr D. F. Crouch*** *had several billets before he found any sort of continuity of family life:*

We arrived after dark at the village of Cwmfelinfach. We must have been on the train for at least 12 hours, after numerous stops along the way. I shared my first billet with another boy. I can't remember much about the house, except it must have been a young couple we were staying with, and they had a rather ugly bull terrier. The first morning we went out full of excitement to explore the place – and promptly forgot where our billet was! I don't think I stayed there long and moved to another billet in the village. The only memory I have of this billet was spending one night in the landlady's bed for mutual comfort when there was an air raid. Well, I was only ten years old! Her husband must have been on night shift at the mine.

The next stop was a very unpleasant one, with a very houseproud woman. The husband was a miner and they were in an older age group than the first two. They had a boy, who was a bit older than me, and the husband was henpecked. I was discriminated against and I was always hungry. It was not a happy place! One episode that sticks in my mind is that, during that hot dry summer of 1940, we played alongside a small railway line where trains shunted to and fro. We used to jump on the wagons for rides, and I can remember being dragged off by brambles alongside the track, and lying with the wheels of the wagons passing just inches away.

We were generally rather scared of the local children and I can remember running the gauntlet of the local gangs, on the way back to the billet after school. It was not a very happy time and I can't remember much about school, but I must have done well enough to get through to the Dover Boys' County School. This was a rather different world and I suppose we were a bit tougher by then. The first billet in my new location was in a household with one other boy from Dover and one local lad. I was not there long and moved again with the other Dover boy to a rather staid, elderly, childless couple. It was an onslaught for them, to have two young teenagers. It was not very homely there but I hope we were polite and well behaved.

School was shared part-time with the Ebbw Vale Boys' School, so it must have left us with an awful lot of free time. I can remember hanging about in the park and in the streets quite a lot. There was a some school sport and an introduction to rugby football. The school cadet force also filled much of our free time. We always came back to Dover for the holidays and the train journeys via Newport were an adventure but not quite as exciting as the final journey home.

***Ivy Campbell*** *(now Mrs Pieri) went with Stella Maris Catholic Primary School, Folkestone:*

When I arrived in Dowlais I stayed with a Mrs Jones, who had a daughter about the same age as me. I wouldn't say that it was a happy time. The daughter was always telling tales on me and getting me into trouble. Mrs Jones was always busy. Every night she had to get the bath out in front of the fire and boil great pans of water for her miner husband's bath. Then she polished a huge black cooking range every day. I realise now how hard it must have been for them.

After about 18 months, my sister, who had been billeted in Pennydaron, returned home, so I moved in with Mrs Mahoney to be with my brother. This lady had already brought up a family and she was very strict with us. She gave us porridge every morning, even though the milk was sour. I remember it was awful. We were also given lumps of fatty meat and they were horrible but I suppose they didn't do us any harm. We didn't have much schooling. We just had half days sitting around a table. My teacher, Sister St John, who came with us from Folkestone, was very good to me and used to play table tennis with me. I felt very attached to her.

I didn't enjoy being evacuated but eventually we all returned home, and things got back to normal. After I got married I went back to Folkestone and saw Sister St John who was still at Stella Maris School. She showed me round the school and bringing back lots of memories.

*Jean Hayward (now Mrs Hampton) went
with her two sisters and younger brother.*

I remember very well the day we were all
evacuated. Mum had packed a small brown
case for each of us and I particularly
remember her putting a bar of Lifebuoy
soap in each one. I was with St James'
School in Dover and we were all taken to
Dover Priory Station to be put on the train
for Wales. Miss James was the only teacher
from our school who I remember going
with us to Wales – in fact, she stayed there
and married a clergyman.

When we arrived in Blaenavon, we had
to walk through the streets, like poor
orphans of the storm, up to the High School

*Jean, Pearl and Peter Hayward, taken in
Newport in 1941 – Peter Hayward collection*

where we received glasses of milk and sandwiches, before we continued around the streets with
the billeting officers. It was very, very late before we managed to find a billet. Pearl, my eldest
sister, had been told by mum that she was to look after us and we were to stay together. Well,
nobody wanted four evacuees, but one kind woman said she would take us all in, just for the
first night. Next day Mrs Martyn came and took my sister Mary away; someone else came for
Pearl and baby brother Peter and I eventually ended up with Mr and Mrs Lewis who lived in
Gladstone Terrace. He was the manager of the Co-op and they had a lovely home. I enjoyed
myself there and I was very unhappy when I had to leave.

Then I had a succession of billets where, although I was treated well, things were not ideal.
For instance, I was put into a dirty bed where there were bugs and I caught scabies. I was put
into an isolation hospital in Blackwood for six weeks – and I didn't have one visitor!

I came out of hospital to another billet – and promptly caught head lice. I remember mum
coming down to see me and she had to cut my hair by candlelight. She then decided that I
should go back to Dover with her, but after three weeks I couldn't stand the terrible bombing so
I was sent back to Blaenavon to a new billet! It was horrible! It was hell and I was very
unhappy. Eunice Crofts from Dover was living there together with our hostess's niece,
Margaret. We were all of the same age, but it was Eunice and I who had to get up in the
mornings to light the fire to get hot water for a cup of tea.

We then had to go over the railway to the Garn to collect dirty washing, then when we came
home from school we would have to wash it! We were just like slaves. The school was always
sending the welfare officer around because we were in such a state.

A typical day would start before breakfast, with one of us going to collect the dirty washing,
while the other would go and stand in the fish queue. When we returned to the house we would
have our breakfast, consisting of not more than one and a half slices of bread with home-made
chocolate spread – and that's what we virtually lived on. We would come home at lunchtimes
for our hot meal of the day, which would consist of one slice of bread and some gravy – and
that would be our dinner! After dinner we would have to get on with the washing.

After teatime, which used to consist of boiled rice and molasses, Eunice and I would have to
sit until midnight making rag mats. We used to sew until we had blisters. Our hostess used to
sell the mats. This routine continued day after day, month after month. I was in that billet for
two years and I believe Eunice was there a lot longer.

If mum sent anything to me it was taken from me and given to Margaret, the niece. I would
come home to find that parcels from Mum had been opened and Margaret would say to me, 'Do

you like my new clothes? They came from your mother!' This used to really upset me and one day I got so angry that I hit Margaret and the hostess. For this outburst I received a severe thrashing with a cane; I had been beaten so hard that she couldn't send me to school.

I ran away once and got as far as Pontypool before the police found me and brought me back – and I received another beating. I hated it at that billet, absolutely hated it! I was sick one day, vomiting everywhere, and instead of letting me stay in bed, this terrible woman made me go and sit outside on the step. Mum always sent me a 2/6d postal order every time she wrote to me, but I never received the money. On one occasion I remember, I was made to write to my mother for a new pair of shoes. When they arrived, they were a size too big for me, so my hostess gave me a pair of Margaret's old shoes, and Margaret had my new ones.

I used to write to mum, but our hostess would read my letters before I was able to send them. It was not until I went to my brother Peter's billet to see his foster mum, 'Aunty Tilly', that I was able to put down on paper everything I was feeling. Aunty Tilly made me sit down and write to mum and tell her everything. Then Aunty Tilly's husband, who was a postman, said he would make sure that the letter got posted.

Instead of writing back, my mother came down to Blaenavon and saw the state I was in. My

hostess wouldn't even ask mum into the house, so mum sent me in to get my belongings and I walked out with everything in a cardboard box. Mum took me back to Dover with her. Poor Eunice, the other evacuee, begged mum to take her back too, but mum said she didn't dare, as the bombing was still very bad in Dover. I stayed home for good this time, even though mum had been bombed out and our house in St James Street had been destroyed. We stayed for a while with friends at Coldred, a village just outside Dover. I don't think I could live those terrible years again; I have never had any desire to go back to South Wales.

*Peter, Pearl and Jean Hayward, taken at the Evacuees' Reunion in Dover in September, 1994*

*Jean Hayward's mother also remembers the unhappy time her daughter had:*

Jean couldn't settle down in Blaenavon. She used to write me pitiful letters and of course that worried me. In fact I went down once because I didn't believe her. She was living with an unmarried woman whose father and two brothers were all miners – and my Jean was down there, washing the shirts of these miners! I didn't believe it until I saw it with my own eyes.

I told Jean to pack her things and I brought her back to Dover. I didn't realise until we were on the train coming home, that Jean was 'lousy'! She scratched and scratched all the way home. As soon as we arrived home I contacted Nurse Grey, who used to visit me in Dover, and I showed her Jean's hair. 'Oh, Mrs Hayward,' she said, 'Bring her down to Victoria Hospital this afternoon at three o'clock.' I took Jean down at three and Doctor Nickolls examined her. He took the name and address of where she had been staying in Wales and told me that he would make sure that no other evacuees were sent there. He then asked if they could cut some of Jean's hair off. I said, 'I don't mind at all – as long as you get rid of that lot!'

When I went back later to collect Jean, I hardly recognised her. They had cut and shaped her hair beautifully and had given her a fringe – and it was spotless. I thanked the hospital staff and said, 'Well, I'm not sending her back to Wales – not to go through that again!'

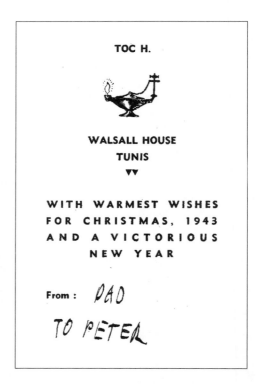

*Card received by the author from his father who was serving with the British Army in North Africa. Christmas, 1943 – Peter Hayward collection*

**Eunice Hoy** *(now Mrs Walton) was another pupil who was evacuated with St James' School:*

We lived at 12 Clarence Street, Dover. My mother had a sweet shop in the front room and, as we lived next door to an undertaker, she asked him to make a counter for the shop. Anyway, in 1940 my sister Ann and I were evacuated with St James' School to Blaenavon.

Ann was eight and I was nearly ten years old and I found the whole business of the evacuation very traumatic to say the least. We were very tearful on arrival in Blaenavon. I had instructions from my mother not to be separated from Ann. We were finally billeted with a Mr and Mrs Jenkins, who didn't have any children of their own. I can't remember the address, but I can picture the little terraced houses perched on the side of a mountain.

Some weeks later, our younger sister Janet followed us. Father brought her down because mother was expecting our brother, who was born in September 1940. Janet was just two years and a few months old when she arrived in Wales. After my father had left, I found it very distressing because Janet was missing mother so much.

As our foster parents had never had children of their own, I was the one who had to look after all of Janet's needs, which I found very hard. Anyway, I took the 'bull by the horns' and wrote to my mother, who by this time had been evacuated to Dartford, Kent. So after just six months we were all collected by father and took our chances in north Kent, as Dartford was horrendous during the war. We all survived and returned to Dover at the end of 1944. I think being evacuated did have an effect on me in that I was very insecure for a long time afterwards and I often accused my parents of not wanting me!

*Rosina Wells* (now Mrs Elson) was evacuated with St Andrew's School for Girls, Dover:

They teamed me up with a girl called Winnie. It was a nice little village where we were. I remember we had to cross the railway line to get to school. We made friends with the local 'Bobby' and the milkman. After I had been with Mr and Mrs Jones for a while, I had a letter from mum, saying that my sister was with nice people in Risca but I never saw her until we were both home in Dover. I remember we had to write our letters to home in school, then the teachers would read them and sometimes we were told to write them again. In the end I used to write home before I went to school, and would post them on the way.

One thing I remember about my billet was that there were always sides of bacon hanging on the walls of the kitchen – and we had bacon every day for dinner! But I still like bacon, after all these years. Church was compulsory on a Sunday. We had to go in the morning, at midday and back again in the evening, but I suppose we all got used to it.

While I was in Undy a German aeroplane dropped a few bombs near the village. We were told not to write and tell our mums about the bombs – but I did! Shortly afterwards, I was swinging on the front gate when two women came up to me and asked if Rosina lived in the house. I told them she did and Mrs Jones took them inside. A few minutes later she called me in and told me that it was my mum and aunty who had come to take me home! I hadn't recognised them – and they hadn't recognised me! When I realised, I just sat down and cried. I was going home to be with mum and to see dad and gran again. My mum took the view that if bombs were being dropped in Wales then I may as well be home with my family.

It was lovely being home again, but I remember that after a couple of days, mum took me to the 'Welfare' and showed them my head. I have never forgotten the look on that lady's face when she examined my hair and found that I was lousy! I had to have all my hair shaved off and I started crying when I saw all my curls lying on the floor. Still, I was home, that was the main thing. I was eleven and I had been away for fifteen months.

*Alma Collis* (now Mrs Cork) was evacuated from Folkestone, with her two sisters, to the village of Grosmont. Their host and hostess were Captain and Mrs Pope:

Within 48 hours of arriving I had sprained my ankle and so had to be carried up and down stairs by Captain Pope. That Saturday, a woman took Helen away to live in a large house in the village, with other teenage girls, leaving Anne of five years of age, and myself of ten years to our own devices. This didn't please me and it upset my mother when Helen wrote to her.

Our only contact with Mrs Pope was in the mornings, when she brushed our hair before school, and again just before we went to bed. We often saw Captain Pope who was a real gentleman. He was very tall and upright and had a lovely smile. There was a son called Scott who attended boarding school, but was the plague of our lives when he was home on holiday. He was always chasing us, teasing us, pulling our hair and calling us names. It was not unknown for him to turn the water hose on us, then get us into trouble with Mrs Pope for being wet through. He was encouraged by cook, who upset me badly by saying that we were gypsies. This brought my mother post haste from Folkestone to Grosmont, to assure both Mrs Pope and the cook that we were very respectable, well brought up children and not gypsies!

Obviously we wanted to go home with mum but she told us that it wouldn't be long before we could return. My father worked at RAF Brize Norton and he used to come and see us more often. We would go for lovely long country walks and one of our favourite places to visit was the ruins of Grosmont Castle. Then we would go back to dad's hotel for tea.

I found it a terrible drudge having to walk three miles to school and back, especially in the winter when the snow was deep. I frequently had to carry Anne on my back – and she was getting heavier as she was getting older. We would sometimes be given a lift to school by a dear old chap who owned the only taxi in the village – I think his name was Mr Baldwin. He would always stop when he saw us, either going to or from school. Letters from home usually went to Helen, so I had to get any news from her. There was often a packet of ginger biscuits for me to take back to my billet and over a period of two and a half years I grew to hate ginger biscuits!

The housemaid Eileen left the house very suddenly; Anne and I were upset to see her go as she had been so nice to us. Weeks later we found out that she had taken a new position and, after being there two weeks, had been found strangled. It seemed she had given up a boyfriend who objected. All newspapers were kept out of our way and there were policemen constantly at the door, but they never spoke to Anne or me.

One Saturday morning I discovered two women in our bathroom and they had called Anne to go in with them. When I questioned them, I was told that they were to cut off her lovely long auburn hair. It seems that she had caught some unwanted 'visitors' from the local children. Knowing that my mother would be absolutely furious, I kicked and hit the nearest woman to me in my efforts to save Anne's lovely hair. I didn't succeed but ran all the way to the village to tell Helen. She wrote to mother who demanded an explanation. I didn't get off scot free as I was ordered before our own headmistress and, no matter what explanation I gave, I was in trouble.

Following the incident with Anne's hair, my own hair was promptly put into plaits, which I knew would spoil the natural curl. I hated it so much that I took out the plaits when I reached school. It was just my luck that Mrs Pope came into school that morning – she was a school governor! I was hauled out into the lobby, told off and my hair re-plaited.

One night I woke to see a figure in a white gown standing in the doorway, smiling at me. Thinking it was Mrs Pope, I smiled back and went to sleep. The next morning I asked Mrs Pope why she had called in. She looked surprised, then asked me several questions. When my sister Anne went back to Grosmont in 1990 for a visit and was telling the owner of the tea shop who she was, the young lady ran to fetch her mother. The mother then said to Anne, 'So it is your sister who has seen the ghost of Part-y-Seal!'

The atmosphere grew worse with cook, who would frequently be very rude to us, so we asked to be moved. In November 1942, we were moved to the opposite end of the village next to a dreadful run-down village pub and were put in the attic to sleep. Helen came to see us at the end of the first week and found me in the yard, doing washing in a wash tub. I showed her where we slept and the old toilet 'half a mile down the garden'. She was so shocked that she wrote to mother to fetch us home. A week later mother arrived and soon we were back home in Folkestone. When I asked mother why she had us evacuated, she would only say that it was one of the most miserable times of her life – and she didn't want to talk about it.

*Joyce Doolin (now Mrs Howell) was twelve when she was evacuated with her brother:*

I was evacuated with Barton Road School. My mother agreed to us going on the understanding that we would be kept together. Mother thought I would keep an eye on Leslie, my seven-year old brother. As it turned out, I went to Ynysddu and my brother went to Blackwood!

I had a very good billet with an old gentleman and his daughter, but my brother was in a very rough place where the woman had a son the same age as Leslie. My brother was made to do all sorts of work. He hadn't been there long before the woman looking after him wrote to mum and said that all his clothes had been stolen from the washing line, and that mum would have to send more. She had taken my brother's clothes for her own son.

Anyway, mum came down to Wales to take Leslie home and there was no way I was going to stay if he went home, so mum took us both back with her. We had been in Wales for just six weeks! When we got back, mum sent us out to Uncle Arthur Nelson in Mill Lane, Nonington, which was a much safer place than Dover at that time. I remember helping the Land Girls with the harvest that year, and also going hop-picking to earn money for a bicycle.

We went home to Dover for Christmas – and stayed. In May 1943, our house at 128 Mayfield Avenue was hit by a bomb and we were all buried in the debris but nobody was really hurt. We had lost everything, but we had survived.

*Michael Cox from Deal recounts his time in Wales:*

We had been despatched from a nice middle-class home in a nice middle-class seaside town to a small mining community in South Wales. At home the miners had been treated with some contempt by the locals when they came to work in the Kent coalfield in the 1920s and 1930s so, on reflection, Wales was probably the worst place to send us. We were soon to discover the hardship of the Welsh mining community. Mrs Hamer, my hostess, was a strict chapel lady and we were forced to chapel three times every Sunday. But the services were totally incomprehensible since they were all in Welsh! Although we were taught Welsh at Sunday School, all we could do was to watch the dramatic and extravagant behaviour of the preacher. As one can imagine, the services were interminable. On other days during the week we had to help clean and polish the chapel and schoolrooms; visit old ladies and listen to conversations in Welsh; or go to other places of worship in the village to see if they were better, or worse, than ours! Cinemas were banned as was any form of entertainment that was not chapel-orientated.

Bullying by the Welsh children was rife for we were strangers in a strange land and tended to keep together. As the phoney war continued, one of the London evacuees in my billet returned home, leaving just Dennis and myself. Escaping from the dark confines of the house, we would wander all over the fields, farms and railway sidings. The countryside was an escape from the stifling atmosphere of the billet. Our favourite place was Kenfig where there were miles of sand dunes and a mysterious pool where it was said the original village was submerged because of its debauchery and whose church bell could be heard on windy nights!

During the same period my family was coming apart. My grandmother died on the 9th of June and within a week my mother joined the ATS. This new-found freedom created some sort of independence and in the summer of 1941 my parents came to Kenfig Hill to announce their separation. I was not to see my father again until 1948 and only intermittently after that until he died in 1965. Meanwhile my mother had been posted to Donnington in Shropshire and achieved the rank of sergeant. Difficulty in travel was the reason given for her lack of visits. I believe the number of visits I received from my mother in four and a half years were in single figures. The war was a good excuse for dropping responsibilities and having a good time! I am sure the psychological effects of all this showed itself later in life.

However, back to Kenfig Hill and my schooling. My best memory was having to sit in front of the class because of difficulty in seeing the blackboard. When the school medical officer visited, the teacher told me to return after the examination to get my eyes tested. Such was my state that when I went back and was asked what I wanted – I had forgotten! So I said the teacher wanted me to have extra milk, which I received. It was very useful for we were always hungry! I didn't get spectacles for another two years and, when I did, what a revelation!

The only other memorable thing about school at that time was that I took and passed the scholarship examination to Sir Roger Manwood's School, which had been evacuated from Sandwich to Carmarthen. So off I went, on my own, to Pyle to catch the train to Carmarthen and I remember having an hour's wait at Swansea. This is imprinted on my mind, for every school holiday I went back to Kenfig Hill, to Mrs Hamer's, and to the regime. Most of my fellow students went back to Kent for the holidays, so one can see how my resentment built up. In addition, effectively I had no parents, except those I feared in Wales. It is no surprise then that my time in Carmarthen, which I enjoyed, was punctuated by being kicked out of billet after billet because of bed-wetting! It seems to me now, more than fifty years on, that bed-wetting was a form of comfort and perhaps a desire to get back to the hostel in Quay Street – to be among all the other reprobates.

The evening walk back from prep at school was always an event; shepherded by the older boys, we were a match for any of the Welsh kids who wanted to make trouble. At Carmarthen I re-discovered the cinema, which I had been denied for two years. I spent all my pocket money in the cinemas of the town, revelling in the golden years of Hollywood. I wonder what is so psychological about the cinema? A frightened boy in the darkness, solitary, living the life of the silver images on the screen.

My other memories of Carmarthen are the cattle market and the market hall with its religious maniac, who was still there some twenty years later! I remember the twice-yearly fair on the cattle market site, and I remember the River Towy and the coracle fishers. I remember the ladies at one of the billets putting on liquid stockings and trying to draw seams at the back of the legs with a pencil. I remember the ox-bows of the river having posts put on them to stop gliders from landing, and I remember the night thousands of American troops arrived, including a black contingent. These troops stayed for several months before leaving to take part in the Normandy landings. After they had left the Carmarthen area, the camp where they had been was surrounded by barbed wire and turned into a prison camp, so I saw my first Germans.

Most of all I remember going into hospital at the age of twelve to have my tonsils out. Not a very good experience. Being the eldest of the group, I was the last in and had to wait and listen as the four younger ones went in and screamed as the chloroform hit them. With my own operation I have vivid memories of the smell of the chloroform and then waking up vomiting black blood. I got no better for it seems I had an infection that would not respond, so they gave me penicillin and sent for my mother. I finally recovered and came out of hospital on the 6th June, 1944. We went to Deal for a few days and then I was sent to a convalescent home in Porthcawl. Then it was back to Carmarthen and to Manwoods for one last term before coming home to Deal for good. I say 'home', but that's not strictly true for my mother could not, or would not, get demobbed, so my brother and I stayed with my aunt and uncle for six months. My mother eventually arrived with two ex-army bikes and we set up house together.

How did the war impinge on me? Well, apart from being dumped in a strange land and left, I saw little of the war. In the early days we would hear the German bombers raiding the steel works at Port Talbot fifteen miles away. The biggest excitement was when a German aircraft dropped a stick of bombs on a hill-side and splattered a row of houses with mud.

Did evacuation have a lasting effect on my life? Of course it did. Anger, resentment, fear and rejection have all had dramatic effects on my life, most of all, rejection by my parents! The effect of evacuation has coloured both my brother's behaviour and mine all our lives. One cannot dwell in the land of 'what ifs', but had it not been for evacuation, perhaps, in the words of Marlon Brando, 'I could have been a contender!'

*Joyce Spratling (now Mrs Bignell) recalls the unpleasant time she had in Cefn Forest:*

On the first morning in my new billet, the woman of the house came into my room very early and said, 'You will have to get up, you have got to get my son Billy and my husband off to work! Before you go off to school, this floor will have to be polished!' The woman was expecting a baby so she made me do a lot of the other housework as well.

*Joyce Spratling (now Joyce Bignell). Picture taken by Ted Green at an evacuee reunion in Dover, May 1995*

My next shock was when I discovered I had head lice. I said to my teacher, 'I think I have got things in my head.' Miss Jenkins couldn't believe it. I didn't mind who cut my hair as long as they got rid of the lice. After that I developed a rash. I showed it to Miss Jenkins, who confirmed that I had scabies! I went to the clinic for sulphur ointment to rub on the skin. I think I caught scabies because the people I was staying with had been using my soap and flannel.

I felt as though I had the plague! I kept saying to my friends, 'Don't get near me or you will catch it.' But they were very good to me. The next thing to go wrong was during a routine medical examination of all the school children. I had been examined and then told not to get dressed, but to go and stand behind a partition and wait for the doctor. I was re-examined and was told that I had a 'bad heart'. I was banned from playing netball and rounders and all other outdoor activities. But that didn't stop me and, after a time, I seemed to have recovered.

We had to be inoculated against diphtheria. We all walked over to Bedwelty Park and, as I was the smallest, they pushed me in front to be done first. On the way home one of the girls said to me, 'Joyce, your arm is swelling up.' Suddenly I couldn't lift my arm and, as Miss Esling and Miss Jenkins took my coat off, I passed out. Some time later we all had to have a booster inoculation, and this affected me worse than the first one. Everything seemed to swell up this time and all my clothes had to be stripped off of me because everything was so tight. And then I went blind! I was rushed to Newport Hospital for observation and, once the swelling had gone, I returned to Pengam to convalesce. I was still blind but, by this time, I had moved billets and was staying with my cousin John Flood. The teachers visited me regularly and many of the girls came to sit and read to me, so that I wouldn't feel alone.

Nobody was sure if I would get my sight back but I woke up one morning and I could see light. The doctor came later that day and examined me. Afterwards he spoke to 'Aunt Nell', our foster mother, and said, 'I think she is going to be alright.' Anyway, during that period of convalescence I learned to play the piano accordion and tap dancing. I was allowed to do anything I wanted and everyone was marvellous to me.

That year I went hop-picking in Herefordshire with Reggie Skingle, John Flood and my foster parents. When we arrived home from hop-picking, there was a knock on the door. It was the woman with whom Pearl, my sister, was billeted in Blackwood. Apparently, this woman was very house-proud, and had treated my sister very badly, so badly in fact that Pearl had run away and was found at the railway station in the early hours of the morning. Anyway, this woman said to Aunt Nell, 'It's all your fault, you have encouraged her.' I found out later that the woman had told Pearl that she would never see her mother again, that her mother would be killed by the shells and that Pearl would have to be adopted.

It wasn't long before mum came down to Wales to take us home, but not before she had 'a few words' with Pearl's foster mother! We never talked about Pearl's traumatic time in Wales, but when we got back home she used to have terrible screaming fits. My young brother Ernie had been billeted in New Tredegar and he had a wonderful foster mother who loved him like a real mother. I had three billets in the short time I was in Wales, but I ended up with a good one. Mrs Morton was really good to me, and she didn't mind any of my friends coming in. However, in October 1941 mum came down to Wales to collect us and we all returned to Dover.

*Joan Beal, evacuated with the Dover County School for Girls, recalls her time in Caerleon:*

As an only child I suppose evacuation 'knocked the corners off me', and being billeted with an elderly lady who had never had children was quite an experience for an eleven year old. Her cats took priority. One of the things I remember about that billet was always having to wake my host so that she could light the fire to boil the kettle for breakfast. There was no gas or electric cookers. I used to hate being late for school; no one would believe me that it wasn't my fault.

My host had a habit of keeping food, for example cake, until it had grown 'whiskers', then she would give it to me. She used to give me a plate of spinach for tea; nothing with it, just spinach. More than fifty years later and I still hate spinach! There was an enormous garden with a six feet high hedge, which I had to cut, balancing on rickety steps. Picking fruit was another activity I had to do – and she always inspected my mouth to see if I had eaten any!

Schooling was a bit chaotic. Lessons were in shifts; mornings one week and afternoons the next in a variety of locations: the local school, church halls and Caerleon College, and we spent quite a bit of time running between these places. The staff arranged various activities for us, of which the Girl Guides were very strong. We also knitted scarves, etc., for the troops, and picked rosehips to help the war effort. On Saturday mornings we would play organised games – usually netball. At one of these sessions I was fetched as the old lady I was living with had died.

I was moved to a temporary billet and then to Llantarnum where our school had opened a hostel for about 25 girls with two staff and a housekeeper, travelling to Caerleon by train every day. While we were there we had an outbreak of scarlet fever which confined us all for several weeks and the staff tried to give us lessons. Evacuation was a way of life we all had to put up with! We made our own fun and went home to the bombs and shells during the holidays. The school returned to Dover in 1944, just in time for Christmas.

### Ruby Jeffries (now Mrs Horton) was evacuated privately:

When the Dover County School for Girls in Dover was evacuated to Caerleon in 1940, I remained behind with my family. However, I eventually went to stay with an aunt in Hertfordshire. The move to Hertfordshire proved unsuccessful so I returned to Dover. My next move was to stay with friends of the family at Eythorne, a few miles outside Dover. Here, the daughter of the house and I attended Elvington School. She was slightly younger and had also taken and passed the entrance exam for the County School. After much discussion, we left Kent in September, 1941, to join our school in Caerleon. When we arrived, we both managed to stay together in the same billet. Our new home was not a happy experience. We never sat down for a meal with the family, but had to have our meal after they had finished. Our homework had to be done in a cold bedroom because our books 'made a mess' in the living room.

The family were staunch churchgoers. The foster father was an organist and his son was a choir boy. We had to go to church three times every Sunday and we had to be seen to be there. Occasionally, the son would say we weren't in church and we would be in big trouble.

Eventually, the lady of the house had to go into hospital so we had to move and, as there were no billets available, we were put into a hostel. This, as far as I was concerned, was the last straw. So I persuaded my mother to take me back to Dover.

When I returned to Dover in 1943, some of the schools had reopened, and I ended up going back to Barton Road Girls' School. Being one of the older girls, I helped with the younger children, listening and reading to them – and we spent a lot of time in the air-raid shelters! I had left school and was working as a shop assistant by the time the war finished.

### Pearl Hayward (now Mrs Walter) recalls the time she spent in Wales:

I was thirteen years old when I was evacuated with St James' School, Dover, to the village of Blaenavon in South Wales. My two sisters and baby brother also went with me, and I had strict instructions from mother not to be parted from Peter who was only three years and four months.

My sisters, Mary and Jean, went to separate billets, but I managed to keep Peter with me. We stayed with Mr and Mrs Daley at Forge Side. However, I was only destined to stay in Blaenavon for about a year. I remember one afternoon during the winter of 1940/41, about six of us kids went up the mountain to do some skating on the frozen ponds. We came across a hollow where about twelve miners from the village were all sitting in a circle. They were playing cards and gambling – and we all got chased away! I found out later that it was considered to be a sin to play cards indoors, which is why they all went up the mountain to play.

Whilst I was in Blaenavon I caught diphtheria. There was an old mine at the top of the road where I was billeted, which was going to be made into an air-raid shelter. Well, there was this awful smell coming from the old mine, and we kids, being nosey, went inside to take a look. I was the only one to go down with diphtheria, but I am sure it was something to do with that old mine. We had all been vaccinated against the disease, which they said saved my life, but I was very ill just the same. They took me to hospital and I was in isolation for about two months. In the meantime, dad had been evacuated from Dunkirk and was in a military hospital at Gleneagles in Scotland, recovering from an injured back and foot.

Anyway, mum went up to Scotland to visit dad and, whilst I was in hospital in Wales, they both came down to see me. They weren't allowed into the ward and could only see me through a window. All the mothers were throwing gifts through the windows on to the children's beds.

Mum went back to Scotland with dad for a few days, then returned to Dover – and the bombing! She was in our house when the bombs fell on St James Street. Houses collapsed just like a pack of cards and mum was buried in the rubble. Luckily she survived without serious injury, but she was in hospital for a while and had to have her eyes taken out and put back to remove all the grit and dust from the blast of the bomb.

When mum recovered, she went to live with a friend for a while, then she came down to Wales while I was recuperating. While she was there, she went into war work at the munitions factory at Usk. Mum eventually went back to Dover and managed to get another house, this time at Mayfield Gardens. In the meantime I had come out of hospital but had paralysis in my leg. I couldn't walk properly after the diphtheria.

While I was in hospital, I had heard gunfire in the distance – ack ack fire, and I heard the nurses saying that thousands of incendiary bombs had dropped near the hospital. They weren't big bombs but I didn't know that then. The nurses had put blankets on all our beds ready to take the beds out to the shelters. Well, I wrote to my mother after I came out of hospital saying there were thousands of bombs dropping in Wales and I wanted to come home to Dover. I told her that if she didn't let me come home, I was going to jump in the river. I hated it down there.

I think mum panicked and told everyone she knew with children in Wales. The police went to see her and told her to stop causing panic, otherwise all the evacuated children would have to come back! I think mum received a caution from the police because of that incident.

Anyway, not long after, mum sent me a parcel which contained a dress and blazer – and my fare home! She sent the same for my sister Jean. So we packed our things and caught the train – I was only fourteen years old and Jean was ten. Mum met us in London and from there we returned home to Dover – and I have never been back to South Wales since!

*Here, Pearl's mother, **Mrs Elsie Hayward**, tells her side of the story:*

Four of my five children had been evacuated to Blaenavon. After they had been gone a while, the local police came to see me and asked me if I had children in Wales. I immediately thought that something had happened to them, then the policeman said, 'We have just found out that you are responsible for many mothers in this area sending for their children and demanding that they come back home! You have been telling the mothers that the Germans are bombing the mountains where the children are living.' I told the policeman that I didn't know what he was talking about, then I remembered that a letter from my daughter Pearl, in which she said that the Germans were bombing and setting light to the mountains, and that they all wanted to come home. I didn't know what to do at the time and, in any case, I couldn't afford their fares home!

Anyway, it appears that many of the mothers in the St James Street area had written to the police station, and some had even written to the mayor, demanding their children back. When they got to the bottom of it all, they found that Mrs Hornsey, who had three children of her own in Wales and who lived in St James Street, was the only person I had spoken to concerning Pearl's letter – the rumour had spread from that point!

The policeman asked me if I still had the letter from Pearl and luckily I did. I showed it to the policeman and after he read it he laughed and said, 'And you took this seriously?' I replied, 'Well wouldn't you if you had a child down there? – And I've got four in Wales!'

Anyway, the policeman said that I was breaking the Defence of the Realm Act and I should stop spreading rumours about the bombing. He told me that one German plane had flown over the mountains and had dropped a flare – that was all! Then he informed me that I was being let off with a caution this time. I was very careful of whatever I said after that!

*We can see from Elsie Hayward's account that the experience of evacuation was also very mixed for parents, especially when disputing the idealised happy image of the safety of their children as it was portrayed in the press. As we have heard, most children's letters home were censored by foster parents and sometimes by teachers. Children's complaints rarely reached their unsuspecting parents. Mrs Hayward's account shows what could happen when the façade of utopian safety and hospitality was threatened by an individual.*

**Winnie Delahaye** *(now Mrs Barrow) recalls the time she and her sister spent in Aberfan:*

Our first billet was with a strict Catholic family with a nine year old daughter. We would go to church three times on a Sunday. Although my sister and I were from a Catholic family ourselves, we never used to go to church very often in Deal, so the novelty soon wore off.

Within a week of arriving, a school timetable had been worked out. Some non-teaching 'helpers' had travelled with our party and they dealt with problems of health, clothing and homesickness. I remember Mrs Trice and Mrs Delahaye coping with many problems. I think we all settled down well to the rest of our schooling. My sister and I went to Pantglass School where, some years later, the terrible Aberfan disaster occurred. We all got on well with the local children and made some good friends in Aberfan. We acted in the same plays and pantomimes and had sports matches between them and us.

In October, 1940, terrible news came that we had lost our dad. He had died of a heart attack. I can still see him on Deal Station on the day of our evacuation, which was to be the last time we ever saw him. I still have his last letter telling us to be good girls in our billet.

*Some of the Deal children evacuated to the Aberfan area of South Wales.*
*Photograph taken early in the evacuation – Peter Hayward collection*

Many of the evacuees had several billets but most were in the same village. We stayed at our first billet for nine months, then we moved on to a lady in her late sixties. It was another strict billet. What wasn't eaten at one meal, we had to eat at the next, until it was gone. When Peggy wet the bed one day, our landlady brought the wet bedclothes to school and opened them out in front of the class! Whenever we received any money, we had to hand it over to our landlady.

There wasn't a great deal to do in the village. In the summer on fine days, we had our lessons on the mountains and we went for lots of rambles. Once or twice a year when it was possible to arrange it, the Deal children would all get together for the day in Cyfartha Park.

By 1941 when there was a lull in the raids in Kent, some of the evacuees were taken home by their parents. It was probably at this time that our headmistress, Miss Rutherford, was recalled to Deal to organise emergency classes for those who had returned. Other Deal teachers I remember were Mr Mainwood, Mr Musk, Miss Newton, Miss Baldry, Miss Sewell, Miss Seymour, Miss Griffith, Mr Pittock and Mr Green. Eventually, my mother and two other sisters joined us in Aberfan and we all stayed until August, 1944.

We all made many friends during our time in Wales and to this day I still write to some of them, but we didn't keep in contact with our foster parents. We were never happy in the two billets that we had, so there was no point. In 1988, I returned to Aberfan for the first time since the war for a nostalgic visit, 44 years after I had left!

Chapter Five

## ON THE BRIGHTER SIDE

*FORTUNATELY, NOT all the evacuees experienced difficult or unhappy billets. Many found a new family and the adventure of a lifetime. For some, the saddest part of the evacuation experience was to be the separation from their host families when the danger of war had passed. Many foster-parents wanted to adopt their evacuees, never really letting go of their borrowed children and often keeping contact with them for the rest of their lives. Parents in war-torn areas made the difficult decision to evacuate their children, only to find that some of the youngest did not want to return to them. For many evacuees, their natural parents had become strangers.*

*This chapter relates the experiences of evacuees who mainly enjoyed their stay in exile and who, for many, made happy and loving relationships with the people who were good enough to have given them sanctuary. It also tells of the adventure of growing up in an exciting new environment of mountains, tall ferns and black water, and of making life-long friends with the Welsh people. For most of these children, the evacuation was a success.*

**Alan Avery** *relives some of his fondest memories of his Welsh foster-homes:*

*Alan Avery pictured with one of the original shoes he wore on the day of his evacuaton in June, 1940 – it is now a pin cushion! (Alan Avery photo)*

As all the other children went off to their billets, no-one wanted me! The Holiday brothers, Peter and Alan, and I were the last three children left standing in the hall. I was beginning to feel frightened and wanting my parents. What I didn't know was that our billet was right at the end of the line, not in the small town, but halfway up the mountainside to a large stone-built house overlooking Upper Cwmbran, Pontnewydd, Cwmbran, Newport and the Bristol Channel in the distance. When the Germans bombed Newport and Bristol, we had a magnificent view!

When we were taken into our billet, Mrs Elizabeth Jones, who was in her 60s, and many of her sons and daughters with their families were gathered in a very large room to welcome us. At this stage I became very frightened and cried when I heard Mrs Jones' brother, 'Uncle Jim', who had such a deep voice that I thought he must be a policeman!

After six months or so, Alan and Peter Holiday returned home to Dover but I remained with Mrs Jones at 'Belle Vue' until July 1944. For the first year (1940-1941) I attended Upper Cwmbran Infant School and then when I reached junior age, I went to Pontnewydd School, which meant a daily walk of more than two miles each way. Because I lived so far away from any other evacuee I made many lasting friendships with the local children, who lived about half a mile away. My best friend was Walford Edwards whom I last met in 1980 while on holiday with my family. In 1944 I passed for the Dover County School, so it was time for me to leave the Jones family in Upper Cwmbran. I came home to Dover for six weeks holiday. I was delighted to come home though terrified by the shelling and doodlebugs, and I was quite happy to return to Wales even though it meant a new billet and a new school.

My most vivid memory of those six weeks in Dover was being taken to the Regent Cinema to see the film *For Whom the Bells Toll*. During the film, which was showing mountain warfare and aeroplanes dive-bombing, an extra loud bang was heard. Immediately a notice flashed on to the screen which said, 'Shelling in progress, please evacuate the cinema'. As we fled out of the cinema we discovered the houses opposite had been demolished by a shell! As we scurryied home over Tower Hamlets another shell landed near Dover Priory Station. During the six weeks I was home, I also watched a doodlebug fall on the Three Horseshoes pub in the Hougham area.

Until July 1944, my parents visited me once a year. One would come in the early spring and the other during the summer/autumn. They were never able to come together because of war work commitments. I had an idyllic four years at 'Belle Vue' with my Welsh foster parents. They were wonderful to me and treated me as if I were another son in the family. To this day I still think of it as my second home and second parents. Nancy is now in her eighties and I still love her as much today as I did more than fifty years ago. On my return to Dover after the war, it took me a considerable time to readjust to my town surroundings after the joys of the open countryside and mountains. I have been back to Wales many times since the war.

*Ted Green tells of his time spent with his foster parents in Pontllanfraith:*

On the first morning I woke up with the sun streaming in through the windows. I looked around the room and I couldn't make out where I was. Henry Plant, my friend, was still asleep in the next bed. Then I saw my gas mask and my jacket, still with the label attached, and my carrier bag. I felt happy and free. I looked in my bag and there tucked between my clothes was a tin of condensed milk, which we had been given at school, with strict instructions, 'This is for your foster parents!'

As soon as I got up I was greeted by a small girl's voice, 'Good morning, I'm Geraldine.' She was about my age and perhaps a little taller with fair hair. I soon learned that my foster parents were Mrs Sarah Williams and her husband John. Geraldine was their grand-daughter.

After breakfast I gave Mrs Williams the tin of milk. She was grateful but surprised. Mrs Williams introduced her husband John, a dear old man, with a broad grin on his face and rosy cheeks. I remember that first day so well, sharing details of my home life in Dover with this lovely family and trying to learn certain bits of Welsh. I found that I was billeted at 38 Sir Ivors Road, Pontllanfraith, Newport, Monmouthshire. The first full day in Wales was spent being shown around by Geraldine. Then on Tuesday, 4th June, we had to report at Pontllanfraith School. All the evacuees had to gather in the playground where our teachers were waiting. We then assembled in the main school hall where we were told that we had been allocated two classrooms, and that we would work mornings one week, and afternoons the following week.

Some of the meals back at my billet were of tripe and onions, which at times made me heave. We also had tea sop and cheese. This was a basin of diced bread, covered with tea, milk and sugar and, as we ate this, we had a bite from a small square of cheese. It all tasted very good.

Mrs Williams (Aunty Sarah) was one for good health. Every morning before breakfast she would drink a cup of clear hot water. She would always enquire if we were 'regular' or not. If the answer was 'No', we would be given a cup of senna pod liquid. Aunty was one for saving tins of all sorts. In the living room was a sofa, the seat of which lifted up on hinges. Inside were tins of food of all descriptions as well as boxes of dried fruit.

Aunty Sarah was firm but kind towards us children and a loving Christian lady. John, her husband was just as kind. He had worked hard all his life as a miner and he was a joy to be with. He would sing in Welsh and English, and teach us about Wales and its beauty. Often he would take us boys up to Mynyddislwn to the woods, to cut firewood. On wet days we would sit in his 'den', and chop up wood ready the winter. We had been in Wales six or seven months when we heard the bombing of Newport, Cardiff and Bristol. The rumbles in the distance were continuous at times. We were told not to worry because they were a long way off. At night, on occasions, we would stand in the garden, see the flashes in the sky and hear the explosions. This was the time when I used to think of my sisters: Marie at Undy and Margaret at Rogiet.

After about two years it was decided that the Dover children would have to move from Pontllanfraith to Blackwood about four miles away. It was a very sad day for me because I was leaving behind all my Welsh friends, who were very dear to me. It was hard to say goodbye – I felt as if I was deserting them. Upon arrival at my new billet at 3 George Street, Blackwood, I was greeted by several other evacuees: the Graham brothers and Leslie Hutchins. My host, Mrs Teagle, was very kind and loving, although I later found out that she never enjoyed the best of health. Mr Teagle, who came home later in the day, was a real gentleman. He was a bricklayer by trade; he was jolly and made me feel very welcome.

We boys all shared one large bedroom, each with our own space for our belongings, in wardrobes and chests of drawers. The house was very spacious, with a lounge, where Mrs Teagle had her bed. The dining room was huge, with a red ceramic tiled floor which was highly polished. The kitchen or scullery had a huge, black, highly polished cooking range where all the cooking and baking was done. There was also an elderly gentleman, Mr Blunt, staying at the house. He had his special high backed chair near the cooking range, where he often sat smoking his pipe. Mr Blunt was a very kind-natured man and he used to talk to us about the culture of Wales and the love in the Welsh people, which I found to be very true.

Chicken were kept in the back garden and one of my jobs was to boil the potato peelings, mashed with chicken meal to feed to them. So we had fresh eggs and, occasionally, chicken for Sunday dinner. School was just three minutes away in an old mission hall. Mr Bell, one of our teachers, had a favourite selection of songs which included *Sussex by the Sea* and *Old Father Thames*. He said they were good for exercising the vocals. He

*Ted Green pictured outside his old billet, 38 Sir Ivors Road, Pontllanfraith. Photograph taken in 1990.*

was a brilliant teacher, but very strict. Later during our stay at Blackwood, an additional building near to Cefn Road Chapel was allocated to us. Here we had an old radio from which we had a regular lesson on current affairs.

My Christian life was continued at Blackwood. I attended the Baptist Church, where the minister was the Reverend Owen Williams, and I also attended Elim Sunday School. Time was also spent with the other evacuees and the Welsh boys, playing rugby behind the gas and waterworks. Between Blackwood and Pontllanfraith, was a spring-filled pool, where in the summer months we would swim. We had great fun. During my stay I met Dorothy who was about seventeen years old and came to attend to the needs of Mrs Teagle about three times a week. Dorothy would invite me home to visit her mother and father who lived in a lovely country cottage on Mynyddislwn. I will never forget her kind and loving ways.

When I reached the age of fourteen, Mr Teagle asked, 'How would you like to come to Newport Docks with me. We need a tea boy on our site. You would earn eight shillings a week.' I had to go and see Mr Twyman, my headmaster, about leaving school. He wasn't very happy about me leaving, but finally agreed to let me go. My job was to collect each person's order for tea, pies, cakes, etc., and take the list to a huge canteen on the site – and then take the orders back to the men at break time. I did several trips a day to the canteen at set times.

One day I had a letter from my parents saying arrangements were being made for me to return to Kent. All the people whom I met in Wales were wonderful. They came to the rescue of thousands of children – and many adults during those long war years.

*Pontllanfraith School, 1990,*
*with Ted Green in the foreground – Ted Green photo*

**Margaret Green** *(now Mrs Brian) remembers her arrival at her foster home:*

I remember Mrs Walker undressing me, washing me on the draining board and putting me into my nightgown. It was incredible to me to see such lovely food she placed on the table, on top of the whitest tablecloth I had ever seen – jelly and blancmange in individual glasses, sponge cake, fruit and bread and butter, cheese, lettuce, tomatoes and spring onions. I really began to think I was in fairyland, especially when she took me upstairs and settled me into a large bed with a down mattress which I sank right into. I remember her telling me that I looked like a bird in a nest. She was kind but when she left the room it was quite lonely. I had always been used to my brothers and sisters being with me at bed-time.

The next morning I was awakened by birds singing and 'Aunty' came in with a cup of tea and some biscuits. I had never had a cup of tea in bed before. At breakfast I saw 'Uncle' properly for the first time and found myself being very shy but they soon put me at ease.

They wanted to know about my brothers and sisters and parents. It was only then that they realised I had been separated from Teddy and Marie. They were soon making telephone calls to establish where they had both been taken, and it was not long before uncle was making arrangements for me to visit them. Aunty and uncle introduced me to their relatives within weeks of my arrival. Aunty's relatives were mainly in the Chepstow, Newport, Bulwark and

Risca areas, while uncle's were in Worcester. Suddenly I had dozens of new relatives – aunts, uncles, cousins, and even a new set of grandparents, the latter being a novelty as I had never met any of my own grandparents. With all these new people who showed me a lot of affection, I still pined, at first, for my own dear family. During the five years in Wales, I had a wonderful life that was full of love and care. I was taken on holiday with them every year and treated as if I were their own. Aunty made all my clothes on her sewing machine. She also knitted all my winter woollies. I had clothes for every occasion.

Uncle was fond of teaching me and he was always teasing me and making me laugh. Aunty and uncle took me to St Mary's parish church every Sunday, where I got to know the rector, the Reverend W. Morris. After church in the evenings, we went for a walk into the woods to pick violets, primroses and bluebells. At other times we would find bee orchids and wild straw-berries near the quarry at Rogiet. Moon-daisies and poppies grew in abundance, and the walk up Windmill Lane always ended up with a peep into the old windmill. Tuesdays were exciting as the farmers came to the cattle market, with their calves, cows, bullocks and sheep.

My foster parents were kind enough to send me to piano lessons, which were the highlights of my week. Once during the war we had a competition for 'Salute the Soldier' week. It was to draw and then embroider a picture of our own design on to a cushion cover. I loved embroidery and art, so I was entered in the competition which was in the Urban and Rural District of Chepstow. The winning entrant would receive a prize and have the cushion cover exhibited in the centre of a window in Chepstow near the old town arch.

On my cushion cover I had the regimental badge of the Royal Engineers in the left hand upper corner and, in the right, the regimental badge of the 'Buffs'. In the centre was a picture of a large tank and across the bottom were the words 'Salute the Soldier'. I sat for weeks in the evenings embroidering my cover, and I was thrilled when I won first prize.

We had many air raids, because the Germans were trying to hit the marshalling yards at the Severn Tunnel. The raids on Avonmouth and Bristol could be seen from my bedroom window and once when oil tanks at Avonmouth were hit, they were burning for three days. Aunty used to put me in the table-shelter to bed on nights when the raids were bad. One of the village boys was killed by shrapnel and blast. It was very sad because he happened to be a son of Mrs Pritchard, the lady in the Red Cross who had found me my foster parents.

On VE day we had a marvellous time celebrating the victory. We had street parties, beautiful church services and dancing in the village hall. My feelings were of looking forward to going back to Dover and at the same time sad at leaving such wonderful foster parents. They were sad too, because they had never had a child of their own and they loved me as if I were theirs. I returned to my family in Dover, and to my school, St Andrew's at Buckland. Later I went back to Wales to train as a nurse. I met and eventually married my husband who was from Newport – and we stayed in Wales!

*After a disastrous start,* **Bob Cain** *left Pengam to join his new school at Ebbw Vale:*

I lugged my suitcase about two miles to Blackwood where I caught a bus to Tredegar and transferred to a bus to Ebbw Vale. I arrived just before lunch.  There I was greeted by the headmaster, Mr J. C. Booth, who, after taking details, asked if I had any money. Very proud of the fact that I had saved the princely sum of one shilling and ninepence, I assured him that I had, so he told me to go and buy some lunch in the adjacent cafe. Feeling very much the 'grown up' I walked into the cafe and ordered a ham sandwich (4d) and a glass of orange squash (2d); it was the first time I had ever 'dined out' on my own.

After lunch, I found there was a problem with my billet. I had been earmarked for Mr and Mrs Phillips of Fairview Road, but it transpired that he was about 90 years of age and his wife was in her mid-eighties, so it was decided not to lumber them with me! So I was put in the care of a very large policeman, who took me round practically every street in Ebbw Vale, knocking on doors and asking, 'Can you take this boy overnight?' Eventually, we found a house where the mother-in-law had gone away overnight, so I could use her bed. It was paradise!

They were a young couple and they treated me wonderfully. He took me into his study and showed me his shotguns and fishing rods, which were displayed around the walls, and then they gave me a slap up meal. After tea they took me to her sister, who owned a sweetshop, where I was presented with a cardboard Tate and Lyle sugar box filled to the brim with sweets, and then it was off to the 'pictures'. There we sat in the best seats and I remember the villain was eaten by an alligator!

The next morning, after a wonderful night's sleep, I reported back to the billeting office and was again put in the charge of a very large policemen, with half a dozen other boys, and this time it was a 'delivery service'. The policeman had a list of people to receive evacuees, so off we went. The first house we went to was 97 Mount Pleasant Road, which was on the corner of an alley. While the policeman was knocking on the door, I went round the side of the house to peer in a window and when I got back to the front, the lady of the house was just taking her pick from the others. 'No,' she said, 'I won't have that one – I'll have that one,' pointing to me, so my (pleasant) fate was sealed.

Mrs Evans was about fifty and her husband a little older. They had a son, Harry, who was a surveyor by profession, but at this time was a sergeant in the Royal Engineers, so I only saw him a few times. This was just as well, because he was married to my Sunday School teacher, with whom I fell madly in love the first time I saw her, and I was green with envy whenever I saw them together! Mr Evans was in hospital when I arrived. He had been in a colliery accident. His foot was badly injured and he was having one of his toes amputated. Sometime later he was involved in another pit accident and received a deep cut in his arm. It took two hours to dig him out, and he later told me that he had watched his artery pumping away. A large part of his arm remained numb, and he could stick a needle in it without feeling any pain. He went back yet again to mining but, shortly after the war, he was involved in yet another fall, which broke almost every bone in his body.

Although Mr Evans was a coal miner, there was no evidence of that in the house. Many miners went to and from the pits in their working clothes, but not Mr Evans. He went in a suit, with starched shirt and tie. He always showered at the pit and returned home spotless – he could have been a 'city gent'. I can still remember his glittering cuff links and tie pin.

The fourth member of the family was Mrs Evans' father, Mr Miles. He was in his early seventies, had been a coal miner from the age of ten and was stone deaf. His grandfather had been batman to Nelson at Trafalgar, and had been left a carved ball of ivory and Nelson's shaving mirror and teapot in his will. The ivory ball and teapot had pride of place in the front room, and the mirror hung on the wall next to the gas mantle.

One weekend Mr and Mrs Evans took me to stay with some relatives in Cardiff. As soon as we arrived the sirens went, and we spent the whole night cowering under the stairs, listening to the bombs whistling down and hoping one wouldn't drop on us. We never repeated that visit!

Mr and Mrs Evans were extremely kind and looked after me wonderfully. I had as much food as I could eat, a very cosy bedroom, no chores to do and I was allowed out to play with my friends whenever I wished. I probably had one of the best billets in Ebbw Vale.

***Peter Elgar*** *talks of his life in Blackwood and later in Ebbw Vale and back in Dover:*

My host, Mr Williams, was a very good musician who played the organ at the Methodist Church. He taught piano and singing and, as my bedroom was directly over the music room, I soon became acquainted with the music of Mozart, Beethoven and many other composers. I always attribute my love of music to this early experience.

Although surrounded by coal mining areas, Blackwood itself was relatively free of industry and there were pleasant country walks. I developed a great love of the cinema – and the admission prices were well below those at home. The best seats at the Maxime were 8d, but we went mostly to the Capitol where seats for children were only 3d. The only snag was that we were restricted to the front rows and were in danger of getting a permanent crick in the neck. The usherette, who was quite strict, was for ever chasing us out of the better seats at the back where we used to scuttle when her back was turned. Nevertheless, we enjoyed a wonderful diet of the 'B' pictures of the day, series such as *The Saint, Mr Moto, Hopalong Cassidy, Boston Blackie, The Bowery Boys* and countless others.

Mr and Mrs Williams were still able to run their car, a Morris 8, and I was taken on outings around the South Wales countryside and as far afield as the Brecon Beacons, the Black Mountains and the Forest of Dean. One particularly enjoyable trip was to the little town of Nelson, which had one of the many Italian cafes which existed in the area. Their wonderful ice-cream was well worth the twenty miles or so round trip. My mother was able to visit in the summer of 1941, and I was taken on a caravan holiday to Ross-on-Wye. The war seemed very remote indeed on the peaceful banks of the River Wye. Listening to such programmes as *Letter from America*, the news and Mr Churchill's speeches enabled us to keep up with the progress of hostilities, but it almost seemed as if I was on another planet.

Two classmates and I won scholarships to the Dover County School. It was a mixed blessing for me as it meant leaving my lovely Blackwood home and my kind foster parents, which almost broke my heart. They were equally sad at me leaving as they had no family of their own.

My new school had been evacuated to Ebbw Vale about fifteen miles away. Again I was very fortunate in my new foster home, a large house called Sunnybank, overlooking the railway station. The town was very much in the centre of a large industrial and coal-mining area, being at the northern end of the four-mile long Richard Thomas and Baldwin Steelworks. Instead of green fields and woods to play in, we had to make do with waste coal and slag tips. Everything, including the surrounding mountains seemed black or grey. Sliding down the loose shale on old tin trays was great fun, but must have had elements of danger, bearing in mind some of those dreadful accidents which have occurred through tips becoming unstable.

At first we spent our school days in a portion of the local county school which had been set aside for us. Later we moved to Pentwyn House, at the other end of town, where we remained for the duration of our stay. For a while I used to walk to and fro for lunch at home, but after a while I went with the rest of the form to the local British Restaurant. I suppose the meals were as good as one could expect during rationing, but afterwards we always trooped across the road to the Italian cafe for a cup of their wonderful chocolate or a delicious ice-cream.

My host, Tom Llewellyn, was an electrical engineer who had an important job at the steelworks. He was often called out in the middle of the night for emergencies. The Llewellyns had a car, but it was laid up for the duration. The local bus services were cheap and frequent however, and I was often taken on shopping trips to Newport and Cardiff. The house was large enough to have a games room and I received my first introduction to the delights of billiards and snooker. There were many diversions to be enjoyed – after I had completed my homework.

Ebbw Vale was also well endowed with cinemas. We had the Plaza, Astoria, White House and the Palace; as some changed programmes midweek, it was possible to see six or seven different shows on my 2/6d per week pocket money. Being in Wales I was soon drawn into the religious life and became a regular attender at the local chapel, where I developed a love of Welsh choirs and the stirring sermons of the ministers.

Surprisingly the Welsh valleys largely escaped the blitz apart from a few stray bombs on the mountains. Everyone thought the steelworks would have been a prime target, but the Germans turned their main attention to the cities of Cardiff and Swansea, and they suffered badly. I remember seeing the shattered ruins of Llandaff Cathedral after one very heavy bombing.

*The plaque which was presented to the people of Ebbw Vale by Dover County School for Boys, in appreciation of the kindness shown to them during their period of evacuation.*

My parents were able to visit in the summer of 1942; at Easter 1943 I returned to Dover for the school holidays. With hindsight it was a risky thing to do, with Dover under bombardment from bombs and shells. It led to my closest wartime shave during the following summer holiday. In August, 1943, our house in Dover was shelled. When the siren sounded I was out cycling towards the country, and would normally have kept going because it was relatively safe out of town. On this occasion however, something persuaded me to return home. When I got home I suggested that we all went to the Anderson shelter – also unusual as, by now familiarity had bred contempt, and we usually stayed indoors during attacks. Half an hour later came the deafening explosion. My main recollection is of my father opening the shelter door to inform us that the house had been destroyed, giving us all a mouthful of dust! We thought our cat, Gandhi, who had just gone outside, must have been blown away by the blast, but on returning the next day to salvage what we could, we found that a kindly neighbour, had rescued and secured him safely in her cellar. Needless to say, from that moment on he was permanently deaf. Our large striking clock which had been blown from a high mantelpiece, was found still ticking and with the glass front unbroken. It still goes well more than fifty years later!

In 1944 we had the flying bombs to endure. Most of them passed overhead en route for London, but sometimes they were brought down by anti-aircraft guns or the RAF pilots, who used to fly alongside and gently tip their wings so that the bomb went off course and fell harmlessly in the country or the sea. Later, back in Ebbw Vale, there were many anxious days when Dover came under heavy shelling in the late summer of 1944, with much damage and heavy casualties. It was a great relief to receive letters from my parents and to know they were alright.

There were many other things I remember vividly about South Wales, such as the heavy and sometimes continuous rains, which seemed to soak one much more than anywhere else that I can remember. We had wonderful, unrestricted areas for play – all the rivers and the mountains were our playgrounds. One day we could be intrepid explorers, the next day Cowboys and Indians, riding the range and acting out our adventures with all the variations our young imaginations could muster. There were torrential streams to be dammed up with stones and we had disused townships and old mine workings to add to the realism.

I remember also the wonderful kindness of the people which has for ever given me a love of all things Welsh, especially the country, to which I have been able to take my family on many holidays over the years. Eventually the Channel Ports were liberated and the threat of shelling was lifted. Victory was just a matter of time and it was soon decided that it was safe enough for the school to return to Dover. Although some fellow evacuees didn't enjoy their experiences very much, most of us grew to love the Welsh people and kept in touch with our host families after leaving. A commemorative plaque was presented by Dover County School in recognition of the great kindness shown to us by the people of Ebbw Vale.

*Jean Randall* (now Mrs Lilly) from Deal remembers her foster home with affection in Merthyr Vale, which she shared with her older brother, Eric:

The lady of the house was Miss Ainsworth, and we soon started to call her Aunty Millie. She lived with her brother whom we called Uncle Fred. He was a lovely man. He had lost a leg in the first world war but still worked in the coalmine opposite where we lived. He had a lovely voice and was always singing. I remember when he used to come home from the pit, Aunt Millie would have a big wooden tub full of hot water and she used to scrub him. The Welsh water was lovely and soft, and you hardly ever had to use any soap.

Two days after arriving in Wales, it was my twelfth birthday, and for breakfast we had

*Eric, Jean and Dennis Randall, taken in Abercanaid with Mrs Hill, evacuees' welfare helper – photos from Jean Randall collection*

bananas with bread and butter. When I told Aunty Millie that we didn't have bananas for breakfast, she said, 'Well you do now!' We didn't have them for long because you couldn't get them later. The River Taff ran behind the houses and we had to go over a bridge to the Aberfan school where that terrible tragedy occurred. We had our own teachers and soon settled down.

Aunt Millie was very kind to us and she was a good cook. I learned how to make Welsh gravy and Welsh cakes; in the autumn we went up the mountain to pick blueberries and Aunt Millie would make lovely tarts. We had to go to chapel three times on Sundays and we were not allowed to play. We had to be quiet by reading or writing letters home. I was very homesick at times and sometimes I used to cry myself to sleep. I was very upset when my mother came to visit us and didn't take us back with her.

*Eric, Dennis and Jean Randall, Christmas, 1940.*

Aunt Millie had a sister and brother-in-law living two doors along the road and we called them gran and grandad. They were lovely, but gran was the boss and ruled over everybody. They had a daughter and son-in-law living with them, and they had two little boys. Grandad was caretaker of the chapel and Eric would help him. Another job Eric did was to help get the coal in. When the coal was delivered, it was dropped at the front door, then it had to be shifted through to the back. By the time Eric was finished, he looked just like a miner!

*'Gran' and 'Grandad' Guard with Aberfan in the background.*

We stayed for a year. Eric upset Aunt Millie so mum had to come and collect us. How brave mum must have been; it was the first time I saw my dad cry when we came in the door. So we came home to all the bombing and shelling. My dad was badly injured in the bombing of Betteshanger and died in 1943. Brother Eric later went into the Fleet Air Arm. I have been back to Wales several times since the war. It is all changed, no pit, no coal tips, and everywhere is clean. The daughter of gran is now in a home, but I still keep in touch with one of the boys.

***Marie Green*** *(now Mrs Pucknell) was introduced to farm life during her evacuation:*

Having been separated from my brother and sister, I finally arrived at a farm house at Undy Magor. There I was greeted by Mr and Mrs Beard, their son the Reverend Arthur Beard, his wife Pearl, their two children Robin and Anne, and Aunty Kate who was the sister of Arthur Beard. I remember they made me very welcome. They had another girl evacuee at the farm, but I can't remember her name. Before going to school we used to get up early and take the cows down to the field. Then we would come back and have breakfast. In the afternoon at about half past four we would go down to the field again, open the gate and the cows would follow us into the milking sheds. They all seemed to know which stall to go into.

One night we were all on our way to bed, Robin and Anne, my friend and I, when there was a terrible explosion. It seemed to shake the whole farm house. We were all taken back downstairs to a safer part of the house. We heard a lot more explosions after that. Mr Beard and other members of the family went outside to look, and I heard them saying the Germans were bombing Bristol, which was just across the River

*Marie Green (Pucknell) and her sister Margaret Green (Brian), taken at Blackwood in 1990.*

Severn, but he said that a few bombs must have gone astray. One fell further down the lane in someone's garden, but nobody was hurt. After that the German planes came over quite often. I remember seeing the big gasometers in Bristol burning and clouds of black smoke billowing into the sky; they seemed to burn for days.

Another job on the farm that we used to love doing was collecting the eggs from the chicken coops out in the field. Most of these eggs were taken to market in Newport on a Saturday morning, and I think it was all under the control of the Ministry of Food. But we children always had plenty of fresh milk and eggs. We were very lucky to have been billeted with such a wonderful family. We were so happy there; we couldn't have wished for better foster parents.

Behind the farm was a large apple orchard; when the apples were ready for picking we would gather up the ones that had fallen to the ground and Mrs Beard would make delicious apple pies with them. Each day Mrs Beard would make a great big pot of soup for all the family – there were nine altogether including us two evacuees. The only thing I didn't enjoy was teatime, when we would be given a big plate of cabbage to eat. This happened every day while we were in Wales. 'Eat it up,' Mrs Beard would say, 'it will do you the world of good, there is a lot of iron in it.' I would look at my friend and make a face at her, and she would do the same to me, but we had to eat it or go without our sandwiches and piece of home-made cake afterwards

There used to be crab apple trees in a field at the back of the farm house, and Mr Beard would get us to pick up buckets of apples which he would put into a machine. I remember asking him what he was doing with the apples and he said he was making a nice drink, although he would never give me any. I know now that it must have been cider he was making.

In 1943 I was told by my teachers that I would be going home. It was then I had to say my goodbyes to my foster parents who had been so wonderful to me, and there were sad faces as I boarded the train to leave. My mum and dad and little sister Rosemary were at Paddington Station to meet me and it cheered me up no end to see them.

*Joyce Hawkins (now Mrs Purssord), was evacuated with Barton Road Girls School, Dover:*

My hostess, Mrs Jones, was a retired headteacher, and married to David Jones, a winder at Wyllie Colliery. They had a five year old son, David. The house was in a terrace. The lavatory was just outside the backdoor. The kitchen was small, with a larder on one side, and a combination of washbasin, bath (covered with a board when not in use), and a wringer attached to the far end of the bath. There was a small front room and boxed-in stairs, at the top of which to the left was my boxroom bedroom, then there were the front and back bedrooms.

I was up early on the first morning and was allowed out to play. There were no houses opposite, only a gently sloping grass bank which led down to the railway line. Later I was taken up to see where my sister Jean was living. She was in the very last house in Glanhowy Road. As things turned out, Jean was not so fortunate as I was. She always seemed to look uncared for, whereas I was taught to clean my shoes and fold my clothes up. I wore black shoes and stockings for school, and brown for Sundays. I attended chapel on Sunday mornings and evenings; I can remember Mrs Jones putting her arm around me during the sermons.

It was during my early days with Mr and Mrs Jones that I learnt to eat porridge without sugar – to save the rations and help the war effort! I remember the slogan 'Dig for Victory' because Mr Jones dug up his front garden to grow potatoes. There were six or seven steps up to the back garden, and beyond these there were soft fruit bushes of all kinds. There were also onions, cabbages, lettuces and all manner of vegetables. All the produce looked lovely to me, as I had never seen such a garden.

In the kitchen of the house was a large range with a hob and oven where the family cooking was done. Above the range was a high mantle shelf with a narrow frill round it, to cover the line where washing was dried or aired. On the mantel, among other things, was always a box of chalks. The free side of the range was painted black to act as a blackboard and when any of my friends came to play, they were invited to do their 'tables', sums or writing on the wall. That wall proved a great blessing to me.

Our school lessons were held in a tin hut behind the chapel. It was there, in needlework classes, that I made my first dress for my sister Janet aged three years. It was pink. Our other lessons were held in the primary school at Ynysddu, a small village close to Wyllie, and at Cwmfelinfach in the church building. There we all had our photographs taken to send home to our parents. We used to walk to school but I suppose, being children, we thought nothing of it. We played about, or stopped to drink at the mountain spring on the way down to the main road.

Our swimming lessons were taken at the outdoor lido at the bottom of the hill in Wyllie. The water always felt very cold and I can still hear my sister Jean screaming as she caught her fingers in the large wooden mangle outside, where we wrung out our wet bathing costumes.

Poor Jean didn't last very long in Wyllie. Her foster father was rather fond of his drink, as I discovered during a visit from my parents. I must have written a letter home asking them to 'come and fetch Jean as I think she is dying!'. My mother told me this years later. When my parents arrived, they found Jean in an awful state, with sores and boils, not to mention general neglect – and Mr Davies none too sober! My foster parents tried to keep these things from me, telling me all about the evils of drink. They were so kind, and tried gently to tell me that Jean was going home with mum and dad, but I would be staying. Once again, being in a happy home, I accepted it all. Jean was bedridden and in need of medical care for several weeks afterwards; it was a long time before she fully recovered.

I sat for my 11+ scholarship in the school at Ynysddu. The desks and chairs were meant for five year olds and I was tall for my age. I remember how difficult it was to get my knees under the desk. However, I passed, thanks to my tuition from Mrs Jones at 'the blackboard wall'. I started at the Dover County School for Girls in Caerleon in September 1942.

I have been back to the Wyllie/Ynysddu area several times since the end of the war. On one visit I took my children to see Mr and Mrs Jones and later I went with my husband to stay for a week. The school at Ynysddu is no longer there, the community centre and chapel at Wyllie have gone, and the railway station and pithead are derelict. Our grassy bank was overgrown, as were the railway lines. The lido is derelict and the open fields leading to Pontllanfraith have been built on. Soon after our last visit Mrs Jones had a fall from which she never recovered; she died at the age of eighty-seven. Mr Jones never got over her death and went to live with David and his family, but died shortly afterwards at the age of ninety. It was the end of an era for me.

Anyway, off I went in September 1942, to Caerleon, a new school and a new billet. I went to live with another Mrs Jones, a widow, and her daughter Dorothy. I occupied the middle bedroom and Mrs Jones and Dorothy slept in the front bedroom. There was no bathroom – we used a tin bath in front of the living room fire. On my very first Sunday I discovered the difference between here and my first Mrs Jones. I was not allowed to read comics or anything resembling magazines or newspapers. They took neither, so I was not tempted! I was not allowed to sew or do French knitting which my first Mrs Jones had taught me.

I was allowed to attend chapel in the morning, Sunday School in the afternoon and chapel in the evening – *every* Sunday! However, I soon got used to the routine and came to love them both. Mrs Jones had been a ladies' maid, so her standards were high. The table was always correctly laid and, after meals, I was sometimes allowed to use the crumb tray and brush.

Our schooling at Caerleon was at various locations. Morning assembly was always held in the Baptist Chapel, and from there we would walk in 'crocodile', to our allotted place for the day. Sometimes we would meet in the Methodist Hall or the tin hut by the Anglican Church. On the days we met at the tin hut, I remember the class standing outside with our hands out-stretched for inspection for scabies, which was rife during the war. Imagine my horror when I was discovered to have it – just when I was about to start having piano lessons. I was sent, with several other girls from the school, to a large house in Blackwood, which acted as a hospital for us. I was there for a few weeks, but when I returned, my piano teacher had given my lessons to another girl. So I never learnt to play the piano! Other lessons, such as cookery, were taken at the elementary school in the main square of Caerleon. The place I remember most was training college at Caerleon. Here we had science, biology, gymnastics, needlework and others.

In the science room the desks were arranged in tiers and I used to sit at the very top row during needlework lessons. It was here that I lost my thimble. It was difficult to get at, so I was advised to report the loss. It was not until many years later, when I was married with two small children, that a small package arrived from Caerleon – it contained my thimble which had been found during alterations at the college.

We had a thriving Girl Guide company. At the time I was due to be enrolled as a guide, there was a terrible accident. Our beloved teacher Miss Rusbridge, also our Guide Captain, was riding to school on her bicycle when she was crushed against a wall in the narrow main street by one of the long trailers that passed through. She died and we were all devastated. After returning home to Dover in 1945, I continued to write to Dorothy and Mrs Jones. I visited them twice, but they are both now dead. Once again, the end of an era.

***Jean Smith*** *(now Mrs Fuller) lived at 45 Crabble Hill, Dover and went to Barton Road Girls' School at the time of the evacuation:*

I remember that Sunday morning, having a label tied to me and the train journey from Dover Priory Station. My father was in the Royal Navy so there was only my mother to see me off. She was very worried about me going. We arrived at Cwmfelinfach near Newport late in the evening. We had a meal in a large hall, then the nurse came to 'look us over'. We went then to our billets. The lady of the house where I went to wanted a brother and sister, but took me and my friend, Margaret

*Jean Smith, second from right, pictured with her foster parents in Cwmfelinfach*
*– photo from Jean Smith collection*

Lowden, instead. Our host was a deaconess of the local chapel. Once we had settled in we had to go to chapel every Sunday morning and afternoon, and to the Pentecostal of an evening. We were not allowed to knit or sew on a Sunday.

We were treated very well while we were with our foster mother, only sometimes we were a little hungry. They had a spare front room at the house which had no furniture in it – just lots of tinned food! I could never remember any of it being opened while we were there.

We went carol singing one Christmas, and the money we got, which wasn't much, we spent on sweets. Our school was at a village called Ynysddu, near Blackwood, and we only attended part-time. I was in Wales for about three years and very homesick. My mother moved from Dover to a safer area in the village of Ash. She then agreed that I should join her. I was put in the charge of the guard on the train, and that was a lovely feeling – I was going home!

***June Harrison*** *(now Mrs Bartle) was evacuated with her school from Sandwich:*

My family all lived in Sandwich, before the war. When evacuation came in June 1940, our parents decided that my sister May aged seven, my brother Fred aged six and myself aged eight should go. Our first billet in Wales was at a place called Stout Hall. I think most of our school was with us as our headmistress, 'Madam', and her two cocker spaniels were also there.

I can't remember much about the place or how long we were there, but my brother was ill and was moved to Madam's bedroom. I wasn't allowed to see him and I was caught wandering along the corridors looking for him. I eventually got to see Fred before they packed him off to hospital. May and I and a lad named Dicky Brett were then moved to a place called Pwll-Du-Bay. It was just two houses in a valley with hills on three sides and the sea on the fourth. I can remember after Madam had left us at Pwll-Du-Bay, we went into the garden, sat on a seat with my arms round May and Dicky, and cried our eyes out.

The people we were billeted with were a Miss James, Aunty Maud and Uncle Basil. Mrs Jenkins lived across the grass at the other cottage. Everyone was very kind to us. We had a lot of fun on the beach, and chasing the sheep up over the hills. We collected oranges that had been washed up on the beach and, if they weren't too salty, we would eat them. We used to gather blackberries which Aunt Maud would make into jam.

After a couple of months Fred was well enough to join us and, when he did, I think we got up to a lot of mischief! School was a long trip up the mountain and into the village. On windy days

110

the journey could be a bit frightening. We were in Wales eighteen months altogether. I never went back to Wales to visit my foster parents – nor to my home town of Sandwich.

*Marjorie Taylor (now Mrs Cockerill) went with St Mary's Roman Catholic School, Deal:*

My billeting arrangements were delayed because a younger girl, Janet, who was only four years old, refused to be parted from me. I was so upset at the thought that they kept me with her and took us both to her new family where I stayed for a couple of days. This house was some way out of Aberkenfig. What I remember most about that house was the flagstone floors and the outside pump for the water. The little girl was subsequently moved from the house and went to the local chemist's shop where she was really made to feel one of the family.

In the meantime, I was taken to St Bride's Road in Aberkenfig, where I met my 'new family', Mr and Mrs Knight and their son and daughter. I was made very welcome, not only by them, but by the uncles, aunts and grandparents. I thoroughly enjoyed being part of their extended family. The war didn't affect us too much. We saw the flames of the Port Talbot Docks and Swansea Docks when they were bombed, but luckily no bombs dropped on the village.

My father and my eldest sister, who was by this time in the ATS, were both able to come and stay with me during their time off work, thanks to the kindness of Mr and Mrs Knight.

I left school while I was still in Wales, but I stayed with Mr and Mrs Knight and got myself a job in Bridgend Woolworths office where I made many friends. I finally left the village and returned home to Canterbury in 1944 and stayed with an aunt. My reaction to the bomb damage of Canterbury was complete horror and shock. I had heard about the damage to the city, but to see it really brought it home to me. Layer I joined the WRAF and met the man I was to marry.

*Bob Dunford from Dover recalls his billeting experiences in Blaenavon with brother Sam:*

The first family we went to, the Challengers, were strict chapel people, and drinking, gambling or cards were strictly out, but Mr Challenger's brothers who worked in the pits, were much more liberal. We got on with all the people there, but it was quite a culture shock.

My brother and I used to have to take the Challengers' two young children, John aged seven and Keith aged three, out for walks on a Sunday – much to our annoyance! If we took them up to one of their uncles' houses on a Sunday afternoon, they would all be sitting round a table playing pontoon, and that's where I learnt to play! During the three months we stayed with the Challengers, we used to go to Sunday School in the morning followed by the

*Robert and Sylvia Dunford, pictured at an evacuee reunion at Dover, May 1995 – photo by Ted Green*

morning service, then we went home to lunch and at half past two we went to Sunday School again. If we were very unlucky, we would go back to chapel again in the evening!

Our next billet was in a mining home on the council estate. Our host was Mrs Davis and she let part of her house to her daughter and son-in-law and their two children. They were nice people and they were more relaxed about things. They didn't want to know where we were every minute of the day and we used to go out and roam over the mountainside all day long.

The only serious sign of war in Blaenavon was when there was a raid on Newport and a bomber, during the night, either got lost or just wanted to drop his bombs. He dropped two which exploded on top of Coity Mountain overlooking Blaenavon.

Blaenavon had two railway stations – lower level and upper level, each run by a separate company. The upper level station had a little halt on top of the hill that reckoned to be the highest station in Wales. The stations have now gone and there is no railway up to Blaenavon.

We had some good times down in Wales. There was an open-air swimming pool up by the playing fields. It was a lovely hot summer that year (1940), and we had great fun. I can remember the Co-op stores down at the bottom near the Working Men's Hall. I used to be fascinated by the contraption they had for handling money. When a customer handed over cash, it was put into something like a wooden ball, then they pulled a lever and it shot round to the cashier's office – then the change would come back.

Schooling arrangements in Blaenavon weren't very good. We attended a local church school which we shared with the Welsh children. One week we went in the morning, and the Welsh in the afternoon, and the following week we would change about. After nine months in Wales our parents wanted us back home. The journey back to Dover was quite an event for us because we had never ever done any travelling on our own. My father had arranged with a woman in Dover, a Mrs Burrows, to meet us at Newport Station. She was coming to Wales to visit her son who had been evacuated. Our host had promised to get us to Newport Station to meet Mrs Burrows. We travelled down with one of her sons who had been home on leave from the army. As soon as we got to Newport, he looked at his watch and said, 'I'm sorry lads, but I've got to catch my train now. Cheerio!' We were left, like two little orphans, sitting on our kitbags on Newport Station! We must have been on the station more than two hours before we eventually saw her. I don't think there were ever two kids in Britain more relieved than we were when we saw that good woman. We came back to London with her and for the first time in our lives we went on the London Underground. When we finally arrived home at the end of Lewisham Road at River, we went in and someone said, 'Oh, your tea is in the oven, go and get it.' There was no emotional greeting or anything. We were home!

*Jim Cullen* had been evacuated with Sir Roger Manwood's School from Sandwich to the Welsh village of Penclawdd but soon it moved to Carmarthen:

On the evening before we left Penclawdd the village put on a concert for us. Just think of it – a concert! Funny stories, conjuring and a bit of singing perhaps; we really looked forward to that evening. The concert was to be held in one of the chapels but, to our increasing consternation, the concert consisted of sacred music and poetry readings, most of which were in Welsh! Nevertheless, we were sorry to leave Penclawdd, with its cockles and warm-hearted people. As we left, the rumour spread that the local fish and chip shop was closed for the duration, as the proprietor had been interned when Italy entered the war. This amounted to a local disaster because fish and chips seemed to feature strongly in the local diet.

A fleet of coaches took us to Carmarthen where once again we went through a selection procedure, which I suppose could have been quite humiliating, rather like a slave auction. But our skins were thick. Dennis and I were very fortunate as we were billeted in a beautiful Georgian mini-mansion on the outskirts of the town. Our hosts employed a maid and a gardener whose principal task seemed to be to keep track of the peacock which had a roaming disposition. Life became more orderly, lessons were quickly resumed and then it was time for the summer holidays. Kent was a restricted area because of the invasion fears and we were not encouraged to go home. It was put to us very firmly that we should stay put! Queen Elizabeth's Grammar School, where we shared accommodation, had a flourishing Scout troop and a number of us were invited to join their summer camp at Wiseman's Bridge, near Saundersfoot.

It was one of the happiest holidays I have ever had. We were under canvas by the cliff edge, cooking our own food, collecting milk from the local farmer, having expeditions to the countryside and searching the rock pools on the shore. In the evening, before it got dark, we would sit around the camp fire and have songs, sketches and competitions . . . did he really eat 48 prunes? The fire was doused at dusk, but that was no great hardship as the country was on double summer time, two hours ahead of GMT. The war was coming closer. We read of the battles in the sky over Kent and the bombing of Ramsgate and Dover. One evening the German bombers set on fire the oil installations at Pembroke Dock. The following day the air was heavy with thick black smoke and then it rained and our tents were covered with an oily soot which got everywhere, even in the food as we were cooking it, but we ate up just the same.

Just after going back to school I contracted measles and was despatched to an isolation hospital near Swansea. My stay there coincided with the arrival of the last banana boat, because I have vivid memories of eating bananas at every meal and in every conceivable form – banana sandwiches, sometimes with jam, bananas and custard, sliced or mashed with jam or without, banana fritters and, a rare treat, bananas embedded in jelly. It was well over 40 years before I ate another banana.

At Easter I was allowed home for the holidays. Burton and mother were at the station, Tibbles the cat was in the sitting room, and I was home for three weeks, but something had changed – me! For in those nine months I had grown up a good deal and I gave away all my toys. Apart from school holidays, when I worked on farms which enabled us to buy a thermos flask and get increased cheese and butter rations, I spent the next three years nine months in Carmarthen, which was at that time a very grey town, washed all too frequently by the rain.

Looking back, time seemed to have gone quickly, but in reality it probably dragged. Our billets changed from time to time as our hosts got fed up with us – or we with them and relations became strained. The billets varied considerably. The first was wonderful but then Dennis and I moved to another fine house only minutes from the school. This house was ruled over with a rod of iron by the housekeeper who spent most of her time sitting on the kitchen fender, chain-smoking and supervising us whilst we did the washing up or cleaned the silver, or helped to prepare the food which came on two levels. The first level was for her employer, a widower who ate in state, alone, and who would dine on lean meat and green peas, whereas we made do with the fat and what seemed to be a mush made from the pods. It was at this billet that I skinned and paunched my first and last rabbit while the housekeeper rooted about in the innards, flourishing bits and pieces, giving us a lesson in practical anatomy.

In another billet I slept in the bath for a few nights; fortunately the taps didn't drip, but it meant that I was the last to go to bed and the first up in the morning. Generally though, we were very well looked after. As a school, we were pretty close knit. Few friendships were formed with local boys – or girls for that matter! It was almost Manwood's 'contra mundum'. None of us returned to Sandwich with any trace of a Welsh accent and we picked up little of the language. There was a book available, priced 6d, entitled 'Welsh in a Week', but I doubt that today it would meet the requirements of the Trades Description Act.

We were kept pretty busy. In the evening I would go back to school for 'prep' which ensured that I devoted adequate time to my homework. Games were compulsory, but I preferred the alternative which involved hauling a handcart around the town collecting salvage, or at times giving the local farmers a hand. Our sins were quite trivial. I can remember only one really serious piece of mischief in the early days at Carmarthen. One of the 5th formers 'took a bicycle without the owner's consent'; he was given a beating by the head in front of the school but, to our regret, we 2nd formers were excluded from the spectacle.

Like most youngsters we enjoyed a cigarette. A beating was automatic if you were caught and the same penalty was inflicted if we were caught eating fish and chips in the street, but of course the blackout gave us a measure of protection. The great thing though was to walk out to a remote country pub on a Sunday afternoon – when they were not allowed to open! We would go round to the back door and after a discreet look through the window the landlord would admit us to a back room where we found most of the males from the neighbourhood. After we had drunk our bottle of cider we would leave as quietly as we had come, for being caught would have had dire consequences. It was widely believed that some of our masters also made the journey on a Sunday but, thankfully, we never met; if they knew about us, they didn't let on.

In those days there stood in Carmarthen the ruin of a mighty oak, trousered in concrete and girdled by protective ornamental railings. Carmarthen was very much a Georgian town, and beautiful railings and balustrades were a feature of the place, but as war progressed these were removed and melted down. But not those surrounding the old oak. There was a plaque set into the concrete support which bore a legend:

When Merlin's oak shall tumble down
Then shall fall Carmarthen Town.

We gave serious thought as to how we could put the prophecy to the test, but felt on balance that if it was fulfilled by actions on our part then the consequences would be dire indeed as far as our immediate future was concerned. Many years later the stump was removed to the local museum and Carmarthen came into the hands of the developers who destroyed the character so perhaps the prophecy was fulfilled after all.

The war dragged on. Old boys earned decorations for heroic deeds and we stood proudly in assembly. Some, mercifully few, died and we bowed our heads in their memory. Alarms and incursions in the early days of the evacuation were hectic. Swansea was very badly bombed – my elder half-brother was there as an ack-ack gunner at the time. A lone and probably lost German plane loosed a small bomb at the town, which fell harmlessly on a hillside at Llangunnor and, when the explosion wakened Dennis and me, we found we were alone in the house; our hosts had taken to their heels! Without compunction, we helped ourselves to a mouthful of the master's whiskey and one of his cigarettes – to quieten our nerves!

Back and forth went our army in the desert. Crete fell and Dennis misheard the announcement of its invasion, thinking the Germans had landed here and we went outside to listen for the church bells to ring, for they had been silenced in 1940 for their sound to be an invasion signal. They did ring out in 1943 to mark the Alamein victory and how pleased we were to hear them. Churchill said, 'Not the beginning of the end, but the end of the beginning.'

D-Day dawned as we prepared for our School Certificate examinations but there were no signs of a return to Sandwich. We took our summer holidays at home against a background of the Allied advances in France and the impact of the flying bombs which at the time posed a serious threat to our home front. Exam results were posted – mine were mediocre. At that time I contracted jaundice so I was late returning to school. It was particularly annoying having jaundice at that time because father had a share in a pig which was killed and eaten while I was feasting on a fat free diet of dry toast and Oxo!

Back in Carmarthen the head suggested another complete year to improve on my results, stressing that, in his opinion, my maths results were the worst recorded since the school's foundation in 1563! I then decided to leave school at Christmas; another decision which very much shaped my future. Later, in the autumn of 1944, it was announced that the school would return to Sandwich after the end of term. As December approached, the mood lightened. Once more the books were packed, the stationery cupboards stripped, under strict supervision of course, for what schoolboy would not wish to 'win' a few pencils or exercise books. The JTC band instruments were cased for the return. The band had proudly participated in many of the parades: Remembrance Sunday, War Weapons Week and Wings for Victory, to mention a few.

My final few months had been spent with two delightful ladies. One, a widow with a son at a merchant navy college, and the other a telegraphist with the Great Western Railway. They were the epitome of kindness. We used to save the top of the milk and on Saturday evenings it was poured into a jar. A wooden peg would be added and the jar shaken as we listened to Saturday Night Theatre, at the end of which we would be rewarded with a small amount of butter.

I remember the last night spent in Carmarthen. Disturbed and restless, I seemed to spend the time trying to get to sleep. Was it excitement at the prospect of going home? No! The local timber yard, Blands, had caught fire during the night and it had been the noise and the flickering of the fire that had kept me in a state of wakeful drowsiness. The smoke was still heavy in the air as we went past the still smouldering ruins, to catch the 6.30am train to Paddington and home.

*Another Manwoodian, **Furley Spanton**, remembers those days in the 1940s:*

At the end of May 1940, Sir Roger Manwood's School left the various form rooms situated around Sandwich town, having been dispersed from the main school buildings for safety reasons, to travel away from their mother's apron strings for the first time in their lives.

By the time we had passed through Minster, Canterbury, Ashford, Tonbridge, Redhill, Reading, Cardiff and Swansea stations, and stopping to get out at Gowerton, most of us had got over the trauma of leaving home. We then embussed with our masters for the small cockling village of Penclawdd on the northern shores of the Gower Peninsula. Our stay here was short-lived due to lack of facilities for schooling and to some extent accommodation. This does not detract from the typical Welsh welcome from our hosts – nothing more could they have done to make us happy. As bathing facilities were not plentiful, the school had a weekly bath parade in the local Penclawdd Rugby Football Club's changing rooms.

The school moved in June to Carmarthen, where we were given a warm welcome. The boarding side plus a few others took over a farming institute complex at Pibwrlwydd; the remainder were put into billets around the town and close by. My brother and I were billeted with Mr and Mrs Evans at Heol-y-Delyn. Our home was on a high hill above the town and overlooked the River Towy wending its way out to sea in the distance.

The school shared form rooms in the Queen Elizabeth Grammar School for Boys and also had rooms in the adjacent Queen Elizabeth Grammar School for Girls, used by the 1st and 4th forms. I was lucky enough to be in the 4th form because here I met a lovely Welsh girl, who later became my wife and we have had a happy and wonderful life together. Two other Manwood boys also met Welsh girls whom they later married.

The school sports teams were rather neglected at the outset, but when Mr D. O. Griffiths joined the staff, things altered dramatically. In a short while we were playing rugby matches every week in the winter and cricket in the summer against such schools as Cardigan, Llandilo, Llandovery, Whitland, Gwendraeth, Llanelli, Haverfordwest and against English schools at Lampeter (Wycliffe College) and Whitland (Erith County School).

During school holidays various functions and activities took place to keep the boys occupied. Mr Brown the chemistry master was a keen cyclist and took groups of boys for tours around Carmarthenshire. Often it happened that the cycle was taken for a walk due to the hills! During summer holidays a few pupils were allowed home if permission was granted, in fact two boys cycled home using hostels along the way. During the years 1941/42, senior boys under the direction of a master, had to do fire-watching duties if the siren sounded within the school precincts – fortunately this didn't happen very often. Carmarthen only received a few incendiaries dropped on Llangunor Hill just outside the town. Where my brother and I were billeted, we could see the red glow in the sky as Swansea was bombed. I came home in 1942, my brother returned home in 1943, and the school returned to Sandwich in December 1944.

***John J. Smith*** *was aged almost eleven when he was evacuated from Dover to Blaenavon:*

At the outbreak of the war I was attending St Mary's Boys' School in Dover. I was also a member of the church choir and when the first siren sounded at 11am on Sunday, 3rd September 1939, there was a hush from the congregation; I remember my father coming to the side door with our gas masks. We hurried home as fast as our legs would take us, and made straight for the air-raid shelter. Eventually, all St Mary's Boys were evacuated to Blaenavon in South Wales. On 2nd June 1940, we were put on a train at Dover Priory Station and set off on our long journey. When we arrived at Blaenavon we were taken from the station in private cars to the centre of the town and faces of women appeared through the car doors and windows, choosing the child that they wanted. I was the last in my car and I could hear the people outside saying, 'I can't take him, I've already got one.' It seemed that no-one wanted me.

Eventually, Mrs Trott of Lower Duke Street said she would have me, as well as an older boy from Dover, Johnny Laury. The house was very old and we had to draw our water from a tap in the garden. When we had a bath we had it in front of the fire – she had a great big Yorkshire range fire and I can recall her making Welsh pancakes on it. While in Wales I joined the local choir. Schooling was not entirely satisfactory. I can remember that we had our classroom in a corridor because we had to squeeze into the local school house. I learned to play snooker in the Blaenavon Working Men's Club; when my father visited, I took him there and we had a game.

I was continually writing home to my parents, asking them to come and bring me home, as I didn't like being evacuated one little bit, but I had to stick with it until one day I had a letter from my parents. They told me that our house in Stembrook, Dover, had been hit by a shell, and that dad had been allocated a miner's house in Elvington, which was some miles out of the town. As it was considered a slightly safer place than Dover, my parents said they were going to come and fetch me. So after eleven months in South Wales, I returned to Kent.

***Frank E. Davies*** *was a Dover County School pupil and he tells of his life in Cwm:*

The day after we arrived in Cwm, a train took us to Ebbw Vale. It was a lovely day and soon we enjoyed a walk to Ebbw Vale Grammar School which we were to share with the Welsh pupils on a shift basis. Having come from an all-boys school, I was very attracted by the sight of so many girls in the school and I was told later that the attraction was mutual.

We had to get down to work quickly, since our vital exams would soon be on us. We had to go to another school to sit the exams. This was in Tredegar, a small town at the head of the next valley. I never minded exams and life seemed very pleasant. We had been well taught, so there was time for recreation which, for me, was mainly walking the steep hills – right to the top. My favourite was the mountain called 'Old Man Noel'.

There were many sheep and they always looked dirty and wild. There were also 'wild' ponies which used to come into the village, pushing over dustbins, mainly at night. After I had been with Mr and Mrs Worthing for a while, Mrs Worthing told me that she was expecting a baby, so they arranged for me to go and live with the Vicar of Cwm, the Reverend Basil Williams. They had a daughter Joan, roughly my own age. The vicarage was a lovely house and they had a grand piano that I was able to play. I also had the use of the church organ next door.

*Ebbw Vale Grammar School, now a comprehensive – Peter Hayward collection*

Cwm was a mining village and the colliery was below the village. A small river ran between the village and the mountain. It moved quite rapidly and always smelt strongly of chemicals. Between Cwm and Ebbw Vale was the huge steelworks and we travelled through it every day. It was always a busy scene, even at weekends and at night; trainloads of molten slag from the works were tipped out on to the mountainside, a bright red glow lit up the sky. It seemed a strange thing to do at night during wartime but while I was there we had no air-raids. German bombers did dreadful damage to Swansea and Cardiff and we occasionally heard the drone of the bombers returning home.

When the summer holidays came I was allowed to go home to Aylesham. It was great to get home. Nothing had changed and it was a glorious summer, but there was no opportunity to visit the seaside. The coast was out of bounds. Concrete obstructions, gun positions and mines had been put in place to help prevent German troops from landing in the expected invasion.

It was while I was home that I saw the start of the Battle of Britain in the skies over Kent. Glistening shapes of aircraft, friend and foe, could be seen twirling and turning. Tracer streaks and vapour trails wove fantastic patterns against the blue sky, and the shrieks and whines of diving aircraft, hit and out of control, added to the spectacle. It was a tremendous fight that I shall never forget, but tragic, as we watched aircraft with young men unable to escape, plunge to their death. By the middle of September the Battle of Britain was over.

I returned to Wales knowing that I had done well in my exams, but I couldn't help worrying about my father back home and often wondered what would happen if Snowdown Colliery, where he worked, was destroyed by enemy action. Meanwhile, here I was living in the safety of a Welsh valley and falling for a Welsh girl, Mary, the first of a few! Several of these romances resulted in marriages later. One of the boys, Roy Howard, lived in Aylesham near me.

When I was studying for my Higher Schools Certificate, I had a serious accident. I was cycling back from school on Friday, 13th June, 1941, and coming down the hill from Ebbw Vale to Cwm, my front wheel hit an object in the road, and I was thrown over the handlebars. The result was a fractured skull and broken collar bone. I was several weeks in Ebbw Vale General Hospital and suffered severe concussion. I was just recovering from this blow when, in the autumn term of 1941, I was back in hospital to have an operation for the removal of my appendix. My sport, studies and music were all affected and subsequently my exam results. However, my 'matric' results were good enough to allow me to go to college.

I left Wales in July 1942 and, after working on a farm for the holidays, I went as a student to Nottingham University. In June 1944, I left there to join the Royal Navy.

*Violet Lamoon*, *of Astor Avenue Girls School, Dover, recalls her stay in the Pengam area:*

I was with a nice family, Mr and Mrs Tom Jones. They had three sons, two of whom worked in the coal mines. My foster-parents kept pigs out in the back garden; sometimes they would kill one and I used to help rub salt into the meat to make bacon. I watched them kill the pigs and I helped shave the hairs off. I also watched the pigs giving birth. I also remember having lots of Weetabix in bowls of cocoa. I thought that was lovely. I was in Wales for nearly three years and the older I got, the more I wanted to come home. After a lot of pleading with my parents, they arranged for me to return home. My younger sister and brother, who were with St Barts School, remained in Blackwood for a long time afterwards. I don't think my parents could afford their fares home. While I was away in Wales, my parents had to move because our house was badly damaged in the shelling, but thankfully no one was hurt. I think we were all home before the end of the war because I can remember us all running to the shelters – but that's another story!

***Dee Croucher*** *was evacuated with St Martin's School, Dover, and billeted in Argoed:*

The day after our arrival in Wales, we were told to report to the school for lessons. I got lost on the way home and had to ask my way to the billet. We were all different ages in school; the youngest being only four or five, and the oldest up to eleven years of age. The youngest girl in the class was always crying. Her name was Shirley Bradbury and she had a sister June who was nine years old – the same age as me. Shirley didn't settle, and soon returned home. We had two teachers, Miss Page and Miss Harmer. I remember a small, very thin girl named Doreen. She was always being picked on and pushed about. I used to feel sorry for her. I think she must have gone home early because she wasn't around for long. After a while our school moved to the Miners' Welfare Hall. I don't remember many lessons, but we went for lots of nature walks. Miss Harmer had two dogs and they came too. Miss Page and Miss Harmer stayed at the Argoed Arms Hotel, and my 'Auntie' used to do their washing.

As numbers dwindled we were sent to Markham School. There we were joined by some London evacuees. Finally those who were left were sent to Argoed School. By this time our teachers had returned to Dover. We were treated well at Argoed School. The only lesson we didn't like was cookery. The teacher always got on to us, saying that our aprons weren't ironed properly. It wasn't our fault, we couldn't even do our own washing.

We heard the German planes fly over when they bombed Cardiff and Birmingham. We watched the sky that night and knew the bombing had been bad. I stayed in Argoed until Christmas 1944, when we all returned home. I remained in contact with my foster-parents after the war, but now they are both dead. I shall never forget all their kindness towards me.

***Mr W. Skelton*** *spent time in Cwmbran and Ebbw Vale:*

While I was in Cwmbran I sat the 11+ exam and when I passed – the first Holy Trinity boy for many years – the headmaster gave the school a half day's holiday; I was a hero! Father, when he heard, decided that as the school was in Ebbw Vale and not in Cwmbran, I should return as an evacuee. Thus, I arrived in Ebbw Vale in October 1941, some time after the school term had started. I was billeted in a large house with four bedrooms, along with another boy, Brian Pursey. Our hosts were Mr and Mrs Lewis and their daughter Phyllis. They were a wonderful family who tended our every need. We were well fed and well clothed. As two normal lads, we often got into mischief and were threatened at the end of each term that we would be re-billeted, but each time a promise of better behaviour did the trick.

There are many things I remember about life in Ebbw Vale, such as half-time schooling, church attendance, the billiard hall, lunch times and the girls, rugger and soccer – and many more! I stayed with Mr and Mrs Lewis until I returned to Dover with the school in 1944 and, on saying our goodbyes to them, I was surprised to find them, and us, in tears!

***Joyce Pellett*** *(now Mrs Pascoe), from Folkestone, speaks of her life in Croesyceiliog:*

My sister Vera and I were lucky to get the same host family when we were allocated billets, so we managed to stay together. We were put with Mrs Kidner, and our address was 36 The Woodlands, Croesyceiliog. Her husband worked in the Avondale Steelworks. The home was very clean and Mrs Kidner was a very good cook. I often think of her and the delicious fruit cakes she used to make. To get our drinking water we had to pump it from a well. Most of our washing and bathing water was rainwater, caught in a big tank. I can recall Monday mornings as washday, with Mrs Kidner heating the water in a copper, and scrubbing the washing on a scrubbing board. She was a very religious lady and we were made to go to chapel three times on a Sunday. She had had two daughters of her own, but one had died from tuberculosis and the other had died in childbirth. She would often say that having Vera and me was like having her two girls again. She was very kind to us and I think in one way we were very good for her.

Schooling wasn't much fun, in fact I hated every minute of it! In the beginning we were kept separate from the local children and our classroom was in the hallway of the school. We had our own teachers from Folkestone. The ones I can remember were Mrs Wicke, our headmistress, and Miss Ewell. After a while we were mixed in with the local children, who, although not Welsh speaking, spoke with a very strong Welsh accent. We didn't like this very much. We were teased about the way we spoke. We were called 'posh' because we spoke so differently. We were also called 'vaccees', and this I think, had a lot to do with my education – or lack of it.

Although Mrs Kidner was very kind to us, we missed our family very much. We would cry ourselves to sleep most nights. Mrs Kidner was very deaf and, when we had air raid warnings in the area, she would leave us in our bed feeling very frightened. After some time our parents and older brother and sister also came to Wales. Our parents rented a property and my sister and I then went to live with them. Eventually, our parents were allocated a council house in Pontnewydd which remained the family home for many years.

On leaving school I had various jobs. When I was seventeen I joined the Land Army and that is where I met my husband. We have been happily married for 44 years. Sadly, my sister Vera who was evacuated to Wales with me, died in December, 1994. I never returned to Folkestone to live after the war, but I did go back some years ago, just for a holiday. I enjoyed my brief visit and it was nice to see my old home again, but I have thoroughly enjoyed my life in Wales.

*Jean Pidduck (now Mrs Arnold) was an evacuee from Sandwich:*

I was eleven years old and my cousin Constance was nine when we were both evacuated in 1940. Constance was at Sandwich Primary School, and I was at Sandwich Secondary School.

I remember going to the railway station, on the day of evacuation. We weren't supposed to take suitcases so the owner of the second-hand furniture shop in Dover Road made up some large haversacks in a type of oilcloth. I don't remember much about the long journey, but we stopped somewhere and were given sandwiches. Mr Sage, who later became headmaster at Sandwich Junior School, was one of the teachers who travelled with us. I think we left the train at Swansea and then travelled by bus to Three Crosses. I remember being in a hall and the children being chosen by the locals. My cousin started to cry when it seemed that nobody wanted us. Eventually, we were taken by the minister's wife to live in the manse.

*Jean Pidduck and cousin Joan in the Manse garden, August 1940 – Jean Arnold collection*

On Sundays we were expected to go to both chapel and Sunday school, and were not allowed to play. We were, however, encouraged to sit and read quietly, which suited me! They didn't have any children of their own, and I think they probably found us difficult to look after. When Swansea got badly bombed, my uncle came to Wales to take us home, probably because our families thought we would be just as safe in Sandwich. It must have been in 1942 when we returned, because I can remember watching Canterbury in flames.

119

*On the Beach*
*A group of Sandwich school children (including Jean Pidduck) enjoying a day at the seaside in*
*Wales during their evacuation – Jean Arnold collection*

**Edwin Henry Brown** *remembers his time in Aberkenfig and Cardiff:*

My sister and I were attending St Ethelburgha's Convent in Queen Street, Deal. We left Deal one morning by train. I was five years old and I missed my mother immensely. On one of the many stops on the way to Wales we were given lemonade to drink. The gas from the lemonade went up my nose and quite frightened me. I thought in my childish way that this was the war, so drinks would always be like this – and would I ever see my mother again!

We finally arrived at a small mining village, Aberkenfig, assembling in the village hall to await our fate. My sister and I stood with our labels long after all the other children had gone to their various billets. It wasn't that we were undesirable, but the people we were intended for didn't turn up for a long time. As it turned out my sister and I were billeted in separate houses, but in the same terrace. I was very homesick and was reluctant to leave my sister's side.

I remember my first evening in my new home. My hosts gave me a bath in a tub on the table, and all the family stood round to watch this spectacle. I don't know if they thought we were differently formed from the Welsh people! Anyway, my hosts, Mr and Mrs Davis, turned out to be good and kindly people. I gradually settled in and, after some time, my longing for my mother was not quite so painful. My foster-parents seemed as old as the hills, but looking back I expect they were in their forties. Mr Davis' health was completely broken through working in the pits and I think he had very little strength to do anything.

Once I got badly stung and Mrs Davis put a small tub of soapy liquid on a chair for me to put my hand in. She even made me a small paper boat to push round in the water with my poor hand to ease the pain. After some months I remember an air raid siren sounding and saw

120

screaming women rushing and running by me for safety. I was left walking casually up Main Street all on my own. It was of course a false alarm. I had heard plenty of sirens and seen many aircraft from the early days of 'Hell Fire Corner'.

Well into my stay I caught pneumonia, due I suspect to the damp climate, and my mother and father came to see me with some urgency. Our parents were missing us and wanted to get away from the bombing in Deal, so my father got a job in a factory in Cardiff. My happy stay with Mr and Mrs Davis therefore came to an end. We all moved to Cardiff and stayed there until the end of the war. Ironically, our first house in Cardiff was bombed, but none of the family was hurt. Our school was near the docks and, although the buildings around it had been flattened by the German bombing, we never missed a day. Going over the bridge I used to look longingly on the way to school, between picking up shrapnel, but the school was always missed in the bombing, and the teacher was always waiting for us. Being a Roman Catholic school, we had ten minutes of chanting 'Jesus give us peace,' and then it was into our lesson, war or no war! We stayed in Wales until January 1946 and then returned to Deal.

*Peter Prescott* met his future wife in Ebbw Vale:

On the morning after our arrival in Waunlwyd, we went by train to Ebbw Vale where we assembled at the County School and were told that we were to share the school premises with Ebbw Vale County School pupils on a half day each basis and this continued for all my time at the school. When we were not actually working in school, the staff kept us occupied and many weary miles we, and they, tramped over the mountains. I marvel at the hours they put in and it shows their devotion to their charges. True professionals to a man – and woman!

We soon settled into a routine and got to know the 'natives'. Curiously the local lads were not very willing to fraternise, but the girls were more amenable and many very innocent liaisons took place. A few long-term relationships developed – ours for one: 55 years this year (1997).

Each week we were taken to the pit-head baths at Waunlwyd and indulged in a shower. Many of the houses then did not have bathrooms and baths were taken in front of the kitchen fire – we were privileged. One courtesy was afforded us which some found of great benefit. We became members of the Institute. At any time we could go to the 'Stute' for a game of billiards or snooker or play cards. Many a happy hour was spent there and some of us learned to play billiards or snooker to a good standard. I discovered Ebbw Vale Library and began to read voraciously – which I have done ever since. Those of us in Waunlwyd began to attend the church and joined the choir. We also attended the youth club and learned to dance.

Each day we would go to and from school by train. Sometimes we would go to a local cinema and return in a blacked-out train with the munitions workers on their way for the night shift. They sang very well! I recall that a sporting rivalry developed between EVCS and our school. They thrashed us at rugby and we thrashed them at cricket. There was the Army Cadet Force and this took up a great deal of time for many of us. Various schemes were arranged over the mountains and there was a drum and bugle band and it was very good indeed. I recall playing a drum in the front row of the band which lead a great parade through Ebbw Vale to celebrate the victory at Alamein. At the church service after the parade I sang with the bass section and I remember the tremendous verve of that congregation. It was as if a great weight had been lifted from us. I cannot now listen to 'Guide Me O Thou Great Redeemer', sung to *Cwm Rhondda*, without feeling a wave of emotion – and that service was over 50 years ago.

While in Ebbw Vale I heard Aneurin Bevan, then MP for Ebbw Vale, talk about socialism at the Palace Cinema. It was a spell-binding performance. I also saw Sybil Thorndike and Lewis Casson in *Macbeth* at the Workmen's Hall – a truly brilliant performance. The school put on *Androcles and the Lion* by George Bernard Shaw, at the Workmen's Hall. The play was in modern dress and cadet uniforms came in handy for the Roman soldiers.

Some abiding memories of my stay in South Wales are: the smell of the coke ovens, the lights of the steel works and the Bessemer Converters spewing out great sheets of flame and orange smoke; the molten slag pouring down the mountainside; the rain; the singing; the long walks over the mountains; the staff of Dover County School – John Booth, a gentleman; W. E. Pearce; Billy Baxter; Coulson; Kendall; Archer; Darby, etc. etc. All of them true professionals for whose care and devotion we must all be truly grateful. Finally, I remember the great kindness and forebearance of the Welsh people.

*Jean Simpson (now Mrs Gladish) from Dover recalls time with her sister in Cwmfelinfach:*

The lady who had taken us in was a widow with a grown up family, and it was a very clean and comfortable home. We were well looked after and had our own bedroom. Sunday tea was always something special, such as stewed rhubarb and custard with bread and butter.

They were a devout chapel family; we had to go to chapel three times on a Sunday and we were not allowed to play. When we did go out to play it would be by the 'black' river, or on the slag tips that were at the bottom of our street. Little did I know that the evacuee boy next door with whom I played, would one day become the last mayor of the Borough of Dover and, later, chairman of Dover District Council. His name was Peter Bean.

I remember my sister and me coming home for the Christmas holidays and, as she had never been happy in Wales, she persuaded our parents to let her stay at home. However, I went back quite happily for another year and came home the following Christmas, travelling all on my own. Then my mother received a letter from my landlady which upset and shocked her. It was a request asking if she could adopt me! This really frightened my parents and they decided, shells or no shells, I shouldn't go back, so I stayed with my family in Dover. I went back to Wales for a holiday after the war when I was twenty years old and again I was warmly welcomed by the foster family. They made a considerable fuss of me once again. I also called to see them when on holiday with my husband in 1992 when we went to the Ebbw Vale Garden Festival. The area has completely changed. The slag heaps have gone, the river was running clear, and there were fir trees on the hills – entirely different from the black days of 1940. The mother had died, but the sons and daughters were considerably thrilled to see us and kept saying, 'You have come home again.' We still receive Christmas and Easter greetings cards from the family.

*Duncan Turner was evacuated with St Mary's Boys' School, Dover, to Blaenavon in Monmouthshire – where he and many other evacuees were destined to stay after the war!*

Joseph May and I were billeted with Mr and Mrs Williams at the Avionic Bakery and shop in Broad Street, which was one of the main shops in the town. Once we were settled in, schooling became a priority, although we didn't attend full-time school for quite some time. Many of us went to St Peter's Church School, in Church Road. This school was split into the girls, boys and infants. The school time was shared by us evacuees and the local children.

We had our own teachers while we were at school and I remember our headmaster, Mr A. J. Wheldon, used to live in a large house at the lower end of Cwmavon Road. He always reminded me of a colonel in the army, being very upright and with a waxed moustache. One of the other teachers was Mr Carter. Benny Haines was a fine friend and companion, and he was another evacuee who stayed after the war. Ben worked underground at Big Pit for many years. He met a young lady from Dover while on holiday abroad and decided to return home shortly afterwards!

Tommy Law, from a large family in Dover, was yet another boy who stayed on in Blaenavon after the war. He got a job in the lamp room at Big Pit and worked there until Big Pit closed. In about 1993, he returned to Dover. Other boys I remember from those schooldays in Blaenavon are Edgar Kearsly, John Hoy, John Steel and John Ashly.

Eventually, we started full-time schooling, but this was not until we transferred from the church school to Penual Chapel where we had more room. By this time I believe that some of the older boys had gone to Park Street Secondary School. We would begin school with morning assembly and hymns and occasionally we would sing our old Dover school song:

> Success to all St Mary's Boys,
>     Of Dover by the sea,
> So sing together one and all,
>     And that right heartily.
>
> We love the time we spend at school,
>     And strive to do our work,
> So let's be earnest in our aims,
>     And never, never shirk.
>
> Then let us give three hearty cheers,
>     Resounding near and far,
> And wish good luck to our old school,
>     Hurrah, Hurrah, Hurrah!

Later, we boys had to vacate Penual Chapel and resume school with the Dover girls, which resulted in mixed classes. Our school now was in the Sunday School classrooms situated behind the Wesleyan Chapel. I can recall the headmistress, Miss James who was very tall, prominent, dark-haired and very efficient. It was during this period that I got to know some of the Dover girls. There were Dora Hedges and her sister Brenda, two very pleasant girls, whose mother was also in Blaenavon, and who was in charge of an evacuee hostel at Forge Side. Then there were Dawn Terry, Ruby Crofts, Betty Nicolas and Joyce Morrisey.

Soon there was a further intake of evacuees into Blaenavon. They came by Top Line Station, This time the evacuees came from Walthamstow in London. Our foster-parents, Mr and Mrs

*Big Pit, Blaenavon, drawn by Don Lewis*

Williams, took another lad in, by the name of Roger Bacon. He turned out a fine young fellow. Mrs Williams' daughter Jane took in two more; Roy Miller and Eric Turner.

We didn't see much of the war in Blaenavon but there were a few incidents. We had a Royal Ordnance factory at Glascoed, near Usk, which was about thirteen miles away. It was a difficult place for the Germans to find, but one did slip through on one occasion and drop a few bombs, but little damage was done. Another time, a German bomber came over and dropped eight bombs right on top of Coity Mountain which rises above Blaenavon. The bombs dropped near Carlo's headstone, a local monument erected in 1864. The last visit from the Germans was when, on a beautiful sunny day, a single bomber came in so low that his markings could be clearly seen, dropping some incendiary bombs, which caused a few fires but no serious damage.

Eventually I reached school-leaving age, and our headmaster, Mr Wheldon, wrote me a reference. Mr Carter, our teacher, accompanied me to my first employment which was at Pontypool Road Station. This was to be the first of many jobs I had in the area. After working underground at Big Pit in Blaenavon, I was drafted into the Welsh Guards, being demobbed in 1950. I eventually settled down and married a local girl and we have a daughter and two sons, all of whom are now grown up. When I think back to those days in 1940, I also think of how little has been said about the way the people of Blaenavon opened their hearts to us evacuees. They gave us refuge, hospitality and love in those dark days, and we should be eternally grateful. I never returned to Dover after the war, but instead I put my roots down in Blaenavon. This is my home now, with my wife, family and many friends. I hope the following poem that I have written shows the love I feel for my adopted home:

### THESE ARE MY MOUNTAINS

These are my mountains, they are my home,
Wherever I wander, wherever I roam.
To the top of the Coity all covered in snow,
I and my sons for a walk we did go;
By the headstone we rested, of Carlo the dog,
Who worked for his master in sun, rain and fog.
A tribute to a Kennard, a man of the past,
Who helped build Blaenavon which still stands fast.
Way down in the valley by rivers and trees,
Echoes the laughter, so gay and carefree,
Of the people who live there and toil in the town,
Deep in the coal mines and steel mills around.
Way out on the Blorenge, what a beautiful sight,
Bathed in God's sunshine, and moonlight by night.
Just alongside the car park, lies Foxhunter's grave,
Sir Harry Llewellyn, his name he made,
And now down yonder lies Llanover Estate,
Just round the bend, Abergavenny its mate.
At the heads of the valley lies the town of Brynmawr;
Who lived there first, no one knows now.
To the north lie the Beacons,
Their peaks capped in snow.
It's the same in Blaenavon, wherever I go,
These are my mountains, they are my home,
Wherever I wander, wherever I roam.

*James Mack, evacuated with Barton Road Boys' School, Dover, shared his billet two other Dover boys, Gordon Saunders and Tony Lay in Cwmfelinfach.:*

My foster-mother, Mrs Pritchard, was a natural motherly sort, I suppose mid-fifties, iron-grey hair, small, quite plump – not fat! And she was a very good caring mother to us three boys. I guess we added to her grey hairs as time went by, but it was all taken in good part. Then there was Mr Pritchard, tall, very upright, sandy coloured hair with not the slightest hint of grey. He was a banksman at Risca Colliery, some three miles down the valley towards Newport. He always walked to and from work, whatever the shift or weather. He would never use the pit head baths, but preferred the old way – the tin bath in front of a roaring open fire.

Also in the household was Gertie, Mrs Pritchard's sister. She had been born with a speech deformity but she did her share of looking after the three of us. This, then, was the family that we joined, at 17 Arthur Street, Cwmfelinfach, and we very soon became part of that family. Meanwhile, the Barton Road Girls had been taken to the next village of Ynysddu, up the Tredegar Valley. It wasn't too long before we got back into the school routine, but we were unable to join the local children in school – there just wasn't enough room for us all. There was no room at all in Cwmfelinfach, so we had to walk daily to Ynysddu. I think teachers and pupils did quite well in difficult circumstances. For all the disruption we must have caused in the quiet life of the people of these two villages, I don't recall any outbreaks of trouble.

After we had settled into the routine of our new life, one of the teachers realised 'Boys need haircuts,' and with most of us lacking in money, a solution had to be found. That solution was me! I'd been given a pair of clippers, scissors and a comb – and then a head to experiment on. I was, from then on, the make-shift barber. My victims never looked too bad!

After a few months a trickle of evacuees began returning to Dover. I suppose parents felt less threatened by invasion fears than they had earlier in the year. Sadly, in November, Gordon received news that his eldest brother had been killed in action. Naturally his mother was keen to have him home, so off he went. Shortly after this, Tony's mother sent for him, and I was then alone with the Pritchard family. I didn't want to return home as I had no father there, but now I had one in Cwmfelinfach and I wanted so much to stay there. I felt that the Pritchards had taken to me and they didn't want to lose me. I was extremely happy with this. As we got into 1941, our school was asked to enter some of us for an essay competition. Mine was on 'National Savings and the War Effort', and I was amazed when this appeared in the post office window. I had won first prize – 15 shillings in savings stamps! I kept these stamps for a good few years.

I had to start thinking of life after school as I had now turned 14 and I knew the end was approaching. My two brothers had joined the army as apprentice tradesmen, so I decided to try. I was eventually successful and received my joining instructions to travel to Aborfield Army Apprentice School near Reading on 14th April 1942. I had the privilege of having almost two very happy years of being part of a homely, happy family. The Pritchards couldn't have been better to me if I'd been born to them. My memories are still very vivid. Like having a glass of cider and a cheese sandwich before going to bed that first night. Of Tony Lay playing the piano, particularly the tune of *The Blue Danube*. Of wandering up the mountain paths and looking down the valley. Stacking the free issue coal in the coal shed to save Mr Pritchard a job when he came home from work. Of standing in the kitchen one day and cooking a whole basketful of sprats. And of my slow walk to the bus stop to go to Newport to catch the train on 14th April!

They were happy days for me. Sadly I have never returned to Dover to live and consequently I have had no contact with those who boarded the train at Dover Priory on 2nd June 1940.

*Eileen Neville* (now Mrs Lacey) *was evacuated with the Dover County School for Girls to Caerleon. Her sisters Pam and Betty, were at other schools to different areas in South Wales.*

My friend Ellen and I had been taken to a Mr and Mrs Cook on our arrival in Caerleon. The next day we posted off the cards to our parents telling them our address, then we assembled at the local junior school, where we were told that this would be our place of education for the time being. I continued to be very homesick. Ellen was the eldest of six children and she seemed to come to terms with being away from the family better than me. I still cried every night, missing my family very much. I received a letter from my parents saying that my sisters had been sent to Llangynwyd near Maesteg. They had been billeted together with a Mr and Mrs Williams and seemed to have settled down well. My cousin Josie was at Cwmbran, just a few miles away, so I didn't feel quite so lonely. Letters from home seemed few and far between. The blitz on London continued and the shelling of Dover intensified. We heard all this on the radio and in the newspapers; we could only hope and pray that our families were safe.

My dad decided to move from the coast, so he got a job working for the railway, taking the office workers out of London. He qualified for cheap fares. It was ages before I learnt where mum and dad had gone because the first place they moved into was destroyed by a land mine and they were a long time finding new accommodation. Eventually, I had a letter telling me that they had moved into a flat in South Harrow, Middlesex, their home for the next six months.

Back in Wales schooling continued in a haphazard fashion. We even used a school in Pontypool for a while. After I had been in Caerleon for three months, my host Mrs Cook became pregnant and it was decided that one of her evacuees had to go. Ellen and I were split up and I was sent to a Mrs Dixon, together with Grace, another friend of mine. Mrs Dixon had three daughters of her own living at home, Edna aged 7, Christine aged 5 and little Noreen who was about two, so as Mr Dixon was away in the forces, it was a truly female household.

We were each given our own ration of butter, marge and cheese, while the rest of the rations, such as tea, sugar and meat, were pooled. We weren't supervised with regard to cleanliness or homework. Our washing was done for us, but we did our own ironing and were expected to help with the family's ironing. All in all, we were left to get on with life in our own way.

Each host family received a weekly allowance for looking after evacuees, which must have been a great help to Mrs Dixon while her husband was away. We helped with the children of course and became quite fond of them, especially little Christine. She was a pretty little dark-eyed girl and full of mischief. One day Christine became ill. At first it was thought to be influenza, but she became progressively worse. I remember being sent to the district nurse's house to get some Thermogene wadding to put on her chest to help her to breathe. We evacuees were sent away temporarily to another house, as poor Mrs Dixon couldn't cope. Her other children went to relations. Unfortunately, Christine died. It was so sad. It was my first brush with death and one I will never forget.

After this sad time we were all moved yet again. This time I went to live with Mr and Mrs Strong. They had two sons at home and a married daughter whose husband was in the forces. Another girl called Ivy was billeted with me, so it was quite a houseful. Ivy and I shared a bedroom with the married daughter. I stayed with this family until I returned home.

During the first year of evacuation my mum came down on the train with Kit, my youngest sister. I hadn't seen them for eight months. It was also Pam's 9th birthday. I met the train at Newport and travelled down to Bridgend with them. We never stopped talking and hugging. At Bridgend we caught the bus to Maesteg to see my other two sisters. As it was the school holidays I was able to stay with them for a week, but the time flew by and soon it was time to leave. We said our goodbyes and left for the bus stop, then all of a sudden there was a commotion as Pat and Pam came running down the road crying, 'Don't leave us, mummy.' They were followed by their host, Mrs Williams, shouting, 'Don't come here again if its going to upset them so much!' We were all crying and, as the bus pulled up, we managed to get on amid more tears as we waved goodbye, leaving poor Mrs Williams to cope with the children.

When we got to Bridgend we boarded the train. Soon it was my turn to get off and, as we approached Newport, there were more tears and frantic hugs. I was once again on my own heading back to Caerleon. It was to be another ten months before I was to see them again.

Back in Caerleon in the summer of 1941, the Agricultural College closed down for eight weeks, so we were able to use their premises to catch up on some school work. I was being taught French and Latin by then, as well as all the normal subjects. During this time we all had a medical at school. I was very underweight and had really outgrown my strength partly due to the food situation and partly because of my home-sickness and the stress I had never come to terms with at being separated from my family. I was told to stop doing games for a while and was given iron tablets to take. Letters from home continued to be slow in getting through. Whenever I received one, it usually contained a postal order for five or ten shillings, depending on how long it had been since the last letter. I would eagerly watch out for the postman each lunchtime hoping and praying that there would be a letter for me.

We kept hearing of the bombing of the cities: I remember once standing by a signpost, feeling very lonely; the signpost pointed the way to London and said something like 200 miles. I wondered how long it would take me to walk there, and what clothes and food should I take! Fortunately common sense prevailed. I resigned myself to more months of being parted from my family – and went home to tea.

I still went over to see my sisters whenever my dad sent me the tickets. I also visited my cousin in Cwmbran. She was billeted with a family with four grown-up sons and was so spoilt that she didn't want to come home. In October 1941 I had a letter from my mum saying that they had moved into a larger flat and I could come home for Christmas. Maybe they would let me stay for good. I asked my parents and they said that I would have to get permission from my headmistress. I took the letter to Miss Gruer, who was not very pleased but relented due to my low health and home-sickness; she added the proviso that I carried on my education at a suitable grammar school in Harrow and gave me a letter to this effect. Mid-December came. I packed up all my belongings, said goodbye to all my friends and foster parents and caught the train from Newport to Paddington, to be met by my mum and sister. It was a happy reunion.

**_Dick Langford,_** _at the Dover County School for Boys, was billeted in Beaufort:_

Mrs Williams was a piano teacher and Mr Williams was a very good tenor singer. They were both on shiftwork: He was at the steelworks and she at the munitions factory at Usk. Whenever this caused problems, Mrs Williams' mother, Mrs Price, looked after us.

The Ebbw Vale County School couldn't accommodate us all so the schools operated a shift system. Later, Pentwyn House was acquired and most of the Dover school moved there. The sixth science form remained at Ebbw Vale school where the laboratories were.

I remember morning prayers were held in an outbuilding of the Ebbw Vale school, built largely of corrugated iron, and which rapidly became known as the 'Tin Tabernacle'. Because of the shift system, various activities were arranged when we weren't at school. They were mandatory and run by our schoolmasters. On bad weather days we assembled at the Welfare Hall on Beaufort Hill and played board games. On fine days we went for long rambles over the mountains and moors. Each form had a 'curfew', in that we had to be off the streets by a given time, which grew later as we got older. This curfew was mainly monitored by the prefects. There were many excuses for being out after curfew – for example, going to the local shop for one's hostess (some shops would stay open quite late). Our hostesses didn't always want us hanging around the house, especially on summer evenings. Anyway, we soon found things to do. In Beaufort the billiard hall and Carini's Cafe were relatively safe havens.

On the whole, except for a very few isolated cases, we were extremely kindly received into the community and very well looked after. Homesickness struck some boys severely and quite a few made 'home runs', getting back to Dover safely without tickets or much money. Some were intercepted at Newport whilst waiting for the London train. Being at a loose end after school certificate had been sat, I and a few friends decided to gatecrash the Ebbw Vale school sports day. Guarding the entrance gate was a young lady named Pauline – I had met my future wife! We were married in 1952, and now have three children and five grandchildren.

Dover County School returned to Dover in 1944; I was a member of the Lower VI by then. What an experience we had had in Wales! I look back on it as a pleasurable adventure and have no doubt that it helped to mould my character – for the better! Our evacuation was, I believe, much more traumatic for our parents. In later years it became clear that my parents, my mother especially, thought they would never see me again after we said our goodbyes as I left Eythorne on that June morning in 1940. Fear of invasion had gripped the South-East, and they hoped at least that I would survive.

*Brian Hedgecock was evacuated with River Elementary School to Aberbargoed:*

At Aberbargoed I had been taken in by Mr and Mrs Idris Jones who sent my mother and father a telegram straightaway to say where I was and that I was alright. I had really fallen on

*Pentwyn House, the old mansion used by the Dover County School for Boys whilst they were in Ebbw Vale. This picture is reproduced from a drawing by Mr C. Rowlands, who was art master at the time of evacuation*

my feet. The house was quite large, stood in its own grounds, was surrounded by a fence of iron railings and couldn't be seen from the road. Mr Jones was a senior manager for Powell Duffryn who, prior to nationalisation, owned many of the coal mines in South Wales, including the one down the valley below Aberbargoed and Bargoed. He was almost regarded as the squire.

Mr and Mrs Jones had a daughter, Esme, who was about twenty, and who really took me under her wing. There was also an older son, Cliff. Both worked for Powell Duffryn and were, it seems, in reserved occupations. There were three cars at the house: Mr Jones used a small black Austin for work and had a nice green MG saloon for other purposes; Cliff had an MG sports car, similar to those used by the police at that time. Use of the cars for leisure purposes was restricted of course, because of the growing petrol shortage. Nevertheless, I remember being taken out from time to time, often when Mr Jones or Cliff made a work visit to one of the mines in their area. Back home there were only two cars in the whole of our road!

Food was not really a problem at this early time in the war. I was introduced to Caerphilly cheese fresh from the farms up in the hills; and then there were Welshcakes, which I had never tasted before, and whinberry pies, the fruit for which we picked on the mountainside.

Aberbargoed was a large village which boasted the largest coal tip in Europe. There were sometimes scares that the slag tip was moving, particularly after heavy rain. The worry was that it might engulf the houses built below it. The village was on the Monmouthshire side of the River Rhymney, the border between Monmouthshire and Glamorgan; the town of Bargoed was on the Glamorgan side and the pit was in between, on the floor of the valley. Water, already black with coal dust from pits upstream, was taken from the river for washing the coal and then returned to the river blacker still. The river banks were thick black sludge. All this was rather different from the Kentish village and the soft, green countryside we had left behind.

Having got over my homesickness and the strange surroundings, I settled down into my new life. I was well looked after by the Jones family, although it was nothing like being at home with my mother and father. As we got to know the area, we found that much of the countryside away from the pits and coal tips was really quite lovely. I am sure that it was here that my affection for the more rugged sort of landscape was born. In the meantime, my parents were also forced to undergo some changes. By September 1940, Dover had become quite untenable for local industry. My father worked at Buckland Paper Mill, owned by Wiggins Teape; the workforce was redeployed all over the country to other paper mills. Dad was sent to Overton Paper Mill in Hampshire. My mother went with him and she was able to pay me several visits while I was at Aberbargoed. So 'home' now was Overton and was to remain so for some years.

My cousins, Colin and Jean, were billeted about half a mile away from me, but in opposite directions. Colin and I, being boys, had more in common with each other and so I saw more of him than I did of Jean who went back to River sometime in late 1940. I also had other friends from River with whom I used to go about and made new friends with local boys and girls.

My cousin Keith had been evacuated with Dover County School to Ebbw Vale, to the north of Abergoed. Early in 1941 I learned that I had been accepted for the County School and, together with Colin, was to start in September 1941. This meant leaving Mr and Mrs Jones, to be billeted with someone else in Ebbw Vale. Colin's and Keith's father moved to St Neots in Huntingdonshire and lived in the village of Eaton Socon. They also had my grandmother living with them because her house in River had been demolished by a German shell in August 1940. At the end of my time in Aberbargoed, my parents and I went to Eaton Socon for a week and then went to Overton in Hampshire until it was time for my mother to take me to Ebbw Vale.

My new billet was quite different from the Jones's. Mr and Mrs Lewis didn't have any children of their own and lived in a pleasant but small terraced house owned by the Duke of Beaufort. There was only gas lighting downstairs and none at all upstairs, so we had to take a candle when going to bed. Mr Lewis did labouring work connected with the new electricity pylons that were being erected over the moors near Beaufort, Brynmawr and further east.

129

My new school was just up the road from the billet and we shared it on a shift basis with the Ebbw Vale County School. And so really serious schooling began. The shift system enabled us to retain our school identity. Sport was well organised and I played soccer from the beginning. We were introduced for the first time to rugby (soccer being regarded locally as being a 'cissy' sport), but I didn't like it at all and managed to avoid playing it most of the time! Later on, I found that I had rather a natural inclination for cricket and that became my favourite summer game. There was intense rivalry between the locals and the evacuees, mainly in the area of sporting activities. The shift system obviously created considerable problems for both schools and within a year or so another building was found – although the sixth form remained at the Ebbw Vale school because of its need to access laboratories, etc.

Our new school was a large old house called Pentwyn House, situated at the far end of town. I remember the toilet facilities at there being totally inadequate for so many of us – they were filthy! But at least we had left behind at Ebbw Vale school the dreadful school dinners. Now we had two sittings to the local British Restaurant each day – a considerable improvement.

A number of us spent some of our leisure time in the evenings at the local working men's club, where we could look at the papers or play billiards or snooker. Other time was spent going to the local park, or to the cinema, or just wandering around. As time went on I had a greater awareness of girls, so not all spare time was spent at the club, etc! Some time in 1942 or 1943 my hosts decided that they had had enough of evacuees, so another billet was found for me, this time much closer to Pentwyn House. My new foster parents were Mr and Miss Edwards, a brother and sister. I stayed with them for the rest of the time we were in Ebbw Vale.

We followed the course of the war with more interest than other youngsters, since the sooner it ended the sooner we would get home, so we listened to all the news bulletins. Then came 6th June 1944, D-Day. There was a radio in the British Restaurant and this would always be on for the one o'clock news while we were eating our dinners. On D-Day there were two local workmen sitting at a table eating their dinners among all of us boys and they were talking to each other very loudly when the news came on. I can remember quite clearly one of our teachers telling them in no uncertain terms to 'shut up' so we could listen to the first reports about the landings in Normandy. You could have heard a pin drop! We hung on to every word.

As the days and weeks went by, it seemed that there was light at the end of the tunnel at last. Then came the news that the Canadians had cleared the Germans out of the Channel ports, from where the Germans had been shelling. We were told that we would be going back home to Dover in December 1944. I was almost 15. This presented another problem for my parents since my father had not heard anything about his work returning to Dover. So there was to be a different separation. Mum moved back to River to look after me while dad had to stay in Overton until Wiggins Teape reopened the paper mill in Dover later in 1945.

It was a strange feeling to return home after all that time. Everything seemed so much smaller than I remembered it. We were lucky that our house had suffered no more than the windows being broken once or twice by blast from shells landing nearby. The Dover County School for Boys had been requisitioned by the navy, was full of WRNS personnel and was called HMS something-or-other! So we started back to school in a motley collection of buildings in several parts of our shell- and bomb-scarred town. We moved to our school later in 1945.

**Brenda Rainsley** (now Mrs Brown) was evacuated with Buckland School from Dover:

My foster parents were Austin and Eileen Howell, who lived in Priory Road with their two children, Betty and Martin. Mr Howell was a miner. They were both very strict and went to chapel every Sunday. I can still remember the chapel; it was lovely with a gallery all the way round. I liked it up there because of the echo. When Betty and Martin had new clothes, so did I. My foster parents bought me a beautiful blue coat with velvet trimming on the collar and cuffs.

130

*Evacuees at Cwmbran – Bob Hollinsbee collection*

It was only to be worn on Sundays. They also bought me my first rainproof cape, wellingtons and an umbrella. Such delights! I also had black patent shoes.

Every day before we went to school, Auntie Eileen would brush our hair and Betty and I would have two matching ribbons each. These ribbons were always lined up on a cupboard door and were all the colours of the rainbow. They must have bought me lots of dresses, but at six years old I took that all for granted. My foster parents were very kind to me.

The school we went to was Danygrieg. Some days we used to go to private homes and sit around a table to do our lessons – and we would have milk and biscuits. On those days we would probably do more reading than anything else, which was my favourite lesson anyway.

My strongest memory is of something that happened on our way home from school one lunch time. It was raining heavily and I was wearing my beloved cape and wellingtons. Thunder and lightning started and Betty and I stopped to shelter in the doorway of a corner shop. We would normally take the cobbled road opposite to go home. A horse with its rider came down the road and the horse slipped on the cobbles when the thunder frightened it. It reared up on its hind legs right in front of where we were sheltering and I thought it was going to come down on us. I was very frightened and, even today, I have a terrible fear of horses!

I remember my foster parents took me by car to see my sister at Rogiet, where she was staying in a bungalow. I hadn't been in a bungalow before and was utterly fascinated by everything being on one floor. My sister had a lovely home. On another occasion, I was taken to see my brother in Ynysddu. That again was totally different. He was staying in a row of older houses and great stacks of coal seemed to dominate everything.

When my father went into the army, my mother and baby sister went to live in Worcestershire with my aunt. Gradually my brother, sister and I went to live there too. We returned to Dover some time in 1942 and stayed there for the rest of the war. However, in 1944 I won a scholarship to the Dover County School for Girls and that September I went back to South Wales – this time to Caerleon. I hated my stay there but, as it happened, the whole school returned to Dover in December 1944, so I was back home with my family, this time for good.

*Evelyn King (now Mrs Jenkin) was evacuated with the Dover County School for Girls to Caerleon and was billeted with Mr and Mrs Pritchard:*

I think some effort was made to keep the school forms together by billeting them in the same area. Ours was billeted in council houses in Lodge Avenue. I shared my billet with a girl named Marie who came from Deal and we were treated as part of the family. We even went on holiday with them to their relatives in Hereford. Some of the evacuees were not as fortunate as us. They would be made to go out all day and had to live in the kitchen when they were in. Fortunately this was not common and, in any case, a child could always ask to be moved.

Our school remained a self-contained unit, and we couldn't feel lonely when there were so many of us in the same boat. Schooling was on a half day basis to begin with, sometimes in the village school, sometimes in the Teacher Training College, and latterly we went on the train to Pontypool Grammar School. I was in Wales for about two years and never actually returned to Dover to live, although the rest of my family returned and all survived the war. I think being an evacuee made me get on with things and stand on my own two feet. The Land Army was much worse – but then, that was war!

*Alan J. Bell, from Deal, was attending the Dover County School for Boys:*

My friend and I were taken to a part of Ebbw Vale called Garden City, about a mile down the valley from the main town. Garden City consisted of about forty houses on the side of the valley, some 400 yards from the huge ovens which produced coke for the steelworks. When there was an easterly wind we had to keep all windows closed due to the large amount of smuts and soot which used to settle on

*1st Cadet Coy, Cinque Ports (Fortress) Royal Engineers, Dover County School for Boys Ebbw Vale, 1943*
*– Alan Bell collection*

everything. At first we shared the Ebbw Vale County School premises and you can imagine our excitement when we found that it was a mixed school! Later our school acquired a large empty mansion, Pentwyn House, and most of the classes were held there. It took us quite a long time to understand the Welsh people and their sense of humour, but we gradually learned to like them. The next five years of my life were spent there, and we settled into a routine, not vastly different from peacetime, at least, as far as school was concerned. School holidays tended to be tedious as we missed the sea and the beaches of home, but we found a lovely place called Gilwern, on the Brecon Canal, where we used to hire rowing boats. I have since been back to Gilwern for canal boating holidays. It is a lovely canal which has been restored and which I would never have known about had I not been evacuated.

The school had a Cadet Corps with a bugle and drum band, in which I was a drummer. Much of our time was taken up in attending parades. We were the only band for miles around and, until other bands were formed, our services were much in demand. In fact, the only photograph

I have of my time in Wales is one of the school band, taken in the main street of Ebbw Vale. It was taken by an American soldier who kindly sent us the negative. At the age of eighteen I joined the Royal Navy. By then my mother and sister were living in Ebbw Vale, so I used to spend my periods of leave there. During one spell of leave I met a girl, whom I had known at school; we were eventually married and had two sons. By then we were living in London, so used to return to Ebbw Vale occasionally to take our boys to visit their grandparents.

Although we had been evacuated to an area so vastly different from home in Kent, my lasting impression is of the kindness of the Welsh people. The local lads would call at our billets to invite us to join their activities and we made many lasting friendships. Any rivalry between us was mainly friendly and chiefly centred on rugby and cricket – at the former we always seemed to lose! Twenty years ago I went back to what was once the family home at Upna Lodge, Upper Gladstone Road in Deal, whence I was evacuated – the only time I have ever been back 'home'.

*Dot Larkins (now Mrs Parrett) was evacuated with Barton Road Girls' School, Dover:*

It was after midnight before I got to bed on that first night away from home and before I was up the next morning, Mr James was out looking for my sister Linda. He found out that she was in the next village up the line called Pontllanfraith and, in the afternoon, Mr James took me up to see her. I was much happier then, but although Mr and Mrs James and their daughter were very kind to me, I never stopped missing mum and dad. As I've grown older I try to imagine what it was like for our parents, who one day had a home full of kids and, the next day, nothing! My parents told us years later that, on the day we were evacuated, they walked up to Bunkers Hill in Dover and sat and cried. The schooling in Wales was quite disorganised to start with. All of us living in Wyllie, no matter what our age, attended school in the local village hall but eventually we walked from our village to Ynysddu, where most of the evacuees attended school. We were taught by our own teachers from Dover and we were kept separate from the Welsh children. Our school in Ynysddu was a very large church hall.

During my time in Wyllie I used to go to church every Sunday; once I even stood on my own and sang 'The Holy City'. Eventually we all returned home to mum and dad but I kept in contact with Mr and Mrs James for many years. Then one Christmas there was no card from Wales, but a letter arrived in the January from Mrs James to say that her husband had died – she didn't want to tell me until after Christmas. I felt very sad, as I could remember him as a very kind and happy man. After that I lost touch with Mrs James. In 1987, while on holiday near Ross-on-Wye with my sister Kitty and her husband, we returned to the village of Wyllie, 45 years after leaving. The church was gone! Destroyed apparently by vandals. We called into the local shop in Wyllie, told them that we were on a trip down 'memory lane' and that I had lived in Pen-ny Cwarel Road. 'Oh yes,' they said, 'Hannah James still lives there!' I remembered exactly where to direct my husband. I knocked on the door and Mrs James opened it. She invited us all in and we had a lovely tea while we talked about the old evacuation days.

*Bob Hadley was evacuated with Holy Trinity Boys' School, Dover, to Cwmbran:*

The people who took us in were Mr and Mrs Burchill. Also in the house were their son Frank and his wife Nellie; they had another son named Pat who was serving with the South Wales Borderers. It was a four bedroomed house, with a front room, middle room and kitchen – and an outside toilet which was up the garden! Frank kept pigeons and there were also ducks, chicken and a pig called Ginney. Ginney was killed off every year for meat. I can remember sitting over a bucket, cleaning the chidlings. Needless to say, another young pig soon arrived, another Ginney! It was my job to go around the village and collect waste food which we fed to the pig. Another job I had was to clean out the chicken, by scrubbing on my hands and knees.

Eventually, two more evacuees arrived from Dover. They were Tommy and Bill Houlton, also from the Ropewalk area. Bedspace became desperate, so we finished up four in a bed – two at the top and two at the bottom. You can imagine the squabbles that caused.

Mr and Mrs Burchill often fancied a drink and a regular thing was for me to go down to the pub for a flagon of draft beer from the tap room. This entailed quite a long walk across a railway line, down a rough embankment and over the canal – and this was all in the blackout! For this I was allowed to sit in the middle room with Mr Burchill and listen to an episode of 'Into Battle' on the wireless. When they filled their glasses with beer, they used to put a red hot poker from the fire into them. Another little job was to take the accumulator battery from the wireless to the local garage to get it charged. Nellie had a baby while I was there, but it was stillborn. I was allowed to see it lying in a box of cotton wool in the front room. Soon there was another evacuee in the house. By way of a change it was a girl, from the pier district of Dover. The house was getting a bit crowded now!

School was really something! We had classes in one school in the morning and in another in the afternoon. There were also houses close by which had undertaken to take us for safety when the air raid warning went. My mother, who was a widow, came to visit us while we were in Wales. She stayed with my sister in Llantarnam Road and we had a nice couple of days with her. She took us shopping and rigged us out with a few clothes. There were also times when we were given clothes which were sent by the people of Canada. On another occasion, Mrs Houlton came to visit and she took us and her two boys to Newport, where we had faggots and peas – and she left a silver threepenny piece as a tip.

My brother Len, who was in the Royal Navy, was courting a girl in Bristol and he came to visit us. When he came to the billet, I answered the door and stood there with a broom in my hand. He looked surprised, but didn't say anything. Len was taking us both out the next day, so my brother and I got up very early and walked to Llantarnam Road. We were there before they were up and Len wasn't very pleased with us. Mrs Burchill didn't know that we had gone, so we were in trouble when we got back to our billet.

Len wrote to mum to tell her about me answering the door with a broom in my hand and it wasn't long before Ray and I were back home in Dover. Our sister Mary stayed on in Cwmbran until after the war. In fact, the couple she was living with, Mr and Mrs Cowley, wanted to keep her! I kept in touch with Mr and Mrs Burchill with Christmas cards, etc. Later I also wrote to tell them what we were all doing after we left school. I did get a reply, but soon the Christmas cards stopped. We went back to Cwmbran after the war and paid Mrs Burchill a visit; some time later I went down alone. A few years ago I was with friends and we went out of our way to drive to Clomendy Road in Cwmbran. I got out of the car and stood outside the house, just looking and thinking to myself.

Chapter Six

## CONTINUING THE BRIGHTER SIDE

*THIS CHAPTER CONTINUES the theme of those who found caring foster parents, but it also includes those whose mothers were also evacuated, those who were evacuated at a later date than the majority of school children, and those who were evacuated privately.*

**Dora Hedges** *(now Mrs Riley) was evacuated with St James' Girls' School:*

My sister Brenda and I were billeted with Mr and Mrs James who lived in Upper Waun Street, Blaenavon. They had a daughter named Claire. The day after we arrived I remember asking Mrs James what we should call her, and she said, 'Auntie will do.' After breakfast it was out the back gate to have our first look at Blaenavon and to try and find our friends. At first we shared a school with the local children and only went for half days. The other half was spent having talks and lessons up at the park. It was a long, hot summer that year and we enjoyed being out in the fresh air. Later on we had our own school at the bottom of Park Street.

I liked living in Blaenavon, although some of the local girls didn't want to know us evacuees. My mother, who had travelled with the evacuation train, volunteered to take charge of a hostel for evacuees in Algood Avenue. She was known as Mrs Hedge to all the children and they all seemed very happy with her, but I longed for the day when I could have my own mum back again! My brother Billy lived with mum in the hostel; I think he must have been quite a handful

*St James Street, Dover, showing St James School on the left of the picture, as it was before the war – Peter Hayward collection*

at the time. Dad, meanwhile, was with the 14th Army in Burma for most of the time we were in Blaenavon. After a while some of the children started to drift back to Dover and rumours would go round the school, saying that we were all going home. Miss James, the headteacher, would then tell us that we were not going and everyone would be 'down in the dumps' for a few days.

We did eventually leave Blaenavon to return to Dover, but this wasn't until just a few months before the end of the war. We had been away for more than four years. When we got back to Dover, our school in St James' Street had been destroyed by enemy action, so we all had to go to St Mary's School. We always kept in touch with our foster parents and even now I write to my foster sister, Claire, who still lives in Blaenavon.

Barton Road Girls' School, Ynysddu, South Wales, July 1940
BACK ROW: Joan Simpson, Doreen . . . , Diana Ramsden, Joyce Heath, Sheila Rogers, Jessie Gimbert, Betty Parkinson, Audrey Ash, Kathleen . . . , Lily Tucker.
SECOND ROW: Pat Donald, Gwen Woodbridge, June Groombridge, Lily Fisher, Maureen Donelly, Peggy Lowden, Margaret Pelham, Daphne Lehan, Eileen Ellis.
THIRD ROW: Alice Cooper, Ada Luff, Jean Fisher, Yvonne Spain, Ruby Hedgecock, Edith Baker, Gladys Addenbrook.
FRONT ROW: Pansy Hatcher, Connie Funnel, Sheila Lester, Josephine Kirby, Pat Deegan, Audrey Gilham.

Barton Road Girls' School, Ynysddu, South Wales, Winter 1940

136

*Sylvia Dunford was evacuated with Barton Road Girls' School, Dover, to Pontllanfraith:*

My sister and I were with our foster mother, Mrs Jones, for about three months, then mum decided to come down and join us. She found rooms so we all moved in together. Mum managed to get herself a couple of cleaning jobs for a while, then she got a good job in a large house but we all had to uproot again to live there. I always seemed to suffer from bronchitis while I was in Wales. By April 1941 we heard that dad was to be based at Donnington, near the Wrekin. Mum decided to go up there and join him, so we packed our bags once again. We spent two months in a room in Trent, had six months at Millishull and, finally, through friends, we managed to get half a farmhouse in Donnington. The farmhouse was very primitive – no gas or electricity, only cold water in the sink in the scullery, and a toilet at the bottom of the garden – which was a three-hole loo! We used to go down there for a chat! I think the toilet used to be cleaned about once a year. It was dug out and the contents were put on the fields. However, it was pleasant living at the farmhouse and I think we quite enjoyed it.

When I think back and work it all out, I went to about ten different schools in five years, which didn't do my education any good at all. Still, I was probably one of the luckier evacuees, because I had my mother with me for most of the time. I was twelve years old when we came back home to Dover. I had been away for about five years and, although Dover had been hit very hard, I don't think I really noticed much of the war damage. I started back at Barton Road School and gradually our family life got back to normal.

*Hillary Humphreys joined her new school, the Dover County School, in Caerleon in 1941:*

Before being evacuated I lived at East Studdal, near Dover, and went to school at Ripple – a small village school of two classrooms with an age range of five to fourteen. In 1940 when the schools were evacuated, I went with my younger sister to Bath, to stay with relations. I went to Wales in 1941 with two other girls from the village. My mother escorted the three of us to Caerleon. I had more than one billet and it seemed that life was very difficult for both hostesses and evacuees. One billet I had was with two other girls. The hostess was at least 65 years old and the three of us girls slept in a double bed. There were two bedrooms, no bathroom and no flush toilet. She had obviously taken on more than she was capable of.

Many evacuees were in this position and often had to move on. Another hostess became pregnant and so I had to leave that billet. Often life in billets was difficult because there was no place to do homework and, after we were fed and watered, we were expected to go out. This eventually was recognised by the school so a church hall was provided where a teacher took on an extra duty to sit with us. Hostesses did have a difficult time fitting in with meal and school times. For school we used three church halls, the infant and junior school, and some rooms at the men's training college. We had to keep all our books, having no desk of our own. Every day we would meet in the Baptist Church for our assembly. It was a very unsettled environment.

We did not generally make friends in the village unless they were the children of the family we were billeted with. Caerleon, at the time of our evacuation, could be divided into three areas, the new council estate on the hill, a very old middle part and the other side of the River Usk, where the properties were mostly privately owned. The village boasted a Roman amphitheatre, mental hospital and a men's training college which was on the top of the hill and took ages to get to. My only health problems were head lice or scabies. Every holiday I went home to be 'cleaned up', and this happened until a permanent hostel for about 20 girls was opened in Llantarnum, two or three stations up the line. This hostel was supervised by two teachers, a cook and a helper, who were all from Dover. We helped with the washing up but here we were able to have baths. Sheets and towels were changed regularly and things became more stable.

We all returned to Dover at Christmas 1944, when we had half-time schooling for a while –

and came home with heaps of homework! Yes, it was good to be home. People were pleased to see you when you came home, and were interested in you and your school work. I was also able to have piano lessons again, which had been denied me since 1940. I have never returned to Wales. Nothing there held any pleasant memories for me.

*Kathleen Fletcher, Marie Green and Patricia Tee at an evacuee reunion, Dover, May 1995 – Ted Green collection*

***Patricia Tee*** *(now Mrs Hackney) from Dover, wasn't evacuated with the bulk of the children who left on the 2nd June 1940, but the authorities persuaded her mother to let her go a few months later. Here is a copy of the letter sent to Pat Tee's mother informing her of Pat's evacuation arrangements, which is followed by Pat's own personal account of her evacuation:*

Brook House,
Dover
30th September, 1940

Dear Madam,

With reference to previous letters, arrangements have been made for your child, PATRICIA TEE, to be taken to the reception area in Monmouthshire on Thursday next the 3rd October. She must be at the Market Square (near Westminster Bank) at 8 o'clock in the morning on that day to join a school party which will make the first part of the journey by bus. The party will be in the charge of responsible 'escorts' selected by the Authority. I enclose two labels, one of which must be securely attached to the child's clothing, and one securely attached to the luggage.

Yours faithfully,
R. J. Briggenshaw, Secretary.

At first, my mother didn't want me to be evacuated but the police paid her a visit and told her that it was her duty to send me away. That made her feel very guilty. My father, who was in the Royal Air Force, also put pressure on mum by saying that because he was away from home and that mother was working at Buckland Hospital, I wouldn't be looked after properly and, besides, there was the bombing and the shelling. Anyway, on the 3rd October 1940, I was put on a bus in the Market Square, destined for the village of Rogiet, between Chepstow and Newport. I was nine years old, and I remember clutching a doll which had knitted green clothes.

When we arrived at Rogiet, I was billeted with a Mr and Mrs Davies and their grown up daughter. Mr Davies was an engine driver. The memory I have of my arrival at the billet is sitting on a stool, nursing a cat. At first we had our own teachers and went to school for just half days – doing very little as I remember, but as some of the children started to drift back home, we were put in classes with the village children. The headmaster was very keen on Shakespeare and, at ten or eleven, we were made to learn *Henry the Fifth* before Agincourt – but it never put me off liking Shakespeare!

One day at school we were given a lovely gift, sent by some school children in Newark, USA. It was a parcel about the size of a shoe box, and it was filled with many different things.

There were cherry flavoured Lifesavers (I had never seen sweets with a hole in them), a tooth brush, soap with a picture on one side, a face flannel and, best of all, some American comics. There were also many letters written by the children of Newark. One day my friend Margaret Green and I were caught stealing apples from the vicarage garden. As a punishment, we were made to weed the garden, but the vicar did give us a lovely tea afterwards.

Once a week I was given a cascara pill – to keep me 'regular' so Auntie said! I hated that pill and once I held it under my tongue and spat it down the toilet, only I forgot to pull the chain and was found out. I did go home a couple of times during the war, but each time I was pleased to get away from the bombing and having to go down to the shelter.

On Sundays, my foster parents made me go to church in the morning, Sunday School in the afternoon and sometimes to church again in the evening. On summer evenings we went for long walks in the woods and fields and I was taught the names of wild flowers, for which I have always been grateful. In 1945 I returned to Dover. My father came home from the RAF, so we were a family again, but mother has always said that she regrets not being able to watch me grow up during those years I was away in Wales.

*Vanda Brown (now Mrs Martin) went with her younger brother from Deal to Aberkenfig:*

Our new home was a tiny cottage at the end of a terrace. All our water came from a tap just outside the door. We attended school in the same church hall where we first assembled to be allocated billets, but later on we went to the village school. We never met any hostility or unfriendliness in Aberkenfig. We used to go to Saturday morning pictures for 1d, which seemed very cheap, even then. I can remember feeling very homesick at times. My parents had a small shoe shop in Mill Hill, where we made clogs for the miners and did shoe repairs. Trade dropped, so mum and dad decided to go to Cardiff to be near my uncle, who was a civilian attached to the RAF in Barry. Dad managed to get himself a job at Currens as a fitter.

My parents hadn't been in Cardiff long when my young brother Teddy caught pneumonia. The police contacted them and I remember mum and dad coming to Aberkenfig to see Teddy. It was the first time I had ever seen my father cry. My brother was so ill that I was allowed to stay off school to be with him. When Teddy recovered from his illness, we went to join our parents in Cardiff – much to my delight! We lived in a basement flat, with very little furniture or anything. I remember well being in bed with mum and two younger brothers, hearing the bombs dropping on Cardiff. It was a terrifying experience.

I went to the local St Cuthbert's Catholic school for a while. Soon afterwards we managed to get a semi-detached house close to the bridge over the River Taff and very near to the docks. There were many air raids on Cardiff. Somehow we took it all in our stride. It was the norm! We spent a lot of time after an air raid, collecting and swopping shrapnel. We used to have to practise putting our gas masks on during lessons and often got the giggles, but we soon got used to the rubbery smell and we even managed to read with the gas masks on.

The air raids got worse and we were to be evacuated yet again. This time to Abercynon. I remember having a very good billet at Station House with Mrs Barwick. Before I was evacuated this second time, I sat for a Kent scholarship. I took it on my own in the headmistress's study; it was quite an ordeal at first, but I got through it. I went to Cheshire to help my Aunt Maggie who was having a baby. While I was there I heard I had got a place at Dover County School for Girls. Before I started at my new school, I went home from Cardiff on my own. When I travelled back to Caerleon, I was actually a week late, and I wasn't very happy about that!

I had a billet with a childless couple who seemed very kind, but my parents weren't very happy about it for some obscure reason, so I went to a hostel for a while. I was then given a billet with a Miss Bunting, who lived with her father and brother. I was very happy there. I went home to Cardiff at weekends by train and I used to love to go shopping there. My family stayed in Wales until January 1946, then we all returned home to Deal.

***Hazel Pittock*** *(now Mrs Smith) was at St Bart's Infant School, Dover:*

I was evacuated at the age of seven with Gladys Gatehouse. We went from Dover Priory with other pupils from St Bart's Infant School and I remember our teacher, Miss Humphreys, came with us too. We finally arrived at our destination and everyone looked tired and forlorn. We had arrived at New Tredegar and were immediately taken to a school hall where our billeting arrangements were made. We were allocated to a Mr and Mrs Panes. He was a miner and I remember how each day he came home from work covered in coal dust, to a large wooden round tub full of water heated in buckets on the large black range, and had his bath in the kitchen. The only water came from a single cold tap in the kitchen. There wasn't even a sink.

We all went to chapel three times every Sunday and once during the week. Aunty and uncle were vergers at the chapel where we used to help them clean the communion glasses. Most Sundays visiting ministers would come to dinner and tea and we had to behave ourselves.

We were very well treated and had new clothes bought for us, especially at Whitsuntide. We had Sunday School outings to Barry Island and Abergavenny and I can remember a holiday we had in Gloucestershire where we helped bring the cows in for milking. We went to school in Cwmsyfiog and joined in classes with the local children. While we were there I can remember learning the Welsh national anthem and 'Baa Baa Black Sheep' in Welsh. We had a lot of fun playing on the mountains and collecting whinberries. We also collected sheep manure for the garden! The sheep used to roam everywhere, even into the village. One of our favourite places to play was on swings on the coal tip, where we used to get absolutely filthy. Eventually, when the shelling of Dover had stopped, all of us evacuees returned home.

***Leonard Fry*** *was late in being evacuated from Folkestone, but he eventually joined his sister on a farm near Abergavenny:*

The farm was really isolated, with no running drinking water, no electricity and no indoor toilets! The farmer and his wife were Mr and Mrs Cross and they had several sons and one daughter still at home. I was soon incorporated into the scheme of things. During the war years, farmers were under great pressure to produce more food, so some of the evacuees became a vital part of a pool of part-time workers – in my case, part of the work force of Llynos Farm.

We attended Brynderi School about a mile away and we walked there and back every day. The school was jammed with children. It is difficult to see now, how anyone learnt anything, with three classes being conducted at once in one room, but learn we did. I don't recall very much friction between the three distinct groups of children, namely the Welsh children, and the Folkestone and Birmingham evacuees. One of my friends there was John Wade, who was originally from London, went to live in Folkestone at the outbreak of the war and subsequently was evacuated to Llantilio Crossenny. Another friend was John Nott, whose whole family had moved out of Birmingham and had a cottage on Llynos land nearby.

I never fell foul of the headmaster but I did see him punish a few people very severely. It was outside school that was a revelation to me, having been born in the middle of a town. Though I had a certain amount to do every day on the farm, I was learning all about country life. Mr Cross's sons taught me all about birds – something that still holds my interest. Godfrey Cross was a little disturbed mentally. He apparently blamed himself for a friend's early death. I became his friend and confidant. Norman, another son, taught me about country craft, such as rabbiting. Mervyn Cross was the gardener of the family, so I learnt a bit more from him. Tony Cross, the youngest son, worked for his married sister and her husband. They had a farm a few miles away but, when he was home, we were great pals. Enid, the youngest daughter, worked in the farmhouse with her mother, catering for quite a large household!

The father, William Cross, was a short, stocky man. He certainly didn't suffer fools gladly;

he had a very short temper, but he had taught his sons well and they ran the farm very efficiently. Mrs Lucy Cross was much the same as her husband, but she was very kind to me.

In 1941 my sister and another evacuee moved out to take jobs while two Birmingham evacuees, Joyce Wheeler and Pat Smoult, joined us. Rationing on the farm almost didn't exist! The food was a revelation to me. I sat down to roast duckling, new potatoes and new peas, in the spring of 1941 – one of my all time memories of Llynos Farm; totally unforgettable!

The war certainly came to the area a few times. We weren't far from the industrial areas of South Wales and I believe there were aircraft factories at Hereford. There was enemy air activity at times. One night a stick of incendiary bombs fell across the farm, one landed about 50 yards from the farmhouse. Another time two bombs dropped about a mile away. The army defused one but the other bomb exploded shortly afterwards, shaking us during tea.

When John Nott and I reached eleven years old, he was allowed to join the newly-formed Scout Group down in Llantilio Crossenny – but I wasn't! That is when disillusionment began to set in. I was increasingly expected to do more on the farm, because I was getting bigger and stronger. I'm afraid I resented this very much and I 'simmered' for a long time. When my mother and aunt came to visit in the summer of 1943, I plucked up the courage to ask to return to Folkestone. Surprisingly, my mother agreed and so I returned home in the September – right smack into the shelling! I kept in touch with the Cross family for a long time after I returned home and so did my mother. The last time I saw Mr and Mrs Cross and the boys was in 1951. After that, contact was sporadic. The story of my evacuation is unremarkable but my stay with the Cross family shaped my life for ever. I realised afterwards that the resentment I felt at the time was unjustified. I had become part of the family and was expected to pull my weight with the chores on the farm, like everyone else.

*Christine Taylor (now Mrs Knight) was privately evacuated from Dover:*

After a hospital ship was bombed in the Channel in 1939, my father decided to send my mother, my two sisters and me to mum's relatives in Blackwood. We stayed in Wales for about six months, attending local schools. My sister, Jean, gained a place with the Dover County School for Girls and went on to Caerleon to join her new school.

My father was working in the Duke of York's Royal Military School at Dover when they too were evacuated, this time to the Saunton Sands Hotel near Barnstaple, Devon. Eventually we followed our father to Barnstaple, although sister Jean remained with her school in Caerleon until a place could be found for her in the Barnstaple Grammar School. I suppose I was one of the lucky ones, being with my own family for most of the war. We eventually returned to Dover in 1945, still with the 'Dukies', where we lived until my father's death in 1953. He was organist at the Duke of York's Royal Military School from the age of 21 until his death. He was Sydney Taylor, the son of Harry James Taylor, Dover's borough organist at St Mary's church.

*Jeanne Fairweather (now Mrs Ruddick), went from Dover to Blaenavon with her sister:*

During the first few weeks in Blaenavon we had schooling for only half of each day, until a suitable building was found. We had our own teachers from Dover with us and they were wonderful to us all. They looked after our welfare in place of our parents. The war continued, of course, but gradually children began to drift back to Dover and, eventually, the authorities had to reopen some of the schools there. Mr and Mrs Edmunds, our foster parents, were very kind and good to us. However, our parents must have missed us because they wanted us to return home so, after sixteen months of being separated, mum and dad came to Wales to collect us.

We stayed in Dover for the rest of the war and went to school throughout the bombing and the shelling. One night the school was bombed, so we had to have lessons in another school for a while. We even had the windows of our house blown out by the shelling but thankfully my family all survived the war. We kept in touch with our foster parents until Mrs Edmunds died in 1993, aged 93 years; Mr Edmunds had died about ten years before. Our friendship with our Welsh foster parents lasted fifty years.

**Bill Collard** *joined the Dover County School in Ebbw Vale in 1941 and had already had two billets before moving to Mrs Domin at 3 Aynho Place:*

Mrs Domin already had three other evacuees, so there were four of us in one room. Evacuation then became quite fun. She was a funny little old lady; she had her husband and her brother Charlie living in the house with her, and there was a little sweet shop in her front room! She confiscated my sweet coupons as soon as I got there, which upset me until I realised that, because of the sweet shop in the front room, we did well for sweets!

The four of us evacuees all slept in one room, in two double beds, and I lived at that billet for eighteen months. I was required to go to chapel three times every Sunday and it didn't stop at that because on Mondays it was the Band of Hope, Tuesdays Youth Guild and Wednesdays something else. My whole social life as an eleven and twelve year old seemed to revolve around the chapel. I was mad keen on cricket and I also played soccer – I got my teeth smashed playing soccer! When I was about thirteen years old, we were playing in a house competition. There was a miners' strike on and there was a lot of miners with time to spare hanging around the football field. A group of these young Welsh miners invaded the pitch, broke our game up and took our ball. We remonstrated with them and one took attacked and beat the hell out of me! The other guys of the team shot off down to the next playing field where our sixth formers were playing, and they all came back ready to do battle, but by the time they arrived, the miners had gone. Apart from that, we generally got on well with the Welsh children of our own age.

I remember seeing the glow in the night sky over Newport when it was bombed, but the huge steel works at Ebbw Vale were, to my knowledge, never hit. The war seemed very remote. The other glimpse of war that I remember was towards the end of my evacuation, when I walked right over the mountains towards Blaenavon, because a Lancaster Bomber had crash-landed. I found it, but it was guarded! We used to walk a lot on the mountains; it was great exercise.

One of our teachers whom I particularly respected was Tom Archer, probably because he was a sportsman. He married Mary Sullivan, the Welsh Latin teacher. Our teachers were all devoted people: Billy Baxter, Charlie Rowlands, Tom Archer, the Reverend W. Uncles and 'Weary' Willis, (history and music). During my evacuation, we lost two members of staff, Mr Allin (Latin), Mr Watt (French) – and several boys of the Ebbw Vale community to tuberculosis.

After eighteen months with Mrs Domin, I was moved to Mr and Mrs Rees. I was with another evacuee and we slept in the box room of this council house. We shared a single bed which we made larger by packing our suitcases down the side of it! We both stayed at this new billet until the school was repatriated in December 1944.

When we all came back for good in December 1944, our train picked up the Dover County School for Girls on the way and I remember de-bagging one of my friends and taking his trousers through to the girls' carriages. We were all wildly excited to be going home. We can't have done too badly at school during those years of evacuation, because when we got back home, I think our year was the first to take the School Certificate when we finally got back into our old school premises – and we were the first form ever to get 100 per cent pass rate.

**Edna Maynard** *(now Mrs Gibbs) recalls life in the mining village of Wyllie:*

My foster parents, Mr and Mrs Morgan, were an elderly couple and had never had any children of their own. They were very kind to me. I wasn't homesick but I did miss Dover, particularly the sea and the countryside. Somehow, the mountain behind Wyllie and the coal mine didn't have the same appeal! We fitted in with the Welsh children very well and made friends almost at once. This was just as well as no effort had been made to keep friends in the same villages and, in some cases, not even brothers and sisters.

We had one teacher, Miss King, billeted in the village and she taught us in the village hall, which was not ideal because our ages ranged from about seven to thirteen. Miss King was later succeeded by Miss Prior. Later we were told that we had to join some other evacuees at school in Ynysddu. After a while the Welsh Education Authority decided the local children should return to full-time schooling, so it was back to Wyllie village hall for us evacuees!

We were expected to attend the local chapel and Sunday School every Sunday. On Saturdays there was a bus that left Wyllie at 2pm for Blackwood returning at 8pm. This enabled the people of the village to go shopping or to the cinema. I don't think many of the village people went out of Wyllie very often – my foster parents certainly didn't!

The Welsh girl with whom I had made friends went to the grammar school in Blackwood, so the only time we were able to play together was during some of the evenings. I can remember her teaching me to knit and we would spend many moments knitting socks, gloves or balaclava helmets in khaki, navy or air force blue. We were allexpected to do our bit for the war effort!

In 1944 my father died of coronary thrombosis. There had been no known heart disease in my family, so I think his death must have been caused by stress. He had had a very hard and busy time after Dunkirk. When I finally left Wales, I joined my mother at Brenchley, then later moved to the Medway towns. I never returned to Dover to live. So when I left Dover Priory on that Sunday morning in 1940, things were never to be the same again!

*Olive Hopper (now Mrs Divito) was evacuated from Deal to Merthyr Tydfil:*

My next billet was a lot different to the first one. My new foster parents were Mr and Mrs Bull, the butchers! They must have been quite wealthy as they had a maid and a daughter who had music lessons – and who played the grand piano beautifully. We seemed to live on every kind of fowl, including duck. It was lovely! Mr and Mrs Bull were very good to me.

Later on my mother and sister came to Merthyr and I finally went to live with them. We had two rooms at 11, Park Place. Mrs Evans, our landlady, worked in the munitions factory. She always looked a sort of yellow colour, caused by something she was handling in the factory, but she was very kind and we all got on well. Her husband was away in the Royal Air Force.

Mum started to look after the welfare of the evacuees and she used to visit them in their billets to see if there were any problems. If problems did arise, she would try and get them moved to another billet. Often she would have to go at night and bring back a distressed child.

I can't remember the name of the school we went to, but I know it was halfway up the side of a mountain which we climbed twice a day – I suppose it was good exercise for us! We didn't take our education too seriously. I think we were more interested in the Folkestone Grammar boys who were also in Merthyr! I left school when I was fifteen and I had various jobs before joining the army. My mother returned to Deal in 1944, but sadly died the following year.

*Harry Stevens almost falls into a category of his own. He was put into an orphanage by his father in 1932 and, eventually, arrived at the Gordon Boys' Home in St James' Street, Dover:*

I left Newcastle for Dover and ended up in the Gordon Boys' Orphanage in St James' Street. I remember that above the front door of the home was a stained glass panel with an effigy of

143

Jesus holding a lamb, with the words, 'Suffer little children to come unto me.' We had a lovely chapel in the basement which was always highly decorated at harvest time.

War finally came in 1939 and within months evacuation was being talked about. The day finally came and Harry Friend and I finished up on a poultry farm at Guston – just outside Dover! While we were there we seemed to live on eggs, cooked every way possible. I think it was Barn Tye Farm. As the war progressed, we were moved again, this time to the village of Nutley in Sussex, and during the next four months I never saw another egg! We were to move yet again, to the Gordon Boys' Home in Woking, Surrey. This was a wonderful place and it was to shape the rest of my life. There were about 350 boys at Woking where they taught a variety of trades – cooking, carpentry, engineering and many others. The school was run on army lines, with the bugle ruling your life from reveille to lights out – but that's another story!

*(As a point of interest, all the Gordon Boys from Dover were dispersed during the early part of the war. During the war, the home in St James' Street was destroyed by enemy action, and the Gordon Boys never returned.)*

**Bessie Laurie** *(now Mrs Newton) recalls her time in Caerleon:*

Having walked out of my first billet after only one night, the authorities were furious with me because they thought we were all settled. I was then taken to Brook House which was almost upper class. The owners even had a double-barrelled name, Mr and Mrs Humphrey-Davies. They were quite elderly and had a daughter in her late thirties named Doris, and three sons.

The house was large, very posh and they had their own maid. My hosts were wonderful to me

*The Gordon Boys' Orphanage,*
*St James Street, Dover –*
*Sylvia Dunford collection*

and so kind, in fact it spoilt me and made me discontented with my lot in later life. I always kept in touch with mum and my brother – I never stopped missing them.

In the beginning, they had great problems with me at school. Miss Gruer, the headmistress, soon wrote home to mum and said, 'If Bessie doesn't pull her socks up, she will have to return to Dover! She is disrupting the other girls.' In those days a teacher told you to do something and you did it! But I didn't see why we should! That summer was particularly hot and we were taken for long walks, which I hated. On one occasion I just sat down and said, 'I'm not going!' If I had gone into a billet less grand, something like my home in Dover, I probably would have adjusted better. I was only fourteen, and we were very immature fourteen year olds in those days. After receiving the letter from Miss Gruer, my mother wrote to me and said, 'You are not coming back to Dover, you are going to pull your socks up and you are going to behave!'

We had two mistresses who ran the Girl Guides company in the school. They were Miss Rusbridge, who was later tragically killed, and Miss Swain. Miss Rusbridge was one of those charismatic persons and, apparently, Miss Gruer had said to her, 'Could you get Bessie into your Guides? It might do her some good.' So one Saturday morning Miss Rusbridge took me out and we walked for miles. When she asked me if I wanted to join the Guides, I said, 'No, I'm not joining – I don't want to be in anything!' But she was marvellous and, as most of my friends were already in the Guides, I decided I would join. This was the calming influence I needed. I later became a patrol leader and loved it. My school work improved and I did quite well.

For a time we shared a school at Pontypool but that didn't last long. Then we used huts which were situated in the playground of the primary school and we also used the Men's Training College in Upper Caerleon. In addition, we had the use of the Baptist and Methodist halls. Our schooling was so fragmented it was incredible how well we all did! The teachers were 'heroes'.

Eventually I became a prefect and I remember taking a small group of younger pupils into Newport to see the film *Bambi*. When we got there we couldn't get in because of huge queues. I went to see the cinema manager and said to him, 'Look, these poor children are all evacuees and I have brought them in specially to see *Bambi*.' And he gave us our own box in the cinema – so we saw the film after all!

We used to go to the youth club in Caerleon for table tennis. We also played netball and tennis, and we walked a lot. It wasn't all fun – some of us had great difficulty in just growing up away from home. Adolescence was not mentioned in those days, or the great difficulty of coping with menstruation. It was things like this, plus the fact that we were developing physically, that we didn't know how to cope. My parents visited me once while I was at Caerleon. I was quite independent by that time, and I secretly hoped that they wouldn't embarrass me. My foster parents were marvellous to them.

My evacuation made me mature very quickly and made me independent in a way that wouldn't have happened back in Dover. It also made me aware of the divisions in the social classes. I had a wonderful billet, but some of the evacuees were badly treated. I remember one girl in particular. She apparently had to get up early every morning to do the housework and, when she got back from school, she had more housework to do before trying to find time for her homework. She was always so tired but she was too frightened to say anything to the teachers. Other evacuees were often shut out of their billets all day!

My brother Harry had a nice billet in Cwmbran; his foster parents used to invite me up to tea and Harry would also come to Caerleon to see me. He returned home in about 1943 and eventually joined the Royal Air Force. Mum always said that seeing us being evacuated broke their hearts. How could I have ever been ashamed of her!

When I was almost eighteen I left the Dover County School in Caerleon, and returned to Kent. I remember going apple picking that year to earn some money. We stayed in huts on the farms. From there I went to London and into a nursing career so, from the day of evacuation in 1940, I never actually lived at home in Dover again, except for holidays.

*June Gilby* (now Mrs Smedley) was evacuated with her mother and grandmother to Blaenavon. She was just three years old at the time:

I was evacuated from Deal to live with my aunt and uncle in their flat in Blaenavon. My uncle, Ted Dash, was a miner at Big Pit Colliery. The flat was at 1a Lion Street, over a news-agent's shop. I remember Dando's the grocers on the opposite corner, and a greengrocer in the opposite direction. On the other side of Lion Street was a parking area where Harry the ram regularly came and I enjoyed feeding him with cabbage leaves! When I reached school age I was fortunate enough to be able to attend a Dover Primary School which had been evacuated to Blaenavon. It was a church school, St James', I think. We learned to recite the catechism and I always omitted the bit about godfathers and godmothers because, as a Methodist, I hadn't any!

The reception class teacher was rotund and motherly. Of course the teachers had to be very much *in loco parentis* since many of the children had been evacuated away from their parents. There were two classes in the same room and, when I got bored with what my class was doing, I just used to 'tune in' to what was going on in the other one. I particularly remember being deeply involved in the poem 'Cargoes', when I should have been doing my own class's work.

The reading scheme which we used was about a black Scottie and a white Westie called 'Mac and Tosh'. I also remember feeling very proud when I was promoted to cupboard monitor. This involved pasting strips of paper across the doors of the cupboard on Friday afternoons – and wet-sponging them off first thing on Monday mornings.

I was very happy at the Dover school with its warm and caring atmosphere. Unfortunately the school returned to Dover before my own family returned to Deal, so for two terms I had to transfer to a Welsh school called Hillside. This I found quite frightening as the atmosphere was so different. Everything was so regimented. We used to queue up in the playground and then proceed round the cloakroom, slinging our coats on to the appropriate hooks in passing. Any child who was even a minute late was publicly caned on each hand. There seemed to be very little personal interest or care for me or the other Kentish child who also remained.

One of the great joys was receiving American Red Cross parcels. What excitement there was as we opened the boxes to find the little toys, crayons, etc., inside. There were also the days when we were instructed to bring a jam jar to school. This would be filled with chocolate powder. I think it was supposed to encourage us to drink more milk, but most of us had the lids off as soon as we left school – and arrived home with sticky brown fingers and faces!

One of the great horrors was being supplied with my Mickey Mouse gas mask. Everything about it conjures up that nauseous rubbery smell. I am glad I never had to wear it other than in practices. The links between the East Kent coast and South Wales did not end after the war. Apart from those evacuees who kept in contact with their Welsh hosts, many of the Welsh miners, including my uncle, moved down to Kent to work in the Kent coal field.

*Patricia Avery* (now Mrs Weymouth) and her younger brother were evacuated from Dover:

What I remember most about leaving is seeing my mother standing at the top of the steps as we all trooped down towards Dover Priory Station. Alan looked such a little boy. He was carrying a tiny case, but I had all his things in my case. Mrs Keenan, a great family friend, had come to the top of the steps with my mother and had given a bag of comics for Alan and a bag of books for me. We left quite early in the morning and I remember when we got to Basingstoke, everyone came out to see us with great big jugs, mugs and food. It was a long journey to Wales, where we finally arrived very late in the afternoon. By this time younger ones were very homesick and tired.

We went as far as Blackwood by train and then by bus to Pengam where some of us were billeted out. I went to a Jones family who lived in an old three-storey house. I remember seeing

146

half a side of bacon hanging in white muslin just inside the front door. Old Mrs Jones had lost her husband the year before. She had a daughter, Choice, and a son, Meldwin, living with her at home. The family was very typically Welsh chapel. We went to chapel mornings and evenings on Sundays, but I didn't mind, in fact I quite enjoyed it. I was not allowed to read any book on Sunday except the Bible, and I was only allowed to play hymns on the piano.

The house had an outhouse in which was the first washing machine I had ever seen. It was operated by turning a handle round and round. There was a large kitchen with a flagstone floor. I had to clean this floor with a hearth stone every Friday or Saturday morning. I used to help with the washing up and do my own washing. I didn't have a hard life like some evacuees.

We would have things like currant cake for breakfast. We would have a meal of potatoes and meat at lunch time, but we would have the vegetables at tea time with bread and butter. It was most odd really, but I soon got used to it. I learned to like beetroot cooked with white sauce and in the summer we would have cooked runner beans with butter on.

Schooling was a little difficult. We had our classes in the main hall of Pengam School. Our teacher, Miss Jenkins, would do extra lessons in the evenings, with subjects like French, or mending and sewing, and we had quite a lot of music. The boys from St Martin's School sometimes joined in our activities at school. I remember Mr Twyman, who was a sort of headmaster for all the Dover evacuees in our area. He always encouraged 'Digging for Victory', and he always made sure that all the children were entertained and well looked after.

Mr Evans was the billeting officer as well as being a teacher, but it was Mr Twyman who used to check on our billets. It was just as well that I had a fairly strict billet, because I really grew up in those two years. In March 1942 I returned to Dover. I was sixteen and I wanted to train as a nurse. My brother Alan had a good billet and he stayed on in Wales.

***Bernard Burgess*** *recalls his short time with Sir Roger Manwood's Grammar School:*

At about 10pm on the first day of our evacuation, my friend Ron Southey and I were finally allocated a billet. We had piped water in ours but not everyone was so fortunate. Our hosts, an electrician, with his wife and little girl, were astonishingly kind considering they had to accommodate two hungry sixth-formers at short notice. Our hosts tried lava-bread on us for a joke (I had to eat Ron's!). They told us all about the village and the dreadful drowning of the cockle-girls and their donkeys many years previously. They seemed quite sorry when we left after a few weeks and gave us a folding picture postcard of Llanfairpwllgwngyllgogerychwyrndrobwillantysiliogogogoch, which they cut in two, giving us half each.

The head of our school was determined that the boys should be under strong discipline and not run riot. Those who were nominally Church of England had to go every Sunday to the English-speaking Episcopal Church, while Non-conformists had to attend the bi-lingual Methodist Church. The Methodist minister encouraged the boys to join in the Welsh hymns, explaining that Welsh is spoken exactly as it is written. Some of the old people in the village spoke English only with great difficulty. It was arranged that we would share the facilities of Gowerton Grammar School, about five miles away – but they could not accommodate all of us so the senior boys had lessons outdoors. Fortunately it was a marvellous June and I remember revising the poetry of Lamartine, sitting on a Welsh hillside, and thinking how strange it was to be studying French poetry while the world was falling apart.

While we were in Penclawdd an unknown benefactor gave the school the treat of a bus ride around the Gower Peninsula, before the unnecessary use of fuel oil was discouraged. I remember one of the buses got stuck under a bridge. Our head, who was a great 'fixer', got us moved a few weeks later to Carmarthen, where the billets all had running water and the boys could walk to the nearby Carmarthen Grammar School, which had good facilities. This time Ron and I were billeted quite palatially. Getting two schools into one building and sharing the facilities must have been a nightmare for those who had to organise it. Lessons often had to be

*Sir Roger Manwood's Grammar School cricket team on the Gower Peninsula, South Wales, 1940*

switched suddenly or cancelled because of some unforeseen emergency. I remember 'Sudds', the old English master, who had taught me since the age of eleven, almost crying with frustration and anger when I was sent by the second master with a message that he had to move his class to another room. He rebuked me for treating it as a joke but I remember thinking how trivial a matter it was compared with Dunkirk. Sudds had been used to a regular, ordered life and did not long survive the trauma of evacuation.

My schooldays were soon to come to an end. I sat the Higher School Certificate and said goodbye to Ron, who would now be the head boy. I called on the headmaster and took my leave. He gave me one last commission. When I got back to East Kent he wanted me to collect the keys of the school from the local solicitor, go into the school library and make a selection of a few hundred books from the shelves. These I was to send by rail to Carmarthen for the use of the boys. I was glad to do so, although it was a strange experience to wander round the silent, empty school, and thinking, 'Would Sir Roger Manwood's boys ever occupy it again?'

**Ron Southey**, *another sixth-former of Sir Roger Manwood's, recalls his time in Wales:*

My experience of evacuation was fairly short. I was already in the VIth form for the third year, spent vainly in search for a scholarship at Oxbridge. On the Sunday when Manwood's evacuated to Wales we caught glimpses of soldiers returning from Dunkirk.

The school was billeted first in Penclawdd, a small village on the Gower peninsula. The school captain, Bernard Burgess, and I were in the same billet. I remember that at the first breakfast we were given with our bacon a portion of lava bread, made from the local seaweed. Fortunately, while our hosts were out of the room, I managed to slip my portion on to Bernard's plate! 'Greater love hath no man . . .!' After a few weeks we moved to Carmarthen and I remember a farewell meeting in one of the village churches at which the headmaster, Mr E. P. Oakes, expressed the thanks of the school to the village and tactfully spoke as if the move to Carmarthen had been imposed upon him from above. The fact of the matter was that, as soon as the school had arrived in South Wales, the headmaster had searched the area for a place where he could maintain the boarding side of the school. This he found on the outskirts of Carmarthen.

During our short time in Penclawdd the school still managed to stage a cricket match against the village. The school XI were not as well turned out as they would have been on their own ground, but I expect that we had left much of our kit at home. While in Carmarthen I spent several weeks in a school, observing and teaching as part of my pre-university training course. I retain an impression of rather tough teachers and working in a room separated from two others by glass partitions, which made teaching an experience suggestive of a goldfish bowl!

During the summer holidays I cycled from Carmarthen to Caerleon, near Newport, where my girl-friend (and now my wife) was evacuated with the Dover Girls' County School. En route I stayed a night at Llangynwyd with the village postmaster, who had served with my father in the first World War. It was in this village that my old elementary school, Deal Parochial, was evacuated. One final point that I must add is that a Carmarthen man, D. O. Griffiths, joined the school staff in Carmarthen, remained with the school until his retirement and, as one might expect from a Welshman, made a huge contribution to the school's rugby over many years.

*Joyce Markwick, evacuated with the Folkestone County Technical School to Treharris:*

My best friend and I were very fortunate to be billeted with the local dairyman and his wife, Mr and Mrs Stephens. They had been expecting two small girls, so when two fifteen year olds walked into their home, they were somewhat surprised. Nevertheless, they were most kind and welcoming. We were given a good meal and then we had a lovely bath. Our billet was one of only a handful of billets which had a bathroom. Many of our girls were expected to wash in the kitchen in full view of the family – and, in one or two cases, to wash in the back yard!

We were extremely tired after the excitement of the long journey and once we were settled in bed we slept for fourteen hours! One of the things we did the following day was to write a short message on our pre-printed cards and post them home to our parents, to let them know we were alright. Later the whole school met in the local park. It was a scorching hot day and the first thing our headmistress told us to do was to wear ankle socks instead of the customary stockings. This was a great relief to all of us. We were also instructed about curfew regulations – no girl was to be out without an adult escort after 8pm in the summer evenings. The curfew time was subsequently altered to 6pm during the winter months.

It was arranged that we would share the building of a mining engineering school for some of our classes and the adjoining secondary school for others. The former school had all male pupils and we were warned that there was to be no fraternisation with any of these boys.

The schools were situated in a hamlet called Quaker's Yard, situated at the foot of a small mountain – and we had to practise running to the top of this mountain, to a clump of trees for cover in the event of an air raid. This had to be done in three minutes and we did this several times one hot afternoon after school, until we got it right.

We soon settled in although it took a little while to comprehend the very strong Rhondda accent. I learnt to speak a little of their language by going to chapel and singing the hymns in Welsh. I found it quite an easy language to read, but more difficult to understand. I was glad to return to Kent of course, but I look back with great happiness to my time in Wales. My foster parents treated me as their own daughter and I kept in touch with them for the rest of their lives.

*David Bates was evacuated with Deal Central School to Merthyr Tydfil:*

We assembled in Deal Railway Station yard, mainly in small family groups. I was with my two younger brothers. We each carried a small amount of personal belongings, ration books, gas masks, etc. Lots of the younger children were crying but I thought it was quite an adventure

*A group of children from Deal Central School. Photograph taken in Wales shortly after evacuation. David Bates is on the extreme left of picture – David Bates collection*

as I was aged twelve and had never been on any long journeys before. However, the journey proved long and tiring. My form teacher, Mr Rich, travelled with us and his wife, cried for most of the way! We must have used the same route as the troops from Dunkirk, for people were at the bottom of their gardens with flags and messages like 'WELCOME HOME'.

After hours of travelling we reached Merthyr Tydfil. Some railway coaches had been added to our train at Folkestone, and I remember a banner over Merthyr Town Hall which read, 'YOU WILL GET A FAIR DEAL HERE, FOLKESTONE.' There was no mention of the Deal children! Anyway, we were arranged into groups and taken by bus to Merthyr Vale where our foster parents were waiting for us. I and my younger brother were billeted with a miner's widow, in a typical back-to-back house. My other brother was billeted just a few doors away, so we were all fairly close to each other. We were treated very well by the Welsh people. They were very generous and kind, and chapel was a 'must' on Sundays.

That first summer we went tractor driving and working on farms in the Brecon area. Later, my younger brother was taken to Plymouth by our mother, as our foster parent found two boys too much to cope with. Dad was in the Royal Navy and was stationed in Plymouth. While in Wales I went to Pont Glas school, where the children of some of the friends I had made, lost their lives in the Aberfan tip disaster some years later. I stayed in Wales for two years and then I travelled the country working on communication cables, which was a reserved occupation. I returned to Deal in 1944 but only for a visit, so I never really lived at home again.

Although the people I stayed with in Wales have long gone, I still keep in touch with members of the family and I have made return visits over the years.

***Hazel Gillett*** *(now Mrs Russell) has vivid memories of being evacuated to Caerleon:*

I remember the Sunday we left home. It was eight or nine o'clock in the morning and I went on the longest journey I had ever made anywhere before in my life. I was 12 years old. My

150

younger sister had to go with another party because she was at another school. I didn't see her for some weeks, then I found out that she was at Blackwood. We reached Caerleon in the early evening and I can remember the local Girl Guides serving us cups of tea in the village hall. Then we lined up and marched round the village until we were sorted out into billets.

My friend and I stuck together like glue. We became 'cousins' for the occasion and nothing was going to separate us. As we got further and further away from the village we were dwindling in numbers, but they were still leaving two at a time at each house. Then my turn came and my bosom pal and I were taken into the same billet. We stayed 'cousins' for the rest of the war – we were so afraid of being split up.

I was one of the many who found a comfortable billet and a caring foster mother, although we had some very sad moments when we thought everything was against us. My cousin wasn't used to helping with the household chores whereas I came from a family of six and my father had only just got into full-time regular work, so we were all used to helping at home. We went to school in all kinds of venues, church and chapel halls etc., so there was a lot of moving about between lessons and, I must admit, quite a lot of lesson dodging as well!

Out of school hours were filled with many activities. Some of us were taken over by a local music teacher, and formed a choir which became known as the Dover Girls' Choir. Miss Slater, our leader, must have worked very hard with us because we became much in demand at local functions. One Christmas we raised £25 for the Red Cross by singing carols. This was a terrific amount but it took a lot of hard work. We had one very sad moment when one of our beloved school teachers was killed in a road accident. That tragedy took a long time to get over. Mostly, however, memories are happy. I used to go at weekends to visit my younger sister at Blackwood. Later, I travelled home for school holidays.

There are so many things I recall about my stay in Wales, not least the little boy in whose home I was billeted. He was the same age as one of my sisters so I suppose an affinity was already there. I must admit, I missed being with all my family, but this little boy did have some funny little sayings, which I remember to this day. One was, 'It's as white as snow only a little bit darker!' Another favourite little act of his was to climb on to his dad's knee, then call us to join him. His mum, my friend and I all had to snuggle together while he chanted 'Happy Family Circle'. Somehow this little act meant more to me than any other thing anyone did. He was a loving little chap – just four years old when we first met. We all finally returned home, but I have never forgotten the kindness shown to us during our evacuation to South Wales.

*Victor Mowles* was evacuated with St Bartholomew's School, Dover to Blackwood:

The long journey to Blackwood was very tearful for many of us. It was the first time most of us had been parted from parents and friends. When we finally arrived at our destination, we were put into groups and were soon handed over to the families we were to stay with. Our first billet was with Mr and Mrs Morgan at Holly Place. My sister Hilda (Midge) was so upset on that first night that Miss Clout, one of our teachers had to come to the billet and help put her to bed. We moved about four times during our stay in Blackwood.

After we had been in Wales for a few weeks, mum came to stay and on that day the air-raid siren went. It was the first time we had heard it since leaving Dover. Mum soon got a job at the munitions factory at Usk, where she worked shifts and eventually became shift leader.

After a shaky start in South Wales, we finally settled down, especially now that mum was with us. Sometimes the kids would gang up together and go up to the Black River to see the pit ponies being washed. When I had my ninth birthday in June 1941, I received a tricycle as a present. It didn't take me long to try it out. What I didn't realise at the time was that the tricycle only had one brake, but I soon found out when I went down the hill near our house and tried to stop! I went over the handlebars and dislocated my left thumb – and ended up at Newport

*Boys of St Bartholomew's School, Dover, pictured in Blackwood, South Wales.*
*BACK ROW (left to right): Bert Voller, Gordon Goldsack, Buster Davis, John Scrivens, Reg Wakefield, Fred Decent, Fred Fagg, Ron Chapman, Norman Piddock, Maurice Taylor.*
*MIDDLE ROW (left to right): Jack Decent, Les Hogben, Ron Alexander, Roger Medgett, Gordon Noremac, Pat Robson, Ron Hadlow, Dennis Wells, Percy Sheaff.*
*FRONT ROW (left to right): Bobbie Bruce, Bert Thompson, Peter Elgar – Peter Hayward collection*

*St Bartholomew's Boys' School, Dover, taken at Blackwood, South Wales, May 1941*
*– Vic Mowles collection*

Hospital. When I got back to my birthday party I wasn't allowed any food because of the anaesthetic, so I had to watch all my friends tuck into the party food.

Down in the main street, there was a shop called 'Conti's Ice Cream Bar'. They were very good to us evacuees. We could get broken wafers and a drink called sarsaparilla, which was something we had never tasted before. The other drink we could get was Tizer. Just down the hill near the school was a garage called Chastow's, where I used to go sometimes to see the men repairing cars. Once I played truant for a whole week, but the truant officer visited mum and I got into trouble. Eventually of course, we all returned home. I went back to Wales in 1990 and visited Blackwood. It seems a bit different now. Most of the surrounding area is covered with fir trees and there is no sign of the old pit tops. The school was nearly the same as I remembered it – mostly tin buildings and small classrooms. And the garage is still there!

*Peter Williams* was another pupil evacuated with Sir Roger Manwood's School:

Evacuation was quite an experience for us all – and it was also done in a hurry! Just a fortnight before we left Sandwich, we had been sharing our school with boys evacuated from Gillingham! When Sir Roger Manwood's School left Sandwich, we went by a special train and I remember we pulled alongside a train in Tonbridge which was packed with troops just back from Dunkirk; most of the troops were exhausted and asleep. Our train took us to Gowerton and somehow we finally arrived at Penclawdd on the Gower Peninsula. After a lot of waiting about – and hair inspection for nits (at which we were very indignant) we were allocated billets.

While everyone was extremely kind and helpful, Penclawdd was much too small to accommodate the school and the head, Mr E. P. Oakes, found accommodation at Pibwilwyd and Carmarthen, whence we moved after just two or three weeks. When the school reached Carmarthen, most of the pupils were placed as evacuees in private houses, but we also took over a farm institute at Pibwilwyd. The institute, which presumably had closed due to the war, consisted of a main building with a dairy attached. I remember that at first the dormitory was in the dairy, rather like the naval barracks I was to experience later. Pibwilwyd was a fine building facing south and was considered most suitable for our needs. I think about sixty Manwood's Boys were boarded there. All the boys attended school in Carmarthen where the grammar school had fine premises and was kind enough to find room for Manwood's as well. Most of the boarders cycled from Pibwilwyd to Carmarthen daily – about one and a half miles each way.

My brother and I left Pibwilwyd after a few months to live in a top floor flat at Llangunnor, as our parents were retired and came down to South Wales to be with us. I remember Carmarthen as a congested market town where every other building seemed to be a public house! I also remember the fairs in the streets. The countryside around Carmarthen was beautiful and we used to explore it on bicycles and with the school OTC – with boots and puttees! I left Wales in the summer of 1943 but Sir Roger Manwood's School stayed in Carmarthen until the end of the war.

*Roy Crofts* evacuated with his elder brother William to Blaenavon:

We all had our own little suitcases or kit bags with our own personal belongings that mum had packed for us and we were all taken up to the school. From there we went to Priory Railway Station. We had to have our kit and gas masks labelled – as well as ourselves! Mum had come to the station to see us off and we all said our farewells. I was almost seven years old and it seemed to me that this was a holiday. I don't think we fully realised what was going on.

We stopped at several stations along the way and I remember the Red Cross, nurses and volunteer people giving us refreshments through the windows of the train. We finally reached the mining town of Blaenavon in the early evening. Here we were met by a miners' band and it seemed as if all the people of the small town had turned out to greet us. I remember us smaller children being put on to a bus and being taken to one of the local schools where we had a meal. I think the older children marched from the station to the school.

After we had all been given refreshments we went out into the playground. Families like my brother, myself and my sisters kept together, and the local people came round and were just selecting the children they wanted. You can imagine how traumatic it was when brothers and sisters started to get separated. William and I went to a miner and his wife, Mr and Mrs Hill. They had a daughter of about 18 years of age living at home – her name was Ivy. They only wanted two boys, but they were persuaded to take our youngest sister Daphne as well.

It turned out to be a marvellous foster home but unfortunately my brother William couldn't settle. As a boy of thirteen he took a bit of controlling; they just couldn't cope with him and reluctantly he had to go. It was some time afterwards that dad came down to see us and within a year William was back in Dover. My foster parents also had problems with Daphne and she eventually went to another billet, but I was to stay with them and Ivy for the whole of the war. My foster parents were a very religious family and I used to go to the Horeb Baptist Church three times every Sunday – morning service, Sunday School in the afternoon and church in the evening. I also went to 'Band of Hope' on Tuesdays and 'Rope Holders' on Thursdays.

My foster father, Mr Hill, had been a deputy at the local coal mine for years until he had to give it up through ill health. While I was in Blaenavon, the firm of McAlpine brought in heavy machinery to start open-cast mining for the war effort, and Mr Hill got himself a job as a shot-firer. He would sometimes take me with him as he went over the mountainside placing the charges, then a horn would sound and everyone would take cover; just ten feet from the surface would be rich seams of coal up to eight feet thick. It was double British summer time and that particular summer was beautiful. They worked practically around the clock getting the coal out.

I remember an engineer who came to work with McAlpine's who was billeted with my foster parents. He hadn't been in Blaenavon long and we started to get on well. One day he said to me, 'When I come back from holiday we will get you started on some schooling in the evenings.' Unfortunately that never materialised. He went home on holiday and then we had a letter from his wife to say that he had died. He was a lovely man and everybody liked him.

We only used the front room on a Sunday. After returning from church, I would be allowed into the front room to sit at the table. There was a marvellous library of books all round the room and I was allowed to look at them because I was clean and in my 'Sunday best'. I also remember the organ they had which was set in the wall of the house.

Mr Hill had an Austin Seven motor car which he kept at his garage near the civic restaurant. He took me up there this particular day and because petrol was in short supply, we jacked the car up on to blocks and took the wheels off. Mr Hill used to receive a few petrol coupons each month, enough to go only a few miles. So he used to save the coupons up until his summer holidays when he would put the wheels back on the car and we would go through the Welsh valleys, exploring the old quarries and picking the fruit that grew wild – it was really lovely.

When I look back, even though there was food rationing during the war, we always seemed to have plenty to eat. I had an exceptional home where they treated me as one of the family. Unfortunately, my five sisters weren't as lucky. They had a hard time of it during their stay in Wales. My oldest sister,

*Broad Street, Blaenavon drawn by Don Lewis*

Sylvia, returned home after a couple of years, and my sister Iris never really got over the traumatic time she had during her evacuation.

When we all finally returned home, mum was at Dover Priory Station looking out for us. Dad and mum had both been down twice to Wales to see us so she obviously knew what we looked like, but she didn't recognise poor Iris! She had gone away a plump girl – and she came back thin as a rake! But I was very lucky; I don't mind admitting it.

At one time I am sure my foster parents wanted to adopt me. I spent five years  and they became more like my own parents. When I did return home I was not happy and it took me a long, long time to settle. My mother was very upset because she could see how unhappy I was. She even said to me, 'You might have to go back.' I didn't of course but that initial period when I first returned home was quite traumatic. I went into a family where there was an only daughter who made a fuss of me – something I never got at home – there were too many of us! I had a wonderful life in Wales, had my own bedroom and then I came back to Glenfield Road, Dover, where there were thirteen of us in a three-bedroomed house. I still don't know how we all managed! Mum and dad did their best and I just had to get on with it.

I kept in touch with my foster parents after the war and they came down to Dover to see me on one occasion. After that we lost touch. But I still have my memories of those happy days.

*Ciceley Beer* (now Mrs Thomas) *stayed in Kent for most of the war but was evacuated to Wales in order to join her new school:*

I had lived through the Canterbury blitz; seen the damage in the village and the craters made by bombs dropped in the fields nearby; studied in windowless bunkers at school; seen enemy aircraft, their swastikas clearly defined, fly overhead; watched many a dogfight in the sky and then, in the autumn of 1944, in order to join the Dover County School for Girls, I was to become an 'evacuee'! I had never heard of the word before and I had no idea what it meant. However, I was a fairly placid child and took most things in my stride, so off I went to Wales.

My mother travelled with me to Paddington Station, where we all piled into the special carriages set aside for the boys and girls of the Dover County Schools. We each took a few personal belongings, plus the ever-present gas mask in its brown, square, cardboard box. The boys and girls were supposed to travel in separate compartments, but in fact quite a lot of mixing went on – and quite a lot of smoking too! On our arrival in Caerleon we were given a reception in a large hall with long tables covered in white tablecloths. We were treated to tea and buns. Those who had already been allocated to families were then taken off to their new homes, while those of us who had not been placed were taken to the hostel until homes were found for us. My friend and I slept in the same bed, in a large room with several other girls. We were reasonably happy there, but I remember feeling hungry for most of the time.

After a few days we were placed with foster families. Several of us went to homes in Christchurch, near Newport. I was cared for by a middle-aged, house-proud couple, whom I called 'Auntie' and 'Uncle'. They were kind to me, but they had no children of their own and didn't understand the needs of a shy eleven year-old girl. I remember being reprimanded for leaving finger prints on the banisters and was told not to touch them when walking down stairs!

It seemed a long journey to school, one bus from Christchurch to Newport and another from Newport to Caerleon. Once there we walked from place to place for our lessons. Some were in schoolrooms, some in the college at the top of the hill, others in a variety of church halls scattered around the town. We had plenty of exercise! One church hall, I recall, opened on to the bank of the river Usk. We were allowed to sit out there on sunny days while we ate our sandwiches. Soggy lettuce and Marmite sandwiches seemed to be my standard diet. Occasionally, during the summer, we walked to school a much shorter distance as the crow flies, up a steep hill (Royal Oak Hill) and down Catash Road, a long ashy path on the other side.

155

We sometimes paddled in the clear, fast-flowing River Usk. This must have been a dangerous thing to do and we were told not to do it, but we were disobedient. Sunday School was encouraged and the outings were fun. One such outing was a trip to Goldcliff, on the Bristol Channel. We had a picnic and then walked along the muddy rocks. A sheep had fallen from the cliff on to the rocks below and had died. What strange things we remember!

Other highlights were visits made by the niece of the family. Her name was Beryl and she lived in Cardiff. She was then about eighteen years old, golden-haired and glamorous. Beryl collected pictures of film stars for me and together we made a much-treasured scrapbook. Betty Grable was a favourite then and we tried to copy her dance routines.

I was very fond of reading and was encouraged to get books from the library. I would break my journey home from school to collect a new set of books. Later, when auntie became ill, I moved to a different family, just along the road. This time I was cared for by a young couple with a little boy called David. He was about five years old at that time. We became friends and I would spend hours telling him stories which I had read in the books I had got from the library. I lived happily with them until it was time to return to Kent and my home in Aylesham.

My impression of being an evacuee is that it was not especially awful or particularly exciting. It can't have been much fun for all the families who took in and cared for us 'war refugees' during those years. It was certainly good to be back with my real family at the end of the war.

*Marjorie Easter (now Mrs White) from Sandwich was one of twelve children. She was only five years old when she, an older brother and two of her sisters were evacuated in June, 1940:*

On the day of evacuation the whole family came to see us off. I can remember being terrified because I thought I would be in trouble if I lost my tag with my name on it. The journey seemed to go on for ever. We finally arrived in Three Crosses, a small mining village in South Wales. We were then taken to a hall where we all stood and waited to be chosen. When we were billeted out, my brother went to another village called Killay. My sister Kath was billeted in a house in Three Crosses and was very happy there. I

*Children of the Easter family. Picture taken at Sandwich prior to their departure to Wales*

stayed close to my older sister Margaret and, because we didn't want to be separated, we were left until last.

We were eventually billeted with Mr and Mrs Thomas. I don't think we were there long because Mrs Thomas became pregnant and couldn't cope, so we were sent to stay with her mother, Mrs Long, who lived at the post office in Three Crosses only a few doors away from our sister Kath. Nearby was another family of evacuees from Sandwich, the Mays.

Mrs Long was quite strict with us, but I think she only smacked me once. Her husband was the headmaster of a local school and he used to help me with my sums. I remember knitting an egg cosy and sending it home to mother. I remember we had a school outing to Mumbles on the Gower Peninsula, with Mr Sage who later taught in Sandwich. That winter I had terrible chilblains and I remember being lifted into a car to go to school. I also remember singing in the chapel and I always equate my love of music to the time I spent in Wales.

I was taken to Swansea Market just before Christmas, 1940, where I bought a little doll nurse for ten pence. That Christmas was really good because many of Mr and Mrs Long's family came for the celebrations, and Margaret and I were included. At Easter 1941, my foster mother made me a beautiful blue satin dress with a big bow on it. During 1941, Mr and Mrs Long's son, who was in the Royal Air Force, was lost in action. In November 1941, my mother wanted us back home and we returned to Sandwich. I never kept in contact with my foster parents and I have never been back to Three Crosses, but overall I have nice memories of my stay in Wales. If one were to ask me what effect did evacuation have on my life, I would say that it gave me inner strength throughout my life, and it has made me more independent.

***Kath Easter*** (*now Mrs Attryde), sister of Marjorie above now gives her account:*

With the threat of invasion in 1940 it was decided that the Sandwich school children would be evacuated to South Wales. Mothers with children under school age were also encouraged to go. I come from a large family. My eldest sister, who was fifteen, was already working when the decision to evacuate was taken, so it was decided that my brother Harold, thirteen years old, my sister Margaret aged eleven, myself aged nine and young Marjorie, who was only five, should go, on the understanding that Marjorie and Margaret would not be parted.

Mothers travelling to Wales with their own children were asked to be helpers and were allocated up to seven children to look after, which included their own. We were looked after by Mrs Marey who came from Woodnesborough. She was travelling with her daughter Joy. Apparently, the helpers were also to check the new foster homes from time to time and to make sure that the children wrote home regularly.The journey itself seemed like a great adventure. I don't think any of us had travelled much before the evacuation.

It took most of the day to reach Swansea, where we left the train and were put into buses to take us to the villages. Our destination was a place called Three Crosses, and my brother and his friends went to Killay about six miles away. When we got to Three Crosses we were taken to the village chapel where one by one we were put on to a table to be looked at by prospective foster parents! It was dreadful, especially after a very long and tiring day. I think it would have been less humiliating if the children could have been assigned to families through paperwork rather than put them through the 'cattle market' procedure.

I was chosen straightaway, but my sisters had to wait a long time for someone who would take both of them. I was billeted with a coalman who had his own business and, by my own family's standards, my foster parents were very well-to-do. Their names were Mr and Mrs Davies and they had a large house. Their married daughter had her own rooms in the house while her husband was away in the army. Unfortunately there was no bathroom in the house! Mr Davies always used a large tin bath in the scullery every day to wash off the coal dust. There was no main drainage in the village and the toilet was halfway down the garden!

The family was very kind to me and treated me as their own. Mr Davies was the organist at the chapel and on Sundays I was expected to attend morning and evening service as well as Sunday School in the afternoon. One thing that none of us liked while we were there was the habit of some of the Welsh people suddenly switching to the Welsh language, as though we weren't meant to understand what they were talking about. We stayed in Wales for 18 months, during which time my mother managed to visit us once and stayed with me for a couple of nights. An aunt also visited when she came down to take some children back home.

Towards the end of our stay in Wales, Swansea was bombed heavily for three nights running. I remember being woken up and being taken downstairs to sit under the dining room table until the all clear sounded. I think this was the turning point for our parents who decided that we might as well be home as bombed elsewhere, so as soon as arrangements could be made, we all returned to Sandwich. It is over fifty years since I returned home, but I still keep in touch with the daughter of Mr and Mrs Davies.

*Frank Stevens was six when he and brother Sidney were evacuated from Folkestone:*

I joined the evacuation process at the time of Dunkirk and, as I was only six years old, I was not fully aware of what was going on. I didn't even know what the term 'evacuation' meant until years afterwards. We were told that we would be travelling in parties, which I thought was great! Parties to me at that age meant cake, jellies and lemonade!

In Wales we got out of the train at some unknown station and gathered in the 'cattle yard'. There we were viewed by local people and selected for placement. My brother Sidney, who is two years older than me, was also there and we were selected by Mr and Mrs Rees and taken to their smallholding home near Crick. Our first meal was of freshly boiled eggs and bread and butter. It was wonderful. The local school could not take us so we moved to the village of Pwllmeyric near Chepstow. Our new carers were a very old couple who no doubt did their best, but who found it hard to cope with two young boys. We walked to the village school a short distance away and picked wild strawberries from the banks on the way.

At this time we were visited by our mother who was appalled at our poor condition and made arrangements for us to return to her care. Mum took us to London – we sat in

*Photograph of Frank Stevens (sitting) and his older brother Sid, taken just before evacuation – Frank Stevens collection*

shelters at night, listening to the shrapnel fall around us and, by day, we would go through the streets picking up bomb and shell fragments. Eventually we went to Doncaster where dad was stationed and, in July 1944, we returned to Shorncliffe Camp which we had left four years previously.

*Raymond Harris and his elder sister Rita were evacuated from Cheriton and were billeted with Mr and Mrs Jehu on a farm in the village of Grosmont, not far from Abergavenny:*

We awoke early on that first morning to the sound of a rooster crowing and some strange noise that we couldn't fathom out until we were told it was Benny the bull roaring. We felt very strange going down to breakfast and, after being greeted by our hosts, we learned that Mr and Mrs Jehu had been checking on both of us all through the night to make sure we were okay.

After breakfast they took us on a tour of the farm, which I really enjoyed. I was shown a very young calf and was told I would share the

*Raymond Harris, centre-front of photograph, with sister Rita, top-left, taken at Grosmont during the evacuation – Raymond Harris collection*

job of looking after it with their young son Derek. We then met Bonnie, a dear and lovable horse who never tired of having Derek and me riding on her back. We all had little tasks to perform, mainly to keep us busy and to take our minds off being away from home. Derek and I helped to clean the stables and do a few other small jobs, while my sister, Rita, apart from a few household chores, fed the chicken and geese with grain from a bucket. The first time she tried to feed them, the flock of geese chased her, so she threw the bucket at them and ran – much to the merriment of Mr Jehu and Ivor their farmworker.

After a few days, the escorting teachers, having made sure that we were settled, returned home. The only unhappy memory of that time took place when I attended the village school. Whether the Welsh teacher didn't care for the extra workload, or just didn't like English children, but we evacuee boys were in mortal fear of him, and beatings were commonplace.

The rest of my memories of that period are mainly very happy ones; the harvesting,

*Raymond Harris's foster parents, Mr and Mrs Jehu, and their young son Derek – Raymond Harris collection*

*The farm near Grosmont where Raymond Harris and his sister Rita were billeted – Raymond Harris collection*

getting the cattle in for milking, watching Ivor milk the cows by hand – and getting squirted with milk as Ivor aimed an udder at us! Mrs Jehu made sure that we wrote home to mum and dad every week. She also wrote to them with a progress report every so often. After a while mum and dad managed to find a house in Shropshire and naturally wanted us back with them. Mr and Mrs Jehu were very sad at the prospect of losing us and begged mum and dad to let them keep us, but to no avail. My mother, father, two brothers, sister and I settled in Shropshire and never returned to Folkestone after the war.

**Colin Bailey** *recalls a few memories of his many billets in Wales:*

I was evacuated with River School, near Dover, on Sunday 2nd June, 1940. We left River early by double decker buses for the Priory Station. The waiting train took us via Canterbury to Ashford, then to Tonbridge and Salisbury (where we were given a drink of water by Boy Scouts). We left the train at Blackwood in Monmouthshire and went by bus to Aberbargoed in the Rhymney Valley. Here we were billeted with local families and shared the local school.

Relationships were good and I was fortunate to have a very homely billet. I stayed there until I left to join the Dover County School in September 1941 at Ebbw Vale. For some time, schooling was on a shift basis. We did mornings one week and afternoons the next, sharing the local county school. We were forced to learn rugby – and mostly lost to the locals.

I spent school holidays with my parents who had been evacuated to the St Neots area. I had five billets during my stay in Ebbw Vale. The last billet was in Lilian Grove where I stayed with three other Dover boys. The four of us shared two double beds in one room for fifteen months. It did have its fun aspect! We left Wales in December 1944 when the school returned to Dover. During my time in Wales I found the Welsh people to be very hospitable.

*Joyce Heath (now Mrs Larner) and her brother returned home within eighteen months:*

My brother and I were billeted in Ynnysdu with Mr and Mrs Williams who already had six children of their own, although their oldest son was away in the army. It must have been a bit of a squash but, at twelve years old, these things didn't worry me.

We were treated well by our foster parents, in fact we were just absorbed into their large family and treated just the same as the other children. However, my parents visited us in the summer of 1941 and my mother was horrified when she discovered that I had head lice. Mother was so indignant that she even went storming up to my school and confronted poor Miss Parkinson, our headteacher, who was very upset about it. She told my mother that it was not the first instance of this sort and it was the reason why some children had already returned home.

Anyway, my mother made the necessary arrangements and we returned home to Dover about a week before Christmas, 1941. I think my mother would have used any excuse to have us back with her again, despite the bombing and the shelling.

*Helen Crick (now Mrs Gerard) left Deal for Merthyr Vale:*

I had been billeted with 'Nana' Sullivan, Nodene and family on my arrival in Merthyr Vale. On the first morning I went downstairs and Nana said, 'Go and wash in the bosh.' I opened the back door and there outside was the bosh – a square sink placed on bricks, with just a cold tap. I washed at the bosh every morning. Our lavatory was at the bottom of the garden and the toilet paper was squares of newspaper hung on string.

The milkman came around with his horse and cart every morning. His milk was in large milk churns and we would take our jugs out to be filled. I went to Aberfan School which the evacuees shared with the local children. I used to stand in the playground and look up at the huge ugly coal tip which seemed to loom over the whole of the school. After the war, there was to be a terrible tragedy at the school when the coal tip moved and buried many of the children.

Eventually we left Aberfan School and amalgamated with the boys of Merthyr Vale. I was also reunited with my brothers. Walter and I were in the same class. Mr Mainwood was the headmaster and our teacher was Mr Bradley. The people of the village had their coal delivered in huge loads, dumped outside the houses. When Nana's coal was delivered, it was the job of Nodene and me to bring all this coal through the house and stack it in the coal shed. Some of the coal was great big pieces. When we had finished, we had to clean the pavement outside and the passage through the house before we had tea. This happened every month.

Eventually, my mother, new baby sister, gran and sister Sarah all joined us at Merthyr Vale. Gran died while we were in Wales, and she is buried in Aberfan Cemetery. We returned to Deal when the war finished.

*Ena Colquhoun (now Mrs Colquhoun-Flannery) and her sister Jean, evacuated from Folkestone to Caerphilly, reflects on her short time in Wales:*

We had a lovely billet and Mr and Mrs Davies, our foster parents, were very kind to us. We went to chapel two or three times on Sundays and most of the service was in Welsh. Weekdays were fine – only half-day education, sharing the school with the Welsh pupils. But the night times were awful. Jean and I became very homesick and cried a great deal.

Mum visited us once and I remember feeling shy when she arrived. My dad came back from France and was stationed in Yorkshire. He and mum must have discussed our problem because, eventually, dad found rooms for us all where he was stationed. I could not believe my mother years later, when she told me that we were only in Wales for about nine weeks! It seemed like an eternity. We eventually came back to Folkestone in 1942, amid the bombing and shelling, and finished our education at Harcourt Girls' School (now known as Pent Valley School).

*Another Folkestone girl, **Margaret Hodges** (now Mrs Brooker), evacuated with St Mary's School to Croesyceiliog, remembers well her two and a half years in Wales:*

I stayed with Mr and Mrs Charles all the while I was in Wales, but my foster-sister Edith with whom I had been evacuated, eventually moved to another family. Mr Charles played the organ at the church we attended, St Mary's Church of England, and Mrs Charles was the Sunday School superintendent. She introduced me to the world of drama; I was entered for a poetry competition in Newport at the age of nine – and I came second. Later, in adult life, I performed in many productions at the Swan Theatre in Worcester.

I was very happy after the initial period of settling in and for the whole of the two and a half years, we never saw our parents, but we did keep in contact by letter. In November 1942 my real mother obtained accommodation in Worcester, and arrangements were made for me to join her. Another traumatic time for me! I was being separated from Edith and going to live with someone who was a stranger. I had been a foster child with Edith's parents from the age of a few weeks, as my own parents had split up before I was born.

Anyway, I was taken to Newport Station on a cold November morning and I remember pleading with Mrs Charles to let me stay with her, but she talked to me and insisted that my place was now to be with my mother. I don't think I stopped crying throughout the journey to Worcester – and for that first night. My mother was so distressed that she wrote to Mrs Charles to ask her to have me back, but Mr and Mrs Charles were very sound thinking people and said I must be given more time to settle down. During the next few weeks I made friends and it wasn't too difficult to adjust. I stayed in communication with the Charles family, but never visited them for a very joyful reunion until many years later, when I was married with two small sons.

Mr and Mrs Charles are now both dead. I did visit Croesyceiliog once since their death, but with all the changes the place is hardly recognisable. I have no wish to return.

***Keith (Mac) McInnes** spent some time in Cefn Forest before going to Ebbw Vale:*

When I started at the Dover County School in Ebbw Vale, I was in trans prep class. This was for 10 year olds prior to taking the common entrance exam. Miss Rookwood ran this class; she was known to many as 'Old Ma Rooker' and was described as looking like a battleship going into action. A large woman with her hair combed straight back.

I lived right by the school at first. After about a year I moved down to Cwm where my brother Ian was in a billet at 127 Canning Street. Our hosts were Mr and Mrs Wilkinson. He was an overman at the Marine Colliery, and Ron, their son, worked in the steel works nearby. They had another son, John, at school. Each week we walked the longest straightest street in the country (or so we thought), with its whitewashed cottages on either side. Marine Colliery was at the end of the street and we had our weekly scrub down at the pithead baths.

Mr Kendall, a form master, lived in Cwm and was always about to see we behaved ourselves. We went to school by train, which was a tank engine on a single line. I can remember riding on the engine and having a go at stoking the boiler. Another memory I shall have for life is the only time I ever had the cane. I had been involved with other lads throwing sticks at each other during a break between classes. Three strokes of the cane was the punishment, given by Spud Slater. He decided we had shamed the school. I have always bruised easily and this was no exception. I was all colours of the rainbow for weeks after the caning.

Phil Buss was our sergeant major in the school Army Cadet Force and my boyhood hero. He went on to fame in the Korean War and being a prisoner of war. Later he was chairman of Dover District Council. In Cwm we lads had a special privilege bestowed upon us. We were allowed into the miners' institute to play billiards or snooker at 6d a game. Other kids had to go to the local Stute Hall. Anyway, we stayed in Cwm until our school returned to Dover in December 1944. I have discovered that my evacuation produced wanderlust, but I have always suffered from homesickness.

*Mercy Webber* (now Mrs Batchelor) was evacuated with Dover County School for Girls:

During the four years I spent in Caerleon I stayed at three different billets. At the first address I stayed with an older childless couple. On the other side of the road was a large mental hospital and most of the houses opposite were occupied by male nurses. On rare occasions when there was an air raid at night, we would cross the road and go down into the basement of the hospital, which we shared with the patients. After a few months there was an influx of more children, this time from London. A much younger girl called Josephine came to live with us.

Our only communication with our parents was by letter. We had sixpence a week pocket money, out of which I had to buy a postage stamp. I used to write long letters home and keep them in my wardrobe until I was ready to post them. It was about a year after I had arrived in Lodge Road that I wrote an unhappy letter to my mother. My hostess found it in my wardrobe, half finished, and after reading it she told the school that I must leave her house. This was after an episode some time previously which at the time affected me deeply. For my first birthday since being evacuated, my mother sent me a full length, pink party dress. What luxury! I'd never hoped to possess such a garment. Before I had worn it my hostess took it and hung it in her wardrobe 'for safety'. My birthday was on the 3rd December and when the school holiday came I was to travel to Exeter where my mother was staying with relatives.

Obviously I wanted to take the dress with me and when my hostess produced it, the hem to a depth of about three inches had become stained with dark brown creosote. She kept a tin of the stain in her wardrobe to keep the moths away and the dress had fallen into it. I did wear the dress that Christmas, but only after a sizeable chunk had been cut off. There was a subsequent episode when my hostess alleged that I had broken a thick glass tray which stood on her dressing table, in spite of the fact that I would never enter the room without her permission.

Further down Lodge Road, was a hostel for girls who were temporarily without a billet and this is where I went next. It was run by Mrs Wootton, a large lady with a strong Welsh accent. Apart from her sitting room and bedroom, the large house was mostly unfurnished except for camp beds in the bedrooms and bare tables and chairs in the dining room. The food was wholesome but very basic as was the majority of food then, except for clever cooks.

After about four weeks I went to live with Mr and Mrs Ainge, a friendly down-to-earth couple from Bromsgrove, with a son named Robert. Mr Ainge worked in Cwmbran. I was very happy there and later two more girls from Walmer, Betty and Joan Martin, came to join me – it was a large house with four bedrooms. However, after about another year, disaster struck (as far as I was concerned). Mr Ainge's job took him back to Bromsgrove. So it was back to the hostel for me, and Betty and Joan too. I had a longer stay at the hostel this time and the standard of the food seemed to have gone down. At one point the only thing we had to spread on our bread and margarine at breakfast and teatime was black treacle.

My last host and hostess were Mr and Mrs Banner in a very large semi-detached house in

Ponthir Road. They were older than Mr and Mrs Ainge and had no children but made me feel welcome. I had a very large bedroom and a lovely view looking over the long garden and towards the distant hill. I had to do my own washing for the first time, but I didn't find this too hard. My history teacher, Miss Fitch, was living next door and Miss Mackenzie, who taught the sixth form commercial subjects, lived across the road with another Mr Banner and his family.

It was here that I was able to do my homework, swotting for the School Certificate Examination. Then I heard news on the wireless of the D-day landings and subsequent battles. I did well in the exam and gained a matriculation certificate. Our schooling had been very erratic but by the time I left Caerleon in July 1944, our education was almost normal.

Our teachers were as follows: Miss Gruer, headmistress; Miss Fisher, deputy head and English teacher; Miss Gambrell, music; Miss Smith, French; Miss Fitch, history; Miss Rusbridge, maths; Miss Swain, geography; Miss Cox, English; Miss Menie, science and biology; Miss Laurie, gymnastics and games; Miss Anderson, domestic science; Miss Mackenzie, commercial subjects. Three other teachers did not come to Caerleon and I understood that they had been called up for national service.

From time to time we were taken to concerts in Newport, where I was lucky enough to hear Eileen Joyce play the piano. On another occasion we went to the University at Cardiff for a performance of Purcell's opera, *Dido and Aeneas*. Sometimes we were taken to the cinema in Newport. Much interest was shown in the film of Handel's life until it transpired that a small section of girls believed the title of the film to be *The Great Mr Handley*. Understandably, we were never allowed to travel without the company of a member of staff.

My mother had obtained a residential post as cook at one of the halls of residence at Exeter University and my brother and I were allowed to stay during school holidays when most of the students were away. While she lived at Hope Hall I was there when the big incendiary raid on Exeter occurred, which was very frightening. The big house next door was burnt down. I remember a group of students manning the hoses. I returned to Caerleon the next day, because of the raid. Our headmistress used to get very angry about girls going home for the long school holidays. She was quite right to do so, because we had been evacuated for our own safety. I suppose everyone became rather blasé about any possible danger.

During the war everyone had to carry their gas mask with them wherever they went. All sorts of different containers became available from shops which were better than the original cardboard box in which the masks were distributed which tended to wear out. I spent a year in the sixth form and finally left school in July 1944. An interview had been arranged by the school for a post at the Deal Library. I started work two weeks after I returned home. The main library in Deal had been destroyed by enemy shelling so I worked at the smaller Walmer branch. Later a very small branch was opened in Upper Deal in an empty fish and chip shop!

*Margaret Ward (now Mrs Griffiths) recalls being evacuated to South Wales with Folkestone Technical School for Girls – and of the 'memento' she brought back from Wales:*

When the war started in September 1939 I had just started going to the Folkestone Technical School for Girls for a two years course in typing, shorthand, book-keeping and commerce. I was 14 and living in the village of Sutton, near Deal. I cycled to Walmer Station to catch the train to school every day. By 1940 the situation had got worse with many air raids. It was finally decided that our school should be evacuated to Wales. On Sunday, 2nd June, 1940, I cycled to Deal Station, leaving my bike at a friend's house to be picked up by my mother. I caught the train to Folkestone where we assembled at the school with our cases, identity cards, ration books, gas masks and a label with our name and school on it.

What a journey that was! I had started from my home at 7.30 in the morning, and did not reach our destination in Wales until 4.30 in the afternoon. It was a very hot and sticky day but all the while the train was moving we were alright but we would suddenly be diverted on to sidings to let troop trains pass. We then had to sit in the heat of the day until we could start again but at last we reached Merthyr Tydfil in Glamorgan. We were met and welcomed by a local committee who led us to coaches and we were off on the last stage of our journey to a small mining town called Treharris. We were taken to the primary school where we had tea and waited to be billeted out. My friend Kath and I had said that we would like to stay together, so we sat and waited and waited whilst most of the other children were taken to their foster homes by the local scouts. We were very tired and missing our families so, in the end, Kath and I decided to split up and were immediately given addresses to go to. Our bags were carried by the scouts, who had apparently been waiting for us to arrive at the school since 10 o'clock in the morning. We soon reached the house where I was to live for the next three years. The lady who opened the door looked startled for a moment. She had been expecting a little girl to be company for her two small daughters, but instead she got a tall 14 year old.

But the welcome was there and, in the days that followed, the evacuees were greeted by everyone they met with such friendliness. Life for me in Wales was a very happy time and although I missed my parents and family a great deal, by joining in with the local community the time passed well. The war seemed a long way off but when the bombers hit Cardiff and Swansea, I used to watch the glow of fire from the back yard of my billet.

I joined the local church choir, the Girl Guides and the ATC. There were also dances in 'The Rink' as we got older – and the cinema was well frequented. Letters to and from home told how we were all coping. My parents had a suitcase packed at all times in case they had to leave home at short notice because of invasion. Rationing was hard on everyone. I hardly ate meat as I felt that my foster father, who was a mine worker, needed it more than me. Sweets were rationed, but I was lucky as my parents had the village shop, and would send me parcels – sweets, chocolate and home made jam. I often queued for my foster mother, in order to get some 'off ration' duck eggs from a farmer's lorry. Some people had relatives in Canada or America who sent parcels of food – tinned salmon and processed cheese being the favourites.

I stayed in Wales after I left school and got a job in a factory in Merthyr Tydfil as a typist. The factory, Rotax, was an offshoot of Joseph Lucas, and made spare parts for aeroplanes. When I went home for holidays, I used to be very relieved to get through London safely, especially when the V2 rockets were dropping there. I witnessed several dog fights and I also saw a V1 Doodlebug flying overhead. When the war ended we all returned home.

I managed to bring something back with me from Wales – the tall Scout whom I had first seen on our arrival in Treharris in June 1940 and we have been together ever since! I never regretted that day I travelled to Wales.

*Marion Richardson (now Mrs Boxall) was living in Ashford and attending the Ashford South Central School at the time of her evacuation to Oxford and a little later to South Wales:*

On the 13th of September 1940, I went to the Ashford South Central School with my gas mask, my case and some sandwiches. We lined up and walked to Ashford station with our teachers where we eventually boarded a train for we-knew-not-

*South Central School, Ashford, at time of evacuation.*

164

*South Central School, Ashford, evacuated to Oxford, September, 1940*
*pictured at the University College Pavilion – Marion Boxall collection*

where. It was a hot September day, the train was packed and it seemed to travel very slowly. We had no idea where we were going but, wherever it was, it seemed to take for ever! Eventually we piled out on to the platform at Oxford station but, apparently, we were not expected! With our luggage, we walked with hundreds of other children to Oxford Town Hall which was already crowded. We were issued with a straw palliasse and a blanket and then tried to find a spot where we could rest. Every bit of the floor was covered, even the balconies, corridors and stage. The noise was terrific and sleep was almost impossible. All night long the noise continued. A tiny child of two or three was next to me and she cried for her mummy, so my first night was spent cuddling her. The next day our teachers had our group moved into a corridor outside the main hall.

Gradually the town hall cleared as children were billeted throughout the city. We slept at the town hall for two nights, until my turn came to be walked round the streets to where a friendly home awaited me. I was taken, with a younger girl, Alma Weller, to the home of Mr and Mrs J. Lewis of 23 Edith Road, Oxford, who were kindly Baptist folk.

We all met together each day and our teachers took us on tours round the local colleges. There were many school parties needing rooms for lessons and our group was allocated two rooms at All Saints Junior School. We also had lessons in the University College Pavilion. I remember one art lesson where we had to sit by the river near Folly Bridge and draw the swans. Once our headmistress, Miss Bettison, came to visit us. She wept when she said how empty the streets were in Ashford and there was no-one to pick up the dropped conkers!

My stay in Oxford was far quieter than the Battle of Britain Hell Fire Corner, but we did have air raid warnings when German planes droned overhead on their way to bomb the industrial towns of the Midlands. My mother came to stay for a week and had to share the double bed which I normally shared with Alma. During that week, Alma developed scarlet fever and was taken to the isolation hospital. As I was a contact, I had to stay at home for three weeks. By the time the three weeks were up, I had been 'found' by the Kent Education authorities and was directed to South Wales to join the Folkestone Technical School.

*The Hearsey family – Audrey, Uncle Fred, Auntie Fan and Nancy – Marion Boxall collection*

On the 13th December, 1940, I was escorted to Oxford station, given a ticket to Treharris and put on the train with Madge Sexton from the North Central School, Ashford. We travelled all day, changing at Newport for Pontypool Road, finally arriving at Treharris in the dark. We alighted at the tiny Treharris railway station and asked the one porter to direct us to Mr Rogers the billeting officer. The porter had never heard of him and did not know where to send us, so we just sat on a wooden seat in the dark and cold, and waited. Eventually, a tall lady, Miss Hornsby, the English teacher, turned up; she was to be my form mistress. Apparently we should have gone on to the next station, Quaker's Yard. We walked with Miss Hornsby to Edwardsville, a mile or more away. There we were both billeted at 6 Treharne Terrace, Edwardsville, with Mr and Mrs Fred Hearsey. My new 'family' consisted of 'Auntie' Fan and 'Uncle' Fred and their daughter Audrey, who was one year older than Madge and myself. She went to Merthyr Tydfil County School. Everyone around Treharne Terrace was very friendly.

Our home was a typical Welsh house: stone, with the doors and windows edged with yellow brick. It was a 'two down, three up' with an outside toilet joined to the house. A wooden room with windows and a glass roof had been built at the back, enclosing the toilet. The gas cooker was in that room and 'the bosh', or little stone sink with a cold tap, was under the window. Madge and I would do the washing up with water heated on the fire or gas stove. There was also a gas lamp on the wall in the living room. In the back kitchen was where we had our wash – under the glass; it was very cold in the winter! Outside in the garden was a large, round, wooden tub. This would be put on a trestle and Auntie Fan would use this to do her washing, with a glass rubbing board. During the winter this was done in the back kitchen and in the garden during the summer. This round tub also came into use at bath time on Friday evenings.

The road in front of the house was the main road from Cardiff to Merthyr Tydfil. On the other side of the road was a dry stone wall and then the mountain – the Tump! Just a little way up the road were the Treharris open-air baths. They were in a lovely sunny position but the water was always so cold. We sometimes visited Pont Sarn, where the clear water drops down and creates a whirlpool called the Blue Pool. This was the local place for suicides.

It was always interesting to walk to Treharris via the low road, as it ran alongside the railway line. I would watch the little tank engines shunting their wagons. On Sunday nights, the main street in Treharris would be full of boys and girls parading up and down, just talking and bumping into each other – well, it was all dark because of the blackout! I never knew anything bad to come from this gathering, it

*Some of the girls of Folkestone Technical School, pictured at Quaker's Yard School. Note the camouflage on the school building – Marion Boxall collection*

was just a social occasion. Along the lower road was the cemetery and I was once surprised to hear a band marching away from it playing 'Goodbye Dolly Gray'. Funerals were very solemn occasions and only the men attended – all dressed in black. The women, also in black, would stay at home to prepare the meal and receive the guests.

The Folkestone Technical School, which I had joined, had two streams – Junior Domestic and Clerical. The JDs concentrated on nursing and domestic subjects. My friend Madge was a JD and would recite long lists of the bones of the body, which she had to learn.

There were three schools in Edwardsville – an infants and junior school, the Quaker's Yard county school and the technical school; they were all centred around one site. Folkestone Technical School used rooms in each of the three existing schools. Quaker's Yard county school was a long low wooden building. It was built on low stilts and was erected during the first world war as an army hospital; when I was there, it still wore the camouflage paint. The local technical school was a more modern building, a block with two

*Marion Richardson at Treharris 1941*
*– Marion Boxall collection*

floors. We had two rooms at the junior school and the heating was a lovely fire in a big grate, with a large fender around it.

As we had rooms in each school, we were often walking between schools at change of lessons. This was good in the summer but not so good in the winter. In the summer we would occasionally walk towards Treharris on the Cardiff road, to the local park where we played tennis. In the winter we played hockey. Our pitch was on top of the Tump. There was hardly any flat surface, no lines and very little grass! If we hit the ball too hard, it would roll down the mountainside among the rocks and trees!

My chosen subjects were the clerical ones. The teachers whom I recall were Miss Kay, Miss Hornsby, Miss James, Miss Robbins, Miss Low, Miss French and Mrs Pratt. As Madge and I had only arrived on 13th December, 1940, we were away from home for our first Christmas. My elder sister sent me a very nice writing set. I also had a camera in a leather case and my

*Marion Richardson with her parents and*
*sisters, South Wales, 1941*
*– Marion Boxall collection*

mother made me a lovely warm, long, pink dressing gown. I wore it frequently and it lasted me many years until it finally wore out. One evening, Uncle Fred was asleep in his chair in front of a good fire and everyone else had gone next door. I sat there by the fire listening to the wireless when Bing Crosby sang his new song, 'I'm Dreaming of a White Christmas', and I sat there and cried. I was homesick, but no-one knew.

On Saturdays during the winter we usually went to the pictures. Occasionally we would go to Treharris but more often we would go on the train to Abercynon or Pontypridd. One film I remember seeing in Abercynon, was

*Treharris Swimming Baths, with spoil tips in the background, 1941*

*Rebecca.* In the summer, we would spend some time at the baths. Once we walked to Merthyr Vale to visit Audrey's Aunt Christobel and we stayed to tea. Uncle saw us on to the bus and, just my luck, I sat opposite my form mistress, Miss Hornsby – I received a 'carpeting' for breaking the curfew!

On the way to Edwardsville station was a grocery shop, run by an elderly couple, Mr and Mrs Francis. We were registered there for our groceries. We always had our whole bacon ration for Sunday breakfast. We usually spent our sweet and jam coupons there as well. Auntie Fan would make pikelets and Welsh cakes on a grid iron over the fire. Sometimes there would be a roly-poly pudding for dinner, boiled in a cloth in a saucepan over the fire.

We had no air raids or bombs while we were in Edwardsville; however, we would regularly hear and see bombing activity from Cardiff and Swansea at night. The German planes would come over our valley and then turn away over the coast. Although things were generally peaceful, there was always the underlying worry for the folks back home. Our days were full of schooling, shorthand and French homework, friends and foster family; overall, it was a happy time. On the wireless, Victor Sylvester gave ballroom dancing lessons as his band played in strict tempo. The foot movements were printed in the *Radio Times*. Audrey would push back the table, lift the mat and spin me round the kitchen floor. Thus I learned the quickstep, the waltz and foxtrot. It was fun.

*Old Tram Road and Viaduct, Treharris, 1940.*

*Railway Viaduct from Tram Road, Treharris, 1941*
*– three photos from Marion Boxall collection*

One lovely summer's day I was out in the back garden when a formation of three Spitfires zoomed overhead and tilted up to get over the mountain. To my dismay, the wings of two of the aircraft touched and they fell from the sky. The third one continued on over the mountain. We walked up the Merthyr road and there, in a field beside the road and next to a row of houses, was the wreckage of one of the aircraft. I never heard where the second Spitfire crashed but I suspect it was probably on the mountain.

Normally, I went on a Sunday to the English Congregational Church in Edwardsville. There, we secretarial girls would sit with our

168

notebooks and try to take down the sermon, which was sometimes rather fast! Having to close our eyes for prayers, I would, in thought, write it in shorthand. We were told to write down items from the radio – anything to practise. The best person for dictation was Winston Churchill – slow and deliberate.

On 25th March, 1943, I went home from school as usual at mid-day, to find Uncle Fred eating his meal and reading the *Daily Chronicle*. He looked up and said, 'Look at this: 250 children got out of their school before it was bombed.' I read the article and before I was halfway through, I knew that it

*Edwardsville showing viaducts, 1940*
*Photos from the Marion Boxall collection*

was Ashford and it was also the school where my young sister attended. My legs went to jelly and I was in a state of shock. 'How do you know?' they asked. I had no idea, but I knew that I was right. Auntie Fan went with me to the village phone box and she sent a telegram home, asking if everyone was alright. The next morning a telegram arrived. I panicked – I thought that mine had been returned, but it wasn't. It was a reply to say that they were all safe. Ashford had had its worst raid on 24th March, 1943. Twelve planes had come in fast at low level and had dropped their bombs across the town. My sister was working in the Ashford railway works and a bomb dropped on the road outside the office, badly damaging it and killing several people who were running to the shelters. After being given permission to leave the office, my sister cycled up Newtown Road to the top, where it joined Beaver Road; there the school was just a pile of rubble – and our younger sister had been there that morning. A policeman on duty told her that no-one had been hurt, and she went home relieved, but she suffered from shock pains in the chest for some weeks afterwards.

On 17th April, 1943, I caught the train from Wales for home. I had to go to London to sit an examination in preparation for employment. I did not take all my belongings because I expected to return to Wales. It was not to be, as I went

*All that is left of the viaducts at Edwardsville*

straight into employment – into the wrecked office where my sister worked! My schooldays were over and I was back where air raids, bombs and doodlebugs were the norm. I have been back to Edwardsville many times since the war and each time it has been a joy to return. The old schools have been demolished and a new one built where the Quaker's yard senior school was. The high level railway lines have gone and new houses built in their place. The Tram Road is still as beautiful, but the two huge viaducts on the Merthyr side of the station have gone, just the stumps remain. After the Aberfan disaster, all coal tips have been removed and where we used to watch the spoil being tipped, it is now a grassy hill. For me, the saddest thing to see

*Marion Boxall and her husband, pictured on Pontygwaith Bridge more than fifty years after her evacuation to South Wales*

was the large and active station reduced to a single line and a halt with no staff. The Tump has been forested and the public are no longer allowed there. I shall always be grateful to my foster family and all the friends who made me and others so welcome in our time of need. They will always have a special place in my heart.

***Reg Neill*** *was with the Dover County School for Boys at the time of the evacuation:*

I remember standing on the top of Plum Pudding Hill at Maxton, in Dover, listening to the distant rumblings from across the Channel. It wasn't thunder – it was the guns at Dunkirk! Then in early June, 1940, we all found ourselves being evacuated as the danger of invasion loomed closer. We left by train, travelling for hours and hours and finally found out that the school's destination was Ebbw Vale in the Welsh valleys. However, some were dropped off at Cwm, the stop before Ebbw Vale, including myself and a friend. We were billeted with Mr and Mrs Job Cool. They were nice people but they were expecting two little girls, not two lanky 14 year old youths! We stayed with Mr and Mrs Cool for a week and were then sent up the valley to separate homes where we were to stay for the next three years.

We shared the same classrooms with the Ebbw Vale Grammar School on a split shift system, doing alternate mornings and afternoons. Ebbw Vale was a co-ed school, which was a novelty for us. The Dover girls had been evacuated to Caerleon, some twenty miles away in the Usk Valley – they might as well have been in Siberia! We found out that the Welsh boys lived for their rugby and I have painful memories, being captain of our team, of being beaten by astronomical scores, no matter which valley we visited! One lad from Pontypool ran rings round us in one particular game (we lost 65-0); he went on to play for Wales the following year.

Our school had a Cadet Band in which I was the big drummer and I remember thumping up and down the valleys during the 'Wings For Victory' weeks, raising £5,000 to buy one of the legendary Spitfires. Then there was 'Dad's Army'! The 7th Monmouthshire Battalion, Beaufort Platoon. A far cry from the laughable Warmington-on-Sea Home Guard we have all seen on television. Vickers machine guns, Sten guns and rifles – we had them all – with ammunition to go with them. Our training ground and defence area was part of the Llangenydr Moors which today are cut through by the Heads of the Valleys Road. Our young sixth-formers worked well with the veterans of army experience as we manned our positions on the moors at weekends, enthusiastically ready for the Nazi paratroopers who were about to descend from the skies – and being disappointed when they never came!

'It always rains on Sunday' – and every other day of the week it seemed to us when we were there! The claustrophobic valley had a permanent pall of pollution and smoke hanging over it from the Richard Thomas steelworks and the colliery at Cwm. I remember how glad I was when, in the summer of 1943, I swopped the valleys of South Wales for the flat fields of Cambridge and, subsequently, the hot plains of India and the green and blue of Malaya, when I served with the Madras Sappers and Miners (Queen Victoria's Own!) at the tail-end of the war.

How different that Welsh valley is now. I went back there for the Garden Festival a few years ago. The colliery, where we used to go for a shower on Thursdays, has gone and the slag heaps have disappeared under a carpet of green. While I was at the Garden Festival I sat on a seat dedicated to the evacuees by the people of the valley, who welcomed us into their homes as part of their war effort. I was one of the lucky ones. I could go back. I survived! Many of those who travelled on that evacuation train in 1940 didn't survive – including my brother Bill.

*John Bolt and his family moved to Dover in 1935 and found the next five years in Dover very interesting. He remembers the firework display from the seafront for King George V's Silver Jubilee and the Graf Zeppelin flying up the Channel. Then came evacuation:*

In June 1940 I left my home at 16 Effingham Crescent, Dover, and was evacuated to Ebbw Vale with the rest of the Dover County School for Boys. My sister Anne was evacuated to Caerleon. Her experiences as an evacuee were not happy ones. Her hosts treated her more like a servant than a guest so, when our parents moved to Tunbridge Wells, Anne joined them there.

I was luckier. I was billeted with Mr and Mrs G. B. Parry at 13 The Crescent in Ebbw Vale. They had no children of their own, but Mrs Parry's father, Mr Owens, also lived with them. I remember that there was a car in the garage which was mounted on blocks, because petrol was unavailable. My foster parents treated me as if I were their own child.

It was a school rule that all boys had to go to church at least once every Sunday. I think I went to the Church of England once. It must have been a high church because of the regalia of

**FOLKESTONE EVACUATION SCHEME**

Full Name ~~of Child~~ W. D. TURNER
BLOCK LETTERS

Home Address c/o Mrs Selden, Cresta
Menafield Road, Plympton, S. Devon

Name of School County School Folkestone

School Party Number 15

Group Number 13

*An example of labels issued under the local evacuation schemes. This one might even have been used by the Secretary of Folkestone County School, whose surname was Turner*
*– Peter Hayward collection*

those conducting the service. They looked like the Ku Klux Klan and they didn't appeal to me at all! Mr Owen was circuit steward for the Methodist Church, and Mrs Parry regularly attended the Methodist Chapel and sang in the choir. The minister who preached there each Sunday regularly came to the house for Sunday afternoon tea – so I went to chapel!

During the winter of 1940/1941 we had a few air-raid alarms but nobody took much notice. One night a bomber dropped a string of bombs but they landed on top of the mountain on the west side of the valley. I also used to listen to 'Lord Haw Haw' occasionally, but only as a source of amusement. Nobody had the slightest doubt that, in the end, Germany would be defeated. In 1941 Hess flew to Scotland. Later we heard he was in an asylum at Abergavenny!

In 1941 another evacuee, Francis Szekely came to stay. His mother had run a restaurant in Vienna before the war, although they originally came from Hungary. They were still in Vienna when the German troops arrived and Francis saw Hitler's car pass at the end of the street.

The Dover County School shared Ebbw Vale Grammar School. Their laboratories and gymnasium were modern and very good. The classrooms were rather drab but adequate. We also made use of the 'Tin Tabernacle', a corrugated iron structure in the grounds of the school. I remember a Dover boy being given 'six of the best' before the whole school in this building and then he was expelled! Francis Szekely and I worked very hard on our school work. Since we were at school on alternate shifts with the Ebbw Vale children, we either had long mornings or afternoons out of school. To keep us occupied we were given lots of homework. Our French teacher, Mr 'Froggy' Watt, was particularly feared. He always appeared stern and without humour. Other teachers included Mr Alfred Bertram Constable (chemistry), Mr W. E. Pearce (physics and applied mathematics), Mr T. E. Archer (biology) and Mr 'Spud' Slater (English and English literature). In my opinion Mr Slater was the most liked and the best of the teachers. He had full control because he made the lessons interesting.

One of my greatest pleasures was to go to the pictures. I think there were three cinemas in Ebbw Vale. I particularly remember the one at the southern end of the main street which I think was called the 'Palace'. I also remember Sybil Thorndike performing in *Macbeth* at one of the other picture houses. The whole audience was made up of school children. We were enthralled.

The weather remains indelibly inscribed in my memory – RAIN! Sometimes it would rain heavily for a whole week without ever stopping. 'Raining pouring' the local people called it. I had to have two raincoats so that one could always be drying! In summer the weather could be very nice, sunny and hot. I used to have a two-feet long sailing yacht which I would sail on the 'Blue Lagoon', a small lake on the way from Ebbw Vale to Tredegar. Daylight hours were less than in most places because the sun had to rise in the morning above the mountains of the east side of the valley and set early behind the mountains on the west side.

I remember going to see the doctor once. The waiting room was like a wide passage with wooden benches on both sides. On a high shelf were two large bottles containing red liquid in one and green in the other. I suspect that no matter what was wrong with you, you received either the red or green liquid. It was like a scene from a Dickens story. The small hospital was next door to my billet. One day each week the whole area would smell of ether when the operations were being performed. My host, Mrs Parry, had a maid during the time I was billeted with her. Later she was replaced and then the new maid also left to get a better paid job in the munitions factory at Bridgend. The exposure to the explosive changed the colour of her hair!

Food at Mrs Parry's was excellent. We were never hungry and daily we would have breakfast, lunch and tea – and a large supper in the evening. We would have marvellous legs of lamb for Sunday lunch. Cream cakes would always be served for Sunday afternoon tea when the minister came. As far as food was concerned, we didn't know there was a war on!

In about 1943 I saw graffiti on a wall – 'Start a Second Front Now!' No doubt this showed that Soviet agitation was having a response. It fell on deaf ears (or eyes) because everybody knew we were in no position to open a second front then.

I left Ebbw Vale in July 1943, aged 16, having completed one year in the 6th form, studying chemistry, physics, pure and applied maths. The following October I started a four year course in chemical engineering at the Imperial College for Science in London. In 1945 I visited Ebbw Vale and stayed with Mr and Mrs Parry for a few days. Mrs Parry was quite ill and tragically died later that year. I kept in touch with Mr Parry until he passed away a few years ago.

*Colin Allan started at Harvey Grammar School, Folkestone in September, 1939. His older sister, Kathleen, was a pupil at the Folkestone County School. They were evacuated in 1940.*

It was a long hot train journey on the 2nd June, 1940, and we must have travelled most of the day. We eventually arrived at Merthyr Tydfil in South Wales – the end of the line! In due course we were 'auctioned off', and I went to a place called Dowlais with two other boys, John Verkaek and Neil Hayward. It was a small terraced house on a hill. The woman put the three of us in a double bed; I remember that one of the legs of the bed was propped up on a wooden block and one night the leg slipped off the prop! While I was in Dowlais I went to school at Cyfartha Castle, where we attended mornings one week and afternoons the next. We used to cross a bridge over a small river to get to school and some days the water of the river was bright blue from chemicals that used to come from Hall's Telephone Accessories factory – whose canteen cutlery we found out later was all stamped with the words 'Stolen from HTA'!

I eventually found out where my sister was living and I managed to get moved to Ernest Street in Merthyr, which was just a street away from my her billet. The couple I lived with were Mr and Mrs Butler, both in their 60s at the time. She was short and fairly round, with auburn hair. Mr Butler was about the same height, but was balding and wore spectacles. They were chapel-goers and Mr Butler used to count the collection on a Sunday evening. Mrs Butler baked bread once a week, so by the end of the week it was rather stale and dry. My feet used to get very sore from playing football on the coal tips, compounded by the dust and lack of washing.

Eventually, the junior forms of Harvey Grammar School were moved to the Georgetown Elementary School in Merthyr Tydfil. At the outbreak of the war my father was working in the post office at Folkestone, but during 1940 he was transferred to GPO Telephones at Canterbury. He moved house on his own while we were all away but my mother returned to Canterbury after he had moved. My sister and I went home for the Christmas holidays and on the way home I can remember seeing the light from the fires caused by the bombing of the London Docks.

Sometime in 1941 my mother came to Merthyr to see us. She was horrified at the condition of us. I remember she took me to a barber to have my hair washed and cut. She got my father to come to Merthyr to see what a state I was in. After they went back to Canterbury they must have arranged to have me transferred to the Simon Langton School. I left Merthyr in May 1941, but because my health was so bad I did not start school again until the September. I kept fainting and could not walk very far. I was checked for TB but the doctors decided it was only dust and dirt in my lungs. In May 1942, I had further problems. My four top front teeth snapped in half. I subsequently had eight teeth extracted at one visit to the dentist! At 14 years of age, dentures were not very nice! It was considered that my stay in Merthyr was the cause of the trouble!

Chapter Seven

## THE WELSH CONNECTION

*WE HAVE ALREADY heard from the evacuees from East Kent, who spent many of the war years in South Wales. Now we hear from the Welsh people who still remember the evacuees – the Welsh Connection!*

**Mr T. L. Cowlin**, *JP, FCIS, well remembers the arrival of evacuees:*

I was employed in the clerk's department of Risca Urban District Council and we were responsible for carrying out a survey of the urban area in accordance with the guidelines issued by the government for the 'Government Evacuation Scheme'. A form was left at each house in the area which had to be completed, giving details of the accommodation and the occupants. A canvasser went around to collect the forms and check them; from these a register was made of the addresses and the number of evacuees allocated to them.

I remember the trains arriving at Risca Railway Station bringing school children, teachers and some mothers from the Medway towns, Dover and Ilford. They were transported to the local schools for refreshments and a medical examination. From there they were taken to the homes of the people in the Risca area, which included Pontymister, Crosskeys, Pontywain and Wattsville. Some difficulty arose when it was necessary to split up brothers and sisters if sufficient accommodation could not be found in one house. Also, there were cases where mothers came with their children and a local church hall was taken over and used as a hostel.

We also took over two large properties – 'The Meadows' at Crosskeys, and Brynhyffryd House, Risca – for use as sick bays. The local education authority also had to arrange for the use of church halls for school purposes. I remember two evacuees in particular from Dover, Brian Beer, whose parents had a public house, and Peter Scopes. Brian was billeted with Mr and Mrs A. Thomas at 23 Newport Road, Pontymister; and Peter was with Mr and Mrs Harry Beddow, 56 Ty-Isaf Park Road, Newport. We had a boy whose surname was Baldwin and came from Ilford. I think his Christian name was John, but I am not sure. His mother came to visit on occasions and also his sister who went into the ATS. My mother, being a widow, was directed to work of national importance (as it was called), so the lad had to be housed elsewhere.

If my memory serves me correctly, both Peter Scopes and Brian Beer had brothers or sisters at Portskewett. Unfortunately, I have not seen or heard anything of them for some years now – the host couples have passed away and contact was then lost with the evacuees.

I spent some time in the forces during the war. When I was demobbed, apart from some of the families who had decided to stay in Risca and some children who had been adopted, the evacuees had returned home.

***Mrs K. Wall**, now living in Cwmbran, shared her home in Blaenavon with an evacuee:*

I can remember the evacuees very well. My mother, Mrs Lily Jones, was in the British Legion Women's Section, and she helped to take the children to their billets. There was one little boy from Dover named Joey Higgins. He was very young and very tearful – and he wouldn't let go of mum's hand. His older sister Jean was with him when they arrived in Blaenavon, but then they were split up. The lady at Jean's billet didn't want Joey as well, so you can imagine how upset he was. My mother didn't really have room for an evacuee at our home in Deakin's Row, but she took Joey home with her. I can't remember how long Joey stayed, but he was happy with us and he stayed with us until he returned home to Dover. My mother did write for a while, but then we lost touch.

***John Elfed Phillips**, now residing in Caerleon, recalls his days as a young boy in Markham:*

I was brought up in the mining village of Markham in the Bedwelty Urban Council area. In 1940 my mother entered her name on the council register to host an evacuee, not knowing where they were coming from. On their arrival by train at our small village station, the evacuees were marched in column through the village, accompanied by billeting officers and school teachers. Their gas masks were a prominent feature.

All the people of the village were on their doorsteps awaiting in eager anticipation for their new charge to be deposited with them. Alas, my mother was unlucky that first evening and she shed a few tears of disappointment. The next day however, a little girl was brought to us as she didn't like her billet of the previous day. We were delighted, and took to the little girl immediately. She was seven years old, named Josie Skelton and she came from Monins Road, Dover. She was soon at home and part of the family. Shortly after, Josie's mother and small brother came to visit us to see what kind of home Josie was living in. Thankfully, they were delighted at the welcome and reception given to them. We found out later that Josie's sister Lana was also billeted in the village, with Mr and Mrs Hunt.

Mrs Skelton was so impressed with what she saw, with us and the comparative safety as compared with Dover, that she asked my father and mother if their little boy could also stay. There was no problem. His name was 'Buddy' and he was four years old. Of course, Buddy was his nickname, his real name being Terence. It was after his birth that his father, who was serving in the Royal Navy, thought that, with clenched fists he looked like Buddy Baer, a famous boxer at that time. Both children attended the local chapel with us and joined in all local and family activities. Their mother, grandmother and Uncle Bill used to visit us quite often. As time went by, and the task of saying cheerio to their parents on Newport Station was behind them, they would say to my mother, 'Let's go home now Aunty,' which was back to Markham.

Occasionally Mr Skelton (Wally by now) brought with him his friend and shipmate from Norwich, whose name was George. Amusingly (for us) on their first visit, they started out from Dover via London in the black-out by train. They arrived at Newport Central and asked the way to our address, which was written on a piece of paper. The station porter, a little bemused and in the best of interest, placed them on the Rhymney Valley train (again in complete darkness), and they eventually arrived in the Brecon Beacons at a place called Pontsticill, which was the end of the line! The guard told them the train was now returning to Newport, but on the production of that valued piece of paper, he told them to get off at Bargoed, which they did (in the black-out).

A porter told them that about 100 yards from the station there was a bus stop where they could get a bus to Markham. They found the bus stop and put themselves at the mercy of the conductor. He told them where to get off in Markham, which they did in complete blackness. As they stood there feeling quite lost, they heard the patter of feet. A complete stranger was asked the way to number 37, which happened to be fairly close by, so the stranger brought them to the house. Imagine their great relief when the door was opened and they were greeted with real Welsh hospitality and a cup of hot tea in front of a big coal fire, after sixteen hours travelling! I shall never forget the relief on their faces when they entered the house.

There was great sadness when, at the end of the war, Josie, Buddy and Lana were returned to their family in Dover. It was a great loss to us all as they had become part of our family and we all loved them very dearly. Again there was sadness when their father, Wally, lost his life when HMTS *Alert* was blown up by a mine on returning to Dover just a day after the war had ended. He was 33 years of age. Buddy followed in his father's footsteps and joined the Royal Navy. Josie married a soldier who eventually became a major. She is now, however, a widow. Buddy attended my father's funeral in 1958 and then we lost trace of him. Eventually, we traced Buddy through the War Office and he came to visit us again when my mother reached her 80th birthday. At that time HMS *London* paid a courtesy visit to Newport and Buddy was CPO cook on board. The whole family was invited on to the ship and my mother was piped aboard, which was a great honour. Sadly, Buddy died of a heart attack at 52 years of age.

Josie and Lana (also a widow) live together somewhere in Dover. Young John became a school teacher but we haven't seen him since the war days. Those days when Buddy and Josie shared our home and our lives are a period of my life I shall always cherish and never forget.

***Miss Ruth M. Hill*** *of Pontypool was living in Pontnewydd during the evacuation period:*

During the war my parents and I lived in Pontnewydd, which was in the Cwmbran Urban District Council area. I remember evacuees from Dover arriving and the headmaster, who came with the boys, stayed at my home in Pontnewydd. His name was Archibald B. Taylor and he brought his black labrador dog, Chum, with him. He also had a car which I thought was wonderful. He must have had a special petrol allowance, as he used his car to visit the boys who were evacuated to Blaenavon. When Mr Taylor and Chum arrived, he asked if Chum could sleep under the dining room table to be safe during air-raids. We hadn't had many air-raids and we were surprised at his request. I had heard that Dover had had many severe bomb attacks and when our siren sounded, Mr Taylor made sure we were safe under the stairs.

Mr Taylor's wife had left Dover to stay with relatives in Bristol. After Mr Taylor had been with us for some time, he made arrangements for his wife to come to Pontnewydd. When she arrived, they both went to stay with my aunt and uncle, where they could have their own living room. The Taylors had a son, George, who was in the Royal Navy – his photograph was on the mantelpiece when they were at my aunt's home. Eventually, Mr and Mrs Taylor left Wales to return to their home in Dover. We exchanged Christmas cards for some years after they left.

***Audrey Damant*** *recalls many details of the boys from Dover County School, in Ebbw Vale:*

The boys of Dover County School were very much part of our school in Ebbw Vale during the war years. Lessons were on a shift basis at the start, but altered when the boys moved to Pentwyn House – except for the sixth form who remained with us for access to the laboratories.

Morning assembly took place in the Tin Tabernacle, as it was called, which was in the school grounds. We always sang the Lord's Prayer in Welsh, which quite impressed the Dover boys. Ebbw Vale, like many other towns had a British Restaurant, which was situated in Church Street and the boys had a song about it – although, looking back, it could just as easily have applied to their various billets. I think it went like this:

> There is a spot we know not far away,
> Where they serve awful food three times a day,
> Good food we never see;
> We get slag dust in our tea,
> And we are gradually fading away!

Our town was hardly the jolliest of places to grow up in then, but we didn't seem to notice, although we lacked just about everything. We went to Chapel Guilds where local people gave us talks, held spelling bees, and became panellists on Brains Trust evenings, when we plied them with the most awful questions. One Dover boy actually knew how to weigh the world when the panellists failed the question. Local Defence Volunteers, whom we knew as 'Look, Duck and Vanish', trained in the park. Outside the Red and White bus office stood a kind of totem pole which recorded the progress of the Ebbw Vale Spitfire Fund. Happily, we had four cinemas in the town, showing five films every week. Nearly all the Dover boys were either in the Army Cadets, ATC or Naval Cadets. They always turned out if ever a parade was held through the town. I forget how, but a show was staged in the Workmen's Hall – one of the numbers being 'Lilli Marlene', with the boys in uniform. We really had a great time together. I don't suppose everyone liked being in Ebbw Vale at the time, but the boys were made welcome. One heartfelt quote which appeared in a school paper, read:

> Oh God! Send me a train,
> So I can get to England once again!

Nevertheless, it was a unique and unforgettable time for all of us.

*John Phillips remembers the arrival of some of the evacuees to Blaenavon:*

I was six years old when war began and when evacuees started to arrive in Blaenavon I remember seeing them in the hall of Forge Side Junior School. We had a boy of about ten staying with us. His name was Dennis Cohen; I think he might have come from London. I'm not sure how long he was with us, but what I remember best was that his mother came to visit him. When she was ready to return home, Dennis, my mother and I went to Bottom (Low Level) Station to see her off. As we were waiting at the station, a German aeroplane flew over the town and dropped some incendiary bombs on the coke ovens of the steel works, known locally as the 'Ottoes' – they had been built in the 1930s by a German company! Mrs Cohen said to my mother that if this was going to happen in Blaenavon, Dennis might as well take his chance at home. So when the train left for Newport, both Mrs Cohen and Dennis were on it! Dennis was dressed in only shorts, shirt and plimsolls and later I helped my mother to pack the rest of his clothes to send on to him. We never heard from him again!

*Mr E. Prothero from Risca remembers his parents taking in two evacuees:*

I am the youngest of four brothers and, when the evacuees came to Risca, my mother and father took one of them into our home. Her name was Jean Powell and she was about twelve years old. She had an older sister, Audrey, staying with another family, Mr and Mrs Drinkwater at Taylorstown, Risca, about a quarter of a mile from our house. After some time, arrangements were made for Audrey to come and stay with us as well, at 31 Machen Street, Risca.

I remember that my mother took all six children into Newport, about six miles away, to have our photographs taken at Jerome's; I think they were the only photographers around at that time. Jean used to get us to act in so-called plays that she would think up. 'The Chocolate Soldier' was one of her plays and we used the top of the Morrison air-raid shelter, which was in our front room, as the stage. Jean also used to tell us bedtime stories. I used to wonder how she could tell such good stories without reading them from a book. She made them all up.

Jean and Audrey attended Danygraig School, now replaced. One thing that sticks in my mind about the war years is being frightened to go into the air-raid shelter when the siren went, in case it fell in on me. My brothers used to say that if anything like that happens, the Seven Dwarfs from Snow White will come and get us out! I am not glad that there was a war, but I am glad that I met Jean and Audrey and their parents.

***Violet May Snell*** (*now Mrs Battersby*) *remembers well the arrival of the Dover boys:*

I remember the train carrying the boys from Dover County School arriving at the station. It was the longest train I had ever seen in Ebbw Vale. I was attending the Ebbw Vale Grammar School at the time, and I remember we had to share the school. We would work mornings only one week and afternoons the following week – including Saturdays! Then the Kent County Council obtained the lease on Pentwyn House, which housed most of the Dover boys.

I remember the Dover cadet force, especially the band, because it was in the band that I was to meet my future husband. His name was Alan Bell – 'Dinger' to his mates. He played the trumpet in the band at first and then the drums. His father was a Royal Marine Bandsman at the School of Music in Deal. It was he who obtained the sash for the band which the drum major, Dick Culver, wore when leading the band. Alan was unhappy in his billet. From the way he described his foster parents, it sounded like something out of Oliver Twist! Alan's mother decided to leave Dover and came to Ebbw Vale to live. She had the house next to the Bridge Street Post Office and Alan went to live with her there.

One of the Dover teachers, Mr Baxter, learned to speak Welsh fluently in just about six months. After that, our headmaster would 'earwig' us at every opportunity about how we, as natives of Wales, could not learn Welsh in the four years at school, yet an Englishman (and he always emphasised 'Englishman') could learn it in six months!

The Dover boys would 'knock spots off' the Ebbw Vale lads when playing friendly inter-school cricket, but the tables were turned when the game was rugby. A chum of Alan Bell was Keith Edwards. When I started 'walking out' with Alan, Keith would always be with us. I believe he left school earlier than most of the Dover boys and joined the Buffs regiment. Alan was deferred until he got his higher school results and then joined the Royal Navy. His mother eventually moved to London and Alan joined her there after his demob in 1946. I went to live in London in 1947 and Alan and I were married in 1948. We had two sons but, unfortunately, Alan and I divorced in 1963, although we still keep in touch.

***Eira Stroud*** *has many fond memories of the Dover boys in Ebbw Vale:*

I was in my early teens when the Dover Boys came to Ebbw Vale. They arrived in the area quietly and in a manner befitting their school background. They shared the local grammar school on a shift basis. One of the Dover teachers, Mr Archer, lived next door to me, with the minister of the chapel. I believe he stayed there until the Dover boys returned home.

We got to know many of the Dover boys and many friendships were formed. Staying with the local post mistress, Mrs Maggie Davies, was Dennis Atherden, tall, blond and very reserved. Also with him was Bobby Reynolds, who was much more fun as I remember! John Hurt lived a few doors away from my home. He and another boy, Ray Hewitt, attended chapel each Sunday – and relieved the monotony no end during the sermon! They lived with a well to do bachelor who was an elder of the chapel, so they had no choice but to attend and sit in his pew each Sunday. My mother had no trouble in getting me to attend either! I have to say that when the Dover boys returned to Kent, life was never the same. They were missed so much.

*Marjorie Walbyoff remembers her mother taking in five evacuees on the first night:*

My mother and I stood and watched the evacuee train arrive in Blaenavon. It was about 7pm on a warm Sunday night in summer. Thinking that it would be some time before we would receive our evacuee, we set off for home and waited patiently. My father was working nights, and at 9.30pm it was time for him to leave for work. He was very disappointed that his little girl evacuee hadn't arrived. At about 10.20pm the door bell rang and, when my mother opened the door, there stood a very worried-looking teacher, Mrs Doreen Griffiths, and five very tired children! The teacher said to my mother, 'Mrs Williams, this is your little girl – her

*Lilian and Rosina Norris (ex-pupils of St Mary's School, Dover) pictured at an evacuee reunion in May, 1995 – Ted Green collection*

name is Lily Norris, but I don't know what to do with these other four children. They are all from the same family and their mother told them not to be parted. No-one will take them.'

My mother, being a kind-hearted woman, said, 'They can stay with me tonight; what are their names?' Well, there was Pearl, the eldest of the Hayward family and about twelve years old, then Jean and Mary, and last a dear little fair haired boy, Peter, who was three years old. After some refreshments and hot drinks, we all went to bed and slept soundly until morning.

When my father arrived home the following morning, he was met at the gate by my aunt who lived next door. She said to my father, 'Well, Tom, you are in for a shock. You didn't get just one little girl last night, you have got five evacuees altogether!' Later that morning, Mrs Myra Martyn came to the door saying she would like a little girl, so she took Mary Hayward. Then Mrs Davies called and asked for a girl, so Jean Hayward went with her. When the teacher came back later the same day, she was very pleased that we had found homes for two of the girls. On the way to us she had met Mrs Coles, who lived near Glantorvaen Terrace, and she said that she would take Pearl and Peter for a few weeks. I didn't see Peter or Pearl again.

Other evacuees on the Terrace were Lucy and Olive Heywood. They lived with Elsie and Fred Savigar and would come to my mum for some motherly love. The Savigars were very kind and it all worked out fine in the end. There was also Nora Hoy who lived with Mrs Roberts.

Lily Norris, our little evacuee, had three sisters, Ruby, Sylvia and Rose, and they were all in different parts of Blaenavon. Ruby and Rose had a few foster homes as they sometimes couldn't get on with the families. Lily was very happy living with us. She stayed about eighteen months, then her mother wanted her back home in Dover. Lily's mother did stay a week with us and couldn't thank us enough for the kindness and love shown to her daughter. When the time came for Lily to return home, we missed her very much. In 1959 my parents, my husband and I went to Dover and visited Lily and her family, and we are still in touch today.

179

*Josephine Hartnoll (now Mrs Parry), still remembers the arrival of an evacuee:*

I was brought up in Cwmfelinfach, which was a mining village in the area served by the then Mynyddislwyn Urban District Council. I remember having an evacuee named Bobby Meek. His sister, Shirley, was billeted with my aunt's neighbours, Mr and Mrs Sam Bayley, in Commercial Road. We lived in Mill Street and my parents were Albert and Jane Hartnoll. I don't remember how old Bobby and Shirley were, except that they were several years older than I, and they attended Cwmfelinfach Junior Mixed School in King Street.

I can also remember an attractive dark haired girl named Joan, who came from Dover. She stayed with Mr Barkway in the bakery opposite our house. As far as I know, Bobby was quite happy living with us, but he eventually returned home to his parents. His father came to see us after Bobby's return home bringing me a doll's swing and some doll's furniture which he had made from wood. I still have the furniture after all these years. I used to play with it when I was a child, but I never let my own daughter play with it; it is too precious to me! Sadly, over the years we lost touch with Bobby and his family and if he were to visit South Wales today, he would see a big change. All the pits have gone now and the valleys are dying because there are no jobs to replace those lost. Many people have moved to places like Cwmbran and Newport.

*Ivy Hill (now Mrs Sage) recalls the time when members of the Crofts family from Dover were billeted with her parents in Blaenavon:*

I remember the Sunday evening when the Dover evacuees arrived in Blaenavon. My husband was away in the forces and I was living with my mother and father at 24 High Street. After the evacuees had all been assembled, we took in two brothers, William and Roy Crofts, from Chapel Road in Dover. Later, one of their sisters, Daphne, also came to live with us and we had the three of them for quite a while. They all attended the old British Wesleyan School in Park Street. I remember the headmaster, Mr Wheldon, and Mrs Carter one of the teachers. During the Crofts' stay, we all worshipped at the Horeb Baptist Chapel regularly on Sundays. On Tuesday evenings the boys attended the Band of Hope, and on Thursdays it was the missionary meeting.

Eventually, Daphne and William left for other billets, but Roy stayed with us until the end of the war. We all got on very well with Roy, and when the time came for him to return home, Roy cried and said that he wanted to stay with us! By the time Roy went home, his parents had moved to 42, Glenfield Road, Dover. Unfortunately, during the course of time, we lost contact with Roy and his brother and sister. I often wonder where they are and how they are getting on. The only other evacuees I remember by name are Harry and Albert Fog who stayed with my sister, Mrs Doreen Hares, at 31 High Street, Blaenavon.

*Edna Davies (now Mrs Williams) remembers two evacuees, Peter and Pearl Hayward:*

I remember Peter and Pearl coming to Blaenavon. Peter was only three years old and Pearl was about twelve or thirteen. They went to stay with Mr and Mrs Dan Daley on Rifle Green. Mr and Mrs Daley were a lovely couple who were childless and they treated Peter and Pearl with a lot of love and affection. I remember Mrs Daley buying Peter lots of clothes and, in particular, a pair of fawn trousers and a red blazer that he used to wear when I took him to Sunday School at St James' Church. The church is now used as a furniture factory.

Pearl and I became very good friends. My aunt, who was a dressmaker, made me a brown coat and Pearl wanted one like it, so my aunt made Pearl a navy one. I remember the time when Pearl became very ill. I sat with her in her room all day on the Saturday and Sunday, and had my meals in the bedroom with her. On Monday I called to see her on the way home from school and Mrs Daley was in a state. She said, 'Go home, Edna, and tell your mam that Pearl is going to the hospital this afternoon. She has diphtheria!' I was very frightened, but my immunisations stood me in good stead. Luckily, Pearl survived but I think she must have returned home to Dover when she came out of hospital and Peter was re-billeted somewhere else in the town. I never saw them again. Mr and Mrs Daley are both dead now. Mr Daley was killed in a mining accident shortly after the war. Their house on Rifle Green is still standing.

*Colin Cooper with Mr Lawrence at 'Danybryn', Bridgend, August, 1940 – Mrs Lawrence collection*

***Enid Lawrence*** *remembers Deal evacuees who came to stay with her family near Bridgend:*

We lived in a village outside Bridgend called Brynmenyn. Our home was a large detached house with a huge garden to house our family of ten. It was in 1940 that Colin Cooper and his two sisters came to us from Deal. I remember the day quite vividly. Colin was only three, not much more than a baby! My mother had all three of them for a week, but it was only a temporary measure though she dreaded splitting them up. She was, after all, in her sixties and had already brought up a family of eight. The two sisters moved to a couple down the road, so they were able to see their brother quite often. My mother and father loved Colin. He was a bit subdued at first but he soon got used to us all. Eventually, he went to the local school, where he promptly caught measles. He used to call my mother 'Ubber Auntie'; he meant 'Other Auntie'.

Colin was with us for five years and, when he finally returned home, my mother cried. She missed him so much – we all did. Unfortunately we lost contact with Colin and his family and I often wonder how he is getting on.

***Mrs R. Roberts,*** *now in her nineties, remembers those who were evacuated to Carmarthen:*

I remember the evacuees coming to the town. We lived in Water Street. My husband worked for the Great Western Railway and I was working at the time as a volunteer with the Women's Voluntary Service. Because of this work and the fact that I had two boys and a girl at school, I didn't intend taking in any evacuees. Shortly after some of the evacuees arrived in Carmarthen, a friend came to the house; she had three girls with her and they were all crying. I asked what the matter was and my friend replied that the girls were all sisters, triplets, and they wouldn't be separated. They were Pat, Mavis and Peggy Pattenden. Well, my neighbour came to the door and she offered to take one of the sisters, so I was

*Mr and Mrs Pattenden with their triplet daughters, Pat, Mavis and Peggy*

181

left with the other two. It wasn't long before another sister appeared! She was a few years older than the triplets and her name was Joan.

Anyway, although we were a bit overcrowded, we soon got into a routine. I made sure the girls wrote home weekly and I would often put a note in from myself to their parents. Soon Carmarthen became full of evacuees, especially the Pentrefelin Council Estate. I also remember when the boys of Sir Roger Manwood's School arrived in the town. They were very smart and all were in uniform. The Americans opened a military hospital in the area, so with them and the evacuees, the town became very busy and was to remain so until the war ended. When the sisters finally returned home, Joan, the older sister, kept in touch every year and even came back to see me. We still exchange letters and cards at Christmas.

**Don Lewis,** *now living in Trevethin, Pontypool, was a young boy when evacuees came:*

I was ten years old and living in the village of Cwmffrwdoer when the war started. I remember a family of evacuees by the name of Watson came down from London. I became pals with the two boys and we went to the village school together. We had many adventures together and I remember one day Billy Watson jumped from the bridge in Cwmffrwdoer into a railway wagon of small coal which was passing underneath at the time. The Watsons stayed in Cwmffrwdoer until the end of the war and I am very pleased to say that I have kept in contact with the family ever since. I have summed up my memories in the following poem:

STRANGERS TO THE VALLEY
*Dedicated to Mrs Watson and Family*

It was during the war, the evacuees came down,
They came from a city called London Town.
There was Billy, Victor and the family as well
To escape the bombs that came from hell.

We would laugh at their accent, we didn't understand
That there were other people living in the land,
But we soon became friends and went to school on the hill,
There was me, Connie, Shirley, Victor and Bill.

In the summer when the weather was fine
We would take a walk up the line,
Playing, getting thirsty, our tongues hanging out,
We would run to Plascoed to drink at the spout.

Coming out of the Pavilion, mostly at night,
The blackout was in force, there's hardly a light,
Walking slowly along Hanbury Road,
Sometimes singing, we were never bored.

Sweets were on ration, food was short,
Stealing apples, but never were caught,
Up to the mountain we could go where we please,
Running, jumping, with cuts on our knees

I'll always remember when the days were hard,
At the time long ago when the world went mad,
We spent some of the days playing in the park,
Often staying until it was dark.

As the war ended, came the VE nights,
Shouts of joy when they turned on the lights;
Bonfires burning up there on the hill,
There was me, Connie, Shirley, Victor and Bill.

Memories still linger, it will never be the same,
When from London in wartime, to the valley they came;
Let us remember those days are no more,
When they stayed with us in Cwmffwdoer.

*__Mrs E. M. Randall__ was hostess to two evacuees in Ebbw Vale:*

In 1942, my husband was abroad with the army and I was left at home with two small girls. As I had a house and spare room I was able to take in evacuees. The first one was a boy called Michael Rigden. He came to me in September, 1942, when he was thirteen years old, from his home in the village of Eythorne, near Dover. His family were personal friends of the French master, Mr Baxter, at the Dover school. Roy Hussey, who was a new boy for the school, came to me in September, 1943. He also came from the village of Eythorne. They stayed with me until the school returned to Dover in December, 1944. Michael kept in touch for a couple of years, but I lost contact when he started work. Roy has written to me every year since 1944 and when the Garden Festival was held in Ebbw Vale, he visited me. I was lucky – I had two good boys and I remember them with pleasure.

*__Mrs Clara Whent__, now in her nineties, well remembers the evacuees coming to Blaenavon:*

I helped get all the children into billets. I even ended up having an evacuee myself. Two brothers came from London; I wanted to take them both, but we just didn't have the room in our tiny house, so I took in Alan Clements and his brother went to my cousin nearby.

We loved Alan so much and mother-in-law idolised him. After some time, his parents came to visit. I sent Alan down to the station to meet his parents off the train. It was while we were having a meal together that they announced that they were taking him back home. Alan wanted to stay and live with his 'Aunty and Uncle' for ever – and we wanted to keep him!

Anyway, he went back home when the bombing was bad in London, but luckily he survived. We kept in touch with Alan after the war and we attended his wedding and then the christenings of his children. Alan has also been down to Blaenavon many times to see me and still comes.

I also remember many evacuees from Dover. There were Ben Haynes, John Hoy, Mavis Ashby and Duncan Turner. Duncan stayed on after the war, eventually marrying a local girl and made Blaenavon his home. Another Dover evacuee who stayed after the war, was Tommy Law. He finally decided to return to

*Mrs Clara Whent pictured
in Blaenavon in
February, 1995
– Peter Hayward collection*

Dover in 1994 after his foster parents had died. Although times were hard during the war years, I think the majority of evacuees enjoyed their stay here in Blaenavon.

183

Chapter Eight

TRAGEDIES!

*TRAGEDIES AND DISASTERS tend to occur no matter where you are or what the circumstance is, but it is doubly horrific when one happens during the time of separation from one's family or friends. The following accounts, log book extracts, newspaper cuttings and private letters highlight some of the terrible things that happened during the evacuation of the Kent children.*

**Mr W. Skelton** *was evacuated with Holy Trinity Elementary School, Dover, to Cwmbran, near Newport, and had only been in South Wales a few days when tragedy struck:*

My younger brother John and I were evacuated in true style – gas masks, sandwiches, etc. When we left the train we were taken to the village square (it wasn't really a square – Cwmbran at that time was a one street village in an L-shape!). We were taken in by the village butcher and his wife, Mr and Mrs W. Jenkins. They had one son. As neither my brother nor I had a 'Sunday suit', we were taken out and both supplied with 'chapel uniform'.

It was a glorious summer in 1940 and, during a very hot spell, local children and evacuees went swimming in the local disused gravel pit. It was there that an accident occurred and brother John was drowned. I was immediately recalled to Dover by father, who declared that Dover was probably safer than Cwmbran! As an aside, Christmas cards were exchanged between mother and Mrs Jenkins until the late 1970s, when they both died.

*The following are extracts from the school log book of Pier Infants' School, Bulwark Hill, Dover, which young John Skelton attended:*

Week ended July 5th 1940: At the end of the 2nd week, notice was received from the Dover E.C. regarding stock and stores, and I was absent (with permission of Dover E.C.) for the purpose of selecting and packaging stock sufficient for our use at Cwmbran. During my absence and during a school holiday, one of the children, John Edwin Skelton, was accidentally drowned while out with his older brother from the Trinity Boys' Dept. The body has not yet been recovered.

Week ending July 12th 1940: On Wednesday July 10th, the body of John Edwin Skelton was found in the pond. I was summoned to give evidence of identification etc., at the Coroner's Court at Newport the same day. The verdict by the Coroner was accidental death.

*On July 12th 1940, the* Free Press *newspaper printed an article on the tragic drowning:*

DOVER EVACUEE DROWNED IN CWMBRAN POOL

At an inquest at Newport on Wednesday on John Skelton, a six-year-old Dover evacuee, who had been missing since June 19th, and whose body was recovered on Wednesday from the Clay

Pits Pool, Cwmbran, Mr D. J. Treasure, Coroner, who recorded a verdict of 'Accidental death from drowning', said: 'It is a very tragic case, and I want to express my deepest sympathy with the parents and schoolmistress. It seems the irony of fate that this little evacuee, after being sent from what is regarded as a danger area to a safe area, should lose his life while following peaceful pursuits.'

Miss Dorothy Cheal, headmistress in charge of 40 Dover infant scholars billeted at Cwmbran and attending St Dial's School, said John Skelton was one of the infantevacuees billeted at 31, Oak Street, Cwmbran. He was the son of Arthur Skelton, a bricklayer, of King Lear's Way, Dover. He was a strong, healthy boy, both mentally and physically. She was able to identify the body by the clothes worn. An older brother attached to St Dial's School had returned home since the accident.

The Coroner: That is understandable.

Police Sergeant Edgar Morgan, Cwmbran, said that at 8pm on Wednesday, June 19th, it was reported to him by William Henry Jenkins that John Skelton was missing from his billet at 31 Oak Street, Cwmbran. He made enquiries and obtained the assistance of local swimmers, who swam around the edge of the Clay Pit pond, Cwmbran, where the boy was last seen when he accompanied his eleven-year-old brother to go bathing in the pond. No trace could be found of the missing boy. He continued the search in the undergrowth in the vicinity of the pond, and on the following and succeeding days search parties searched the district. On Friday, June 21st, Cwmbran Council obtained the services of a diver, who operated in the pond from 11am to 3pm, without result. At 11.10am on July 10th, Samuel Eastman, of Commercial Street, Cwmbran, informed him that whilst travelling in the train past the Clay Pit pond he observed something floating on the water. P.S. Morgan said he went immediately to the pond, accompanied by W. R. C. Wilson, where he found the body on the water at the side near the rock where the boy was last seen. P.S. Morgan said his enquiries revealed that the boy was seen at 11.15am on June 19th near St Dial's School, which was a quarter-mile from the pond, and later he was seen in Cwmbran Park. Witness formed the opinion that the boy returned to the pond to look for his brother and accidentally fell in, there being no one at the pond at the time. The pond was private property, owned by the Ponthir Star Brick and Tile Company, and covered about an acre. At some parts the pond was about 45 feet deep. Where the body was found the pond was about 30 feet deep, and there were ledges of rock, underneath one of which the body had no doubt been caught.

P.S. Morgan added that an old workman who had worked in the clay pit told him that at the spot where the body was found there was a part of the rock at the bottom projecting about 6 feet to 8 feet from the side, and that it was under this that workmen used to take shelter from the rain. The probability was that the boy became caught under this rock, and was disturbed by dragging operations. A shoe on one foot was on the verge of coming off, suggesting that the dragging iron had caught it.

The Coroner: Is it not very dangerous for children to bathe there?

'Yes, sir, but the children climb through the fence. Since the accident the fence has been repaired.'

Mr K. G. S. Gunn (Clerk to Cwmbran Council) said the company who owned the property had been very concerned about children bathing there, and of the danger to which they were exposing themselves. Repairs to the fences had been effected, and efforts were being made to stop the practice of bathing in the pond.

P.S. Morgan said that parts of the pond were shallow. It was difficult to fence the pond.

In recording the verdict, the Coroner appealed to the teachers to use their influence to prevent children from bathing there. 'I know it is difficult,' said the Coroner, adding, 'I used to be the same.'

Mr Gunn said he wished on behalf of Cwmbran Council to join with the Coroner in an expression of sympathy. The Council had been very concerned about the matter and had obtained the services of a diver, etc. They wished to express thanks to P.S. Morgan and his

185

colleagues, and to those who had lent material, to the British Legion and St John Ambulance, and many others who had gone out of their way in an attempt to solve the mystery.

Miss Cheal also returned thanks. Mr Gunn added that, if necessary, the Council would meet the cost of a coffin and other incidental expenses.

*On Saturday, 13th July 1940, little John Skelton was buried. The following account of his funeral appeared in the* Free Press *newspaper on Friday, 19th July, 1940:*

### CWMBRAN FUNERAL OF DOVER EVACUEE

Cwmbran Councillors, officials, schoolmasters and boys of St Dial's School were present at the funeral on Saturday of John Skelton, the six-year-old Dover evacuee who lost his life by drowning at the Cwmbran Clay Pit Pool. Mourners and friends assembled at Cwmbran Cemetery chapel, where the service was conducted (and also at the graveside) by the Rev. John Donne (Vicar of Llantarnum). Cwmbran, Dover and Birmingham schoolmates attended.

Mourners: Mr and Mrs Arthur Skelton, King Lear's Way, Dover, father and mother; Mr and Mrs W. Jenkins, foster parents, Cwmbran; Mrs Paul and Mrs Arthur, Cwmbran. Cwmbran Councillors present were Mrs F. Carver, Messrs F. J. Gifford (Billeting Officer), W. E. Brown, JP, CC, and Alex Jones, K. G. S. Gunn, Clerk (who also represented Mr W. H. Hill, JP, (Chairman) and R. T. Lewis (committee clerk). Local Police were represented. Scholastic: Messrs V. Gutsell (Headmaster Dover Schoolboys), T. H. Platt, A. E. Bowden (Dover Teachers), P. J. Hood (representing St Dial's school teaching staff), Nurse Gray, Dover School. Schoolboys present were: Dilnud, Coulson, Butcher, Poy, Barringe, Clayton, Cook, Atkins, Harrison, Cloke, Sadler, Howling and Howland, (Dover); Funell, (Birmingham); E. Hopkins, J. Burr, T. Arthur, J. Ackley, J. Philpott, W. Bouchley, G. Davies, A. Price, J. Daniels, A. Slater, E. Griffiths, G. Smith, E. Slade, W. Cantillo, L. Thomas, J. Hall, Scammells, D. Peard, K. Powell and R. Penn, (Cwmbran).

Bearers: Messrs R. J. Hood, R. T. Lewis, I. Dodham, and P. Compton. Flowers: Membersand officials of Cwmbran Council; Miss Dorothy Cheal, Headmistress Dover Infants; V. Foard and E. Chapman, teachers; Dover schoolchildren; foster parents; and others. The parents' and other wreaths were placed on the tiny white coffin. Messrs W. E. and C. Brown were the undertakers.

\*    \*    \*

*On the 9th July, 1940, barely more than a month after being evacuated with St Andrew's School in Buckland, Dover, two young sisters were tragically killed. The following article appeared in the* Dover Express *on Friday, 12th July 1940:*

### TWO DOVER CHILDREN KILLED IN WALES

Two Buckland School girls, Georgina Thomas aged eleven years, and Joan Thomas aged nine years, who were evacuated with their school to Undy, near Newport, Wales, were killed by an express train while on their way to school on Tuesday.

It appears that the two children were walking hand in hand with their twelve-year-old sister, Julia, and stopped at a level crossing to let a goods train pass. Then thinking the line was clear, they started to cross, when an express train knocked the two younger children against the embankment and killed them.

The father, Mr Thomas, who is employed at the dockyard, lives at Buckland Farm. Mrs Thomas had that morning left for Yorkshire.

*Twin graves of the Thomas sisters, killed at Undy Railway Crossing, June, 1940.*
*– Ted Green collection*

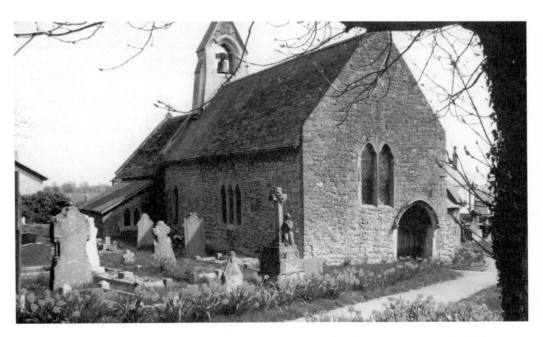

*St Mary's Churchyard, Undy, South Wales where the Thomas sisters are buried*
*– Ted Green collection*

\*     \*     \*

*Dawn Terry (now Mrs Vodka) continues her unhappy memories of her time in Wales, but she also had to cope with some tragic news from back home in Dover. When Dawn was evacuated, she left behind her mother, father and two sisters, Doris and Lena. Doris and Dawn used to write to each other; two of the letters from Doris are reproduced below. Although the letters are not dated, they would have been written between June and September 1940:*

1 Townwall Passage,
Dover

Dear Dawn,

Just a few lines in answer to your most loving letter which I got OK. I think Valerie is very silly in coming home, as it is very bad in Dover and a good many people have been killed.

Mother has got your new coat and it is blue, and it is very nice. They are coming down to see you soon. Well, when Valerie does come home she will not be let out of a night to run the streets, as they wouldn't let you now. Well Dawn, when the war began, I thought it would be great fun, but now I am afraid to go outside the door.

Please do not take notice of my writing this time, as the siren is just going. Well, I must now come to an end.

With lots of love and kisses,
Doris.

1 Townwall Passage,
Dover

Dearest Dawn,

First a few lines in answer to your most loving letter which I got OK. I am so pleased to hear, Dawn, that you are happy with Mrs Bruce, not that I don't want you home, as I do very much. But it is much better for you in Wales.

I was talking to a girl that has come back from Wales, you know her Dawn, Pat Stavely, she said you were very lucky in getting with nice people. She said you were very happy. You know, Dawn, that is a lot off mother's and father's minds when you say that, that you are happy.

There are only about three big shops in Dover that are open. Well Dawn, I don't go with Elsie and Pat as they have both got a boy to go with, so they don't want me, so I go with Barbara. You know, she is not so bad. I was talking to Mrs Hayward the other day and she said Pearl and Mary and the others were happy and was pleased to hear you were well. Most of the people whose children are away say they are happy.

Dawn, do you read this or does someone read it to you? As when you were at home, you couldn't read my writing, but still that does not matter now. We have an air raid about six times a day. Well I must now come to the end.

With lots of love and kisses,
Love,
Doris

*Dawn Terry continues her memories of her time in Blaenavon and of the time the terrible news arrived from Dover:*

Sometime in September 1940, I was told that my cousin Pat's mother was coming to see me. My foster-parents got me ready and I was allowed, for the first time, to take a bath in the bathroom. At any other time I used to take a bath in a big old tin tub once a week in the scullery. After the bath, they gave me a really nice dress to put on, one that I had never seen before. Then I was inspected all over to make sure everything was just right. At any other time I could have worn a sack and it would have been fine with them! All my foster-parents wanted was for my aunt to think I was so well taken care of and what a wonderful place I was living in.

Anyway, my aunt had come from Dover to tell me about the bombing. My two sisters had been killed and my mother was in hospital badly injured. My father was alright because he had been at work at the time of the bombing.

From then on, after my aunt had left, I used to wonder what was going to happen to me. Would I have to stay where I was for ever? There was no home to go back to and I had no idea if my mother would ever get back to normal. My mother was in hospital for six months. She had so many skin grafts it was just a miracle that she survived at all, but she never got over the loss of my two sisters. Their deaths affected her mind and she was never the same person. When my mother was able to leave hospital, she came to Wales to live. She had to get away from the bombing.

*A recent photograph of Dawn Vodka (nee Terry), taken with her husband at their home in California – Peter Hayward collection*

My eldest sister had a young baby. Her husband was in the Royal Navy and she was too frightened to stay in her own home, so she moved in with my mother while her husband was away. The day my sisters were killed, they were all in the house together. They didn't want to go to the shelter when the siren sounded. If they had, they would probably have been alive today. When the bombs hit our home, my eldest sister Lena threw herself across the pram of her baby. She was killed, but the baby, little Jean, survived; she saved her baby's life.

Mother eventually came to Wales and stayed at the farm with me for a while. Finally, she found a place with some really nice people where both of us could live. We stayed on in Blaenavon after the war, because we had no place to go home to. We had lost everything in the bombing. It was a miracle that my mother was rescued out of the debris when my two sisters were both lying dead beside her. For the rest of her life, my mother always said she could hear the girls calling for help. It affected her mind so badly.

I was seventeen years old when I left Wales with my mother to come back to Dover. We returned to nothing. We stayed with my grandfather for a while, but things were never the same. My husband and I came back to the United Kingdom for a visit a few years ago and we drove to Blaenavon. I wanted to see what it was like after all these years, but it didn't seem to have changed much at all. I went to see the farm house where I once lived, but I didn't see the owners. I had nothing but bad memories of that place. We didn't stay long in Blaenavon, just long enough to relive and finally bury some of those memories of long, long ago!

*11th September, 1940, known to many in Dover as Black Wednesday, was the day Dawn's two sisters were killed. It was reported that about twenty bombers were over the town during the afternoon of that day. Dover residents had to contend with the bombers overhead and the German long-range guns were also in action while the bombing was going on.*

*A mention must be made of those involved with the rescue of Dawn's mother, Mrs Terry, and also of little Jean Amos, Dawn's niece. When it was known that Mrs Terry was buried in the rubble, a stoker from the Royal Navy, G. W. Lowe, volunteered to crawl in and locate her. Mrs Terry was finally rescued after being buried for many hours. The following month Mr Terry wrote to G. W. Lowe, to thank him for all that he had done in rescuing his wife. Mr Lowe's reply is reproduced below:*

Monday Night                                          6 Mess
21st Oct 1940                                    Transit Camp
                                                        Dover


Dear Mr Terry,
Thank you very much indeed for your letter received today. I am very pleased to hear your wife is doing fine after her ordeal. She was a very plucky and brave woman. I saw her in hospital at Dover just before she went to Maidstone and she asked me about her daughters. Well, you understand the position. I could not tell her, for her own sake. But now I can offer you my deepest sympathy and regret at your loss. I only hope and trust that you both will understand my feelings when I say, 'But for God's help it might have been worse.'
I must close now wishing your wife and yourself my best wishes and good luck in the future.
                                   Yours sincerely,
                                   G. W. Lowe


*In February the following year, 1941, the* London Gazette *announced the award of the George Medal to Stoker 1st Class, George W. Lowe, for his gallantry in saving lives. He died in 1954. Little Jean Amos, the baby of Dawn Terry's elder sister, Lena, was rescued from the ruins of 1 Townwall Passage by Jack Hewitt, leader of the first aid party and a member of the St John Ambulance Brigade in Dover, who tunnelled through the debris to reach the child. Dawn Terry now lives with her husband and family in California, U.S.A.*

*         *         *


**Dee Croucher** *lost someone very special to her while she was an evacuee in Argoed:*

My mother came each year to visit me in Wales, then in March 1944, she wrote saying that her legs were bad and that she was off work. My mother had a job at Dover Castle, attached to the WRNS and every day she would walk to the castle from Hamilton Road in Dover. Well, I had a few letters saying she wasn't much better, then I had a letter from my elder sister telling me that mother had died on 24th June from pneumonia and pleurisy. By the time I had the letter, my mother had been buried, so I didn't even go to her funeral.
My sister, who worked in Welwyn Garden City, had been called home to look after mum and my brother was also home from the RAF Regiment. I was given a few days off school, and everyone was very kind. When I finally left Wales at Christmas 1944, I went to live with my sister.

*         *         *


**Mrs Gwendoline Byford** *was evacuated with her two younger brothers from Dover to South Wales. She was separated by the evacuation from her mother and father and from her brothers because they attended a different school. As if this traumatic experience wasn't enough, they were to suffer a tragic loss within months of arriving in Wales:*

I was born at 49 Noah's Ark Road, Dover. Later the family moved to Churchill Street, where we were living when war was declared in September, 1939. I lived with my mother and father and my two brothers, Donald aged 10 and Maurice aged 7. I was evacuated from Dover to Fleur-de-Lys, Pengam. My brothers were also evacuated but they went to Cefn Forest near Blackwood. My foster-parents were kind and treated me as one of the family. But in that September, the dreadful news arrived from Dover that mum had died. We were devastated! My foster-mother, knowing about our sad loss, was like a real mother to me and showed me much love and affection. My brothers and I stayed in Wales until 1943. We then returned home to look after father who was hard of hearing. Dover was under shelling and bombing and, later, we had the German flying bombs to contend with. We had returned to a Front Line Town.

*     *     *

*Previous chapters have already included information about Eltham Hill Girls' School, which was evacuated first to Deal, then to Folkestone before finally being evacuated to Abertillery. In the* Folkestone, Hythe and District Herald *for 15th June, 1940 there appeared this report:*

ELTHAM HILL SCHOOL GIRL KILLED
Had been billeted in Folkestone

News of the death in tragic circumstances of Muriel Gower, a pupil of Eltham Hill Girls' School, London, who was evacuated to Folkestone and three weeks ago re-evacuated to Abertillery, has reached the town this week. Miss Gower, who was 14 years of age and resided at 33 Lulworth Street, Welling, Kent, recently accompanied her hostess at Abertillery on a picnic trip by motor car to Newbridge-on-Usk. Returning to the car to fetch a box of matches, Miss Gower passed alongside a wall which collapsed on her, burying her beneath the debris. She was conveyed to the Royal Gwent Hospital and died shortly after admission. An inquest was opened at Newbridge when evidence was given by Miss Gower's father, Mr William E. Gower, a shipping clerk, who stated that he last saw his daughter at Whitsuntide when she visited her home from Folkestone. The inquest was adjourned for further police inquiries.

*The following passage appeared in the Eltham Hill School magazine for September, 1941:*

The people of Abertillery have lived up to the warm welcome they gave us on 19th May, 1940, and we have had a happy year here making lasting friendships. I think we first felt their real kindness on that sad day in June, 1940, when Muriel Gower, aged 14, died as a result of an accident at a picnic. Our own sense of loss and our deep sympathy with her parents and her sister Alice were sincerely shared by our friends here.

*     *     *

**Miss Doris Fisher** *was a member of the teaching staff of the Dover County School for Girls in Caerleon, when a tragedy occurred involving one of her colleagues. She recalls that tragedy:*

The great tragedy of our exile was the death of Miss Rusbridge. Her subject was maths but her greater values, in our situation, was as captain of the School Guides Company. She was an enthusiastic Guide and had inspired many of the girls to join her. With their inevitable lack of interests the movement was invaluable and she herself was much beloved. I think of her every time I go to Caerleon now and remember that the one-way system through the village is the direct result of her death, which was due to the fact that the road was too narrow to take her

191

bicycle and a large lorry. She was crushed against a wall and died later in hospital. We were lucky in that this was our only tragedy.

***Mercy Webber*** *recalls the same tragic loss:*

During our evacuation to Caerleon a Guide Company was formed at the school, with Miss Rusbridge as captain and Miss Swain as lieutenant. I was in the Chaffinch Patrol and I remember weekly sessions on a Saturday morning in a local church hall as being some of my happiest times. I later became patrol leader and felt very privileged to attend meetings in a very small cottage in Cross Street shared by Miss Rusbridge and Miss Swain.

So it was a very shocking time for the whole school, and especially for us guides, when Miss Rusbridge, riding her bike through the narrow main street, was crushed against a wall by a lorry and received terrible injuries. I went with a group of guides to visit her at the Royal Gwent Hospital in Newport, but we were not allowed to see her. She died a few days later.

***Evelyn King*** *also remembers the great loss felt at the death of Miss Rusbridge:*

I remember when Miss Marjorie Rusbridge was killed. A lorry crushed her against a wall by the amphitheatre in Caerleon when she was riding home on her bicycle. She died later in hospital. Miss Rusbridge was a very good maths teacher and a lovely person. She was the Guide District Commissioner in Dover before the war and I went to three Guide Camps with her. In Wales she formed a school Guide Company and I was a patrol leader. Everyone was terribly shocked at her tragic accident

Chapter Nine

EVACUATION – THE SCHOOLS' PERSPECTIVE

*MANY OF THE PERSONAL accounts in this book touch upon the upheaval and readjustment which faced the evacuated schools. However, a more in-depth insight into the experiences and frustrations of these schools and their staff can be gleaned from the log book extracts and the teachers' testimony that form most this chapter.*

*Extract from the log book of Great Mongeham School, Deal:*

27th May – Evacuation of school children ordered for Sunday, 2nd June. Impossible to work to timetable! School open to 7pm.

28th May – Contd. fitting of gas masks 9.30 – 10.30am.

1st June – Children at school 3pm for examination of luggage, etc.

2nd June – Evacuation buses left school 9am. Arrived Pyle, Glamorgan 7pm. Billeted Cornelly.

3rd June – Visited N. Cornelly School. Children to have large room and to keep entity of school for present.

25th June – Headteacher left school 3pm to receive fresh evacuees from Deal.

*Extract from the log book of St Bartholomew's Girls' School, Dover:*

31st May – School closed by order for evacuation.

2nd June – 88 girls of St Bartholomew's Junior School were evacuated with the Staff (4) to Blackwood, Monmouthshire, South Wales.

3rd June – Monday, arrangements were made for those of 10 and 11 years of age to work in a room in the Junior Mixed School, and those of 7 and 8 in a room in the Infants' Department; 4 girls, Hannah Timmins, Rose Timmins, Violet Amos and Rose Amos are at the hostel, while Barbara Colyer is with the Infant Department, New Tredegar.

4th June – Joy Bessent and Kathleen Vassey are also at the hostel.

10th June – Doris Hall and Joyce Wise have been taken home by the parents without reporting.

15th June – Miss Everett, Head Mistress, returned to Dover by request of the Education Committee to obtain some stock.

*Extract from the log book of New Tredegar Mixed Council School in South Wales:*

3rd June – The school was closed today in order to make arrangements for the children of St Bartholomew's C of E School (Infants' Dept.) who have been evacuated from Dover. 63 of the 91 children have been placed in our infants' department – the remainder being sent to Cwmsyfiog.

4th June – The St Bart's children were settled in their classroom ready for instruction today. The headteacher of the school is Miss Agnes Blaxland.

St Bartholomews Girls' School.
At Blackwood.
To the Chairman and Members
of the Evacuation Welfare
Committee.

Dear Madam,
On behalf of
the girls of St Bartholomew's
School Dover, I wish to thank
you and your Committee for
the very warm and useful
garments, which we appreciate
very much. We think it is
very kind of you to give us so
much consideration as there
is so much to do at times
like these. Our mothers are
very grateful for your help.
We wish especially to thank
Mrs Griffith, Councillor Mrs
Booth and Miss Everett for
all they are doing to help us
and for looking after us all
so well.

Yours Truly,
Jean Weatherhead.

*An undated letter of appreciation written to the Evacuation Welfare Committee by one of the pupils of St Bartholomew's Girls' School in Blackwood,*
**Jean Weatherhead** *– Astor Primary School collection, Tom McArdle, Headteacher*

*Extract from the log book of Buckland School, Dover:*

28th May – Preparations for evacuation being made.

2nd June – 94 infants and four teachers entrained for South Wales. 132 girls evacuated to Rogiet, Nr. Chepstow, Mon., accompanied by Miss Radford and six teachers.

5th July – Received air raid warning from Newport. Girls took cover under their desks as recommended by the Board of Education.

29th July – Infants working in two sections in separate schools. Some children already taken back by their parents.

19th Nov – To date 33 girls have left; there are now 37 billeted at Undy and 68 at Rogiet.

[Note: By the end of 1941 only 71 Buckland School girls remained. Miss Beverton left for an appointment at Banbury; Miss Sinclair as well as two of the girls had died; Miss Burn went to a school in Sussex; Miss Packham left to be married; Miss Saunders was recalled to Dover to take charge of the children who had returned to Buckland. When Canon Browne visited on the 14th July, 1942, he found the numbers reduced to 23 girls at Rogiet and 19 girls at Undy.]

*Extract from the log book of Trinity C of E Boys' School, Dover:*

27th May – A very good attendance of boys this morning in spite of the disturbance during the night, when the air alarm signal was in operation for two hours. Boys brought large portions of pom-pom shells, found in the vicinity of the Ropewalk. The Government declared Dover to be an Evacuation Area and invited the registration of all school children with a view to their removal to a safer place at an early date. During the afternoon Registration Forms circulated.

29th May – Returns rendered of 51 boys for evacuation.

30th May – 50 boys have registered for evacuation.

31st May – The school closed at 4pm, possibly for the last time as a separate department for the education of boys.

2nd June – Fifty boys assembled at the school with their kit, and were conveyed in buses to the Priory Station where they entrained and left at 10.40am for their place of evacuation, Cwmbran, Mon., South Wales. On arrival at 6.15pm the boys were medically examined and, after tea, went to their respective billets in the Cwmbran and Llantarnum districts.

3rd June – The boys assembled in St Dial's Boys' Council School at 11am. During the period June 3rd to June 21st no formal education or registration took place, but the boys met on school premises every morning for at least an hour, while the afternoons were spent in taking walks in the neighbourhood, or P.T. and organised games on the sports ground of the Whitehead Engineering Co. (through the kindness of the directors). A rough piece of derelict ground was also acquired and with borrowed tools a school allotment was started. One day was also spent in an educational visit to the Roman Amphitheatre at Caerleon, where the boys were much interested in the recent excavations undertaken by Prof. Wheeler. They afterwards walked to the River Usk and thence to the bathing pool and Bulmoor Lido some two miles to the eastward.

24th June – From this date formal instruction took place at St Dial's School, the senior boys occupying one classroom and the juniors another. The double shift method of attendance has been adopted by instructions of the Monmouth County Education Committee.

15th Aug – The boys assembled at school to receive a visit from the Chairman and Secretary of the Dover Education Committee. Capt. Powell inspected the boys in the playground and afterwards expressed his pleasure at finding the boys looking so well and happy.

4th Nov – A welcome distribution of boots (30 pairs), waterproof coats, 1 dozen, and sundry articles of underwear took place this day. This clothing came from the Canadian Red Cross through the medium of the Women's League of Service.

December 1941

10, Downing Street,
Whitehall.

Dear Miss Everett

I want, with all my heart, to thank you for the gift you have sent me for my Red Cross "Aid to Russia" Fund. From all over the country similar donations are reaching me, & I feel that they are particularly significant because they shew the vivid & intense concern of the citizens of Great Britain for the desperate struggle for freedom, & for the sufferings silently & unflinchingly borne by the Russian People for their national life & ideals. I send you my heartfelt thanks for your help.

Yours sincerely
Clementine S. Churchill

*Letter of appreciation, dated December 1941, from 10 Downing Street, Whitehall, sent to the Headmistress of St Bartholomew's Girls' School, Miss Everett, and signed by Clementine S. Churchill, the wife of the then Prime Minister, Winston Churchill – Astor Primary School collection, Tom McArdle, Headteacher*

10th Dec – Letter received from Secretary, Dover Education Committee, instructing the headmaster to inform the two teachers, Messrs Bowden and Platt, that from January 1st 1941, the school will be supervised by Mr A. B. Taylor, headmaster of Dover Christ Church Boys' evacuated to the neighbouring district of Pontnewyd.

19th Dec – The school closed at 4pm for the fortnight's Christmas holidays. Mr V. Gutsell, headmaster of Trinity Boys' School, Dover, since September 1918, and teacher representative on the Dover Education Committee since April 1919, relinquished the post of headmaster as from December 31st 1940. At the December meeting of the Dover Education Committee, the secretary was instructed to convey to Mr V. Gutsell the thanks of the Education Committee for his past service and to wish him many happy years of retirement.

6th Jan 1941 – Mr A. B. Taylor, Headmaster of Christ Church Boys' School, has been placed in charge of the school as from this date. Full time school commenced at St Gabriel's Church Hall on alternate sessions.

16th May – Family of Cousons, billeted in Cwmbran, were sent to Conisburgh, Yorks, by the local billeting officer without the staff having been consulted. The journey involved two changes for four unaccompanied children. The matter was reported to the Dover Authority.

19th Dec – Mr Platt left today, having been recalled to Dover.

5th Jan 1942 – Re-opened for the winter term. Mr Alcock from St Mary's School replaced Mr Platt on the staff. Miss Cheale (headteacher), Pier Infants, having been recalled to Dover, the scholars were promoted, 9 to Trinity Boys', 8 to Trinity Girls', 4 were temporarily merged in St Dial's Infants' School.

(Note: This was the last entry in the school's log book.)

*Extract from the log book of St Peter and St Paul, Charlton Girls' School, Dover:*

29th May – ARP officials visited and spent the day fixing filters to each child's gas mask.

31st May – Visit of SMO at school for medical inspection of all evacuating children (71).

2nd June – Children evacuated to Ynysddu and Pontllanfraith.

3rd June – Arrival at Pontllanfraith, children fed and billeted midnight – 3am.

10th June – School opened for full-time instruction in following accommodation:
Pontllanfraith Girls' Dept. – 13 of class I in empty room.
Pontllanfraith Infants' Dept. – 28 of class II and III in empty room; 27 of class IV and V in hall.

Miss Thomas absent owing to the death of her mother.

15th Aug – Mr Briggenshaw (Secretary) and Alderman Powell of Dover Education Committee visited

21st Aug – Air-raid warning 10.40, 'all clear' 11.40; Air-raid warning 11.45, 'all clear' 12.15
Previous warnings:  July 15th   10.15am to 10.45am
        July 18th   11.50am to 12.10am
        July 24th    2.50pm to 3.30pm

During each warning children have taken shelter in the lobby between inner walls and have sat on coats and occupied the time singing community songs. The space however is small and, now that both schools are on full-time, it is impossible to crowd all the children in, and it has been decided to allow Class I and Class III to remain in their classrooms.

12th Dec – The children paid a visit to Blackwood to see concert given by St Bartholomew's, Dover and other schools in Blackwood, by the kindness of Mr Smith the retiring headmaster who paid all expenses.

1st Sept – Miss Thomas transferred to Buckland Girls' School.

10th Sept – The Chairman of Managers, Rev. H. Budgen and Mr Paramor, Education Committee representative, visited billets of some of the children and were very pleased both with the condition of the children and the care that was being taken of them.

5th Feb 1942 – Canon Clifford Wilson, Canterbury Diocesan Inspector, visited the school in the morning.

5th June – Miss Kelf out on a visit to Folkestone Technical School at Quaker's Yard.

22nd Aug – Miss McDade recalled to Dover.

5th Feb – Miss Wood recalled to Dover.

20th May – Mrs Goodfellow the school 'helper' returned to Dover.

1st Sept – Scholars merged into local schools. 11 only now on roll. 4 others wish to attend schools at Fair View. Miss Kelf returned to pack stock.

6th Sept – Today I resign my trust of Charlton Girls' School which I took over on December 3rd 1938, and report at Fair View to take temporary charge of Astor Avenue evacuees.

(Signed) J. G. Kelf.

(Note: This was the last entry in the school log book.)

*Log Book extracts from Barton Road Girls' School, Dover:*

28th May – Owing to the serious national situation, forms for evacuation of children have been sent to all parents.

31st May – The Medical Officer and school nurse visited the school to examine all children who have registered for evacuation. Pauline Bedwell who has swollen glands will not be allowed to accompany the first evacuation party.

2nd June – 110 girls in the charge of 7 teachers and 2 helpers left Dover at 12.30pm today. The party arrived at Ynysddu, near Newport at about 11pm and, after being medically examined and entertained to supper, the children were taken to billets already provided. Children and teachers were welcomed very kindly.

4th June – Children and teachers met at Sardis Hall; there will be no formal lessons this week as no school buildings are yet available.

5th June – Children assembled at Sardis Hall and were taken for rambles while the headmistress and Miss Gigg visited various halls in the village and neighbourhood.

7th June – All billets were inspected today.

10th June – School work commenced today:
     (a) At Baptist Chapel, Cwmfelinfach, 57
     (b) At Bethany Hall, Cwmfelinfach, 35
     (c) At Ynysddu Infant School, 18
     54 girls are over eleven years old
     56 girls are under eleven years old.

12th June – J. W. Fisher Esq., H.M.I. visited during the afternoon.

13th June – Mrs Wraith reported this morning that Edna Maynard, who is billeted in Wyllie, slipped on the steps as she was leaving her billet and fell heavily. Her arm was broken. Edna was taken to see Dr McKay, M.O. She will receive subsequent treatment at Newport Hospital.

14th June – Various important and urgent matters make it imperative to hold staff consultations today. The girls will therefore be taken for rambles by the two helpers and the registers will not be marked this afternoon. The consultation is primarily to arrange for details of stock and apparatus to be collected in Dover for our immediate needs.

19th June – Miss Prior went to Dover today to superintend the packing of stock and apparatus. She will be away for three or four days. Further evacuees have now been billeted in this area and it is suggested that a 'shift' system of education shall now commence.

24th June – Commencing today, our girls will only attend from 1.30 to 5pm until other arrangements can be made. The mornings will be used for outdoor activities when the weather is suitable. Afternoon lessons will be in Cwmfelinfach Mixed School where classrooms are allotted to us.

24th June – Miss Prior returned to her duties today. Miss Banks is now well enough to return to duties having been absent since March 7th. As Mrs Wraith (supply teacher) has asked for leave of absence to visit her husband who is home on leave from HMS *Aurora*, Miss Banks recommenced duties at once.

30th June – Mrs Walker (school nurse) inspected heads today.

6th July – Information has been received that Jeanne Kear, Joyce Saunders and Brenda Ward have been awarded special place scholarships to Dover County School. Lucy Niblett took her test at Bristol and has also been successful.

7th July – 14 of the older girls and 5 members of the staff viewed the upper workings of Nine Mile Point Coal Mine this afternoon. Afterwards, Miss Gigg, Miss Prior and Miss Frost were taken down the mine.

14th July – Maureen Donnelly who was evacuated with the Dover school children has been allowed to join her mother at Nuneaton.

16th July – Mrs Lewis asked that her daughter Betty Lewis might visit relations at Pontypridd for a few days. Mrs Lewis has now written to say that Betty will not rejoin the Dover children here. School stock has arrived but owing to lack of storage room cannot yet be made available.

17th July – Sirens interrupted work this morning and afternoon.

18th July – Warnings again interrupted work this afternoon.

19th July – Only 10 mins work was done today owing to warnings.

23rd July – The children were dispersed to houses near the school for about one hour this afternoon.

24th July – Air-raid warnings again interrupted the work this morning and afternoon.

15th Aug – This morning Alderman F. R. Powell, Chairman of the Dover Education Committee, accompanied by R. J. Briggenshaw, Esq., Education Secretary, visited our scholars now billeted in this neighbourhood.

3rd Sept – We are still all working (106) in one room in the English Baptist Chapel at Cwmfelinfach. I attended school this morning to enquire about the children's health and find that Constance Fennell is absent and is suffering from scarlatina.

16th Sept – S. Lewis Esq., H.M.I., visited the English Baptist Chapel today, to enquire into the welfare of our girls. He found our accommodation insufficient and generally unsatisfactory. With the Headmistress, the inspector visited St Theodore's Hall and Wyllie Sunday School, and was of the opinion that both these halls should be taken for the use of our girls.

23rd Sept – Today our girls commenced school work at St Theodore's Hall, Ynysddu. All the girls are accommodated in the one hall temporarily, but it is hoped that girls who are billeted in Wyllie – about 20 in number – may be accommodated there.

30th Sept – Miss K Gigg has been called home to Dover because her home has been bombed and matters need personal attention.

13th Nov – A medical inspection for the purpose of grading according to nutrition was held in the School Hall.

21st Nov – Three pounds fifteen shillings was sent to the Dover 'Spitfire' Fund from Staff and scholars.

25th Nov – Miss E. Frost is redundant and her service will terminate on Dec 31st 1940. Miss E Marsh will be transferred to St Mary's Infant School now at Blaenavon. Miss E. A. Banks will be transferred Astor Avenue Girls' School now near Blackwood. All changes to be made at the end of December.

18th Dec – Owing to bereavement, the Head Teacher, E. M. Parkinson, will be unable to attend school again this week.

19th Dec – The Christmas Party was held today. Nine pence per scholar had been sent for the children's entertainment from Major and Lady Violet Astor. The Dover Town Council sent a further three pence per child, and this was expended on a visit to the local cinema.

23rd Dec – Information has been received today that 'Special Place' Scholarships to Folkestone Day Technical School have been awarded to: Jean Hopkins and Waveney Jacobs.

6th Jan 1941 – School re-opened this morning. On Roll 93. The Head Teacher, Miss D. Gigg, Miss Musk and Miss K. Gigg are at St Theodore's Hall, Ynysddu, while Miss King and Miss Prior are at Wyllie.

14th Jan – Eileen Austin – in the Wyllie Group – is excluded for scabies.

3rd Feb – As local circumstances make it necessary for 'fire-watchers' to guard the local schools during 'Alerts', Miss D. Gigg, Miss K. Gigg and I (E. M. Parkinson) have volunteered for Fire Duty from 5pm each Monday to 8am each Tuesday, our duties to commence tonight.

6th Feb – Councillor Wilfred Williams has sent various items of apparel for necessitous children. These are provided from the Lord Mayor's Fund for evacuees.

27th Feb – The children are very tired this morning owing to a rather severe air-raid last night. The siren sounded this afternoon and the children were dispersed in the usual way. (Air-raid warnings disrupted school work on 5th, 7th, 10th, 12th and 13th of March.)

2nd April – Information has just been received that Eileen Payne, Hilda Wilson and Jean Young have been awarded Special Place Scholarships to Folkestone Junior Day Technical School.

30th June – Mrs Chidwick who came with our Evacuation Party from Dover has today been transferred to work with a London school. A protest showing the scattered billets occupied by our scholars has been of no avail, and I am afraid neither the girls' parents nor the foster parents will be satisfied. A lecture on Tuberculosis was given to the older girls today by a lecturer approved by the LEA.

30th July – Notification has been received that Audrey Ash and Joan Clarke have been awarded Special Places to Folkestone Junior Commercial School now at Treharris. Special Place Scholarships have been awarded to Doris Thorpe, Joyce Hawkins and Eileen Austin. Joan Carey, Marguerite Muston, Barbara Baxter and Sheila Hammond, who were privately evacuated, have also gained similar awards. All are tenable at Dover Girls' County School.

20th Aug – Pamela Newing has been awarded a Special Place at the Dover County School.

30th Aug – Patricia Marquis has also been awarded a Special Place to the Dover County School.

19th Sept – Mrs Walker (School Nurse) visited the school today and found most of the girls very satisfactory. The exceptions were June and Brenda Leeder who are suffering from a skin eruption and have been excluded temporarily.

6th Oct – Miss K. Gigg has been recalled to Dover where schools are to reopen for part of each day.

4th Nov – An unexploded bomb not far from the school is regarded as a source of danger so that the school will not reopen until Thursday.

5th Jan. 1942 – School reopened this morning. Miss Musk, Miss Gigg and the Headmistress are at St Theodore's Hall, and Miss Prior is at Wyllie. Miss King has returned to Dover for teaching duties.

23rd Jan – A grant of two pounds has been received from R. S. Briggenshaw, Esq., for shoe repairs among necessitous evacuated children.

10th Feb – The School Nurse today excluded Joan Ward, Marie Emberton and Joan Plant, all with a suspicious skin infection, possibly scabies. Marie Emberton was the only serious case

13th April – Barbara Lott went to Dover for the Easter Holidays, but her parents have decided that she shall not return here.

23rd April – The School Nurse today excluded Joan Plant for scabies. A grant of three pounds five shillings has been received from the Dover Education Committee to purchase necessary clothing for Ann and Josephine Kirner.

15th July – The Education Secretary, Dover, has sent instructions that the Headmistress, E. M. Parkinson, is to return to Dover to take charge of Astor Avenue Girls' School. (Barton Road Girls' School will be temporarily joined with the Boys' Dept as a mixed school under Mr Roberts.

10th Sept – Miss D. Gigg has been recalled from Wales for duty at St Radigund's School, Dover.

31st Dec – Miss D. L. Musk has been recalled to assist at Astor Avenue Girls' School. Miss Prior is the only member of Barton Road Girls' School staff now remaining in Wales. (Barton Road Girls' School reopened in Dover on the 1st September, 1943, under the direction of E. M. Parkinson, Headmistress, and assisted by Miss C. M. King, Miss K. Gigg and Miss D. L. Musk.)

*Extracts from St Martin's Junior and Infants' School, log book:*

2nd June 1940 – Evacuation from Dover. 123 Children (6 under 5).
3rd June – Arrangements made for children to be accommodated in the following schools:
     Argoed Infants 43. 2 classes in Hall.
     Markham Infants 60. 2 classes in Hall plus 1 classroom.
     Hollybush 20. 2 classes in classrooms.
Staff allocated as follows:
     Argoed: Miss Harmer, Miss Page, Miss Wood.
     Markham: Miss Hall, Miss Fagge, Miss Archer.
     Hollybush: Miss Robinson, Miss Beverton.
(As each group contains children from three and a half years to 11+, staff arranged as far as possible with one infant teacher in each group.)
3rd to 7th June – Children assembled daily for walks, games etc.
10th June – Lessons commenced.
17th to 19th June – Head Teacher in Dover packing stock.
19th June – 2nd evacuation from Dover. 7 children (Markham 4, Argoed 3)
26th June – Stock arrived.
28th June – Miss W. G. Hall left (domestic reasons).
22nd July – Rearrangements of older girls. Owing to difficulties of having girls of 10-11+ in an Infants' school, and also to utilise better the services of Miss Robinson accustomed to dealing with older children, it has become necessary to transfer girls from Markham School to Hollybush. 14 of the older girls still billeted in Markham will attend school at Hollybush from Monday, July 22nd.
11th Sept – Joan Kerry transferred to Dover County School, Caerleon.
19th Sept – Patricia Blackmore transferred to Dover County School, Caerleon.
1st Oct – School closed in afternoon (arrival of London and other children)
7th Oct – Molly Barton transferred to Bedwelty Secondary School.
15th Oct – Nurse Walker visited Hollybush and Markham.
21st Nov – Doctor examined children at Hollybush (malnutrition).
22nd Nov – Doctor examined children at Markham (malnutrition).
3rd Dec – Doctor examined children at Argoed (malnutrition).
16th Dec – Miss K Wood today commenced duties at Sturry, Kent.
20th Dec – Schools closed at noon for Xmas holidays. The Headmistress and Miss Robinson will remain in contact with the children during this period.
6th Jan 1941 – Schools reopened today. Miss Webb commenced duties at Markham. Miss

Paxman commenced duties at Hollybush. Attendance very good (2 absences only). School numbers on 6th Jan:

| | |
|---|---|
| Argoed | 40 |
| Markham | 40 |
| Hollybush | 31 |
| (Total | 111) |

16th Jan Markham School closed in afternoon for Doctor's visit for diphtheria immunisation.

19th Feb – Markham School closed in afternoon owing to arrival of evacuees from Birmingham. In order that accommodation might be made for the Birmingham school, One and Two Groups at Markham are now working together in the hall of the Infants' Dept.

3rd Mar – Alderman Powell, Mr Gales and Mr Briggenshaw visited Argoed, Markham and Hollybush schools in the morning.

29th Mar – War Weapons Week. This school raised £42.

8th July – Headmistress at Newport in afternoon to meet Dover party.

1st Sept – Schools reopened after summer holiday. Miss Harmer absent (internal operation). School numbers: Argoed 33, Markham 36, Hollybush 22. Total 91.

7th Oct – Miss Webb returned to Dover today.

8th Oct – Immunisation of all 3 schools at Argoed in afternoon by M.O.H. 59 treated.

10th Oct – Miss Paxman returned to Dover today.

13th Oct – Miss Pelham (from Barton Road Infants) commenced duties at Markham this morning. Miss Pelham will take the Infants and Std I. Miss Fagge is transferred to Upper Group.

29th Oct – 2nd Immunisation held at Argoed in afternoon.

4th Nov – Miss Harmer returned to duty from Nov 1st.

16th Dec – Children assembled at Baptist Vestry, Argoed and gave programme of carols, etc. to Foster Parents.

19th Dec – Schools closed at 12 noon for Xmas vacation. All staff on holiday, Head Teacher remaining in touch with children.

5th Jan 1942 – Schools reopened today. Owing to recall of Miss Pelham to Dover, reorganisation of schools has been made, the accommodation at Hollybush no longer being used. New grouping is as follows:

| Markham | Infants, Std I & II, | Miss Fagge | 18 | |
|---|---|---|---|---|
| | Upper Group | Miss Robinson | 21 | |
| | | Total | | 39 |
| Argoed | Infants, Std I & II, | Miss Page | 17 | |
| | Upper Group | Miss Harmer | 16 | |
| | | Total | | 33 |

Four children to be merged in Hollybush School. (Tom Kennett, Brian Reader, Betty Tong, Joy Bowman)

20th Apr – Schools reopened after Easter Holiday. Number on Roll:

| | | | |
|---|---|---|---|
| Markham | 30 | Argoed | 30 |

20th Apr – Miss Robinson recalled to Dover. New arrangements:

| | Miss Fagge | Lower Group Markham. |
|---|---|---|
| | Miss Page | Lower Group Argoed. |
| Mornings: | Miss Pumfrey | Upper Group Markham. |
| | Miss Harmer | Upper Group Argoed. |

Afternoons: Misses Pumfrey and Harmer alternating between Argoed and Markham.

1st June – Owing to the Argoed Infant School being overcrowded, the group working in the Infants' Hall is to work in future in Argoed Welfare Hall, sharing accommodation with the L.C.C. group working there, but remaining as a separate unit.

1st July – Number on books, Argoed 25, Markham 27, total – 52.

14th July – Rev. Browne, Vicar of Buckland, Dover, visited us.

20th July – Schools closed for summer vacation. Arrangements were made for teachers to be on duty throughout the holiday weeks, and dinners and milk were supplied at Argoed for 4 weeks and Markham for 2 weeks.

Reorganisation for September: Amalgamation between London and Dover Groups in Argoed and Markham.

Misses Page, Harmer and Fagge returned to Dover for duty on 1st September. Miss Haines (Astor Avenue) transferred to Argoed.

Staffing changes:

| | |
|---|---|
| Argoed | Miss Taff, L.C.C., in charge. |
| | Miss Moy, L.C.C., Infants and Juniors. |
| | Miss Haines, Dover, Juniors and Seniors. |
| Markham | Miss Pumfrey, Dover, in charge, Senior Group. |
| | Miss Ford, L.C.C., Infants. |

9th Oct – Markham closed in afternoon (attendance). (Children went hop-picking!)

7th Dec – Audrey and Bobbie Wilkins examined at Pont. Clinic by Dr Jones. Audrey Wilkins to Sanatorium.

4th Jan 1943 – Schools reopened after Xmas vacation. Head Teacher absent (pharyngitis).

6th May – Visit of Mr Burden, L.C.C. Inspector, to discuss further merge with L.C.C.

22nd May – Local Wings for Victory week. School group raised £32.

24th May – Empire Day. Short service and singing of Empire songs in morning. Schools closed p.m.

1st June – Miss Taff, L.C.C. Head Teacher, having retired 31st May, Miss Pumfrey, Dover Head, to take charge of merged Dover and L.C.C. groups in Markham and Argoed, and to be responsible for welfare of those children of same party merged in the local schools at Hollybush and Oakdale.

11th June – Schools closed at noon for Whitsun Holiday. Josephine Cain gained scholarship for Folkestone Technical School. Blossom Cain gained scholarship for Dover County School.

13th June – Head Teacher took B. Cain and J. Fagg (A.A.) to Caerleon to enter Dover County School in afternoon.

29th Oct – Schools closed for Half Term Holiday at 4pm. From today the group at Argoed is to be closed down. 9 of the 11 children will attend at Markham. Miss Haines to take charge of Dover Group at Risca. (Supervision by Miss Pumfrey).

2nd Nov – Schools reopened after Half Term.

Markham arrangements:        22 Dover,        11 L.C.C.        Total - 33.

Teachers: Miss Pumfrey (Hd), Mrs Kaye L.C.C.

22nd Dec – School closed noon for Xmas vacation. Mrs Kaye to be transferred to Risca and the remaining L.C.C. children merged into Markham Mixed and Infants' depts.

6th Jan 1944 – School reopened after Xmas vacation.

Number on books 21 (Teacher – G. Pumfrey).

19th Jan – Xmas presents arrived from the U.S.A.

16th Mar – Joan Ayers successful in obtaining scholarship for Folkestone Technical School.

3rd April – Mrs Price (66 Thomas Street, Aberbargoed) commenced duty today as Supply. Mrs Price will take charge of the groups on resumption after the Easter vacation.

5th April – Miss Pumfrey left group today.

17th Apr – School reopened after Easter vacation. Number on books 18 (Teacher – B Price).

31st July – School closed (Dover Group) for Summer Vacation. Children to be merged in local schools after the holidays – September 4th, 1944.

(This was the last entry in the school log book.)

*Extracts from the school log book of St Martin's Girls' School, Dover:*

30th Apr 1940 – Mr Morley, HMI, visited and inspected shelters.
13th May – School closed Whit Monday – reopened Tuesday on Government order.
23rd May – Medical Inspection – also May 27, 28, 30.
27th May – Registration for evacuation begun.
1st June – (Saturday) School open.
2nd June – School travelling to Blackwood, Monmouthshire. Government Evacuation Scheme.

(There were no further entries in the school log book until December, 1947. It appears that there was a 'temporary' school log book for the time St Martin's Girls' School was evacuated to Blackwood.)

*Log Book extracts from Pengam Board School, Monmouthshire:*

14th May 1940 – As a result of the national crisis, caused by the War, the Whitsun holiday has been cancelled and the school was reopened this morning (Tuesday).
3rd June – In view of the evacuation of school children, school was closed today.
4th June – Today, 21 boys from St Martin's Boys' School, Dover, and 28 girls from Astor Avenue Girls' School, Dover, were admitted. These were accompanied by their teachers and to facilitate their education and to enable them to maintain their identity, two rooms in the hall have been placed at their disposal. After the children's ration books and identity cards had been collected, they were allowed to return to their billets until Monday next when it is hoped their instruction will commence.
10th June – The education of the evacuated children commenced at this school today.
13th June – In view of the arrival of further evacuees today, school will be closed this afternoon in order to make necessary arrangements.
13th July – At 10.25am an air-raid alarm was sounded. The children were immediately directed to neighbouring houses for shelter where they remained until the all-clear signal was given at approximately 11am.
(Note: Between 19th July 1940 and 30th June 1941, 46 air raid warnings are recorded in the school log book.)
3rd March 1941 – The section of St Martin's Boys School, Dover, which has been accommodated here since 10th June 1940, was today transferred to Fleur-de-Lis Council School. The fall in attendance and the 'calling' to Military duties of the staff have accounted for the change.
10th Dec – The lessons were interrupted this morning for the first hour to enable the children to see their Majesties, the King and Queen who passed by the school while making a tour through the Welsh Valleys.
9th Sept 1942 – The Astor Avenue Senior Girls' School which has been accommodated at this school since June 1940, was removed at the close of the Summer holiday to Fair View School.

**Miss Doris Fisher** *was one of the teachers to be evacuated with the Dover County School for Girls. Her recollections of life in Caerleon during the evacuation days are recorded here:*

About the train journey of the school I can tell you nothing, except that it passed off without incident, for I made it by road. Several staff members had cars and were allowed to travel in them. The Second Mistress was one of these, but in view of her near-retiring age, could not face the long journey alone. I could drive but had no car, so it was arranged that I would travel with her and share the driving. There were no sign posts, as they had all been removed because of the war, but once we were on the A40 I was on familiar ground and we made good time. We met up for tea with the other cars at the Three Salmons Hotel in Usk. After tea I led us in convoy to my home in Pontypool where we all stayed the night. My father had gone to Caerleon to help with the arrival of the train. He soon joined us in Pontypool, bringing with him Miss Gruer, who had travelled with the school.

Before we left Dover, several members of staff had been allocated to other schools, as our own numbers had decreased due to some of the younger children being withdrawn from the school, in the run-up to the declaration of war. In the event Miss Gruer remained in my home for the first few months. My father gave me a car so that we could drive up and down to Caerleon every day. That situation remained until September when the Billeting Officer put us into the Lodge of the Priory, which became empty on the death of Sir Harry Webb. Miss Gruer and I sent for our furniture and moved in together. We were there until January 1945.

The Lodge became the centre of school activity. It was very small. The front door opened into the kitchen where there was an old iron coal-burning range. This kitchen opened into a tiny room on one side and this, in turn, opened into a larger built-on room. On the other side, the kitchen opened into a stone passage containing a cold water tap, but no sink, only an open drain. There was no washing facility at all and the only toilet was a hut at the bottom of the walled garden. This contained a wooden seat and a bucket. (We made an arrangement with the bin-men to look after this for us every Monday and they never let us down!)

Several of the girls' mothers had come to be with their daughters and one of these very kindly became our daily help. Without her I do not think we could have managed, for everything, including lessons for the A-level English group, took place there. We even entertained to lunch the directors of education for Kent and Monmouthshire (as it was then), when they came on their official visit.

I cannot say enough in praise of the Billeting Officer. He was endlessly available, re-billeting, setting up a hostel for girls who could not be fitted in anywhere else, and keeping a constant eye on the whole scheme. His success is shown in the lack of major problems we encountered.

The health of the girls was never a problem. Of course there were colds and minor ailments. In our whole stay we had only one case of serious illness. A thirteen year old developed cerebro-spinal meningitis and the local GP refused to examine her. The Billeting Officer went into prompt action and fetched another doctor who put her straight into hospital where she eventually recovered. Her mother was called and came at once, but the hero of this incident was the girl's host who, when the girl was deliriously flinging herself about the room and in great danger of injuring herself, carried her up and down for several hours until help arrived.

This is, on the whole, typical of the magnificent kindness that was shown to us all by the people of Caerleon. I am glad to be able to say that most of the girls kept in touch for many years with their foster-families and even, in a few cases, married into them.

The greatest problem of all was accommodation for teaching. Caerleon contained three primary schools (boys, girls and infants) and a male teacher-training college. The infant school headmistress was very friendly and co-operative, but all her chairs were for small children and she had none that would seat our older girls. The headmistress of the girls' school was friendly too, but her school was already over-crowded, and we could have used her school only after her classes had gone home. This would have meant having our girls on the loose all day and, when autumn came, going home in the dark. An experiment was tried for a few weeks of giving us a special train to Pontypool for half a day at the grammar school there, but so much time was wasted in travelling and, as bombing grew more widespread, the journey was considered too dangerous. The experiment, totally unsatisfactory from our point of view, was therefore cancelled.

The people who came to our rescue now were the churches of Caerleon. They each had a parish hall and these were put at our disposal for every week-day. Indeed, the Baptists had already led the way from the beginning by giving us their hall every morning so that we could start each day with school prayers. Now each class was allocated a hall and stayed in it for lessons all the morning and the staff became peripatetic. PT suffered from a lack of apparatus, but the staff managed somehow, and the science staff had an arrangement with the training college, which allowed the science sixth to use their laboratory.

The only head who was totally unco-operative was the head of Caerleon boys' school – but even his wife was looking after two evacuees! We had a few teething troubles with some of the teachers' billets. Two members of staff were billeted on one of the self-supposed 'grand ladies' of the village, who insisted on their wearing bedroom slippers at all times in the house. They had to change their shoes in the porch! Another pair, billeted some distance from the village in a large country house, found themselves in the embarrassing situation of being expected to wear evening dress for dinner, a contingency for which, with limited luggage, it had not occurred to them to provide. However, they were soon re-housed and, before long, all the staff, which had been quite early reduced to eight members, were given cottages or flats which they either occupied alone or shared with each other.

No bombs were dropped on Caerleon during the time we were there, but Newport was badly hit and Bristol (not very far away by air) even worse. We all lived from day to day, taking things as they came, and making the most of the good ones. We joined in all the village life, taking our turn in fire-watching, putting on school plays to help local causes, etc. I was exceptionally fortunate in being able to go home every weekend, and take Miss Gruer with me, though we had to do it by train or taxi, as teachers soon ceased to qualify for petrol.

We all returned to Dover at the end of December 1944. By this time I was second mistress. After the kindness to which we had become accustomed in Caerleon, it was hard to be treated as renegades and deserters, and accused of having 'cleared out of Dover to save our skins' by the shops, some of whom refused to serve us! However, as it turned out I had only a short time left in the Dover County School for Girls, because at the end of December 1945, I left them and went to Chislehurst to re-open my own old school, which had been commandeered by the War Office and used as a research station. I took it over, battered and shabby, but full of possibility, in January 1946.

*Extracts from the school log book of Pier Infants' School, Dover:*

9th Oct 1939 – The school re-assembled at 9am. The air-raid shelter is now fit for use if necessary. Air Raid Drill has been taken three times during the day to familiarize the children with the procedure. Air Raid Drill will continue to be taken twice a day until such time as the children regard it as part of their routine work. Gas masks and coats are part of the child's equipment for the Air Raid Drill.

17th Oct – At 1.45 the Air Raid warning was given – such children as were already in school immediately left their rooms, filed to the cloak rooms, took their respirators and coats and walked straight to the Air Raid Shelter. The All Clear signal was heard at 3.10 approx. The time taken for them to get from their room to the shelter was a minute and a half. The children all appeared to enjoy the experience.

30th Oct – ARP warning at 9am, the all clear sounded shortly afterwards.

20th Nov – Heavy gunfire was opened this morning at 11.30am and although no raid warning was sounded, the children went into the shelter as a precautionary measure. The firing had ceased within twenty minutes.

3rd Jan 1940 – The school re-assembled for the Spring Session at 9am. About 10 boys of age were transferred to the boys' dept.

5th Jan – Men from the Borough Surveyor's Dept were occupied Jan 4th in creosoting the sandbag pile.

(Author's Note: Bad weather conditions appeared to have continued until the end of February, 1940.)

10th Apr – The siren sounded an Air Raid Warning at 2.50pm. All Clear sounded after about 5 minutes.

22nd May – There was an air raid warning on May 21st at 10.45pm, lasting for over an hour. This has some effect upon the attendance for the next day.

24th May – On Roll 76.

27th May – Notice to evacuate the school was issued this morning. The children's parents were given to Wednesday to register for school evacuation.

31st May – There are 47 children registered. The evacuation will be on Sunday June 2nd. The Medical Officer of Health and the ARP Authorities have examined all evacuees. By order of the Government the school will be open on Saturday June 1st. Miss Foard and myself will be in charge of the 'Pier' Party, and will have the assistance of one or two helpers.

(Author's note: This was the last entry made in Dover before the actual evacuation of the children to South Wales. The next entry was for week ending 5th July, 1940, in which is described the journey to the reception area, and the period of 'settling in' in their new location.)

Week ended 5th July – The children were evacuated on Sunday June 2nd, according to plan. The children were assembled at school at 9am and at 9.30am buses conveyed them to the Priory Station where they were marshalled into a special train leaving the Priory at 10.45am. After a very long journey via Chatham, Clapham Junction, Basingstoke, Salisbury, Bristol and the Severn Tunnel, Cwmbran was eventually reached at 6.15pm. A halt had been made at Salisbury where the children obtained water etc.

On arrival at Cwmbran Station, the children were subjected to a superficial medical inspection before being allowed to proceed to tea in the R.C. Hall and on to billets. The last of the children left for billets at 9.30pm and I and Miss Foard were taken to a billet at 10.30pm. All the children appear very comfortable and happy. During the first week of June no school was held. The children were called together in the playground of St Dial's School each day.

On Monday of the fourth week, notice was received from Monmouth County Authorities re school working hours. These were to be 9 – 12.30 morning session and afternoon session 1.30 – 4.30, each alternate week. The last week of June we were at school for the afternoon session.

The first week of July the stock arrived on Thursday mid-morning. This had only been delivered to the wrong school, and the Headmistress of Trinity Girls Dept plus myself went up to the next village to make enquiries, with the aforementioned results.

During this week arrangements have been made as to the dispersal of children in the event of Air Raid warning during school hours. It is proposed that older brothers and sisters living in the immediate neighbourhood shall take children belonging to Pier School home. The remainder living too far to get home are to remain on school premises in the safest position, i.e. corridor and cloak room. This is not too satisfactory an arrangement, but a temporary measure till such time as adequate shelters are provided.

There are other evacuees in school – Dagenham and Millwall – these came to Cwmbran a fortnight after our arrival. Hence the necessity for a shift system of school attendance.

The Air Raid siren has been frequently used at night-time during the last fortnight.

Numbers on Roll – 44. Average attendance – 39.8.

Week ended 2nd Aug 1940 – On Roll 43. Admitted Joseph Weir – an evacuee brought with the party 2nd June 1940, but then not of age for school.

6th Dec – On Roll 39. The School Nurse visited the school. There have been numerous air-raid warnings during the last month.

6th Jan 1941 – The children re-assembled after Christmas Vacation at 10am. The whole of the Pier Infants are now accommodated in one room of the St Dial's Infant School and full-time is worked.

18th Dec – I have been notified from Brook House that I resume duties in Dover as from 3rd Jan, 1942. The children on Roll are to be passed on to the Boys' and Girls' depts. Those under 6 years of age are to be enrolled on the Cwmbran Infants' School register.

(Author's note: Pier Infants School reopened in Dover on 5th January, 1942. Bomb damage closed the school for a while in September, 1942, and intense shelling closed the school again for about a month in September 1944.)

*Log Book extracts from Blackwood School, Monmouthshire:*

2nd June 1940 – Boys and Girls of St Bart's School, Dover, evacuated here today.

3rd June – School closed this day in order to give an opportunity to deal with the evacuees.

4th June – Today the Boys' School from St Bartholomew's, and the Junior Girls were accommodated in the temporary building, and Classes I, VI and IX were transferred to the main buildings. Class I sharing a classroom with Class II and Class VI using the Central Hall. Class IX were placed in the music room. The portion of the Junior Girls' School were accommodated in the Infants' Department.

These schools have been supplied with materials such as pens, pencils, exercise books, reading books etc., from our own stock. The arrangements made are working very smoothly and satisfactory, and the St Bart's Schools are able to keep their own identity.

11th June – School was closed this afternoon in order to give the teachers time to find more billets for another batch of evacuees which are expected here on Thursday.

13th June – School closed again today in order to make arrangements for the reception of the evacuees which are expected to arrive today.

1st July – 63 Dagenham children arrived here today.

9th July – Children receive drill in taking shelter under desks in case of an actual Air Raid taking place before they get enough time to run home to their billets.

(Between 17th July and 8th October, the school had 18 air-raid warnings.)

8th Oct – Seven refugee children from London were admitted into the school today. Their attendance will be kept in a separate register.

12th Dec – School was closed this afternoon in order to hold a rehearsal and a matinee for the school concert to be held in the evening in the Welfare Hall. This concert was given in aid of the Fund for the Evacuees' and Local Children's Christmas Treat.

22nd Jan 1941 – In accordance with an appeal from the County Authority to form a scheme for fire-watching at the school, a rota of the male members of the staff with the evacuated teachers has been formed and the first on duty will commence tonight.

*Extract from the log book of St Peter's Infants' School, Folkestone:*

Sept 1939 – Owing to the outbreak of war the schools in the Borough were not opened until September 25th.

25th Sept – Re-opened school this morning and Folkestone children, for the time being, will attend in the mornings from 9 to 12, and the London evacuated children from 1pm to 4pm.

17th Oct – The air-raid warning was sounded at 1.40pm, so the children who had already arrived at school were taken to the adjoining air raid shelter until the all clear was sounded at 3pm.

31st May 1940 – Average attendance for the week: 38.1 ie. 81%. Closing school today for Evacuation under the Government Scheme. 22 children of 47 on Roll have registered for evacuation.

31st Aug – Today, I, Florence E. Knight, resign my post as Headmistress of this school, to take up the position of Headmistress of St Mary's Infants' School, Kettering.

(This was the last entry in the school log book.)

*Extracts from the school log book of St Peter's C.E. Primary School, Folkestone:*

25th Sept 1939 – Opened as Mixed Dept. with myself as Headteacher, Miss Jarvis, Mrs Martin and Miss Pegden. Mr K. Anderson (CM) appointed by the managers to succeed Mr D. C. Thomas, but the war prevented him from attending.

125 in attendance on first morning.

(Signed) F. J. Phillips.

Owing to the war, only morning sessions from 9 – 12 are to be conducted. An LCC school to use the school in the afternoons.

19th Jan 1940 – School closed by order of Education Authority – heavy snow, severe frosts.

5th Feb – School reopened for full-time sessions. Roll 136.

14th May – Returned to school. Change in the war situation.

27th May – Roll now 140.

31st May – School closed for Evacuation.

2nd June – A party of 83 from this department, with Mrs Martin, Miss Pegden and myself and Rev. C. N. Bales and Mrs Tucker (helpers) with 3 from George Spurgen School left for Chepstow.

(Author's Note: There appears to be no log book entries for the period that the school was in the Chepstow area. However, the following passage was included in the school log book, and was obviously written towards the end of the war, dealing with conditions back in Folkestone.)

### THE WAR PERIOD (1940-1945)

Folkestone schools were evacuated to areas in Monmouthshire and Glamorgan; this school being in the Chepstow area. Later, home tuition groups were formed for children still in the town and those returning; and teachers were recalled for this service.

The school reopened 27th October, 1941, with a small number of children, as an Emergency Junior School. In 1942 Miss Whewell was placed in charge of St Peter's and Christ Church Schools, beginning here on 15th June. Emergency Admission and Class Registers, summaries, log books, etc. were brought into use.

Thenceforward, the school proceeded on more normal lines, though much disturbance of routine was caused by air-raid warnings, shelling alerts, and incidents. From June to September, 1944, considerable strain was caused by the period of flying-bombs and the climax of Cross-Channel shelling. On October 6th, 1944, this school was closed owing to blast damage having reached a point at which there was some doubt regarding the structural safety to the school.

The children attended Christ Church School – the Infants, until October 30th, when they ceased because of distance and time taken; the Juniors until St Peter's School reopened. All children returned on November 7th, on completion of repairs.

*George Spurgen School, Folkestone, used as an A.R.P. Depot, was hit during a raid on*
*13th November, 1940 – Peter Hayward collection*

*Extracts from the log book of George Spurgen Infants' School, Folkestone:*

25th Sept 1939 – School re-opened for morning session only. The children of Lancelot Road School, Downham Estate, Bromley, will be using school during afternoons. This arrangement has been made necessary owing to outbreak of war.

26th Sept – Mrs Tibbey, Headmistress of Lancelot Road School called this morning with eight members of her staff to arrange rooms, equipment etc. Only 97 children are expected to attend.

18th Oct – A special air raid practice for children who are to be sent home was taken this morning as the siren was sounded yesterday afternoon.

14th Nov – Mr Woods, Chief Fire Officer, visited the school to give advice as to the safest place for children during an air raid. The trenches are still nowhere near completion.

23rd Dec – School closed after morning session for Xmas holidays.

2nd Jan 1940 – School re-opened after Xmas holiday. This was curtailed owing to war condition.

3rd April – Air raid practice for school. All children in trenches in two and a half minutes.

13th May – Whitsuntide Holiday. School closed.

14th May – Whit Tuesday. Holiday cancelled owing to grave international situation.

20th May – The London evacuees having been removed to a safer reception area, the school is now available for our use during afternoons.

27th May – Notice received that Folkestone is now an Evacuation area and that children registered for this will leave on Sunday next.

28th May – Day spent in interviewing parents. Air raid warning 11.45 to 12.30.

29th May – List of 75 children to be evacuated sent to office.

31st May – School closed till further notice.

1st June – Evacuee children attended school a.m.

(Author's note: The next entry in the school log book is dated 16th April, 1945, when the Infants' Dept of George Spurgen School re-opened after the Easter holidays as a separate department. However, a summary covering the missing years (1940-1945) was also included as follows:)

## SUMMARY OF EVENTS FROM JUNE 1940 TO APRIL 1945

After evacuation, which took place on June 2nd 1940, the school building was seriously damaged during the Battle of Britain and later further damage was sustained – in June 1944 by shell, and July 1944 by flying bomb. Part of the building was occupied as HQ of ARP.

The school carried on in Wales under Mrs Powell until her retirement in June 1941. There was no appointment as new Headteacher; Miss Goddridge and Miss Sansom supervised the children in Wales.

In October 1941, Miss Sansom was recalled as part-time education was to be arranged in Folkestone. Small groups of children met for one or one and a half hours instruction. As numbers increased, more teachers were recalled and additional rooms cleared. Miss Wright was appointed temporary headteacher over the junior boys and infants. Half-time instruction was carried out from Jan 1942 – Jan 1944 when the boys only commenced full-time attendance. Lack of accommodation made it impossible for the infants to attend for full-time instruction until Sept 1944. These arrangements continued until April 1945 when the question of accommodation became acute and it was decided that the junior boys should be transferred to Dover Road School under the supervision of Miss Wright, and infants only remain in the George Spurgen Buildings.

*The following account of a concert, given by evacuees and local children in the Blackwood area, appeared in the* Dover Express *for Friday, 27th December, 1940. The account tends to highlight the magnificent co-operation that must have occurred between the local Welsh schools and the evacuated schools from different parts of the country:*

## EXCELLENT ENTERTAINMENT AT BLACKWOOD

In aid of a fund to provide a Christmas treat for all evacuee children attending schools in Blackwood and district, a concert was held at the Welfare Hall, Blackwood. Every item proved that the children had been well trained. Mr A. W. Twyman, Headmaster of St Bartholomew's School, Dover, presided.

Selections by a percussion band of Dover infant scholars, now at New Tredegar, were followed by a pretty tableau, representing the four seasons, by Dagenham Infants. The girls of St Bartholomew's Junior School gave a display of physical training.

A scene from *Uncle Tom's Cabin* was given by Dagenham Juniors; Miss Ophelia was taken by Jacqueline Norman, Topsy by Pamela Jimack, and Miss Eva by Rita Dove. The Masked Men, played by St Bartholomew's Boys, provided plenty of fun, while the play, 'Fun and Games', by St Bartholomew's Girls, including Jean Weatherhead, Edna Morris (dancer), Joan Collins and Ray Cocks, was another delightful item. The pleasure of this number was enhanced by a number of evacuee carol singers. A character song, 'I Travel the Road', played by children of Blackwood School, with Ivor Edwards as soloist, was excellently performed.

The same school provided good entertainment in giving *Guy Fawkes, Guy*, with Billy Scott taking a leading part. Dagenham School Seniors were amusing in a one act play, *The King who Limped*. Those taking part were Lawrence Manley, John Green, Donald Snook, Charles Rich, Alec Pizzey, Len Green, Florence Weeks, Rose Tolladay, Peggy Gulbert, Lilla Snook and Winnie Maskey. The Welsh National Anthem was sung by Dagenham schoolgirls in Welsh costume, under the direction of Miss Morgan.

Another play, *Blackwood Petty Sessions*, was highly amusing. The cast included H. Dyer, D. Williams, H. Edwards, R. Wakefield, S. Wells and P. Robson – boys of St Bartholomew's.

Children of Blackwood and Dover schools formed a choir of sixty, and sang in pleasing style. The accompanists were Mr D. M. Williams, Blackwood School, Miss Walter and Miss White, Dagenham. In the afternoon more than 900 children of the district attended a matinee.

*Log book extracts from Stella Maris Catholic Primary School, Folkestone:*

1st April 1940 – Sister St John (Miss L. M. M. Brooks – Trained Certificated Teacher) began her duties as Headmistress today.

29th April – Miss Smilie, H.M.I., visited the school and examined the timetable which the Headmistress had drawn up for the 'half-time' school. She said that it was obvious that the children were not losing much, educationally. She also visited the Infants' Class.

27th May – Received notice from the Education Office that the children were to be evacuated from Folkestone.

28th May – The Air-raid warning sounded at 11.50am. The children and teachers went to the shelters until the 'all-clear' sounded at 12.25. There are 100 children whose parents are willing for them to be evacuated.

27th to 31st May – A very busy week preparing for evacuation. A small canvas haversack of books and school equipment made for each child.

1st June – Papers were received from the Education Office stating our destination for evacuation: Merthyr Tydfil, South Wales. The school is to assemble at Folkestone Central Station at 8am, Sunday 2nd June.

2nd June – 95 children accompanied by Sister St John, Sister St Teresa, Miss O'Brien, Miss Burd and 4 helpers, travelled in the train which left Folkestone with 888 children from all the schools of the town. The journey took from 9am until 4.45pm. The Townsfolk and Corporation of Merthyr Tydfil gave us a warm welcome and lined the streets to greet us. We were conducted to the Miners' Hall where the Mayor gave a speech assuring us that we were very welcome. Stella Maris School was taken by omnibus to Dowlais where the children were billeted.

10th June – Owing to lack of other accommodation we were obliged to be 'absorbed' into the Dowlais R.C. School, St Illtyd's. Miss O'Brien has a class of 33 boys of St Illtyd's and Stella Maris. Miss Burd has a class of girls and Sister St Teresa has her group of infants in a class in the Infants' School. The Headmistress takes different groups in the 3 departments for Arithmetic, English, First Aid and Nature Study.

23rd Aug – Mr Wilkinson, Clerk to the Education Committee, visited us today.

November (no date) – The Headmistress, anxious to have the children of Stella Maris less scattered and more completely under her supervision, approached the Reverend Father James, Rector of St Illtyd's R.C. Church, and begged the use of two rooms of the Young Men's Club attached to the church. The permission was granted.

July 1941 (no date) – Miss Burd sent in her resignation in order to take a post in her home town (Manchester). Joan Martin and Margaret Tomsett passed the Technical School entrance examination.

Numbers on Roll have dropped to 39 by September. Miss O'Brien recalled to Folkestone (1/10/41) to assist in 'home-tuition' there. Sister St Teresa and Sister St John have the few remaining children between them.

1942 – Received a letter from Mr Wilkinson (16/11/42) recalling Sister St John to Folkestone. Sister St Teresa to remain.

1943-1945 – Sister St John asked to take temporary Headship of Mundella Council Girls' School, Folkestone (Sept 1943-March 1945).

19th Mar 1945 – The school reopened today as Stella Maris R.C.    Primary School. Sister St John (Headmistress) and Sister St Teresa (Miss M. Neil) form the staff. There are 42 on Roll.

8th May 1945 – Victory is proclaimed and the school closes for today and tomorrow to celebrate the occasion.

*       *       *

*Ken H. Ruffell* *was a master at Dover County School for Boys at the time of the evacuation. He went with the school to Ebbw Vale where he stayed for three or four months before enlisting in the armed forces.*

*Mr Ruffell rejoined his school after the war and he stayed until he retired as deputy head in 1979. However, he has remained in close contact with the school and held the post of editor of the Old Pharosians' Association Newsletter for many years.*

*The following article, written by Mr Ruffell, appeared in the July 1989 issue of the newsletter:*

*Dover County School for Boys. pictured in 1996 by Peter Hayward*

Toward the end of the summer holiday in 1939 the school staff were recalled to Dover to receive from London expectant mothers who were to be billeted in East Kent villages. Air raid shelters for our boys were dug into the chalk above the school and are still in use for storage.

During the winter, Hitler gathered his forces for a spring offensive which proved that concentration of modern armour with air support could penetrate thinly widespread defence lines with out-dated equipment and last-war ideas. By a miracle the British army was rescued from the Dunkirk beaches, using a fleet of small boats, many of which returned to fill Dover Harbour. The triumphant German army advanced along the Channel coast and France capitulated. Invasion of Britain was threatened and authority decided that Dover schools should go elsewhere.

The headmaster, Mr J. C. Booth, and his deputy, Mr W. E. Pearce, told staff and boys that the school would parade on the quadrangle on the following Sunday morning. Mr Booth had army, and Mr Pearce naval, experience so that planning was efficient. Each person was limited to one suitcase of a size that the individual could carry, as well as food and drink for the day.

A long file of boys and teachers, Mr Booth in the lead, walked to the Priory Station, where we were glad to see our sister school who were to travel on the same special train. Boys were placed in the front of the train, the girls in the rear part; and between the two were the teaching staff to prevent any fraternisation. We knew not where we were going. We trusted that the engine driver probably knew. Senior geography master, Mr L. W. Langley and his very junior assistant observed the passing landscape and were able to tell any who cared to listen that we went through the south-western suburbs of London, then across Salisbury Plain and then under the Severn Tunnel to stop at Newport in Monmouthshire. Here the girls' school left us and spent their war-time in Caerleon. Our train continued in the evening through a Welsh valley. We were used to living in the Dover valley, but this Welsh valley was steeper and deeper, with coal mines, waste tips, factories and rows of terraced houses.

On arrival at the head of the Ebbw Vale we were met on the platform by emotional Welsh people who felt we had come from the line of battle. They were more than willing to welcome us into their homes. The best looking and smaller boys were quickly snapped up. For some reason, the present writer was among the last to be placed, but the whole dispersal was effected and the school in a few days, settled to its war-time life in Ebbw Vale.

I spent only three or four months in South Wales. I lodged at first in Beaufort above the head of the valley, so that the school was reached by running down over the slag tips left by ancient iron workings. Later I asked to transfer to Cwm, beside a coal mine, separated from the school by the whole length of the Ebbw Vale steelworks. No doubt these works were engaged in production of national importance so the prospect of air-raids or saboteurs dropped from the skies justified the exercise of wartime precautions.

The rest of this account is largely drawn from the memories of Mr Arch Coulson who was in Ebbw Vale throughout the school's stay there.

The school alternated week by week in its use of the Ebbw Vale County School buildings. In one week we would have the buildings from 9am to 1pm, and the Ebbw Vale school would teach in the afternoon; in the following week we would have the school from 2pm to 6pm.

No one can over-emphasize the problems and achievements of Mr Booth in this wartime situation. His tact and consideration maintained excellent relationships with the host school. He and the staff did their best to arrange walks and games and worthwhile use of time outside the time-table. Mr Booth's honesty in the matter of rationing was legendary in the valleys. When, as was inevitable, some boys were asked to leave their lodgings, Mr and Mrs Booth took a house far larger than they needed and they made a home for displaced boys. Mr Pearce, himself of Welsh origins, gave steadfast support. Mr Langley became well known in the valley as a singer at concerts and for his work in Beaufort for the church. Mr Baxter delighted in learning the Welsh language and did his best to gather news of Old Pharosians at war. He also struggled to maintain war-economy issues of the Pharos and the Old Pharosians' Newsletter.

The school army cadets enrolled more boys than ever before. The band became well known and much used in the valleys. A link was established with 'Dads' Army', at first known as the Local Defence Volunteers and later as the Home Guard. One of their duties was to mount road-blocks and see that everyone had their identity card. On one occasion a somewhat pompous local dignitary was stopped as he drove up in a large car. 'I am Thompson of Ebbw Vale,' was the assertion. 'I am Mentor of Deal,' was the boy corporal's answer, 'and can I now see your identity card, please!' Mr Coulson had taken a store of rifles and ammunition so training in the corps must have helped many young men who left school to go into the forces. Inevitably, the news from Old Boys included casualties from far away places.

In the summer of 1944 as war in Western Europe advanced from the Normandy beaches across France and the Channel ports were cleared, there were thoughts of returning home. Relationships in Ebbw Vale were still extremely friendly and Mr Coulson remembers a dinner given by the local Home Guard to the school detachment, an occasion when Mr Booth made a splendid speech, as indeed he must have done on several similar occasions. He was able to return to Dover to look at the school buildings which, in occupation by the Women's Royal Naval Service, had suffered little or no damage. The school returned to Dover in January, 1945, at first to other premises, including Ladywell where the school had started in 1905. At Easter the school re-entered its own buildings to find the laboratory benches still covered by experiments hastily abandoned in 1940.

The work of re-establishing the school was undertaken by Mr Booth with the constantly reliable and sound support of Mr Pearce and the rest of the staff, some of whom retired but were replaced by younger men who gradually returned from war service, glad to exchange uniform for an academic gown; and anxious to pick up the threads of life in such peace as boys in a school will allow.

*The following poignant article on the evacuation of the Dover County School for Boys to Ebbw Vale was written for the Old Pharosians' Association Newsletter (July 1989 issue) at the editor's request, by* **Mrs J. C. Booth,** *who did so much to help her husband, the headmaster, during the most difficult time in the school's history:*

In early June 1940, Dover County School for Boys had one week in which to prepare for evacuation. During that time I took my three year old son and my five week old baby to stay with my father-in-law in Staffordshire. No one knew the school's destination so I did not know when or where I would see my husband again. At the end of that week I received a telephone call from him in Ebbw Vale. After a month I took the children to South Wales and we stayed until the end of 1944.

It had been difficult to find somewhere for us to live. For the remainder of that beautiful summer and during the first winter we rented rooms in Beaufort. Unfortunately, when it rained the water came up between the flag stones on the kitchen floor so that we had to walk on duck boards. Our landlord and his family entertained us royally on Christmas Day.

It soon became obvious that a base would be needed where a boy could live if he found it difficult to settle, sort himself out after some slight misdemeanour, or even recover from illness. We found a furnished house in Beaufort Terrace, Ebbw Vale, and stretched it to include 2 or 3 boys. This became our home. Everyone seemed contented except the youngest member of our own family who protested noisily day and night for the first year of his life.

A variety of boys came and went. It would be easy to fill a page with anecdotes concerning them, but they might recognise themselves and that would not be fair. I do remember a young boy walking from Cwm one Sunday afternoon to face my husband with the question, 'Please sir, do I *have* to go to Sunday School?'

It was wonderful how the boys adapted to the situation considering how suddenly they had been uprooted from their homes, and they were naturally worried about their parents in Dover.

I am so glad to have an opportunity at this stage to pay a tribute to foster parents. Imagine this town, which had been through a very hard time, suddenly confronted by this horde of boys. With only a few days' notice they were being asked to take them into their homes, not just for a holiday, but for an indefinite period. Fortunately for us they were a warm hearted people who were not afraid of hard work. Without them, nothing would have been possible. Of course, there were misfits on both sides, but most difficulties were ironed out with a little give and take. Their generosity was recognised publicly at the end of our stay.

It is always difficult to give growing boys enough to eat and it was even more so on coupons. Eventually, a British restaurant opened which provided some mid-day meals. Many parents tried to supplement the rations, and I also remember a huge basket of luscious cherries coming from our fruit farming friends in Kent. This we took across to the playing field for a share-out.

It wasn't easy getting used to the climate. According to our doctor, moving from sea level to a higher altitude had an adverse effect. There must have been quite a lot of pressure on the doctors with the increase of population. Dr Stein looked after our whole household without thought or mention of payment. When pressed for a bill before our return, he presented one for £12! I remember him with gratitude.

Recreation could be a problem in the winter. There were a few church clubs, but the younger boys could hardly go out in the blackout. No television, no record player, not even a snooker table; how did they exist? At home we tried to set aside Saturday evening for games, with even the headmaster's homework out of sight. Any picnic arranged by a small stream during the summer would be spoilt by the mountain ponies demanding our food.

The ponies could be frightening. They would suddenly go on the rampage, coming to rest on a piece of rough field behind our house. One pony gave birth to a foal there providing an extra biology lesson for the children coming home from school.

But back to Ebbw Vale and the real world. For two years the Ebbw Vale County School had allowed us to share their premises on a shift system. Our boys then moved to Pentwyn House, a large building which stood in its own gardens. When the boys returned from holidays, they needed time to settle again, but they worked hard and many successes were achieved which gave great joy.

We were always delighted when parents or other friends came to see us. Miss Gruer, the headmistress of the Dover Girls' Grammar School, would sometimes come from Caerleon for the day. Canon Browne from Buckland Church visited the school and lunched with us. We picked the fruit from the hills and introduced him to bilberry pie.

I still remember waiting for a bus to go into town when a neighbour called to me, 'They have landed.' It was D-Day! At the end of term in December, 1944, I went to Ebbw Vale station to see the departure of the school for Dover, leaving me to follow later. I wept, but I did not know then that I would weep again when I saw the state of Dover!

My husband had returned home many times to report to the educational authorities on our welfare and to visit Canon Elnor who was the chairman of the school governors. Just before Christmas he made his last return through the Severn Tunnel to collect me and the children, now aged 7 and 4.

We were to spend Christmas with David and Mona Jones and their family at New Tredegar, foster parents who had moved there from Ebbw Vale. They were among the many people who had shown us great kindness. Mona and I, now both widows, remain firm friends.

In his last report at Speech Day, November 1959, my husband spoke of the 'unforgettable experience' of evacuation and also what a privilege it had been for us to know so many boys personally. To me, at this time, it had seemed that the school became an extension of our own family. The evacuation of the school was a tremendous emotional upheaval for the boys and their parents. It was a great responsibility for all the staff and it was a challenge for the people of Ebbw Vale. In the end it was a triumph for human relationships.

*Miss Edna Meadows was just twenty years old and in her first teaching post at St Mary's School, Dover, when the news came of the evacuation of East Kent schoolchildren. Here she relates her own experiences as a teacher and how she had to cope in a strange place:*

It all began at about six o'clock one Sunday evening when on the radio it was announced that all East Kent schools were to be evacuated. My first reaction was – 'Not me, I'm not going!' The next week was terrible. I thought to myself, 'I'm not going to leave my parents here,' so I spent the next few days persuading my parents to lock up the house and come with me. Had they not done so, I would have given up my job!

It was a very harrowing week for us all. Troops rescued from the beaches of Dunkirk were landing at Dover in their thousands as the threat of enemy invasion grew ever nearer.

We all had to meet at the Dover Priory Station at 8am on that Sunday morning, 2nd June, 1940. We had no idea where we were going. There were lots of weeping mums – and dads! Many of the children had never been on a train before and it must have been purgatory for the little tiny tots to leave their parents in such a way. The sight was pathetic.

My mother came on the same train as a 'helper', and as the train travelled its route we saw other trains full of soldiers from Dunkirk. We chugged all day and eventually realised that we were heading for the Welsh valleys, and I think it must have been about 6pm before we finally reached our destination – a small mining town, north of Newport, called Blaenavon.

We were greeted by the town band and marched through the streets – which was the last thing we wanted! We were taken to a large playground of a school, and there we all stood. It was dreadful; just like a cattle market! The women of the town came up and started choosing the children. All the attractive-looking children went first. Then there were tears as brothers and sisters began to be split up.

The children were gradually billeted and eventually my mother and I seemed to be the only ones left – we had nowhere to go! The Billeting Officer took us round the streets and at Forge Side he stood at the end of the street with his loud-hailer and shouted, 'Would anyone take a teacher and her mother?' How humiliating it all was! Nobody wanted us so we came back to the centre and the local baker took us in for that first night. The next day we again hunted for accommodation and finally found somewhere, but it was really humiliating.

We had to share the school with the local children. One week we would teach in the morning; the following week in the afternoon, and normally the rest of the day would be our own. However, probably because I was young and 'green', I would be sent up to Forge Side to teach during my 'free' time! Conditions for teaching were terrible – I taught in the cloakroom, and I remember the wind used to whistle under the door. I suppose for the evacuated children, to start with at least, it was all an adventure, but gradually numbers diminished as children started to return home.

While we were in Blaenavon we started a Guide Company and it really flourished. It wasn't just for our own girls; we included the local girls as well, and it gave us, the teachers, an interest. We even took the guides camping to Rhondda. Once whilst we were camping, at about four o'clock in the morning, a guide came to the tent in her wellington boots and said, 'Excuse me, captain, there is a cow in the store tent!' And this wretched cow had completely wrecked all our provisions. It was in a terrible state. The local Commissioner of Guides helped us out. As luck would have it, her husband was the chief manager of the local Co-op, and he managed to replace our provisions. Our Guide Company was one of things that made our stay bearable. We all wore white ties with our uniforms and, whenever anyone got a black mark on her tie, we would say, 'That is another 'Jerry' landing on the White Cliffs of Dover!' Those times with the guides were happy times.

The only glimpse of war that I had in Blaenavon was when I was walking over the hills one day and a German plane came over and dropped incendiary bombs nearby. That is the only incident I can remember. At some weekends we used to visit our friends on the staff of the Dover County School for Girls at Caerleon. These visits used to make life bearable!

We finally hired a cottage for the rest of our stay in Blaenavon. It was only a 'two up and two down', with hardly any room to swing a cat! There was no sink and we had to wash by taking a bowl of water to the table. Water came from a tap under the stairs – and the toilet was across the yard. The cottage had a stable door, because sheep used to wander everywhere! We even had one in the house once. We had no furniture of our own, so we had to make do. All our clothes, everything we possessed, were hung on a hook on the back of the bedroom door. They were awful times.

I had to join the Auxiliary Fire Service during my stay in Blaenavon, which meant that one night a week I had to 'man' the telephone till six o'clock in the morning, go home bleary-eyed, wash and change and get to school on time! I didn't really know what I was supposed to do if the telephone rang. Luckily, it never did, but I suppose I would have coped. That was my war work! Mother and the other helpers were kept busy looking after the welfare of some of the poor Dover children – knitting for them and seeing if they needed shoes, etc.

When all the children came home, I was made redundant. The headmaster of the local Welsh school offered me a job, so I stayed on for about a year. I eventually came back to Dover and worked at Barton Road School with Mr Roberts. As the men gradually came back from the war to take up their jobs, I was again made redundant, but I managed to go back to my old school of St Mary's – and stayed there for the next 40 years!

If I were to sum up the evacuation, I suppose I would say it was a necessary evil! I certainly wouldn't let my children or grandchildren go through an experience like that. Parents made a terrible sacrifice!

Chapter Ten

EPILOGUE


SEPTEMBER 1944 FINALLY *saw the end to the horrific shelling of Hellfire Corner by the German guns across the Channel, although it wasn't until Saturday, 30th October that it was announced that the last of the long-range guns had been captured. In the final assault on the German cross-Channel guns at Cap Griz Nez, nearly 30,000 prisoners were taken at a cost of fewer than 1,500 British and Canadian casualties.*

*As the guns now lay silent and the prospect of an early end to the war increased, parents wanted their children to return home. One problem of course, was that of accommodation. Many hundreds of homes in South East Kent had been destroyed by enemy action. Nevertheless, on 9th December, 1944, the Ministry of Health issued the following circular to all local authorities:*

Circ. 178/44.
Ministry of Health,
Whitehall
London SW1

To all Local Authorities

9th December 1944

Sir,

GOVERNMENT EVACUATION SCHEME


1.    I am directed by the Minister to state that the Government have decided that arrangements should now be made for the return home of evacuees whose homes are in the areas listed in the Appendix to this Circular.

2.    The arrangements should be on the lines indicated in Circular 150/44 dated 26th October 1944, bearing in mind that all the areas listed in the Appendix to the present Circular are 'Special Scheme' areas to which the provision of paragraph 9 and 10 of Circular 150/44 will apply.

3.    I am to remind you that, under paragraph 4(c) of Circular 129/44, facilities for return are to be given only to evacuees who have homes or accommodation with friends or relatives to which they can go. It is especially important that this restriction should be observed in the case of the areas listed in the Appendix to the present Circular, in view of the acute housing difficulties in some of these areas.

4.    Schedules of returning and non-returning evacuees prepared in accordance with paragraph 9 of Circular 146/44 and paragraph 3 of Circular 150/44, also particulars of applications for free travel vouchers (see paragraph 5 of Circular 150/44) should be submitted to Senior Regional Officers not later than Saturday, 13th January 1945, and every effort should be made to complete the organised movements by the middle of February.

5.     In the case of certain schools which were evacuated as units and whose premises in the home area are available, special arrangements will be made to enable them to return home in time for the reopening of the schools in the home area at the beginning of the next school term. Particulars of these arrangements will be given to the local authorities concerned by the Senior Regional Officers of the Ministry of Health.

6.     Lists of evacuees whose homes are in areas listed in the Appendix to the present Circular and who remain accommodated under the Government Evacuation Scheme in the reception areas at 28th February 1945, should be sent by the reception area authorities to the Senior Regional Officer of the Ministry of Health not later than 15th March 1945. The lists should give the information indicated in paragraph 12 of Circular 150/44.

I am, Sir,
Your obedient servant.

APPENDIX

Deal Borough
Dover Borough
Folkestone Borough
Margate Borough
Ramsgate Borough
Sandwich Borough
Broadstairs & St Peter's Urban District

\*     \*     \*

In the preceding chapters we have experienced most of life's emotions through the eyes of those children who were evacuated all those years ago. We have read about the sorrow of being parted from our parents, the adventure of the journey and the trauma of arriving in a strange 'foreign' place. Of being selected by foster parents as if in a cattle market, and having to live in the homes of strangers.

We have read of how difficult it was for teachers to give the evacuees an adequate education, and how teachers and pupils had to cope with the serious problem of school accommodation.

We have seen how some evacuees fell foul of bad billets, with the resultant traumatic long-term effects on their lives, but we have also seen the tremendous amount of love and kindness, given freely by the Welsh people, many of whom were very poor, to the majority of the evacuees. I personally remember my own foster parents with great love and affection.

When the evacuees finally returned to their home towns, they were coming back to a changing world. Many family homes had been bombed out of existence, and parts of the towns they knew before the war were now unrecognisable. Some evacuees had lost parents, brothers, sisters or friends to the war and, for many others, their parents, especially their fathers, had become virtual strangers. I personally remember asking my mother who the strange man in the house was. My mother replied, 'He is your father!' For these children the separation from loving foster parents was almost as difficult as it had been in leaving their natural parents years earlier.

The trauma and the need of these uprooted children, really kicked into action the provision of much needed social and welfare reforms. Child counselling and care had become a nationally recognised necessity. Attitudes towards welfare and the State had changed dramatically during the war, as women were left alone to cope while the men were conscripted into the forces. Families were finding themselves homeless and destitute through no fault of their own, as the effects of the bombing and shelling were felt.

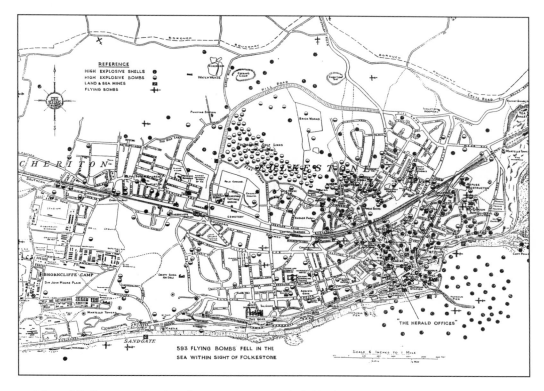

REFERENCE
HIGH EXPLOSIVE SHELLS ●
HIGH EXPLOSIVE BOMBS ◉
LAND & SEA MINES ◼
FLYING BOMBS ✛

593 FLYING BOMBS FELL IN THE
SEA WITHIN SIGHT OF FOLKESTONE

SCALE 6 INCHES TO 1 MILE

*Map of Folkestone showing the concentration of shells, bombs and mines which fell on the town during World War II – Folkestone Herald*

The squalid conditions of some of the evacuated children highlighted the need for basic human rights and standards of welfare for children. The traumatic effects of children being separated from their parents had excited research and assertions about the importance of the family. Research such as that of John Bowlby, about the effects of 'maternal deprivation' was also to be used to encourage women to give up their war-time roles and return to the home where they were 'needed' – so creating jobs for the returning men.

Much of the war-time legislation, for example, the 1944 Education Act, and afterwards the 1948 Children's Act, and the evolution of the Welfare State can be seen to have been greatly influenced by the awareness brought about by the experiences of evacuation. The nation's concern for the children had been aroused in a way which was never to be forgotten. The importance of maintaining their health, welfare and rights to education became national concerns.

It is not hard to imagine the personal traumas involved for families reunited at the end of the war. The young child was grown and changed, the parents unaccustomed to family life and who were, perhaps, grieving for the way it used to be. The father returning from war with romanticised ideals about domesticity, only to find he had a wife who had learned to manage without him – neither parent having any real insight into the war-time sufferings of the other.

What a sacrifice parents made by sending children to a 'safer place', little knowing what kindness or cruelty their children might be met with, or whether they would have a home to return to, and little knowing how long and painful that separation was to be. The following poem imagines the pain of the parents:

FIFTY YEARS ON

by V. M. Cubitt

The sun felt so warm, and blue was the sky,
We all looked the same, Pat, Dad, and I,
And even you Mum – though you'd started to cry,
And no one told me the real reason why,
That life was about to change!

When they who loved wars, gathered us out of doors,
And sent us away for a while,
Kept quiet about strain, anguish and pain,
And only mentioned the journey by train,
Of mountains asleep in Welsh moors!

Just a six year old lad, lovingly clad,
In short trousers, and new shoes and coat,
As you helped me to dress – gentle caress,
And a lump that just grew in your throat,
With a list of the 'dos' and the 'don'ts'!

Not once did I guess, that warming caress
Was the one thing that tears are born from,
For I was but a lad, and secretly glad,
To be leaving this busy old town,
I couldn't wait to be gone!

Grand pastures new – with Pat, but not you,
I didn't really care much at all,
As the train travelled fast – from Dover, my past,
I begged for adventure to call.
But what of the person, I'd left behind,
Did my smile and quick wave, inside you find,
Or was it a sham, and just a dark blind,
To cover my thoughts like a shawl!

And was your safe world ripped open in two,
Did I ever stop to think about you,
And when I cried out when things became blue,
Was I calling for me – or for you?
These memories are false, and yet true!

I never did tell you, and is it too late,
To say to the God that life operates,
That you forfeited more, than many would tell,
And gave up a life, that you loved so well,
And while those brave soldiers fought on foreign shore,
You definitely gave up more!

So, look at me now . . .
Where have the years gone?
From June 1940 . . .
Fifty years on!

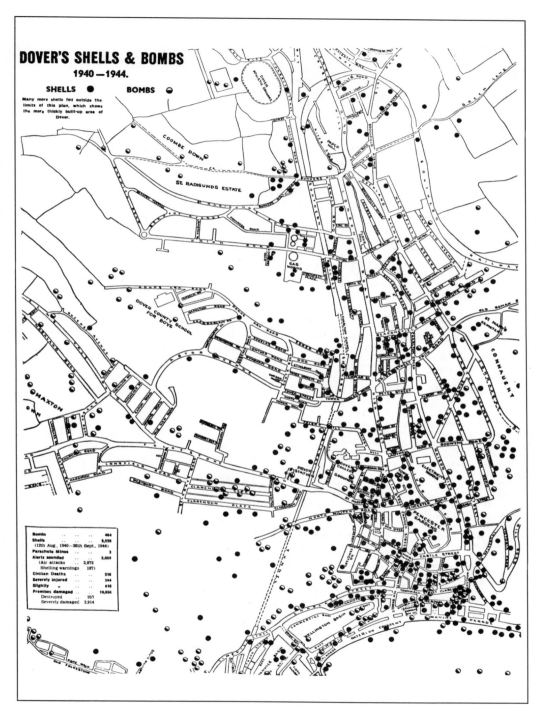

*The Dover Express printed this map in its issue on 4th May, 1945*

223

# DOVER PUTS ON SUNDAY BEST AGAIN

## "HERALD" REPORTER

FOR the first time in four years people in Dover, Deal and Folkestone walked the streets freely in their " Sunday best " yesterday.

Special thanksgiving services were held in the churches.

Churches that for four years had had scarcely a congregation between them, were crowded.

In each the congregation remembered the Armed Forces, particularly the Canadians in Calais who had brought them this freedom from enemy fire.

Only recently some of those Canadians were in " Hell Fire Corner " during a gun bombardment.

" We'll get those guns," they vowed. They had kept their word.

### Call To Prayer

At Dover parish church, the vicar, the Rev. A. S. Spencer, called on the worshippers to " pray for the men whose bravery has brought this long-awaited release —who have stormed and captured the guns which had wreaked havoc in this town."

Altogether, 147 people in the three front-line towns were killed by shell fire in the four years.

Dover had 2,226 shells, 107 people were killed and 341 injured.

Folkestone 2,565 shells, 28 killed, 200 injured; Deal 120 shells, 12 killed, 40 injured.

*Newspaper cutting heralding the end of enemy shelling of 'Hellfire Corner', September, 1944. The vicar's name should be 'Cooper'*

*I cannot end without including an article by **John Talbot**, of his own evacuation recollections, as it seems to encompass and capture the essence of many of the other evacuees' experiences so well. John Talbot was evacuated with Barton Road School, Dover, to Ynysddu in Monmouthshire, and his hosts were the Schull family:*

## A Faint Recollection

It's only a faint recollection now, like a vague flickering image that leaves a huge gap in the detail. Sometimes a mostly forgotten trace reappears from some hidden recess in this imperfect memory. When that may happen can't be predicted. Why this mite and not that morsel return is a great mystery. Perhaps some childishly important point tagged in the event and it remained whilst other, now more interesting relics, have vanished. Anyway, what the weather was like, and how I said goodbye, they have gone. What is still there today are the haversack, the gas mask in its cardboard box, a lot of others of my age, the teachers and the train.

Before that day there are other memories that matter in the telling of it. I can still hear Chamberlain's voice. Or is it that the broadcast has been repeated so many times that I believe falsely that I recall the original? I'm sure about the preparations for war and how absurd they seem now. Paper wetted in some way, stuffed into the cracks 'to stop the gas coming in', the criss cross of brown sticky paper on the windows to stop flying glass when the bombs went off (not so absurd that one). The false alarms from the siren which were to become so familiar, the men enlisting, the uniforms, they're all firmly fixed as if they were background items which help to focus attention where it should be. Only it can't always be made to focus no matter how hard I try. And then the trivia, why does white chocolate stick in the mind as it did on the hands, bought from Arthur Nicholls' corner shop? Why the lead soldiers, mother's curling tongs and Monday washing done in the copper? Another world it seems. And it was.

The train journey took a very long time, just how long I don't know. It was a special train managing to take us from Dover to the Welsh valleys without the need to change. On the way more evidence of mobilisation as we were shunted into sidings to give way to military equipment and troop trains. Lots of schoolboy banter with much shouting out of windows whenever we managed to avoid the close scrutiny of the teachers. I seem to recall refreshments being dispensed by ladies from some volunteer organisation, sandwiches and tea or lemonade. It was all an adventure until the boredom or the uncertainty set in.

224

It was dark when we arrived. The next thing I remember is the school hall in which we were gathered as if in some sort of market, to be 'sold' to the highest bidders. 'Any two brothers?' 'Two girl friends?' And when allocated then disappeared with some strange person to who knows where? Well into the proceedings there was a call for two boys and Teddy and I shot our hands in the air not wanting to be left unsold, nor to be hived off alone in this foreign place. By now, as I recall, it must have been about two o'clock in the morning and we were half awake so that anything was better than staying wide eyed in that uninviting room. I know now that the home we were to be taken into was friendly secure and warm, but then? Despite the tiredness it was no easy matter to go to sleep and morning came with a start. Teddy was sitting up, cold and miserable, and being afraid to find the right thing to do. He'd shit the bed. It was a bed we were sharing. Now we both sat up and just waited. I don't remember the reaction of the new 'aunty', but I imagine how she felt. She must have dealt with the situation well or surely it would stay in my mind.

Days later it was time to write home and paper and pen were provided. It would take a different home and indifferent family for a kid in such a circumstance not to be homesick. 'Dear Mum,' I wrote, 'I'm not happy here can I come home?' But by the time I might have expected a reply I had found new friends and a new environment and all was right with the world. I got no reply. But that only occurred to me much later and I was an adult before I discovered that the letter had been intercepted by a wise and canny 'Aunty' and had never reached its destination. Now it seems that that kind of wisdom would be penalised rather than rewarded in a modern world grown used to discouraging such unilateral good sense.

I had found myself in a very special place and time. This was Welsh mining country with the closeness of community life and the fervour of its commitment to God, singing, the working class and family, that provided a mixture perhaps unique in history and soon to all but disappear. I didn't know it of course, not that is as a grown up, paid up, member of it would. But I could feel it, smell it and even taste it too, and still to this day. It was the slag heap and the coal dust in the alley, the bracken and the whinberries on the mountain, the smell of bake scones for Sunday tea, and chapel. Oh yes, chapel above all. Sardis Congregational. We went en masse and sang the hymns with me singing as loud as any, but those sermons, they were a different matter. The way I see them now reminds me of something someone once said about going to the opera as a social duty. It starts at eight and after it's been going for a couple of hours you look at your watch to find it's ten past eight. Well I used to lean forward and gnaw at the varnished wooden pew in front of me to relieve the boredom and I can still taste that varnish today. What would bring me up sharp was the visit of a particularly fervent preacher who, starting in a modest tone would gradually work up to fever pitch, changing to 'the Welsh' and then breaking into song till there was no one able to ignore him not even me. It was heady stuff leaving its permanent mark like the armourer's stamp on a gun which identifies its pedigree. At the age we were at, we evacuees were like untempered steel, malleable, pliant, open to influence.

It was a sound experience growing up there. There was something of my boyish role model in it. I was Tom Sawyer and I could identify Huck. He came from Alexandra Road of course where the outcasts lived. Quite what was so different about them I can't say, but we were certainly better than them. Even when a community is that close knit there is still a caste system at work. I had to be Tom because as a special treat at the Workmen's Hall and sitting on the hard seats, 'the fourpnees', I had seen the film. To add to the illusion there was my hour of fame when I fought Edgar Weinbaum. Edgar and I had some sort of dispute which it seemed impinged on our honour. However we neither of us were quite prepared for what came next. Some of the offshift miners looking for some entertainment no doubt, in a place that offered precious little, decided to take us in hand. So it became the world heavyweight championship with timed rounds, corners, seconds and betting! It would have been more appropriate for Edgar

225

and me to have posed a little, snarled a little, shaped up and gone our separate ways. We couldn't now, of course, our cowardice would be exposed. So we went several rounds, drew a little blood, mainly from knuckles and noses and enjoyed the moment of fame.

At 'home' Aunty had become our Mam. What a towering image she projects. An earthy mother if ever there was one. 'We don't have failures here; our Jack went to university.' Getting on at school was not encouraged, it was demanded. And we all did get on. Not one in the house that didn't 'win the scholarship'. It was in such circumstances that, after what seemed like a lifetime, but in reality could only have been a couple of years, I had to leave to find a home elsewhere, where the grammar school was evacuated to a different place. It was harder leaving than it had been catching that train with haversack and gas mask. An episode of indelible quality had passed into experience leaving the fading memories which undoubtedly shaped the man.

The transfer to the grammar school in another part of South Wales took place in entirely different circumstances. I was older and a little wiser, but then so were they. The patriotic fervour that led to people taking us in had grown a bit stale. It was compulsory billeting now and it all happened in the cold light of day. The system had the force of law and so it was implemented in that way. A sergeant of police with evacuee in hand arrived at the allocated address to pronounce the sentence.

'I've got an evacuee for you.'

An astounded look appeared on the face of the reluctant new hostess who replied, 'We don't want one here. Got no room.'

'You've got to have him,' was the reply, at which stage I was thrust unceremoniously in through the front door and left with my aggrieved supervisor with whom I was at least as unhappy as she was with me.

A limit was set on the time that the unfortunate family had to put up with the intruder, so that each new term brought another new experience. There was the old maid and her spinster daughter, then the apostolics ever proclaiming the second coming and so on. Not all bad of course, but none living up to that first and happy home in the valleys to which I have returned and which will always be a part of my life that I would readily live again.

Despite being that much older this second phase brings memories just as vague; oddly it's much more the happy times that are readily recalled. Nothing, you see, seemed to be for ever; tomorrow was another day. Soon that other day arrived and the time had come for this passive invasion to end. I remember the ceremony in which we had rehearsed 'Land of our Fathers' only to be swamped when our hosts took up our lead and sang it in their native tongue. It seems now to have symbolised that uneasy relationship, that clash of cultures. More than forty years on the influence might be hard to detect, but whenever certain attitudes, deeply ingrained, collide with those of others too young to remember – well then I know it's there with a certainty that needs no clearer picture. That faint recollection is enough.

*(I am very grateful to the Gwent Association of Voluntary Associations for allowing me to reproduce John Talbot's account.)*

## ACKNOWLEDGEMENTS

MY WARMEST THANKS go to all those ex-evacuees, mentioned by name in this book, who were kind enough to share their evacuation memories with me, and without whose help this book would not have been possible. Special thanks also go to Ted Green and his sister Marie Pucknell for their continued support and encouragement throughout this project.

My grateful thanks also goes to many people of South Wales also mentioned in this book, who submitted their own memories of the evacuees during the course of my research.

Others, whose help has been invaluable, include the editors of the following newspapers for allowing me to quote from many articles on the evacuees:

*Dover Express*
*Folkestone Herald*
*East Kent Mercury*
*South Wales Evening Post*
*South Wales Argus*
*The Free Press (Press Series)*

I am also grateful to the staff of the following Libraries, Heritage Centres and Record Offices:

Centre for Kentish Studies, Maidstone, Kent; Heritage Centre, Folkestone Public Library, Kent; Local Studies Section, Dover Public Library, Kent; Deal Reference Library, Kent; Torfaen Museum Trust, Pontypool, South Wales; Glamorgan Record Office, Cardiff, South Wales; County Record Office, Cwmbran, South Wales; Rhondda Borough Council, South Wales; Gwent Association of Voluntary Organisations, South Wales.

My thanks also go to the headteachers of the following schools for allowing me access to old school records, or for their help in other ways:

Dover Grammar School for Girls; Dover Grammar School for Boys; Astor Primary School, Dover; St Martin's Primary School, Dover; Barton County Junior School, Dover; St Peter's C.E. Primary School, Folkestone; Stella Maris Catholic Primary School, Folkestone; Harvey Grammar School, Folkestone; George Spurgen Primary School, Folkestone; Mongeham Primary School, Deal; Sir Roger Manwood's School, Sandwich (special thanks go to John Cavell and Brian Kennett for allowing me to quote from their book, *A History of Sir Roger Manwood's School, 1563-1963*); Ebbw Vale Comprehensive School, Ebbw Vale; Eltham Hill High School for Girls, Eltham.

Finally, I must thank my wife, Deborah, for her patience, her constructive criticism and the enormous amount of help she gave me during the two years it took to produce this book.

*A Victory party for the children at East Cliff, Dover,*
*to celebrate the end of the war – Peter Hayward collection*

*Victory party at the end of the war, at Mayfield Avenue, Dover.*
*(The author is situated front right of the picture – with his back to the camera!)*

*Evacuee Reunion, taken at the Marine Station, Dover, September, 1994 (Dover Express)*

*8th June, 1946*

TO-DAY, AS WE CELEBRATE VICTORY, I send this personal message to you and all other boys and girls at school. For you have shared in the hardships and dangers of a total war and you have shared no less in the triumph of the Allied Nations.

I know you will always feel proud to belong to a country which was capable of such supreme effort; proud, too, of parents and elder brothers and sisters who by their courage, endurance and enterprise brought victory. May these qualities be yours as you grow up and join in the common effort to establish among the nations of the world unity and peace.

*George R.I.*

*The King's message which was sent to all British schoolchildren in recognition of the hardships they had to endure during World War II – Peter Hayward collection*

# INDEX OF CONTRIBUTORS AND EVACUEES

Hoy, Eunice: 88
Humphreys, Hillary: 137
Jeffries, Ruby: 94
Jones, G. H.: 34
King, Evelyn: 53, 132, 192
Lamoon, Violet: 57, 117
Langford, Dick: 38, 54, 127
Langley, Llewellyn: 34
Larkins, Dot: 50, 133
Laurie, Bessie: 60, 144
Lawrence, Enid: 181
Lewis, Don: 182
Lowe, G. W.: 190
Mack, James: 54, 125
Mainwood, H.: 31
Markwick, Joyce: 149
Maynard, Edna: 74, 142
McInnes, Keith: 65, 161
Meadows, Edna: 217
Middlemass, W.: 18
Mowles, Victor: 151
Neill, Reg: 170
Neville, Eileen: 54, 126
Panes, J. J.: 32
Pellett, Joyce: 68, 118
Phillips, J. E.: 175
Phillips, John: 177
Pidduck, Jean: 119
Pittock, Hazel: 140
Powell, Rowland: 64
Prescott, Peter: 63, 121
Prothero, E.: 177
Rainsley, Brenda: 52, 130
Randall, Mrs E. M.: 183
Randall, Jean: 70, 106
Richardson, Marion: 164
Roberts, Mrs R.: 181
Roberts, R.: 42
Ruffell, Ken: 213
Scott, Miss J. B.: 41, 42

Simpson, Jean: 59, 122
Skelton, John: 184
Skelton, W.: 118, 184
Smith, Jean: 110
Smith, John J.: 116
Snell, Violet: 178
Southey, Ron: 148
Spanton, Furley: 115
Spratling, Joyce: 75, 92
Stevens, Frank: 158
Stevens, Harry: 143
Stroud, Eira: 179
Sutton, Terry: 9
Talbot, John: 224
Tarrant, Brenda:15
Taylor, A. B.: 44
Taylor, Christine: 141
Taylor, Marjorie: 71, 111
Tee, Patricia: 138
Terry, Dawn: 56, 78, 188
Terry, Doris: 188
Thomas, Georgina: 186
Thomas, Joan: 186
Turner, Audrey: 57, 80
Turner, Duncan: 21, 53, 122
Walbyoff, Marjorie: 179
Walker, F. C.: 44
Wall, Mrs K.: 175
Waller, J.: 28
Ward, Margaret: 163
Weatherhead, Jean: 194
Webb, Vivienne: 17
Webber, Mercy: 50, 162, 192
Wells, Rosina: 58, 89
Wheldon, A. J.: 35
Whent, Clara: 183
White, Jean: 48, 82
Williams, Peter: 153
Wood, D. W.: 36
Young, Mary: 34